# OXFORD ENGLISH MONOGRAPHS

# John Donne's Articulations of the Feminine

H. L. MEAKIN

CLARENDON PRESS · OXFORD
1998

Oxford University Press, Great Clarendon Street, Oxford OX2 6DP
Oxford New York
Athens Auckland Bangkok Bogota Bombay Buenos Aires
Calcutta Cape Town Dar es Salaam Delhi Florence Hong Kong Istanbul
Karachi Kuala Lumpur Madras Madrid Melbourne Mexico City
Nairobi Paris Singapore Taipei Tokyo Toronto Warsaw
and associated companies in
Berlin Ibadan

Oxford is a registered trade mark of Oxford University Press

Published in the United States
by Oxford University Press Inc., New York

© H. L. Meakin 1998
The moral rights of the author have been asserted

First published 1998

British Library Cataloguing in Publication Data
Data available

Library of Congress Cataloging in Publication Data
Meakin, H. L.
John Donne's articulations of the feminine / H. L. Meakin.
Includes bibliographical references (p. 241).
1. Donne, John, 1572–1631—Characters—women. 2. Donne, John,
1572–1631—Politics and social views. 3. Feminism and literature—
England—History—17th century. 4. Women and literature—England—
History—17th century. 5. Femininity in literature. 6. Sex role
in literature. I. Title.
PR2248.M34 1998
821´.3—dc21                                98–26941
ISBN 0–19–818455–7

1 3 5 7 9 10 8 6 4 2

Typeset by Vera A. Keep, Cheltenham
Printed in Great Britain
on acid-free paper by
Bookcraft (Bath) Ltd,
Midsomer Norton,
Somerset

For my Parents
and my Sister

# Acknowledgements

I have been supported, advised, and inspired in the writing of this book by many people and it is a pleasure to thank them here. I would like to thank the Social Sciences and Humanities Research Council of Canada for awarding me a fellowship with which to pursue my doctoral studies, out of which this book originated. I thank Professor John Carey of Merton College, Oxford, both for the initial inspiration to study John Donne (in the form of his own book), and for his great kindness and generosity at many crucial moments along the way. I also owe heartfelt thanks to Doctor David Norbrook of Magdalen College, Oxford, and Professor Catherine Belsey of the University of Wales, College of Cardiff. I am deeply indebted to both of them for support above and beyond the call of duty, and for the inspiration of their brilliant minds and large souls. To Professors Mary Nyquist (University of Toronto), Elizabeth Harvey (University of Western Ontario), and Janel Mueller (University of Chicago) I owe a debt of thanks for various stimulating conversations and their encouragement, but also for the models of exemplary feminist scholarship which they have set. I thank Professor Ernest Sullivan II (Virginia Tech) for his wisdom concerning all things academic and his generosity with his own research. Mrs Katie Andrews, Academic Administrator of Trinity College, Oxford, and Mr Paul Burns, Graduate English Studies Assistant of the University of Oxford, deserve my gratitude for consummate professionalism and humanity demonstrated over the years I was in Oxford. The kindness and generosity of Beverly Clarkson and David Pedersen have had an immeasurable influence on this book. I owe an especial debt of thanks to my editors at Oxford University Press, Jason Freeman and Frances Whistler, and to Mr Freeman's assistant, Barbara Thompson. Any errors which remain are of course my responsibility alone. Lastly, I owe more than I can say to my parents, David and Reverend Glenda Meakin, and to my sister Julie. It is to them I dedicate this book: 'All love is wonder'.                H.L.M.

The quotations on pages 2, 13, 15, 16, 17, 21, 97, 98, 99, 121, 134, 135, 136, 144, 213 are reprinted from Luce Irigaray: *This Sex Which is Not One*. Translated from the French by Catherine Porter with Carolyn Burke. Translation copyright © 1985 by Cornell University. Used by permission of the publisher, Cornell University Press. The quotations on pages 2, 12, 16, 17, 19, 21, 22, 97, 134, 135, 138, 199, 219, 220, 222, 240 are reprinted from Luce Irigaray: *An Ethics of Sexual Difference*. Copyright © 1993 by Cornell University. Used by permission of the American publisher, Cornell University Press. The quotations on pages 13, 19, 21, 39, 121, 148, 150, 180, 193, 215, 226–7 are reprinted from Luce Irigaray: *Speculum of the Other Woman*. Translated from the French by Gillian C. Gill. Copyright © 1985 by Cornell University. Used by permission of the publisher, Cornell University Press.

# Contents

# Abbreviations

ACW      *Ancient Christian Writers. The Works of the Fathers in Translation.*
Ed. Johannes Quasten, Walter J. Burghardt, Thomas
Comerford Lawler. New York; Ramsey, NJ: Newman
Press.

ANF      *Ante-Nicene Fathers, The. Translations of the Writings of the Fathers
Down to* A.D. *325* (1885). Ed. Revd Alexander Roberts and
James Donaldson. Buffalo, NY: The Christian Literature
Publishing Company.

CSEL      *Corpus Scriptorum Ecclesiasticorum Latinorum* (Vienna, 1866– ).

DNB      *Dictionary of National Biography* (1885–1900). Ed. Leslie
Stephen and Sidney Lee. 58 Volumes. London: Smith,
Elder.

FA      *The First Anniversary*

FE      'A Funerall Elegie'

OED      *Oxford English Dictionary.* 2nd edn. (Oxford, 1991).

PL      *Patrologia Latina.* (Migne)

SA      *The Second Anniversary*

Periodicals

ANQ      *American Notes and Queries*

CI      *Critical Inquiry*

CQ      *Critical Quarterly*

ELH      *English Literary History*

ELN      *English Language Notes*

ELR      *English Literary Renaissance*

ESC      *English Studies in Canada*

GLQ      *Gay and Lesbian Quarterly*

HLQ      *Huntington Library Quarterly*

JDJ      *John Donne Journal*

JEGP      *Journal of English and Germanic Philology*

MLN      *Modern Language Notes*

MLQ      *Modern Language Quarterly*

MLS      *Modern Language Studies*

MP      *Modern Philology*

N&Q      *Notes & Queries*

PLL      *Papers on Language and Literature*

PMLA      *Publications of the Modern Language Association*

PQ      *Philological Quarterly*
RES     *Review of English Studies*
SCR     *South Central Review*
SEL     *Studies in English Literature, 1500–1900*
SP      *Studies in Philology*
TLS     *Times Literary Supplement*
UTQ     *University of Toronto Quarterly*

# Note to the Reader

All i/j, u/v spellings in quotations have been modernized, including those spellings in the Variorum edition of Donne's poetry. The sole exception to this practice is Elizabeth Drury's epitaph, which is printed as it appears on her tomb and in the Variorum. I have used the Variorum editions published thus far (Volumes vi and viii) when quoting Donne's poetry. For the poetry not yet available in the Variorum, I use the Oxford editions of Gardner and Milgate, cross-checked with the other modern editions for significant variants. Texts and translations of classical works are taken from the Loeb Classical Library series as listed in the Bibliography unless otherwise noted. In quotations from the work of Luce Irigaray, any italics used for emphasis are her own unless otherwise indicated.

# Introduction

> Nor could incomprehensiblenesse deterre
> Me, from thus trying to emprison her.
>
> (John Donne, *The First Anniversary*)

> The Copernican revolution has yet to have its final effects in
> the male imaginary.
>
> (Luce Irigaray, *Speculum of the Other Woman*)

In one of John Donne's most startling love elegies, Sapho searches
for a means of praising her beloved, Philaenis: 'What shall we call
thee then?'[1] The topos of inexpressibility is common in Renaissance
love poetry, but Sapho's question contains radical implications for
what follows here: a feminist reading of some of John Donne's constructions of gender. Donne's sexual politics have yet to be fully
understood in the context of his own work, as well as in terms of how
they illuminate or complicate gender constructions circulating in
the literature of the English Renaissance. Might Donne's reputation
as an 'original and matchless poet' (Carey 1990: p. ix), extend to his
constructions of gender? What were 'the limits of the thinkable'[2] for
this 'Copernicus in Poetrie',[3] this intensely passionate, intensely frustrated poet/priest, writing at a historical moment when anxiety
around the definitions of masculinity and femininity (usually formulated in terms of the nature of woman) was repeatedly registered
in fictional and non-fictional texts?

In the following four chapters I will explore a number of Donne's

[1] Donne 1965: 92, 'Sapho to Philaenis', l. 20. Unless otherwise indicated, all
elegies and *Songs and Sonets* are quoted from this edition, by line number. For
purposes of clarity I reverse Renaissance spelling here. The resumptive conjunction, 'then', was spelled, 'than', and the quasi-preposition or comparative
conjunction, 'than', was spelled, 'then'.
[2] James Turner applies the phrase to Renaissance interpretations of Genesis
(1993*a*: p. vii).
[3] Quoted in Carey 1990: p. ix. See also Milgate 1950: 292, Bodleian Library
MS Malone 14, p. 38.

more neglected works: the early verse letters; the heroical epistle, 'Sapho to Philaenis'; an epithalamium and a wedding sermon; and the epitaph and funeral elegy written for Elizabeth Drury. I will ask how Donne articulates the paradigmatic or individual feminine figures found there: the Muse, Sappho,[4] Eve, and Elizabeth Drury. Using some of cultural theorist Luce Irigaray's strategies for analysing patriarchal culture and language, and testing some of her conclusions/propositions (1985*b*: 152–5; see Whitford 1991: 9–25), I will examine the 'function of the feminine' (Irigaray 1985*b*: 76) in the construction of a (gendered) poetic self, as well as in the transmission of patriarchal, or, to use Irigaray's term, 'hom(m)osexual' culture.[5] I will consider Donne's representations of the relations between gender positions, and his negotiation of gender boundaries. I will ask, what are Donne's strategies for containing the incomprehensible feminine? How does his articulation of the female body aid in the construction of his 'house of language'?[6] When Irigaray asserts that '[s]exual difference is one of the major philosophical issues, if not the issue, of our age . . . which could be our "salvation" if we thought it through' (1993*a*: 5), I suggest that reading Donne as one who confronted a crisis of sexual difference in his own time helps us to better understand 'the limits of the thinkable' for Renaissance constructions of gender as well as to think through sexual difference in ours.

The questions formulated above and the particular orientation of this book evolved out of several general observations of scholarship when I first began thinking about Donne. First, there exists extreme disagreement among scholars about Donne's attitude towards women.[7] Deborah Larson has documented what she admits 'may seem a conventional enough literary dispute, but, in fact', she concludes, 'scholars do not so vehemently disagree about how any other

---

[4] References to the historical figure, or to fictionalizations other than Donne's, will be spelled 'Sappho'. I will use 'Sapho' only when referring to Donne's figure in 'Sapho to Philaenis'.

[5] Irigaray renames heterosexuality as 'hom(m)osexuality'—'[a] single [masculine] practice and representation of the sexual'. Her neologism brings together the French, *homme*, the Latin, *homo*, and the Greek, ὁμός. The call to undertake 'a history of the function of the feminine in the transmission of what Irigaray terms hom(m)osexual culture' is made by Joan DeJean (1989: 22).

[6] Irigaray reworks Martin Heidegger's concept of the 'house of language'. See Heidegger 1971: *passim*.

[7] For examples which show the persistence of particular views as well as the disparity of others, see E. Simpson 1948: 71–2; Mollenkott 1981: 35–6; J. Bennett 1967: 85–104; Scarry 1988*a*: 104; Bell 1983: 129.

Renaissance love poet felt toward women' (1990: 139). Donne has achieved the considerable feat of surviving the manic extremes of critical fickleness with the seductive challenge of his inscrutability still intact, and there are no signs—despite T. S. Eliot's forecast[8]— that interest is waning, yet Donne scholars are no closer to resolving the question of Donne and women (Roebuck 1996: 172). Speaking generally, William Kerrigan observes that Donne 'does not yield very readily to our current passion for being comprehensive. . . . *Comprehension* is precisely what Donne studies have always been forced to defer' (1987: 2–3; see Lyon 1997: 114), especially, it would seem, on the subject of Donne and women. This study seeks to celebrate rather than lament this phenomenon, because it is through the fissures created when Donne's representations of the feminine collide with one another that possibilities emerge for rescuing both the feminine and masculine from essentialism and the false universal, about which more in a moment.

The second observation which motivated this study was that Donne's work seemed conspicuously absent from the feminist re-readings of Renaissance literature which have been ongoing for two decades now. Until the late 1980s, work which theorized gender in Donne's writing could be counted on the fingers of one hand. Most noticeable has been the recent surge of interest in Donne's lesbian love poem, 'Sapho to Philaenis'. James Holstun's 1987 analysis of the poem as lesbian elegy sparked a number of discussions which have sought to address problems of voice and gender (Harvey 1989 and 1992; Revard 1993); establish literary sources and explore contemporary contexts for lesbianism (J. Mueller 1992; 1993); theorize Donne's 'homopoetics' or his 'effort to re-create the other as the self and the self as another' (Blank 1995: 364); and place the poem within the context of Donne's Ovidian elegies (Benet 1994; Correll 1995). Articles written from a feminist perspective have appeared on a few individual poems, such as Janel Mueller's feminist reading of 'The Exstasie', a poem she calls 'the Donnean master text on love union' (1985: 42) which nevertheless proves to be 'a dialogue of one' for the male sex only. In her broader assessment of 'Women among the Metaphysicals: A Case, Mostly, of Being Donne For' (1989), she argues that Donne's poetry demonstrates an inextricable link between female subjects and the metaphysical style (144), and

---

[8] 'Donne's poetry is a concern of the present and the recent past, rather than of the future' (1958: 5).

therefore 'the centrality of gender relations to the constitution of the mind's capacities' (151) whereby femininity is used by the male poet 'as a means of grounding his selfhood' (143). With her most recent work on 'Sapho to Philaenis', Mueller's has been the most sustained feminist scholarship on Donne to date.

Several feminist critics have incorporated chapters on Donne in recent books. Heather Dubrow focuses on the neglected genre of the epithalamium, of which Donne wrote three, in a chapter in her book, *A Happier Eden: The Politics of Marriage in the Stuart Epithalamium* (1990). In *Echoes of Desire: English Petrarchism and Its Counterdiscourses* (1995), Dubrow reads both well-known love lyrics and less frequently read poems such as some of his verse letters to explore Donne's self-imposed status as a 'resident alien' who crosses the border between Petrarchism and its counterdiscourses in their negotiation of gender identity. Dubrow argues that Donne cannot be placed on one side or the other in 'either/or' debates about his investment in Petrarchism. Barbara Estrin also reopens the question of Donne's relationship to Petrarchism in *Laura: Uncovering Gender and Genre in Wyatt, Donne, and Marvell* (1994). She 'reads the female consciousness back into' Donne's Petrarchan lyrics in the *Songs and Sonets* using the postmodern theories of Jean-François Lyotard (on the contingencies of genre) and Judith Butler (on gender as performative), so as to 'uncover' the apparent fixities of Petrarchan poetry as the site of 'something both beyond and within the "available order" its genre seems to foreclose and its genders preclude' (18). In *Ventriloquized Voices: Feminist Theory and English Renaissance Texts* (1992) Elizabeth Harvey uses both French and Anglo-American theoretical and new historicist approaches to investigate what she calls 'transvestite ventriloquism', or the appropriation by male authors of the female voice, and the ways in which gender is perceived as operating between voices and bodies. Maureen Sabine's study of *Feminine Engendered Faith: The Poetry of John Donne and Richard Crashaw* (1992) examines some of Donne's less-often discussed religious poetry—'La Corona', 'A Litanie'—as well as the *Anniversaries*, in her exploration of the ways in which Donne covertly maintains an imaginative connection with the Virgin Mary as a maternal figure. Sabine's book aligns itself with those of John Carey (1990) and Dennis Flynn (1995) insofar as it counters the predominant view in Donne criticism that Donne underwent a relatively untroubled (if thoroughly considered) conversion to Protestantism, and that he accepted, for example, the

Protestant excision of the feminine from models of divine relationships, and the demotion of the Virgin Mary. Catherine Belsey includes a chapter on 'John Donne's Worlds of Desire' in her book, *Desire: Love Stories in Western Culture* (1994). Belsey uses a combination of post-structuralist theory and close reading of 'The Good-morrow' and 'The Sunne Rising' to show how 'Donne's poems in particular belong on the threshold of modernity' (134) insofar as they inscribe an uncertainty as to whether the possession of 'worlds of desire'—the body of the mistress or the 'little room' of perfect union—does not extinguish desire itself. Using various critical approaches, the essays in *John Donne's 'desire of more': The Subject of Anne More Donne in His Poetry* (Hester 1996b) are an interesting and welcome contribution to the question of Donne and one woman in particular, his wife.

Even with the excellent work of these scholars, Elaine Hobby's observation is still relevant to Donne studies as a whole, that 'it is still relatively common to find work on [Donne] paying no heed to the particular contemporary limitations of femaleness and maleness' (1993: 31). Few readings of Donne have gone so far as to uncover the ideological foundations of the naturalization of arbitrary categorizations of gender, which I take to be central to a feminist approach. It is important to emphasize that the term 'feminist' does not apply to all discussions of Donne and women, because these readings often unselfconsciously assume, rather than problematize, gender categories and issues (see e.g. Tayler 1991). Nor does a woman critic writing on Donne guarantee a feminist reading, or even a particular interest in Donne's view of women.[9] It must also be said that I have not undertaken a feminist reading of Donne because, like Mount Everest for Mallory, Donne is 'there'. I hope to join the scholars mentioned above in showing that to read Donne from a feminist perspective is, to paraphrase Dr Johnson, not a 'violent yoking together' but a mutually illuminating exercise.

The third observation which shaped my own focus early on is that less than half of Donne's literary output finds its way into critical discussion with any regularity. Summarizing his compilation of two annotated bibliographies of Donne criticism, John R. Roberts concludes that modern criticism 'concerns itself primarily with less than half of Donne's canon' so that 'we have ... substituted the part for the whole and then proceeded as if the part were, in fact, the whole'

[9] See Scarry's implied correlation (1988a: 104 n. 29).

(1982*a*: 6–3). Happily this imbalance has begun to be addressed in the years since Roberts's assessment, especially with regard to Donne's religious writing (see Frontain and Malpezzi, 1995; Hester 1996*b*; Oliver 1997) and 'Sapho to Philaenis' as I mentioned. James Turner recognizes that our perceptions depend on what we are defining as constitutive texts, the raw data of our investigations (1993*b*: 1). In the case of Donne, if we have been looking at only half of his poetry and neglecting his prose, we 'have not done', especially since some of the more neglected works are highly charged in their constructions of gender.

I respond to these three trends in Donne criticism, then—the disagreement over Donne's attitude to women, the relative paucity of feminist work on Donne, the neglect of parts of Donne's canon—with four exploratory chapters; that is, in the process of answering smaller questions I raise larger ones. In Chapter 1 I explore Donne's relationship with the Muse in the early verse letters, poems which tend to be ignored even in the few studies available on the later verse epistles to women such as Lucy, Countess of Bedford. The poet's relationship with his Muse is fundamental and at least latently gendered. These early poems show us how the young Donne and the friends with whom he exchanged poems imagined the engendering of poetry. Chapter 2 is devoted to 'Sapho to Philaenis', the first lesbian love poem in the English language and yet politely ignored for close to four hundred years. How does this poem change our sense of Donne as the poet of 'masculine perswasive force' ('On His Mistress': l. 4) in the *Elegies* and the *Songs and Sonets*? Chapter 3 marks a change in focus which is continued in Chapter 4, from a classical to a Christian horizon, and also pairs an early epithalamium and a wedding sermon together. Since Izaak Walton's formulation of Donne's life as an Augustinian transformation from the sinful pursuit of bodily pleasures to exemplary saintliness, readings of Donne have frequently operated as if there were a fault line (in the double sense of both a gap, a break in continuity, and a flaw resulting from that gap) in Donne's mental geography; a double but diachronic personality whereby Jack Donne becomes Doctor Donne, a split Donne himself famously cultivated in his letters (1977: 21–2). This chapter asks whether there might be a common foundation, which I suggest concerns the unacknowledged debt to the maternal feminine, for the ways in which Donne in each genre—sermon and epithalamium—represents and defines the marriage relationship. Chapter 4 marks an apparent change in proportion. From a study of the Muse, Sappho, and Eve, we move to Elizabeth Drury, a nearly anonymous 14-year-old girl, a 'nobody' who, some critics have argued (or complained), is transformed by Donne into a Christian 'everyman' (see Lewalski 1973). What questions come into focus when we compare the domestication or the making ordinary of mythical figures of the feminine such as the Muse with the inversely proportional apotheosis of a young female contemporary of Donne? I trace her sexual-/textualization from her epitaph, where she is described as 'sine sexu', or sexless, through to *The Second Anniversary* where she is described as a double-sided scroll and addressed as the 'father' of Donne's poems, metaphorically inseminating his Muse.

Putting aside the goal of comprehension in the sense of neat answers or blanket generalizations, to determine whether Donne is nice or nasty to women is not perhaps the most illuminating approach for an understanding of literary and historical constructions of gender.[10] Elaine Showalter observes that until very recently, 'few feminist critics were analysing *men's* writing as a gendered discourse' (Showalter 1989*b*: 5; see Carr 1988) within patriarchy. Irigaray explains her critique of Freud in similar terms:

It is not a matter of naively accusing Freud, as if he were a 'bastard'. Freud's discourse represents the symptom of a particular social and cultural economy, which has been maintained in the west at least since the Greeks. What we have to question is the system of representation, the discursive system at work in this socio-cultural functioning. And, in this respect, what Freud demonstrates is quite useful. (1990: 82)

Likewise, it is not my project to naively accuse Donne, 'as if he were a "bastard"'. As a product of a particular historical moment, Donne cannot be expected to leap outside his cultural milieu and transcend the contemporary understanding of relations between men and women. In this sense, one must recognize 'the limits of the thinkable'. We also need to heed James Turner's reminder that 'Renaissance discourses on sexuality and gender cultivated a dissociation between ostensible meaning and performative occasion' (1993*b*: 7–8), which could make a text seem, for example, protofeminist.

However, as a poet, Donne's imaginative genius seems to have allowed him moments when seemingly entrenched categories and

[10] 'The assumption that feminism is identical with kindness to women is a common befuddlement' (Woodbridge 1986: 3).

concepts become unstuck and take on new meaning, even if only within the confines of a single poem, and if only because such meanings suit Donne's imaginative needs at the time.[11] John Carey recognizes 'Donne's impulse to reach beyond language and thought into wonder', his 'urge to express the inexpressible, and think the unthinkable' which was 'necessarily the most self-defeating' (1990: 111; see Klause 1987; Hester 1996*a*: 18) of his impulses, but which pushed him to question received notions. Donne was not one to shy away from taboo or uncharted territory, but seemed, rather, compelled to explore it; for example, in his treatise on suicide, *Biathanatos,* or in taking the implications of anthropomorphism to their limit in figuring the sexuality of God in some of his Holy Sonnets (see Kerrigan 1972: 337–63).

I am reluctant, therefore, to adopt wholeheartedly the new historicist hypothesis that it is impossible for poets to transcend their historical circumstances or literary context (see Low 1988). J. B. Leishman's neglected observation several decades ago that Donne is the first to use the word 'sex' in its modern, abstract sense (1966: 224) is a case in point for Donne's particularly subtle appreciation of the psychological implications of the physiological differences of sex, and hence his ability to stretch existing concepts of gender. Helen Carr notes that Donne in his elegy, 'On his Mistris', was using the word 'masculine' to imply gender as well as sex characteristics well before the *OED*'s earliest citation from 1629 (1988: 97). In my reading of Donne's constructions of gender I therefore acknowledge with Claude J. Summers and Ted-Larry Pebworth that 'the relationship of literature and history is always reciprocal and reflexive, and crucially so in the case of literary representations of sexuality, which focus on issues—such as erotic desire, courtship rituals, gender definitions, and sexual and cultural anxieties—that are simultaneously highly localized yet universally, and therefore sometimes misleadingly, familiar' (1993: 4).[12] While one must exercise caution in making pat conclusions about the transposition of literary representations onto historical experience and vice versa, or in assuming a moral position within the text, one must nevertheless allow the

---

[11] For example, Donne used Ptolemaic or Copernican cosmologies in his poetry and prose depending on which schema suited his needs. See Carey's discussion of Donne's use of both theories (1990: 234–9). Carey suggests that 'Sapho to Philaenis' was Donne's 'answer to an imaginative problem' (257).

[12] On the pitfalls of assuming a straightforward exchange between fictional representations of women and historical women, see Woodbridge 1986: 3–7.

question to remain open. There is a relation or an exchange between the two taking place, if one cannot expect simple answers as to the precise mechanics of such a subtle relationship (see Belsey 1994: 10).

One of Donne's epigrams demonstrates the need to move beyond asking whether Donne is nice or nasty to women and to analyse the function of the feminine in his gender constructions. The epigram works against received notions of gender in the Renaissance and reveals Donne's readiness to question even ontological categories. Here is the epigram:

> Thou call'st me effeminat, for I love womens joyes
> I call not thee manly, though thou follow boyes. (Donne 1995*b*: 8)

The epigram appears in only three manuscripts, and only once with a title, 'The Jughler', which has been dismissed as 'pointless' and replaced with 'Manliness' (Donne 1942; 1967*b*); reinstated as a euphemism pointing to 'the rhetorical and sexual facility of the speaker' (Hester 1990); and challenged as a misreading of 'The Inghler' (Halley 1989). Halley's suggestion is compelling, for 'ingler' was a term used by the Elizabethans as a synonym for 'catam-ite' or 'ganymede' to denote a man who favours the company of, and has sexual relations with boys. Interestingly, Patrides's 1985 edition of Donne's poems, which gives the title as 'The Jughler', notes there is confusion in the manuscripts and editions between 'ingle' and 'juggle' in the one other instance of the word in Donne's poetry, line 29 of 'The Perfume'. The editors of the *Variorum* make no mention of Halley's argument and give the title, 'The Jughler'. In its lone appearance, in National Library of Scotland MS 2067, Haw-thornden XV, the scribe seems to have intended 'Jughler'. Although 'I' and 'J' are, customarily, not differentiated and can be read either way, the scribe often distinguishes his 'u' from his 'n' with a short horizontal line above it. The line never appears above an 'n'. Both titles are apposite but we cannot even be sure a title originated with Donne. There is also the possibility that the scribe did not approve of the title if it was 'The Inghler' and so did some easy juggling of his own and mistranscribed it intentionally, but we can only speculate on any censorship that might have taken place.

The speaker of the epigram has been branded 'effeminat', which in the Renaissance was used to describe a man who had become 'womanish, unmanly, enervated, feeble, self-indulgent, voluptuous, unbecomingly delicate or over-refined' (*OED*), as a result of spending too much time in the company of women. In the Renaissance, then, an effeminate man was not homosexual, as the modern use of the term often connotes, but a heterosexual who did not balance his social or sexual intercourse with women with appropriately masculine pursuits. Hence, he risked succumbing to his (feminine) passions and losing control of his (masculine) reason.[13] Donne uses the word in this sense in his elegy, 'The Perfume'. When his perfume betrays the speaker's presence to the father of his mistress, he expostulates: 'By thee, the greatest staine to mans estate | Falls on us, to be call'd effeminate' (61–2). This Renaissance coding of excessive desire for *women* as effeminacy requires further explanation in order to understand Donne's epigram within its cultural context. Thomas Laqueur documents one of several competing theories in the Renaissance whereby male and female sexual organs were asserted to be different in degree rather than kind: the same organs were either outside the hotter, more perfect male body or inside the female body. Laqueur's too-neat division of a pre-Enlightenment 'one-sex' model and a post-Enlightenment 'two-sex' model has been corrected by Katharine Park and Robert Nye (1991), among others (see Traub 1995), who assert that the Aristotelian view of incommensurability between the sexes had always competed with the dominant Galenic notion of homologous yet hierarchical male and female bodies, which in any case was a system of analogies rather than identities (Park and Nye 1991; Park 1997). If he flattens out the complexities of sex/gender theories among anatomists and other writers, Laqueur's description of the 'one-sex model' dominant in the English Renaissance is sound as far as it goes, and he notes that the major paradox of this 'one-sex model' 'is that pairs of ordered contrarieties played off a single flesh in which they did not themselves inhere': male reason vs. female emotion and so on (1990: 61). Ian Maclean remarks on the same paradox: 'the separation of sexual characteristics from gender, which is in fact practised by scholastic theologians ("a manly soul in a weak female body"), seems to result in a pursuit of paradox and a provocation of wonderment in the reader or listener, and not in the development of a new paradigm of psychological characteristics' (1988: 26). The 'fact' of the body was not the bio-

[13] For discussions of effeminacy in the Renaissance, see Rackin 1993; Laqueur 1990: 123–4; Woodbridge 1986: 139 ff.; 158–9; 169–71.

logical bedrock on which cultural meanings were based; rather, it was often used to illustrate previously established, metaphysical truths. In other words, gender preceded sex, rather than as in our own culture where gender is generally perceived as a cultural interpretation of biological sex.[14] Whether arguing the 'one-sex model' or, alternatively, an Aristotelian incommensurability, Renaissance theorists viewed sex as 'a sociological and not an ontological category' (Laqueur 1990: 8).

'The Jughler' appears to be the exception that proves the rule. Supremely confident in his masculinity, the speaker refuses to participate in Renaissance anxiety about men becoming 'womanish' and sliding away from perfection. Rather, he affirms what became a predominantly post-Enlightenment notion that gender is correlative: one attains masculine identity and status by one's conquests of women. The more 'womens joyes' one 'loves', the more manly one is. He's more, rather than less of a man around women, and is even more manly for flinging back the insult with greater force; not only is the addressee 'not . . . manly' in the sense of virile, because he 'follows', that is, sodomizes boys (i.e. he is literally behind them), he is 'not . . . manly' in the sense of being sub-human or bestial. In terms of the hierarchy of being, then, Donne's speaker has intensified the insult from an accusation of womanliness to an accusation of bestiality, and shown his masculinity—his mastery—through his manipulation of language. Like the speaker in the elegy, 'On His Mistress', it is his words which possess 'masculine perswasive force'. This dialogue between men, 'Thou call'st me . . . I call not thee', requires a reference point to distinguish types of men amongst themselves and it is women and boys who function as such. To return to the problem of the title, then, the epigram supports both possibilities, since one man is an 'inghler' and one is, rhetorically, a 'jughler'. Far from 'pointless', the title 'The Jughler', as we must read it in the manuscript, is decidedly pointed.

I want to return to the opening question asked by Sapho, in order to show how my reading of it informs the structure of this book. In Donne's startling lesbian love poem, Sapho writes a letter to Philaenis who has absconded with a male seducer, leaving Sapho desperate for her return. In an attempt to win Philaenis back, Sapho employs two strategies: she both praises Philaenis' beauty and argues

[14] See J. Butler 1990*a*; 1993; Traub 1995; and Park 1997 for examples of the increasingly complex 'troubling' and theorizing of gender and sex.

for the superiority of their woman-to-woman love over love between
a man and a woman. Beginning her epideictic with a comparison of
Philaenis to the gods, Sapho then pauses to reflect:

> For, if we justly call each silly man
>     A litle world, What shall we call thee then? (19–20)

Sapho's question exhibits a typically Donnean virtuosic compression. In these two lines, Donne manipulates at least four poetic conventions: the comparison of one's beloved to elements in nature and
the cosmos; the assertion that the beloved is incomparable (usually
to other women); the poet's assertion of his inadequate ability to
describe his beloved; and the idea that human beings are microcosms
of the world.

Donne plays upon, and thus exposes, the falsely inclusive 'man',
for which, according to the rules of English grammar, we are to read
'a human being (irrespective of sex or age)' (*OED* I.1), a member of
the collective species whose sex is indeterminate or irrelevant. 'Man'
is the official term used in such instances because the male gender is
held to be 'more comprehensive than the female'.[15] But Philaenis is
not a man—that is, a male. Therefore, the syllogistic joke is that*she* is
not comparable to a microcosm of the universe, because only a 'man',
that is, a male, is justly called a 'litle world'. As a woman, Donne's
Sapho subverts, by playing with, the language she must use according to grammatical convention, but which does not represent her
experience. By pointing up 'man' as a false universal and revealing
woman's 'present absence' in the ubiquitous noun which supposedly
refers to human 'being', Donne reveals a radical awareness of the
gender politics which operate in language. Here is the poet of self-
proclaimed 'masculine perswasive force', in the service of jest and
seduction, admitting to fundamental elisions of identity in the very
structure of language, a patriarchal 'language which is neuter [or
universal] only in that it forgets the difference from which it draws
its strength and energy' (Irigaray 1993*a*: 129). Yet implicit in
Sapho's pun, and her attempt, conventional as such, to praise Philaenis above all others, is the notion that woman must remain un-
named or incomparable, for the whole world is already taken up as

---

[15] One of John Kirkby's 'Eighty Eight Grammatical Rules' (1746), quoted in
Spender 1985: 148. Kirkby compiled his grammar long after Donne was writing,
but see Thomas Wilson's *The Art of Rhetorique* (1560) in which he argues for the
priority (because superior) of the male gender.

the vehicle which mediates or reflects man to himself; woman as the symbol of materiality is that which man uses to construct his subjectivity.[16] Donne's language thus exposes the grammatical invisibility of women at the same time as it replicates that invisibility in a poetic convention, the inexpressibility topos.

Before I can relate Sapho's question to the structure of this book, I need to elaborate the workings of patriarchal discourse on a more general level. The questions posed thus far, and indeed the title of the book, suggest that this study of Donne's construction of gender focuses exclusively on his articulations of the feminine. However, analysing gender as a category used to delimit difference (purportedly on the basis of physiology or biology) in a culture where the standard is man/male/masculine means that one almost always encounters texts preoccupied with defining 'a problematic, unstable female body that is either a version of or wholly different from a generally unproblematic, stable male body. . . . [I]t is *always* woman's sexuality that is being constituted; woman is the empty category. Woman alone seems to have "gender"' (Laqueur 1990: 22; see Jacobus, Keller, Shuttleworth 1990: 2). Paradoxically, however, this project is an effect of what Irigaray calls *'the sexual indifference that underlies the truth of any science, the logic of every discourse'* (1985b: 69); hence, the sexual 'indifference' of hom(m)osexuality. Woman is always defined phallocentrically—that is, against the normative male—as man's opposite, or his complement, or an inferior 'copy', as in Aristotle's notion of the female as defective male; in short, as Other. To put it diagrammatically, gender is represented as a reciprocal relation of difference between two autonomous terms, 'A' and 'B', rather than what it is in patriarchal discourse, an oppositional structure of one term and its negation, 'A' and '–A' (Grosz 1989: 106). Irigaray terms these two positions, 'the Same', and 'the Other of the Same' (see 1985a: 32–4; see Whitford 1991: 104–5). Women have no symbolic order or means of representation of their own (as 'the Other of the Other') which does not take the male as its initial point of reference, yet as '–A', when '–A' *is* 'B' or 'C' or 'D', etc., the possibilities for 'woman' are infinite.

Donne's 'Communitie' offers a lesson in women as '–A', as 'things indifferent, | Which wee may neither hate, nor love, | But one, and

---

[16] Irigaray 1985a: 54. See Berry 1994: 232; Woolf 1977: 'Women have served all these centuries as looking-glasses possessing the magic and delicious power of reflecting the figure of man at twice its natural size' (35).

then another prove, | As wee shall finde our fancy bent. . . . | Onely this rests, All, all may use' (3–6, 12).[17] The speaker of Donne's elegy, 'Change', admits he 'feare[s]' his mistress precisely because she is— and, he argues, should be—changeable: 'Women are like the Arts, forc'd unto none, | Open to'all searchers, unpriz'd, if unknowne. . . . | Women are made for men, not him, nor mee' (5–6, 10). Woman is contructed as what David Halperin calls a 'necessary female absence'. 'Nothing in herself, "woman" is . . . an alternate male identity whose constant accessibility to men lends men a fullness and totality that enables them to dispense (supposedly) with otherness altogether. "Femininity" is not referential then, but figural' (1990: 149,150–1), a phenomenon Virginia Woolf noticed in *A Room of One's Own* (1977: 42–3). Insofar as Philaenis is a woman defined as 'not man' or '–A', Sapho should have no trouble 'calling' or naming her, but Philaenis' incomparability is not only an effect of her unique beauty but an effect of her sex as it is signified (figural rather than referential) within a patriarchal world: as 'B'—or 'C' or 'D', etc.—she has yet to be recognized.

Thus, I reiterate Sapho's question in several different voices throughout this book. I ask how Donne names the feminine in re- sponse to poetic predecessors which he tended to regard as rivals rather than models. As a reader, I ask the question keeping in mind Irigaray's understanding of gender, arrived at through a strategic essentialism, or essentialism as 'a position rather than as an ontology' (Whitford 1994: 16; see Schor 1994). Gender is an

index and mark of the *subjectivity* and the ethical responsability [*sic*] of the speaker. . . . It constitutes the irreducible differentiation that oc- curs *on the inside of 'the human race.'* Gender stands for the unsubstitutable position of the *I* and the *you* (*le tu*) and of their modes of expression. Once the difference between *I* and *you* is gone, then asking, thanking, appealing, questioning . . . also disappear. (Irigaray 1993*c*: 169–70)

Such is Irigaray's call for an *ethics* of sexual difference, 'I' and 'you' engaged 'in a collective process of self-definition' (Whitford 1991: 144). In other words, using a strategic essentialism and insisting on the 'feminine' as 'B' rather than '–A' (while at the same time keeping in mind we do not know what 'the feminine' is), we can at least begin to posit two subjectivities, 'A' and 'B', at which point strategic essen-

---

[17] See Mann 1981 who argues that Donne is criticizing rather than colluding in this libertine attitude.

tialism can be discarded to allow for an exploration of how these subjectivities speak, enunciate, and evolve. Once we are released from patriarchy's 'A'/'–A' vicious circle into the 'fecundity' of plural subjectivities, the possibility of creative, ethical relationship truly begins. In his figurations of the feminine, when Donne asks 'What shall we call thee, then?' of Sappho, the Muse, Eve, and Elizabeth Drury, does his writing reveal any acknowledgement of 'the un-substitutable position of the *I* and the *you*', of 'difference as positivity', as something other than the failure of a fallen world? Or, are his feminine figures always just place holders, additional substitutions for the 'not I' or 'not-man', for 'when hee hath the kernell eate, | Who doth not fling away the shell?' ('Communitie', 23–4).

Like Margaret Miles's discussion of St Augustine, my discussion of Donne in its 'reiteration of the male convention of discussing women in connection with sex seeks not to perpetuate but to display and subvert this placement of women as objects of male desire' (Miles 1992: 72) and to trouble the frequently naturalized connection between women and the sexual or material.[18] In other words, the goal is not to replace one *'concept* of femininity' with another, but to read in the optative mood (Burke 1994: 48); to read *as if* there were 'a place for the feminine within sexual difference' (Irigaray 1985*b*: 159), so as to listen for what has been silenced, repressed, or hidden. One way of listening is, paradoxically, to mimic. Criticized for her almost exclusive focus on male philosophers, Irigaray is nevertheless deliberate in her choice of texts. In an effort to recover or discover a feminine 'specificity', Irigaray asserts that one must go 'back through the dominant discourse' (1985*b*: 119). One must deliberately assume the role 'historically assigned to the feminine: that of *mimicry*' or mirroring the masculine, reflecting man to himself.[19] To adopt a strategy of mimicry—this time not in order to parrot but in order to parody 'through amplification and rearticulation' (Schor 1994: 67) —is 'for a woman, to try to recover the place of her exploitation by discourse, without allowing herself to be simply reduced to it. . . . so as to make "visible," by an effect of playful repetition, what was sup-

---

[18] See Munich 1988: 243–4; Showalter 1989*b*: 4–5. Both assert the importance of returning to male-authored texts for similar reasons. See Bynum 1995, esp. 15–17, for a warning against assuming a historical essentialization of body/matter as female.

[19] Whitford explains the psychoanalytic basis for Irigaray's strategy of mimicry (1991: 36). See also J. Butler 1993: 36 ff.

posed to remain invisible: the cover-up of a possible operation of the feminine in language' (Irigaray 1985*b*: 76).[20] Because 'one cannot simply leap outside that [phallocratic] discourse', one must 'situate [one]self at its borders and . . . move continuously from the inside to the outside' (1985*b*: 122). '[T]he issue is not one of elaborating a new theory of . . . woman . . . but of jamming the theoretical machinery itself, of suspending its pretension to the production of a truth and of a meaning that are excessively univocal.' As we saw, Sapho's question seems to implement a mimeticism which exposes and goes beyond what it repeats by exerting a '*disruptive excess*' (1985*b*: 78).

Irigaray speaks of mimicking patriarchal discourse in general, but Carol Neely advocates a similar 'over-reading' of Renaissance texts, to read 'as if for the first time, instead of merely rereading them or deconstructing traditional readings. [A feminist critique] needs to over-read, to read to excess, the possibility of human (especially female) gendered subjectivity, identity, and agency' (1988: 15–16). In the words of Donne himself, 'Nothing is to be neglected as little, from which great things may arise. If the consequence may be great, the thing must not be thought little. . . . Words, and lesse particles then words have busied the whole Church'.[21] While we must recognize that Donne is talking about the Bible, an exceptional text which as the Word of God is subject to a different hermeneutic, his advice is nevertheless relevant to my feminist project, and corresponds to a psychoanalytic view in which the 'unnoticed, the detail that is casually relegated as insignificant or accidental, can usually be reckoned to be significant and revelatory' (Whitford 1991: 106).

Neely's call to read 'as if for the first time' echoes Irigaray's assertion of the need for wonder or *admiration* as a response: 'This passion has no opposite or contradiction and exists always as though for the first time' (1993*a*: 12). '[A]n action that is both active and passive' (73), wonder 'does not try to seize, possess, or reduce [an] object, but leaves it subjective, still free' (13). As part of her strategic essentialism, Irigaray urges a return to wonder between the unsubstitutable man

---

[20] See Irigaray 1985*b*: 144, 151; 1993*a*: 9–10. Whitford notes, however, that Irigaray's 'mimetic strategy makes it difficult to know to what extent [she] is endorsing any of the positions she occupies discursively, and to what extent she is consciously imitating them in order to expose the patriarchal symbolic distribution' (1991: 94–5).

[21] Donne, *Sermons* (1953–62), ix. 71. Hereafter, cited by volume (in Roman numerals) and page number in parentheses.

and woman or the 'I' and the 'you' so as to 'arrive at the constitution of an ethics of sexual difference', but such a relationship of wonder between author and reader can also be extrapolated from her work. One way of 'jamming the theoretical machinery' of patriarchy is to *'have a fling with the philosophers'* (1985*b*: 150) or in my case, with the poet, John Donne, for whom wonder or admiration as an everyday 'process of defamiliarization' was crucial: 'All love is wonder'. To take up such a position in relation to Donne's texts, as one way of reading, is to assume 'a relation of passionate involvement' rather than one of 'detached objectivity. . . . The lover may not be objective, in the sense of "impartial" but does perceive what the more detached observer will never see' (Whitford 1994: 19). In her call to read '*other*wise', Catherine Belsey urges that we treat texts 'with almost infinite respect' (1994: 13). Irigaray's call for a response of wonder and Belsey's call for respect are, for my own reading practice, then, ways of balancing the trend in current critical practice towards 'de-mystification rather than celebration' (Harvey and Maus 1990: p. xi) and an attempt 'to relearn the least fashionable of lessons, a lesson which is indeed anathema to the academy', 'the humility which admits the varying and variable limits of its own understandings' (Lyon 1997: 115).

If Donne and Irigaray seem unlikely bedfellows, there are, nevertheless, uncanny similarities of concern in their work, not all of which can be fully explored in this book. For example, both are fascinated by angels in their role as messengers and mediators between the human and divine.[22] Both Irigaray and Donne recognize the short-comings of Neoplatonic attitudes towards the relationship between body and soul, and offer up possibilities for a more creative mode of being, what Irigaray calls a *'sensible transcendental '* (1993*a*: 32), and what one critic recognizes in Donne as a call for a transcendence 'accomplished not by denial of the body but through its fulfillment' (Guibbory 1993: 137). Both explore the symbolism of thresholds. Both encourage a response of wonder in one's ethical relations. Both insist on the necessity of touch and explore the concept of nearness. Obviously, to point to similar themes and concerns is not to suggest

---

[22] In *An Ethics of Sexual Difference*, Irigaray writes of the angel as 'a representation of a sexuality that has never been incarnated' and suggests that a 'sexual or carnal ethics would require that both angel and body be found together' (1993*a*: 15–17). Compare Donne's assertion that 'Love must not be, but take a body too' (l. 10) in 'Air and Angels'.

that Donne and Irigaray approach them in similar ways or come to
the same conclusions as to their significance, nor that each is consistent in their approach to these issues within their own work. Donne
and Irigaray are both notoriously difficult writers in their own way,
and one constantly struggles to navigate between the Scylla of re-
ductiveness and the Charybdis of vagueness when reading their
work. I want to avoid 'emprison[ing]' Donne's own 'incomprehensiblenesse', insofar as I assert with the postmodernists that undecidability is not meaninglessness, or, to use the terms of an earlier and
influential generation, the mark of a lesser or minor poet.

Undoubtedly, Irigaray calls for a far more radical interrogation of
phallocentric discourse[23] than is possible in a book which implements
feminist historicist approaches to Renaissance texts; that is, which
considers Donne's writing in its local, historical, as well as its generic
contexts. Irigaray's relevance to my reading of Donne lies in the
breadth of her critique, which Margaret Whitford calls 'a sort of
"psychoanalysis" of western culture and metaphysics, seeking what
underpins its fragile rationality, looking for the "repressed" or unconscious of culture' (1991: 33). Furthermore, if there are shared
themes in the work of Donne and Irigaray, critics have also noted
that the Renaissance and the twentieth century share a concern with
the 'inner life' and the ways in which it interacts with the more
external spheres (see Finucci and Schwarz 1994: 3; P. Parker 1987:
5; Howard 1987). Gender paradigms in both eras are no exception.
Caroline Bynum's warning against the danger of transhistorical
comparisons is worth reiterating, however. She urges that we understand the relationship between two historically discrete thinkers (she
compares Origen and Judith Butler) as 'analagous and proportional,
not direct', because 'the past is seldom usefully examined by assuming that its specific questions or their settings are the same as those of
the present'. To paraphrase Bynum, then, Donne is to Donne's context as Irigaray is to Irigaray's, yet we can recognize 'that there is a
large and developing issue with which both figures struggle, each in
his or her own vocabulary and circumstances' (1995: 29).

As I indicate by my choice of epigraph for this introduction,

---

[23] Joanna Hodge notes that Irigaray rejects 'the Anglo-American scholarly
apparatus', refusing to employ footnotes, explicit quotation, or direct references.
Subverting the boundary between one's own text and texts of others thus 'permits
a writing with explicit ethical intent, defying the canons of neutrality', and
questioning 'what counts as authority' (1994: 199–200). See also Whitford 1991:
36–7.

I suggest Donne's writing constitutes one of the fault lines of Western culture in which the struggle of masculine subjectivity to bury the feminine 'ground' on which it depends is especially apparent. Here is the passage from the end of Donne's 'An Anatomy of the World', or *The First Anniversary*, which contains my epigraph:

> Nor could incomprehensiblenesse deterre
> Me, from thus trying to emprison her.
> Which when I saw that a strict grave could do,
> I saw not why verse might not doe so too.
> Verse hath a middle nature: heaven keepes soules,
> The grave keeps bodies, verse the fame enroules. [24]

One way to read these lines is to see them as Donne's recognition of the 'incomprehensiblenesse' or unknowability of Elizabeth Drury in particular—the poem's purported subject—but also, I would argue, of the whole female sex, the incomprehensibleness of 'her'. In Donne's admission (quickly followed by his phallogocentric determination to set limits on 'her' boundlessness anyway) is evidence of Irigaray's assertion that if we go back through the male imaginary and look at woman as she has been defined by and for men, we will find that '[n]o metaphor completes her' (1985a: 229); or, as Whitford expresses it: 'there is something which exceeds all attempts to confine/define her within a system (of discourse, representation etc.), or to appropriate her power(s) within the philosophical logos' (Irigaray 1991a: 27).[25] The same is true for the masculine: 'One sex is not entirely consumable by the other. There is always a *remainder*' (1993a: 14).

Donne defines 'comprehend' in a sermon which addresses the mystery of Christ's birth to a Virgin-Mother: 'for to comprehend is not to know a thing, as far as I can know it, but to know it as far, as that thing can be knowne' (*Sermons*, vi. 184; see iv. 128–9). Here then, is an acknowledgement of what Irigaray calls the irreducible difference between self and other *as* other. However, writing about the relation-

---

[24] Donne 1995a: 17, ll. 469–74. Hereafter I quote the *Anniversaries* and 'A Funerall Elegie' by line number from this edition. When it is not clear in the main text which poem I am referring to, I include an abbreviation parenthetically: FE ('A Funerall Elegie'), FA (*The First Anniversary*), or SA (*The Second Anniversary*).

[25] Irigaray's essay, 'Volume-Fluidity' in 1985a: 227–40 is translated in 1991a by David Macey as 'Volume without Contours', 53–67. We might 'wonder if it is impossible to "imprison" or silence more than half of the world's population' (1993a: 120), Irigaray suggests ironically.

ship between husband and wife in a verse letter to the Countess of Huntingdon, Donne suggests that the Countess's husband does comprehend her in the sense of 'contain' as well as 'know': 'So you, as woman, one doth comprehend, | And in the vaile of kindred others see; | To some you are reveal'd, as in a friend, | And as a vertuous Prince farre off, to mee' ('Man to Gods image, *Eve*, to mans was made', 41–4). As we shall see, Chapter 3 focuses on the 'comprehension' of woman within marriage. In this book I explore the tensions between several kinds of incomprehensibleness: the fundamental ontological incomprehensibleness of self which Donne expresses in *The Second Anniversary*: 'Thou art to narrow, wretch, to comprehend | Even thy selfe: yea though thou wouldst but bend | To know thy body' (261–3); the 'irreducible difference' between individual subjectivities so that we can never fully know another person; the incomprehensibleness of woman as woman, rather than as 'woman-for-man'; and the resulting tension in Donne's attempts to 'emprison' the various figures of the feminine.

One strategy for 'emprison[ing] her' is, paradoxically, by articulating woman; that is, putting her (partly, or in parts) into discourse, but only as she is defined by and for man (see Irigaray 1990: 91). Throughout literature, 'the female body has been feared for its power to articulate itself' (Gubar 1981: 246); feared for its desires and its power to create. The Latin root of 'articulate' denotes the joints or limbs of the body, or more abstractly, 'pieces', which are distinctly divided, yet form a coherent whole; hence, clear, distinct speech itself. An articulation is thus paradoxical, for it is a whole which is only whole or coherent as a result of the differentiation of parts within itself (for similar observations see Garber 1997: 35–6, 42; Hillman and Mazzio 1997: pp. xi, xv). Keeping in mind the bodily metaphor submerged in the notion of articulation, then, I will ask in each chapter whether Donne's articulation of the female body is one which breaks that body into pieces, fearful of the female body's power to articulate or name itself as something other than 'the Other of the Same'. In some of Donne's elegies—for instance, 'The Anagram' or 'The Comparison'—Donne more or less successfully diffuses the female body's power so that Woman becomes not even a disembodied voice or Echo, but a mute and mutilated body, a statistic of male desire.[26] Irigaray asks:

[26] See Nancy J. Vickers's classic essay on Petrarch's scattering of Laura's body (1982).

Must this multiplicity of female desire and female language be understood as shards, scattered remnants of a violated sexuality? A sexuality
denied? The question has no simple answer. The rejection, the exclusion of a female imaginary certainly puts woman in the position of
experiencing herself only fragmentarily, in the little-structured margins of a dominant ideology, as waste, or excess, what is left of a mirror invested by the (masculine) 'subject' to reflect himself, to copy
himself. (1985b: 30)

Woman's fragmentation thus leaves her 'unable to articulate her
difference' (1985a: 228). When Sapho asks, 'What shall we call thee,
then?' and Donne determines to 'emprison' Elizabeth Drury, these
two articulations reveal one of the central paradoxes of patriarchal
discourse: the taking of what is unknown—the 'feminine sexe' in its
own right—and relegating her to what Irigaray calls an 'internal exile'
(1993a: 65). Philaenis is there but we cannot see her. Elizabeth is
incomprehensible but Donne attempts to imprison her in language.
I will argue the same is true for Sappho, the Muse, and Eve, but I also
suggest there are moments when Donne does seem to articulate
something of the 'excess' which is woman beyond the margins of
patriarchal discourse.

Irigaray uses the phrase, 'internal exile', to describe the paradox of
woman's existence as both a symbolic homelessness and an imprisonment in which woman is literally shut up in the house, the
private sphere, controlled as an object of exchange between men. But
Irigaray also talks about the larger phenomenon of the 'dereliction of
the feminine' (1993a: 126). Whitford suggests that déréliction has
much stronger connotations in French than in English, 'for example
the state of being abandoned by God or, in mythology, the state of an
Ariadne, abandoned on Naxos, left without hope, without help, without refuge' (1991: 77–8). Whitford is probably correct in terms of
late twentieth-century society, but for Donne and in a Christian
context, the word, 'dereliction', is extremely resonant because it is one
of the words Christ speaks on the cross at Matthew 27: 46. Donne
quotes the phrase from the Vulgate in his sermons: Ut quid dereliquisti
mei.[27] In 'A Hymne to God the Father' Donne admits to a profound

---

[27] The King James Authorized Version (1611) reads: 'And about the ninth hour
Jesus cried with a loud voice, saying, ELI, ELI, LAMA SABACHTHANI? that is
to say, My God, My God, why hast thou forsaken me?' See Sermons, ii. 92, 141,
161, 300; iii. 267; v. 160. Donne's treatise on suicide, Biathanatos, is cited by the
OED under the definition for 'dereliction': 'the action of leaving or forsaking
(with intention not to resume); abandonment'.

fear of dereliction: 'I have a sinne of feare, that when I'have spunne |
My last thred, I shall perish on the shore'.[28] Borrowing Heidegger's
notion of dwelling, Irigaray considers how dereliction operates differently for men and women. 'To *inhabit* is the fundamental trait of
man's being. Even if this trait remains unconscious, unfulfilled,
especially in its ethical dimension, man is forever searching for,
building, creating homes for himself everywhere: caves, huts,
women, cities, language, concepts, theory, and so on' (1993*a*: 141).
Irigaray points to the nostalgia men carry with them for their first
dwelling, the womb of their first love object, their mother, who
always remains, in some sense, their love object, although taboo
according to the Law of the Father: 'Unmitigated mourning for the
intrauterine nest, elemental homesickness that man will seek to
assuage through his work as builder of worlds, and notably of the
dwelling which seems to form the essence of his maleness: language'
(1993a: 127). Whitford explains, 'Everyone is born into dereliction
through the loss of their original home but men palliate the loss at
women's expense' (1991: 153). Irigaray argues that '[t]his linguistic
home that man has managed to substitute even for his dwelling in a
body, whether his own body or another's, has used women as construction material, but (therefore?) it is not available to her' (1993*a*:
107; see 1990: 96). One of the aims of this book, then, is to explore
the ways in which Donne constructs a shelter for himself out of or
indeed against the female body, leaving the feminine in what is
sometimes recognized as '*internal exile*'.

In this introduction I have used three excerpts from Donne's
poetry to demonstrate the need for a feminist reading which moves
away from simply identifying Donne, the 'great visiter of Ladies'
(Bald 1986: 72) as cynical libertine or tender lover. What follows
subjects his gender constructions to analysis, both within his own
cultural context as well as in the recognition that as twentieth-
century readers, '[t]o read the past, to read a text from the past, is . . .
always to make an interpretation which is in a sense an anachron-
ism'(Belsey 1993: 2). I thus adopt Irigaray's strategy of going
'back through the dominant discourse' in order to read 'suspiciously'
(Turner 1993*b*: 7) but also from a stance of wonder, in the assertion
that there is as much to 'discover' about Donne and our own reading

---

[28] Donne 1982: 51, ll. 13–14. Future references to any of Donne's religious
poems will be cited from this edition by line number.

practices as there is to 'recover' of his literary historical milieu.[29] An assessment of just how Donne is situated in relation to Renaissance discourses of gender will aid in a much needed reassessment of his whole canon.

[29] John R. Roberts's description of the 'major split that continues to divide critics on Donne' is still relevant: 'the recoverers still regard with suspicion the discoverers as dangerously clever, overly imaginative, unscholarly dilettantes, while the discoverers still dismiss with some contempt the recoverers as pedantic, literal-minded, harmless antiquarians who have nothing significant to contribute to the central, important issues of modern criticism' (1982: 64–5).

# Donne's Domestic Muse:
# Engendering Poetry in the Early Verse
# Letters

[T]he Invention of *Young Men* is more lively, then that of Old:
And Imaginations streame into their Mindes better, and, as it
were, more Divinely.

> (Francis Bacon, *Essayes*, 'Of Youth and Age')

[Donne's] Muse suffers continual pangs and throes. His
thoughts are delivered by the Cæsarean operation.

> (William Hazlitt, *Lectures On the Comic Writers*)

This chapter explores Donne's representations of his relationship
with his Muse. Nearly half of the twenty-two references to a Muse
in Donne's poetry occur in the verse letters he wrote during the
1590s, and so my focus is related to certain generic issues because
of the concentration of these references in a single genre. Indeed,
my contextualization of Donne's poetry using contemporary Renaissance texts will show that the adaptation of the Muse figure
which occurs during the Renaissance is connected, in part, with
generic experimentation and the self-conscious definition (in
some cases, the derogation) of a specifically English poetry. Because Donne's early verse letters often self-consciously articulate
the process of their own creation through the use of gendered
imagery, I also consider gender-related images of poetic creation in
these poems, whether or not a Muse is involved.

The verse letters which Donne exchanged with male friends
during the 1590s are a felicitous place to test a feminist reading of
gender dynamics in Donne's writing for several reasons. First,
these short poems to his university and London Inns of Court
friends are Donne's earliest extant poetic work in English.[1] Second,

---

[1] See Flynn 1995 for a persuasive argument that a number of Latin epigrams were
Donne's 'earliest literary efforts' written at age 14. They are printed for the first time
since the seventeenth century in Donne 1995*b*.

they are a group of poems which share stylistic and structural elements, chronological proximity, and contextual similarity, thus making it somewhat easier to isolate gender issues for investigation. Third and most important, these poems experiment with the oldest and most fundamental of poetic conventions: the invocation of the Muse. Placed in the larger context of Elizabethan treatments of the Muse, the early verse letters and their domestic or lesbian Muses are the site, heretofore almost unmapped, of important developments in the convention of invocation and in Renaissance gender dynamics. These early poems show Donne building the foundations of his 'house of language' with, precisely, the feminine as building material. While this book aims to document and discuss, rather than to trace any chronological development in, Donne's representations of the feminine, these early verse letters show that gender dynamics were central to Donne from the very beginning, as both cause for enquiry and as a metaphorical means to explore and convey other ideas. In exploring how gender functions in the exchange between poet and Muse, and in the creative process generally, this chapter will be divided into four sections: (1) a theoretical framework which establishes the co-ordinates of my enquiry; (2) a review of the status of the Muse among Donne's contemporaries; (3) an in-depth discussion of Donne's early verse letters and the Muse's role; (4) a brief coda in which I consider the Muse's 'interre[ment]' and Hazlitt's comment cited as an epigraph for this chapter.

## I. THEORETICAL FRAMEWORK: WHY IS THE MUSE FEMALE?

The apparently inane question, 'Why is the Muse female?' is not solely my own. It is a question asked by Thomas Heywood in his *Gunaikeion; or, Nine Bookes of Various History Concerning Women; Inscribed by yᵉ names of yᵉ Nine Muses* (1624), which I will discuss later in this section. I mimic Heywood's question not only because it is one which Heywood's contemporaries were asking, if not always so overtly; such questions are also being posed in the general 're-visioning' (Rich 1979: 35) of texts by feminist scholarship. Even the most basic structures and symbols of literature are being re-examined from a perspective which foregrounds the role of gender in the construction of meaning.[2] Donne and his contemporaries foreground what had remained a relatively unacknowledged element operating in invocation: the very femaleness of the Muse.[3] That aspect which is now taken for granted amidst much formulaic tedium—the gender of the Muse or Muses—is that aspect with which Donne plays most. As recently as 1991, the Muse figure, when mentioned at all, is still being described as 'latently' female (Humphries 1991: 197). Why is the femaleness of the Muse so often latent, that is, 'hidden, concealed; present . . . but not manifest, exhibited or developed'? And why is the Muse's latent femaleness capitalized on in the Renaissance? The very centres of the words, 'invocation' (L., *invocare*, to call for help), and 'inspiration' (L., *inspirare*, to breathe upon or into), constitute the heart of poetry: the activation of voice and authority in order to communicate human experience and to mediate between the human and the divine, the mortal and the immortal. How does Donne construct his relationship with the figure traditionally considered to activate the poet's voice and authority? What might this poet of 'masculine perswasive force' owe the female Muse? Questions with broader implications arise as well. Why, when Donne engages in textual exchange with his male friends, does he so often depend on the mediatory body of woman? Why is intellectual creation so often grounded in a somatic metaphor when it is supposedly trying to assert its superiority over the body and 'mere' procreation?[4]

Arthur Marotti suggests that the misogyny evident in some of the poetry of Donne and his coterie is a direct result of the challenges they faced while studying at the Inns of Court in

---

[2] An important essay with far-reaching implications beyond its classicist context that phrases a similar question, 'in all innocence', is Halperin's 'Why is Diotima a Woman?' (1990: 113–51).

[3] As several critics have pointed out, a few references to a male Muse do exist. See Graves 1961: 446–7 n. 1. Graves's condemnation of those who do invoke a male Muse suggests that gender dynamics between poet and Muse are not insignificant. He dismisses Milton's reference to a male Muse in *Lycidas* as 'a mere conceit', pointing out that Milton substitutes 'Muse' for 'poet possessed by a Muse'. See *Lycidas*, ll. 19–22. The phenomenon occurs earlier than Milton, in Joseph Hall's 1611 prefatory poem to Donne's 'Anatomy of the World', for example. Female poets seem to invoke the traditional female Muse until around the nineteenth century. See the discussion of Charlotte Brontë's 'Genius' and Emily Dickinson's 'Master' in Gilbert and Gubar 1979: 394, 429–30, 607–11, 636. For a general cultural overview, see Battersby 1989: *passim*.

[4] A valuation which originates in Plato's *Symposium*. See Halperin 1990: 117–18.

London, one of which was encountering the daughters of wealthy London citizens (1986: 53). John Carey has also argued that these women were perceived as both a threat and a promise, 'frighteningly emancipated and self-assertive' (1960: 370) yet desirable marriage matches. In the light of this particular phenomenon and the crisis in the definition of women faced by Donne and his contemporaries (see Woodbridge 1986: 181; Belsey 1993: 185), we might conclude that the poet's Muse was a figure of the feminine over whom he could assert control. She was perhaps a convenient figure to manipulate in their coterie poetry—precisely because she was a figure—as they jockeyed both for career advancement in an increasingly crowded field and for good marriage matches.

A more literary explanation for the Muse's treatment lies in the generic, stylistic, and thematic experimentation taking place in tandem with the 'anticourtly impulse shared by many Inns men' which Marotti (1986) and Harold Love (1993: 224 ff.), among others, have recently discussed. 'The verbal medium for such an attitude was a linguistic style sharply distinguished from that of "complement," a form of plainspeaking with roots in the egalitarian mode of humanist literary exchange, noncourtly genres like the epigram and the Ovidian elegy, as well as the native English traditions of moral prose and poetry' (Marotti 1986: 29, 33). The demoted, domesticated, or debauched Muses we find in the poetry of Donne and his contemporaries are, I suggest, a reaction against the Petrarchan convention of the unyielding, disdainful mistress, as well as the response of young poets to the classical traditions with which their education was saturated. Indeed, Donne's 'masculine perswasive force', and that of some of his contemporaries, was just as likely to be exerted against the Muse as inspired by her. There were innumerable traditional references to the Muse amidst the flood of classical imitation, but there was also an individuality asserted—collectively and singly—in an England Gabriel Harvey calls the 'new Parnassus', and written with, in Alexander Barclay's phrase, 'newe forged Muses nine'.[5]

[5] See below for Harvey's assessment. Alexander Barclay is, however, being derogatory in referring to 'newe forged Muses nine'. In his fourth eclogue, Barclay rails against bad poets who advance at court by flattering their princes (1928: p. 165, l. 691). Barclay's dates (1475?–1552) are earlier than the period with which I am concerned but his phrase anticipates the trend of 'newe' Muses, whether they are corrupt or not.

In his *Defence of Poetry* Philip Sidney considers 'why England, the mother of excellent minds, should be grown so hard a stepmother to poets' such as other countries can boast. His answer is 'that base men with servile wits undertake it who think it enough if they can be rewarded of the printer. . . . For now, as if all the Muses were got with child, to bring forth bastard poets, without any commission they do post over the banks of Helicon, till they make the readers more weary than post-horses' (1973: 110, 111). Sidney's complaint points to another important development which influenced representations of the Muse: the emergence of a class of professional writers. Disdain for these mercenary poets was often expressed as a sullying of the poet/Muse relationship. The Muse's 'fall', whether a descent from the Petrarchan pedestal or from remote Parnassian heights, generally involved a reversal in positions of authority. The poet had always been 'Μοῦσαων θεράπων [servant of the Muses]',[6] whereas Joseph Hall laments in 1598:

> O age well thriven and well fortunate,
> When ech man hath a Muse appropriate,
> And she like to some servile eare-boar'd slave
> Must play and sing when, and what he would have![7]

The classical Muse was associated with higher forms of literature, especially epic and lyric. Renaissance English poets, as they reclaimed classical forms, experimented with new genres in English such as satire, epigram, and the verse epistle. In keeping with a kind of decorum which had some precedent in the Roman poets, Donne and his contemporaries invoke the Muse in these lower genres, but by suitably transforming their inspiring figure. *Les grandes dames* of Parnassus were not expected to waste their time on a mere epigram or puling love poems. The English Muse, besides being more immediate and personal, embraces the whole spectrum of female physicality: sometimes chaste, sometimes fecund and maternal or merrily wanton, even whorish. When authors wanted to condemn the obscene and bawdy writing of their fellow poets, they exploited associations of the feminine with the material and

---

[6] The Greek phrase contains no menial implications, but suggests a close association between the Muse and the attendant poet. See Harriott 1969: 41. The Elizabethans represent the Muse both as a menial servant and as an intimate who participates in the creation of poetry.

[7] *Virgidemiarum*, 6.1.233–6 in Hall 1969: 94. All future quotations of Hall's poetry will be taken from this edition.

sexual, and inscribed their condemnation on the body of the Muse. This development seems part of 'a new and aggressively sexualized form of distinctly English literature', neither 'Elizabethan bawdy' nor 'Ovidian sensual', a form which Lynda Boose suggests was influenced by the infamous Italian satirist and pornographer, Pietro Aretino, and which resulted in the 1599 Bishops' Ban (1994: 185–200).[8] In contrast to the 'shaming' of the Muse in the moralistic and more public genres of satire and epigram, Donne's verse letters present a domestic Muse whose roles correspond to the maid/wife/widow paradigm. Donne's figuration of her seems to relate more to private concerns; or, to use Anthony Low's terms, to 'communal' rather than 'social' concerns (1993: 63). If the classical Muse is denizened within the 'new Parnassus' of England, Donne's Muse is domesticated and familiarized with the poet in the sense of 'having the character or position of the inmate of a house' (*OED*).

The convention of invocation intersects with another convention in Donne's early verse letters and other poetry: the use of procreative imagery to describe the generation of a poem, which we saw in Sidney's *Defence*, above, and which he famously combines in the first sonnet of *Astrophil and Stella* (see below). These two conventions present the relationship of voice, body, and gender in complex ways. In one case, a female deity functions as the source of a male poet's voice. In addition to creative inspiration, the Muse could bestow wisdom, knowledge, and authority. In the other case, the female body's unique function of parturition is used figuratively by a male poet to describe his own intellectual creative process, usually as a difficult, painful, and protracted labour. I will show that Donne and his contemporaries combine the two conventions of invocation and the use of (pro)creative metaphors to the following effect: while appealing to the classical Muse for her traditional gifts of poetic voice, inspiration, or knowledge—that is, in*voking* her—they also (metaphorically) biologize her role in the creative process, and hence in*carnate* a Muse who is less a lofty Greek deity and more a personal attendant, as we saw in the excerpt from Joseph Hall's satires. Although she is never described the way a mistress's body is catalogued, the Muse's bodily presence—insofar as she has been assigned a sexual function—is called upon.

---

[8] Boose does not discuss the Muse figure.

Poetry is thus created in the midst of what seems to be a fundamental paradox. It owes its voice, by its own acknowledgement, to the chaste Sister Muses of Mount Helicon, and its memory to their mother, Mnemosyne (Memory), without whom there would be no poetry and no immortal fame. However, women as historical agents in everyday life—whether in classical Athens or late Elizabethan England—were, with few exceptions, denied their voices, only '[p]ermitted to break their silence in order to acquiesce in the utterances of others', the authority of their fathers or husbands (Belsey 1993: 149). Moreover, male writers appropriate the uniquely physical function of women as childbearers to describe an intellectual endeavour from which women are essentially excluded except as the source of the poet's voice,[9] an appropriation 'perfectly consistent with an ideology that prescribes the strict supervision of female sexual behaviour, and the exclusion of actual women from literary endeavours' (Maus 1993: 274). The transformation of the Muse from autonomous deity to a poet's servant who must 'play and sing, when, and what he would have', would seem to be a phenomenon closely related to the appropriation of the womb as a figure for the imagination. Poets take the generative metaphor one step further (or rather, back), and involve the Muse as a sexual, fertile, female vessel. The Muse is thus one more female 'enabling figure for the production of male artists' and 'thus both that which is not, and that without which there cannot be' poetry, art, discourse (Barbara Johnson 1994: 59).[10]

There is only one reference to a Muse in Donne's *Songs and Sonets* and I want to consider it now. In 'Love's Growth' Donne declares:

> Love's not so pure, and abstract, as they use
> To say, which have no Mistresse but their Muse,
> But as all else, being elemented too,
> Love sometimes would contemplate, sometimes do. (11–14)

[9] For excellent documentation and analysis of the denial to women of discursive subjectivity and 'the demonization of eloquence' in Renaissance England, see Belsey 1985: 149–91; Jardine 1989: 103–40.

[10] Johnson analyses Joshua Reynold's painting, *Theory*, and poses the question, 'What does it mean to personify theory as a *woman*?' (53). Recall Halperin's formulation, 'necessary female absence', and see P. Parker 1987: 132 ff.

These lines reiterate Donne's confounding of Neoplatonic hierarchies of physical and spiritual love in, for example, 'The
Exstasie': 'Loves mysteries in soules doe grow, | But yet the body is
his booke' (71–2). Donne's observations on the necessarily mixed
nature of love are found throughout his *Songs and Sonets*. In
'Love's Growth' Donne points to the unfulfilling—because merely
ethereal—relations which poets conduct with their Mistress Muses
while he plays with the conventional distinction made between
the active and contemplative life, a popular subject in theological
and humanist writings, and, indeed, in his own verse letters to
Henry Wotton. Whether Donne's insistence upon love's physical
and spiritual modalities in terms of 'both/and', rather than 'either/
or', is simply an elaborate seduction lesson for the benefit of the
male sex has been debated by such astute readers of 'The Exstasie'
as Janel Mueller (1985).

Donne's 'incarnation' of his Muse could be one more instance
of performing a literary seduction for the approbation of one's
male friends, or a more sincere manifestation of what Elaine
Scarry calls his 'volitional materialism': '[t]hroughout the poetry
and sermons, Donne is forever tracing and retracing the passage
between the material and immaterial worlds. . . . The passage from
body to voice, or body to language is itself one instance of the
spectrum that leads from the material to the immaterial. . . . It is as
though Donne cannot allow body and voice to become separated
from one another' (1988*a*: 78–9). In his early verse letters, Donne
often insists on the (metaphorical) body's participation in the
creation of poetry just as he insists on the body's participation in
the generation of love in some of the *Songs and Sonets*. Indeed,
what the early verse letters show us, I will argue, is a situation
whereby Donne and his male companion poets imagine themselves both 'contemplat[ing]' and 'do[ing]', i.e. having intercourse
with, their Muses. Unlike the one in 'Love's Growth', the Muse of
the early verse letters is engaged in love that is neither 'pure' nor
'abstract', but rather domestic, or adulterous, or lesbian, as we shall
see. She is not an aloof Petrarchan mistress but a willing and
fecund female, even, at times, 'in control' of her own sexuality.

Some years after Donne, Richard Brathwaite writes of Muses
who become excited by the language of love in terms similar to
those Donne uses in 'Love's Growth'. In *A Strappado for the Divell*

(1615), Brathwaite addresses Venus, Goddess of Love, and notes that she 'hath some aliance with a Poet':

> Yet art thou much endeared to their Art,
> Though they can say nought for the practick part;
> . . .
> Some I doe know, even of the pregnant'st men,
> That love to trade with *Venus* now and then,
> And this the cause why they observe that use,
> (As I have heard) for to enflame their Muse:
> And some I could produce, had their desire:
> For they, their Muse, and all were on a fire. (1615: 12)

Even poets with the greatest imaginative fecundity (still the primary meaning of 'pregnant' at this time, although Brathwaite may be punning, here) desire to write love poetry so as to indulge in a kind of male masturbatory fantasy. Unlike these love poets, however, Donne does not 'enflame' his Muse in love poetry; rather, he uses her as a figure for the poetic creation which enables him to communicate with his male friends in his verse letters.

In their heightened sensitivity to the (im)materiality of the Muses, English writers in the 1590s may have been influenced by several Continental works of literature, including Boethius' rejection of the Muses of Poetry in his *De consolatione philosophiae* (1.1.26–44), where Lady Philosophy banishes the Muses as harlots ('meretriculas'); Boccaccio's *Decameron* (1348) where he compares flesh and blood women and the Muses, and finds real women more inspiring; and Montaigne's *Essais* (1580 and 1588). Montaigne's *Essais*, published in 1580 (Books I and II) and 1588 (Book III), and translated in 1603 by John Florio, reveal that Montaigne was also thinking about the 'latent' metaphorical femaleness of the Muses. Unlike Donne in 'Love's Growth', he wonders in 'Of the affection of fathers to their children', 'whether my selfe should not much rather desire to beget and produce a perfectly-well-shaped, and excellently-qualited infant, by the acquaintance of the Muses, then by the copulation of my wife' (1603: 233). Montaigne also declares in 'Upon some verses of Virgil',

> I know not who could set *Pallas* and the *Muses* at odds with *Venus*, and make them colde and slowe in affecting of love; as for me, I see no Deities that better sute together, nor more endebted one to another. Who-ever shall goe about to remoove amorous imaginations from the *Muses*, shall deprive them of the best entertainement they have, and of the noblest subject of their worke. (509)

Just as the verses from Virgil's *Aeneid* (8.387–90, 404–6) which form the centrepiece of Montaigne's chapter serve to license the 'virile but familiar vernacular literary style' (Boutcher 1996: 198) which Montaigne cultivates, so does Montaigne in turn, it would seem, license the greater freedom English poets take with their Muse figure. Incarnating the Muse was one way for poets to achieve the affective yet heroic familiar style (see Boutcher 1996: 197 ff.) for which Montaigne was so celebrated and which meshed with the other modes of humanist literary exchange Marotti identified, above, as particularly connected with an Inns of Court style. Brathwaite may indeed be alluding to Montaigne in the poem I quoted above, while other poets seemed to take Montaigne's advice to an extreme, as we will see.

The Mistress-Muses mocked by Donne and Brathwaite point to another dynamic in tension with the incarnation of the Muse, whereby the Muse is incorporated within the poet to become, as Donne writes in one verse letter, 'the Soules Soule | Of Poets'. In Sidney's *Arcadia* the 'nearness' of poet and Muse is emphasized in another reversal of poetic 'possession':

> My muse what ails this ardour?
> 'Alas' she saith 'I am thine,
> So are thy pains my pains too.
> Thy heated harte my seat is
> Wherein I burne, thy breath is
> My voice, too hott to keepe in.' (1962: 67, ll. 40–5)

According to the Platonic tradition of poetic inspiration, the poet is possessed by a 'divine frenzy' and taken over by the Muse; that is, she enters his body or his mind for a time and speaks through him.[11] The male poet is no more than a passive vessel or conduit, a ventriloquist's dummy, for the powerful workings of the female Muse. In *Satire I*, Donne's speaker describes the 'Giddie fantastique Poets' (1967b: 10) he reads in his closet but he himself 'conferre[s]' (48) with the Muses, suggesting a more equitable relationship. In *Satire II*, the poet is 'sicke with Poëtrie, 'and possest

---

[11] See Plato (1994), *Ion*, 534a–e (p. 220); *Phaedrus*, 245a (p. 492). A comic variation was Horace's claim that wine, rather than possession by the Muse, makes for better poetic frenzy. See Horace, *Epistles* 1.19.5; Hall, *Virgidemiarum*, 1.3.1–2; Thomas Nashe's Preface to Robert Greene's *Menaphon* in C. G. Smith 1904: ii. 317; Ben Jonson, *Underwood*, 48 in Jonson 1925–52: viii. 220–1. Hereafter all references to Jonson's poetry are quoted from this edition by volume and page number.

with muse | . . . and mad' (61–2). By the nineteenth century, the theory that a poet's inspiration originates outside the poet was very largely replaced by the theory that inspiration originates within the soul of the poet (see Battersby 1989: *passim*). The question already for the Elizabethans, as we have seen in Hall and Sidney's poems, above, is who possesses whom? One could consider the invocation of the Muse and the childbirth metaphor, then, as modes of incorporation, or, to use Irigaray's phrase, '*internal exile*'. Ben Jonson articulates this phenomenon of the '*internal exile*' of the feminine when he talks of 'all the ladies of the *Thespian lake*, | . . . crusht into one forme' (viii. 108)[12] and in this poem finally rejects them altogether: 'No, I bring | My owne true fire' (28–9).

In her study of female allegorical figures Marina Warner provides a gloss for the incorporation of the Muse by the male poet when she analyses the motive behind Zeus' incorporation of Metis. Zeus must 'ingest' Metis for his own survival, and

make [her] one with him. Incorporation is a stronger bond than union and grants total control. As a daimon who dwells within the paternal womb of Zeus . . . her powers remain unimpaired, only differently sited and generated. . . . Zeus' incorporation of her into his being robs her of freedom of agency but does not diminish her force; the *thea* (goddess) loses definition to the daimon, and the personal patriarch with his multiple-faceted valency takes over from the plurality of the earlier pantheon, representing separate powers. (1985: 73–4)

Metis, pregnant with Athena, is sacrificed to the Law of the Father. Zeus' swallowing of Metis is an example of what Irigaray calls '*an appropriation of the relation to origin and of the desire for and as origin*' (1985*a*: 33). Samuel Daniel can thus instruct his poems in his sonnet sequence, *Delia*: 'Goe wailing verse, the infants of my love, | Minerva-like, brought foorth without a Mother'. We will also see Donne producing poems without a 'mother'. Margaret Whitford stresses that Irigaray is not 'positing the maternal metaphor as alternative origin' but rather she is urging that 'the relationship between the two parents has been forgotten' (1991: 112), that of a fecund couple. Both the incarnation and the incorporation of the Muse then, can be understood as the male appropriation of origin and feminine power. This dynamic is also due in part to the

---

[12] Jonson's poem was first published in Robert Chester's *Love's Martyr* (1601): 177–8 (Aa 3ʳ⁻ᵛ).

rejection of the pagan muses in early Christian poetry and their substitution by invocations of the poet's own soul (not altogether exclusive of classical poetry) or Christ as Word (Curtius 1979: 228–46) whereby the Judaeo-Christian all-male deity 'swallows up' representations of the divine feminine (Mollenkott 1993: *passim*).[13]

One critic asks, 'Why should [the male poet] need to do this?' 'Almost as long as poetry has existed, male poets have shared a fantasy: . . . speaking with a woman's voice', a fantasy sometimes 'embodied in the Muse' (Lipking 1988: 127). Initially, it is 'the passive, instrumental male' who acts as secretary under the power-ful agency of the Muse. Alternatively, Lipking recognizes, the Muse is subjected to 'the stealth [and] force' of a tradition driven by male fantasies of domination. He describes the Muse as 'the female daughter [*sic*] of memory who breathes into the male poet, wrapping him in a cloud of sexual confusion and longing until he takes up his pen and tries to impale her' (180). Male fear of a suffocating or engulfing female is overcome with an act of violence which mimics the act of desire, but with destructive rather than creative results. Indeed, the reversal of roles is accomplished by figured sexual violence, as several examples from Donne's con-temporaries discussed later in this chapter illustrate. The Muse is 'forced', that is, raped, before a poem is produced. In one of Donne's poems, she is ultimately 'interre[d]', no longer immortal and her own agent.

Whitford sees in Irigaray's rereadings of classical mythology 'her belief that in mythology we can see a struggle taking place between the maternal and paternal genealogies, eventually ending in the installation of patriarchy' (1991: 102). I would suggest that there is a similar struggle taking place on the body of the Muse figure as patriarchy seeks to erase her connection to her mother, Mnemo-syne, and her sisters, and make her a kind of secretary to each poet, a commodity among men, no longer returning home to Mount Helicon, as it were, at the end of each 'workday'. Like Echo, the nymph scorned by Narcissus, the Muse comes to have no body and no place of her own. Fully to document such a claim is clearly a larger task than the scope of this book affords, but I hope to illuminate its particular manifestations as reflected in Donne's

---

[13] But see Caroline Bynum's discussion of the flowering of medieval imagery of and devotion to 'mother Jesus' (1982: esp. ch. 4).

attitudes towards his own Muse, and to discuss whether or not Donne participates in the larger cultural process.

★

Let us turn, now, to Thomas Heywood's question in his *Gun-aikeion*. After presenting us with a catalogue of the Muses, and discussions by Hesiod, Homer, Plato, and later commentators in terms of their origin, number, and function, Heywood poses a final question:

It may now lastly bee demaunded by those that are studious of antiquities, Why the Vertues, the Disciplines, the Muses, the Devisers and Patrons of all good arts, with divers of the like nature, should rather bee comprehended under the feminine sexe, by the names of Virgins and women, as also their pictures drawne to the portraitures of damosells, than either by masculine nomination, or according to the effigies of men; the rather since not onely the Ethnickes and Morrall men, but even Christians and Theologists themselves, in all their bookes and writings which they commit to posteritie still continue them under the same gender? (1624: 60)

In referring to 'Christians and Theologists' as well as 'Ethnickes', or those who are not Christian or Jewish but heathen or pagan (*OED* B.1), Heywood points to the pervasiveness of the practice throughout Western culture. It is usually taken for granted that personifications of various abstract ideas—Truth, Justice, the Virtues, Poetry—are 'merely' arbitrary or nearly so in being based on grammatical gender assignation.[14] Heywood goes on to ask the same question or a variation of it seven times and indeed he protests too much. He borders on self-parody, and betrays an anxiety which Donne is more determined to assuage in his pronouncement: 'Nor could incomprehensiblenesse deterre/ Me, from thus trying to emprison her'. As constructed within patriarchal discourse, the Muses and female allegorical figures in general function as mere place holders who occupy, without inhabiting, the place of the feminine (Irigaray 1985a: 227; see B. Johnson 1994: 54; and Warner 1985: 238). Their phantom femaleness distracts from what Irigaray asserts is the mode of 'semblance' in which patriarchal societies function:

---

[14]  For various discussions of the arbitrariness of grammatical gender or the 'hidden sex' of words, see Irigaray 1993b: 67–74, 119–31; 1996: 69–78; Warner 1985: 63–70; Gombrich 1972: 125–6; B. Johnson 1994: 66–7, 72–3.

The value of symbolic and imaginary productions is superimposed upon, and even substituted for, the value of relations of material, natural and corporal (re)production. . . . Reigning everywhere, although prohibited in practice, hom(m)o-sexuality is played out through the bodies of women, matter, or sign, and heterosexuality has been up to now just an alibi for the smooth workings of man's relations with himself, of relations among men. . . . Men make commerce *of* [women], but they do not enter into any exchanges *with* them. (1985*b*: 171–2)

Joseph Hall, using language harking back to Pindar, alludes to this 'traffic in women'[15]—including figurative women—at the end of his satire on bad drama: 'Shame that the Muses should be bought and sold, | For every peasants Brasse, on each scaffold' (*Virgidemi-arum*, 1.3.57–8).[16]

Heywood finally answers his question(s) with language similar to Irigaray's, but without the irony. Tautological and anti-climactic, Heywood's answer finally evades by deferring to male authority: 'To all these objections, it is briefely answered . . . [t]hat by the symbole or semblance of such women, much science is begot, and besides much fruit ariseth from the judgment of the soule: besides it was a custome of old for Virgins to play and daunce in companies, which excellently fitted the coupling and sisterhood of the sciences'(60). Heywood's metaphors are markedly procreative or generative, using words like 'begot', 'fruit', 'coupling', yet there is also in his last clause a suggestion of female homoerotic 'coupling' among the sister sciences for the benefit of male scholar/voyeurs, although one would not want to make too much of it. It is as if he unconsciously recognizes the need for two subjective principles

---

[15] The phrase is coined by Gail Rubin (1975).

[16] One of Pindar's Pythian Odes (XI) addresses his Muse who 'didst bind thyself to lend thy tongue for fee of silver' and 'must needs suffer it to flit, now one way, now another' (1989: pp. 302–3, ll. 41–2; see also pp. 448–9). In 1702, an anonymous critic of Aphra Behn encapsulates the attitudes which were gelling in Hall and Heywood's time: 'What a Pox have the Women to do with the Muses? I grant you the Poets call the Nine Muses by the Names of Women, but why so? not because the Sex had any thing to do with Poetry, but because in that Sex they're much fitter for prostitution'. Quoted in Battersby 1989: 39. Women writers of the mid- to late seventeenth century could view the connection very differently. See Evans and Little (eds.), *'The Muses Females Are': Martha Moulsworth and Other Women Writers of the English Renaissance* (1995), esp. Frances Teague, 'Early Modern Women and "the muses ffemal"' 173–9. Moulsworth writes in her poem, 'Memorandum', 'the muses ffemalls are | and therefore of Us ffemales take some care | Two universities we have of men | o thatt we had but one of women then' (30–1). Moulsworth writes that she bid farewell to the 'virgin Muses' (41), i.e. learning, when she married.

for any creation or communication to take place. The feminine principle or its 'semblance' is necessary to high culture, as can be seen in Raphael's frescoes of the Vatican Palace's *Stanza della Segnatura*, to take just one spectacular example, but the implications of letting 'the women of our age' in on the secret (or into the Pope's library) are, for Heywood, hardly to be contemplated:

which (as *Beroaldus* saith) if the women of our age did fully apprehend and truely understand, how insolently would they boast of their worth and dignitie? how would they glorie in vaine boasts and ostentations, how much continuall chidings would they upbrayde their husbands, . . . therefore (I feare) this had beene better kept as secret as mysteries in Sanctuaries, and not to have been published to them in their owne mothers tongue, in which they are so nimble and voluble; least calling a Counsell about this argument, it may adde to their insolencies, who have too great an opinion of their owne worths alreadie. (60–1)

It is significant that Heywood's fears should be of women's voices. His final phrasing is perhaps most significant, for it suggests collective, even political action, and echoes the very gifts of the Muses: memory and eloquence. That he can observe how 'almost whatsoever is good' is represented in female shape or name, and then assert that this ought to be kept secret and 'not . . . published to them in their owne mothers tongue' lest they call 'a Counsell' is either too unconscious or too brazen to be taken seriously. Is Heywood having some fun with his readers? Even if Heywood writes here in the tradition of jestbook literature, Linda Wood-bridge reminds us that literary genres can be used as shields to ward off criticism of misogynistic attitudes: '[m]any theorists of jest have recognized in laughter a tool for asserting and main-taining superiority' (1986: 32). Heywood reveals, however, that there *is* a secret to be kept, and thus at least unconsciously acknow-ledges the cultural construction of gender as it applies differently to Woman and women. As many feminists have suggested, 'mother tongue' is a misnomer; rather, 'the whole of our western culture is based upon the murder of the mother' (Irigaray 1991*a*: 47; see Ch. 3, below); the mother's tongue has been cut out. Is it coincid-ence that Heywood begins his enquiry with Sophia, 'mother' of the theological virtues, and ends with a reference to the 'mother tongue', all under the assertion of paternal genealogies and the shadow of patriarchal censorship? Both a burial of the 'mother's tongue' and a specular relationship in which contemplation of 'the symbole or semblance of such women' takes place are advocated by Heywood, the two acts which Irigaray suggests establish and then perpetuate patriarchal society (Whitford 1991: 34).

In his dedicatory letter to the Earl of Worcester, Edward Somerset, Heywood states he would not dare to approach him,

did I not bring the Nine Muses, with an Armie of Goddesses and Women, to mediate in my behalfe. In these few sheets, I have lodged to the number of three thousand; who (could they speake) would undoubtedly informe you, that they were acquired and sought out for no other reason, than to be exposed to your noble view and most judiciall censure. All which I have charmed with such art, that the fairest amongst them you may admit into your Bedchamber without suspition, and the most clamorous into your Closet, without noyse. (A3)

Heywood's entanglements in the above passage as to who speaks to whom reveals him caught in a difficult position: a male subordinate to the powerful male Earl, yet superior to the female subjects of his History in the simple fact that he is a male; with whom, ultimately, is he to identify? Thus, he speaks for 3,000 women who, he claims, would 'mediate' or speak in *his* behalf, except he has 'charmed' them, indeed confined their voices in a parenthesis. They are only 'exposed' to the view of a male patron who will bestow his 'judiciall censure' on Heywood's labours and reward him accordingly. Irigaray draws a conclusion from the famous opening of Freud's fictional lecture, 'Femininity' (1991: 145–6), which is a perfect gloss for Heywood's question, 'Why is the Muse female?', his answer which must be kept secret from flesh-and-blood women, and his remarks to the Earl:

So it would be a case of you men speaking among yourselves about woman, who cannot be involved in hearing or producing a discourse that concerns the *riddle*, the logograph she represents for you. The enigma that *is* woman will therefore constitute the *target*, the *object*, the *stake*, of a masculine discourse, of a debate among men, which would not consult her, would not concern her. Which, ultimately, she is not supposed to know anything about. (Irigaray 1985a: 13)

If the question for Freud is 'what is femininity?', and for Heywood, 'why is the Muse female?' it is nevertheless the same question, addressed to the same (male) audience, and intentionally excludes women as subjects.

Just a few years after Heywood, but writing in Puritan New England, Anne Bradstreet also ponders why the Muses are female and anticipates her male critics:

> If what I do prove well, it won't advance,
> They'll say it's stol'n, or else it was by chance.
>
> But sure the antique Greeks were far more mild
> Else of our sex, why feigned they those nine
> And poesy made Calliope's own child;
> So 'mongst the rest they placed the arts divine:
> But this weak knot they will full soon untie,
> The Greeks did nought, but play the fools and lie.
>
>                    (1967: p. 16, ll. 31–8)[17]

Unlike Heywood, who at least finds an answer to satisfy his question, Sir Thomas Wroth asserts the whole convention is a mistake, an error in logic, despite classical authority, exactly as Bradstreet suggests. 'De Musis' is an epigram in which is found that ubiquitous couple, misogyny and jest:

> Ye reverend Poets, now but earth and clay,
> And ye the gloryes of this present age,
> Vouchsafe mee leave with due respect to say,
> Ye seemd to flatter in your sacred rage,
> Faining the Muses to be women, when
> Reason approves them rather to be men;
> Those Nine, in men are but a nine-fould skill,
> Which for the head is the supreamest part
> Doe there inhabit, as upon a hill,
> Well nam'd Parnassus, or the house of Art;
> Ther's scant nine women wise; men nine times nine,
> Then reason will, they should be masculine. (1610: H4)

## II. SOME INVOCATIONS OF THE MUSE IN RENAISSANCE ENGLAND

In her study of metaphors of childbirth in Shakespeare's works, Elizabeth Sacks observes that in the sixteenth century, '[t]he

---

[17] In 1650, Bradstreet's brother-in-law took a manuscript to England without her knowledge and published it with the title, *The Tenth Muse, Lately Sprung Up In America*.

English language itself was undergoing rebirth. Rediscovery of the generation metaphor seemed appropriate, and proclaimed the new-found eloquence of the mother tongue in a time of . . . great literary productivity' (1980: 4).[18] Part of this rebirth, I am arguing, was a newly incarnated Muse, examples of which I have already included in the first part of this chapter. Ernst Curtius traces invocational practice from antiquity through to the seventeenth century and Milton, after which point he recognizes that the Muse figure as Greek deity is no longer recognized or respected in English poetry so that the source of inspiration takes other forms (1979: 229). No mention is made of what seems to be a significant development in the invocation/incarnation of the Muse in Elizabethan England. Donne and his contemporaries are also passed over by Walter Schindler in his discussion of the 'sexual overtones in Milton's portrayal of inspiration in *Paradise Lost*' (1984: 28, 109 n. 10). Schindler identifies Milton as the first to portray the poet's relationship with his Muse as a domestic one whereas I suggest that Donne preceded Milton in this domestication of the Muse. In this section, I will review late Elizabethan incarnations of the Muse in order to contextualize the use of the Muse in Donne's early verse letters. There are seeds of an embodied or sexualized Muse in the works of their classical predecessors (to whom I will make reference when appropriate), but late Elizabethan poets seem to develop these seedlings into a new hybrid which continues to sprout new forms in the Stuart period. An exhaustive study of such a ubiquitous convention as invocation is obviously impossible here, and my examples should be regarded as typical or representative of developing trends, rather than demonstrative of every variation of the 'Camelion Muse' (Sir John Davies 1975: 163). For example, space does not permit consideration of the economic, social, and psychological implications of male poets referring to their mistress or patroness as their Muse. Moreover, my argument does not attempt to trace patterns of influence because of the difficulties in dating many of these poems, some of which would have circulated in manuscript prior to being printed.

In his notorious exchange with Thomas Nashe, Gabriel Harvey initially presents a favourable opinion of English letters. In *Pierce's*

---

[18] In ch. 1 Sacks provides many examples of what she calls the 'pregnant poetic' from among Shakespeare's contemporaries.

*Supererogation* (1593), he observes: 'It is not long since the goodly-est graces of the most noble Commonwealthes upon Earth, Eloquence in speech and Civility in manners, arrived in these remote parts of the world. . . . Apollo with his delicate troupe of Muses forsooke his old mountaines and rivers and frequented a new Parnassus and an other Helicon nothing inferiour to the olde' (C. G. Smith 1904: ii. 248–9). Likewise, John Davies of Hereford praises Oxford, filled with student poets, as a place 'Passing *Pernassus, Muses* habitation!'[19] Rejecting what he calls the 'Ah-mees' of Petrarchan convention, Michael Drayton announces at the beginning of his sonnet sequence, *Idea* (1594), that '*My Muse is rightly of the* English *straine*' (1961: ii. 309) and continued throughout his career to promote 'a true native Muse' (1961: vol. iv, p. v). The titles of several late Elizabethan poetic miscellanies suggest a self-conscious nationalism which began with Richard Tottel's own compilation in 1557,[20] and so relocate the *locus poeticus*; for example, *England's Helicon* (1600) and *Englands Parnassus; or, The choysest Flowers of our Moderne Poets, with their Poeticall comparisons* (1600).

But there was something rotten in the new Parnassus. A brief review of the extent of Roman poets' innovations will allow us to appreciate the Elizabethan 'corruption' of the Muse. In classical tradition, especially for the Greeks, an encounter with the Muses was generally a fearful thing, as we hear from Hesiod at the beginning of his *Theogony,* and to challenge them was pure folly. The bard, Thamyris, the Pieridian sisters, and the satyr, Marsyas, all of whom challenge the Muses' skill in song (let alone their virtue) are punished for their presumption.[21] In his *Metamorphoses* (5.273–93) Ovid tells of King Pyreneus' attempted rape of the Muses, and his mad death leap in futile pursuit of them. However, the Muse who relates the story admits she has not fully recovered from her fear, suggesting that at least for Ovid, the Muses can no longer be entirely confident in being beyond the reach of mortal attempts on their virtue. Even if Pyreneus is unsuccessful and dies for his wickedness, the very fact that he attempts to rape the Muses

---

[19] 'To my much honored, and intirely beloved Patronesse, the most famous Universitie of Oxford' in *Microcosmos* (1603) Nn[v].

[20] For a discussion of the significance of Tottel's miscellany, see Marotti 1995: 212–28.

[21] See Homer, *Iliad*, 2.594–600; Ovid, *Metamorphoses*, 5.294 ff.; 6.382 ff.

suggests Ovid manipulates or exposes their latent femaleness more than most authors. Moreover, Pyreneus' 'downfall' may have more to do with his being a usurper, a mortal, and his violation of the laws of hospitality, than with his attempted rape, an act ubiquitous in Ovid. Ovid's eschewal of the holy Muses in favour of experience in his *Ars Amatoria*[22] suggests that the Nine Muses were not to be associated with sexual subject matter. His 'nova Musa' of the *Remedia Amoris* might instruct in sexual matters and hence be described as wanton ('Musa proterva', ll. 12 and 362), but the relationship between poet and this more personal Muse (as opposed to one of the Nine) is still consultative, as it were, rather than sexually active.[23]

Departing from classical models where the Muses are untouchable, Spenser in his *Teares of the Muses* (1591) presents Polyhymnia describing how the Muse has lately been abused in English poetry: 'But now nor Prince nor Priest doth her maintayne, | But suffer her prophaned for to be | Of the base vulgar, that with hands uncleane | Dares to pollute her hidden mysterie'.[24] John Davies of Hereford berates writers' breaches of literary decorum with similar language in 'Stultus stulta loquitur': 'O senselesse Things! will you still Doing be | The Muses, to their shame, thus to deflowr?' Harvey attacks Nashe by disparaging 'the whole ruffianisme of thy brothell Muse, if she still prostitute her obscene ballatts, and will needes be a younge Curtisan of ould knavery' (C. G. Smith 1904: ii. 258–9). While not strictly concerned with Muses, Davies's 'Papers Complaint' presents the abuses of literature as sexual 'villany', endowing the paper on which 'Ballet-mongers' and 'doggrell Rimers' such as Nashe and Sir John Harington write with a female voice. For example, Robert Greene is charged with having 'scraped mee | With Pens that spirtled me with villany, | And made me ope a gap, unto each Gap, | That leads to shame, to sorrow, and mishap' (see *The Scourge of Folly*, 1610: ll. 243–6; and see Love 1993: 148 ff.).

Joseph Hall envisions the bawdy and obscene poetry being written by 'Rimesters new' as the rape of Muses who had formerly been, as we saw in Ovid's *Metamorphoses*, invulnerable:

---

[22] 'Usus opus movet hoc [experience inspires this work]' (1.29).
[23] See *Amores*, 3.1.6, 3.15.19; and Martial's 'Musa iocosa', *Epigrams*, 2.22, 7.8, 8.3.
[24] Spenser 1989: 290, ll. 565–68. See Oram's introduction to *Teares*, pp. 263–7. The poem may have been written as early as 1580.

Whilome the sisters nine were Vestall maides,
And held their Temple in the secret shades
Of fayre *Pernssus* that two-headed hill,
Whose auncient fame the Southern world did fill.
. . .
There did they sit and do their holy deed,
That pleas'd both heaven and earth: till that of late,
Whom should I fault? or the most righteous Fate?
Or heaven, or men, or fiends, or ought beside,
That ever made that foule mischance betide?
Some of the sisters in securer shades
Defloured were:
And ever since disdaining *sacred shame*,
Done ought that might their heavenly stock defame.
Now is *Pernassus* turned to the stewes
. . .
Each bush, each banke, and each base Apple-squire,
Can serve to sate their beastly lewd desire.
Ye bastard Poets see your Pedegree,
From common Trulls, and loathsome Brothelry.

(Virgedemiarum 1.2.1–4; 8–17; 35–8)

Hall figures the decline of poetry due to obscenity and a lack of decorum as the rape of the classical 'sisters nine'; these are not altogether 'newe forged' Muses. Their rape is visually and aurally represented in Hall's shortened line 14, 'Defloured were:', which leaves a blank space on the page or in the poem in which the chaste sisters suddenly/silently become prostitutes or 'common Trulls' who are, moreover, instantly insatiable in their 'beastly lewd desire' and infected with sexual disease (20–2).[25] The Cankered Muse is a syphilitic one as well.[26] Furthermore, rather than expending his vitriol on the poet-rapists, Hall focuses on the Muses themselves. He inscribes the male fantasy of the maid who secretly desires sex onto the classical divine Muses: once raped they decide they like sex. Hall parodies classical invocation with imagery as violent and lewd as anything in Nashe's poem, illustrating that the line between the satirist and that which he satirized could be thin indeed. Such imagery is ironic in the light of another of Hall's

[25] In the original edition, however, this shortened line is the last on the page (B3) so that the visual, if not the aural, effect is lost.
[26] I play on Alvin Kernan's title for his book, *The Cankered Muse: Satire of the English Renaissance* (1959).

satires where he addresses his fellow poets as Muses and appeals to their sense of decency: 'Chast men, they did but glance at *Lesbias* deed, | And handsomely leave off with cleanly speed' (*Virgedemi-arum* 1.9.31–2). Michael Drayton also represents the decay of English poetry as the sexual decay of the classical Muses: 'The thrice-three Muses but too wanton be, | Like they that Lust, I care not, I will none'. Drayton declares, 'Onely I call on my divine Idea' (1961: ii. 330). Yet he also, like Hall, appeals to the purity of the Muses, alluding to the episode of the attempted rape of the Muses by King Pyreneus in Ovid's *Metamorphoses* to justify his status as a professional writer. In 'To Himselfe, and the Harpe' he claims that one need not possess the pedigree of gentle birth but rather be 'borne a Poet' and come 'with hands pure': 'The *Phocean* it did prove, | Whom when foule Lust did move, | Those Mayds unchaste to make, | Fell, as with them he strove, | His Neck and justly brake' (1961: ii. 347).

The emergence of a class of professional writers brought about the charge of 'having commerce with the Muses', a conceit which also often depicted the Muses as prostitutes. John Heath in *Two centuries of epigrammes* (1610) comments on the recent past in his opening epigram, 'In lascivos Poetas': 'Gather the refuse scraps of looser times; | Huddle them up in your lascivious rimes . . . | Runne they that list with this the times abuse; | I scorne it I to prostitute my muse' (D4). John Marston had used the same figure defiantly when he addressed his detractors in 'In Lectores prorsus indignos': 'Nay then come all, I prostitute my Muse, | For all the swarme of Idiots to abuse. | Reade all, view all, even with my full consent' (1961: 98). Marston's editor suggests he was retorting to Everard Guilpin's teasing epigram, 'Of Fuscus' (Guilpin 1974: 46), in which Marston is a 'bawde' 'Who to all sorts thus prosti-tutes his Muse' (Marston 1961: 263).

In *Skialetheia* (1598), Guilpin refers to his epigrams as 'these bastards of my Muse' (1974: 58) but in his epigram, 'To the Reader', Guilpin suggests the criticism his Muse receives would be better directed towards the living women of the times:

> Some dainte eare, like a wax-ribd Citty roome,
> Wil haply blame my *Muse* for this salt rhume,
> Thinking her lewd and too unmaidenly,
> For dauncing this Jigge so lasciviously:
> But better thoughts, more discreet, will excuse

> This quick *Couranto* of my merry *Muse*;
> And say she keeps *Decorum* to the times,
> · To womens loose gownes suting her loose rimes. (1974: 57)

Guilpin[27] neatly deflects possible criticism of himself and his work onto his Muse and onto real women, making the ubiquitous correlation between a woman's sexuality and her speech by aligning the 'loose rimes' of the Muse with the 'loose gownes' of actual women. Likewise Sir John Harington offers an apology for the content of his epigrams at the expense of his Muse and Jane Shore:

> My Muse is like King Edward's concubine,
> Whose minde did to devotion so encline,
> She duly did each day to church resort,
> Save if she wear intyst to Venus sport—
> So would my Muse write gravely, nere the latter
> She slips sometimes into some wanton matter. (1930: 309)

Virgil, Horace, Ovid, and Martial had all established links between genre and the representation of the Muse or Muses, but while the Muses were becoming more personal, they were far more benign. In his *Eclogues*, Virgil refers to his 'agrestem [rustic]' Muse (6.8) while in his *Georgics* he tells of being smitten with love of the Muses (2.475 ff.). In his *Satires* Horace refers to his 'Musa pedestri [prosaic Muse]' (2.6.17). Martial also defends his epigrams and his Muse against the more 'serious' poetry of Ovid, Homer, and the dramatists (4.49). Ovid, as we saw, also engages a 'new Muse'. Many Elizabethans imitated Persius' anti-invocation in the Prologue to his *Satires* and rejected the classical Muses without debasing them. Sonnet 74 of Sidney's *Astrophil and Stella* is a close imitation of Persius' rejection of the Muses, as well as a rejection of Platonic *furor poeticus*:

> I never drank of *Aganippe* well,
> Nor ever did in shade of *Tempe* sit:
> And Muses scorne with vulgar braines to dwell,
> Poore Layman I, for sacred rites unfit.
>     Some do I heare of Poets' furie tell,
> But (God wot) wot not what they meane by it. (1962: 1–6)[28]

---

[27] Donne addresses a verse letter to Guilpin, 'Even as lame things thirst their perfection', to which I refer, below.

[28] See 'Let daintie wits crie on the Sisters nine . . . | For me in sooth, no Muse but one I know' (Sonnet 3, ll. 1, 9); all of Sonnet 15; 'Muses, I oft invoked your holy ayde, | With choisest flowers my speech to engarland so; . . . | But now I meane no

Astrophil's inspiration lies elsewhere: 'My lips are sweet, inspired with *Stella's* kisse' (14). Likewise, Shakespeare's Sonnet 38 shows the traditional nine Muses eclipsed by his addressee: 'Be thou the tenth muse, ten times more in worth | Than those old nine which rhymers invocate' (9–10). Marston's 'Proemium' to his third book of satires in *The Scourge of Villanie* (1598) also shows Persius' influence and the link between the rejection of the classical Muses and generic decorum:

> In serious jest, and jesting seriousnes
> I strive to scourge poluting beastlines.
> I invocate no *Delian* Deitie,
> Nor sacred of-spring of *Mnemosyne*:
> . . .
> I crave no Syrens of our Halcion times,
> To grace the accents of my rough-hew'd rimes;
> But grim *Reproofe*, stearne Hate of villanie,
> Inspire and guide a Satyres poesie. (1961: 1–4; 9–12)

Following the precedent of Tibullus in his elegies (2.1.35), Elizabethan embodiments of a Muse figure could also be innocent or innocently amorous. Shakespeare's young man becomes a substitute Muse, as made explicit at the beginning of Sonnet 78: 'So oft have I invoked thee for my muse'. In Sonnet 80 of *Astrophil and Stella*, 'the Muses bide' in the 'new *Pernassus*' of Stella's '[s]weet-swelling lip'. The Muses are relocated not only to England's 'new Parnassus and . . . other Helicon', but also to the 'new *Pernassus*' of the mistress herself, significantly, to her mouth. In Donne's elegy, 'Love's Progress', his mistress's 'swelling lip' is the place where both 'Syrens songs, and . . . | Wise Delphique Oracles doe fill the eare' (55–6). Donne's figure is darker than Sidney's, and suggests danger in his allusion to the Sirens who tempted men to their death with enchanting song. Thomas Churchyard in 1580 had described his mistress as one whose 'countenance carries sutche a state, full right amid her face, | As though therein the Muses nine, had made their mansion place'. In his sonnet sequence, *Cynthia* (1595), Richard Barnfield writes of his Mistress as one '(In whom the Muses and the Graces strive, | Which shall possesse the chiefest part of thee)' (A4v). The Muses dwelled not only in the

more your helpe to trie' (Sonnet 55, ll. 1–2, 9); *Other Poems*, 4.2–8; 'A plaining songe plaine-singing voice requires', inserted in the 1593 edition of Sidney's *Arcadia* (1962: 493–6).

body of the poet's mistress. Barnfield describes 'Cherry-lipt Adonis' in Sonnet 17 of *Cynthia* in language reminiscent of Sidney's Sonnet 80: 'His lips ripe strawberries in Nectar wet, | His mouth a Hive, his tongue a hony-combe, | Where Muses (like Bees) make their mansion' (C6). In an epigram, 'To my much honored & intirely beloved friend, Sir Basill Brooke, Knight', John Davies plays with the name of his male addressee: 'Cleere *Brooke* wherein the Muses bathe themselves, | And Nectar'd, *Streames of Helicon* do fleete' (*Scourge of Folly*, 1610).

At the other end of the spectrum, examples of embodied Muses may involve scatalogical rather than sexual imagery, as in Sir John Harington's defensive epigram on his Rabelaisian poem, *The Metamorphosis of Ajax* (1596). Harington's epigram is important for several reasons: it is an example of the way in which the Muse was involved in conceits rather than just invocation; it shows that the Muse was figured as possessing a body of fully human working parts; it refers to decorum and the way in which the Muse was re-articulated to fit the poetic form or content:

> You muse to find in me such alteration,
> That I, that maydenly to write was wont,
> Would now set to a Booke so desperate front,
> As I might scant defend by incitation.
> My Muse that time did need a strong Purgation
> Late having tane some bruse by lewd reports;
> And when the Physick wrought, you know the fashion
> Whereto a man in such a case resorts:
>    And so my Muse, with good *decorum* spent
>    On that base titled Booke, her excrement. (1618: I3ᵛ)

John Davies of Hereford writes similarly but combines several conceits: alcoholic rather than divine inspiration, scatalogical decorum, and anti-invocation in the form of his Muse's epitaph:

> Here lies a Muse (was made by Nine)
> That drunken was with Wit, not Wine:
> And yet the Bowells of her Wit
> Being too full of Trash unfit.
> Here, like a Fart, doth let it slie,
> More for hir ease, than honesty. (1617: L7ᵛ)

The indignities the Muse suffers here are increased by the genre itself: writing an epitaph for a figure who was supposed to be immortal is the final indignity which we will see Donne use, below. Donne uses a similar excremental conceit to Davies's, above, in *Satire II* when criticizing poetasters:

> But hee is worst, who (beggarly) doth chaw
> Others wits fruits, and in his ravenous maw
> Rankly digested, doth those things out-spue,
> As his owne things; 'and they are his owne, 'tis true,
> For if one eate my meate, though it be knowne
> The meate was mine, th'excrement is his owne. (1967*b*: 25–30)

This passage, and indeed the whole satire, is Donne at his most derisive on the abuses of poetry, and so the absence of a Muse may be significant in that he does not associate her with the kind of bodily degradation—prostitution, defecation—evident in the epigrams and satires of Harington, Davies, Hall, and others. At worst, Donne in his satires, as I mentioned, is dismissive of the convention.

If the Muses dwell in the lips and bosoms of mistresses, one also finds poets invoking the 'modesty' of their Muses in declining further to detail the bodily charms of their mistresses, usually once they have reached her navel. For example, an anonymous poem, 'In praise of his mistresse parts', begins with a standard invocation of the 'sacred sisters'. Praising his mistress in a blazon beginning at her face, the poet reaches an impasse at her pubic area: 'prohibited for to descend | To praise that part where praises have no end. | For my Muse stops me, and says to me No | Leave that, describe y^e rest: then on I goe'.[29] Or, as in Spenser's description of Duessa in *The Faerie Queene*, the reason for his Muse's reticence is the hideousness of the witch: 'Her neather parts, the shame of all her kind, | My chaster Muse for shame doth blush to write' (1995: 1.8.48.1–2). Ovid also invokes the modesty of his Muse when convenient, for example in *Ars Amatoria*, Book 2, when the couple he describes reach a certain stage in their love-making, at which point a Muse is superfluous. He tells her to stay by the chamber door: 'Sponte sua sine te celeberrima verba loquentur, [Of their own accord, without your aid, they will utter eloquent speech]' (705). Yet Ovid is also proud that his Muse tells the truth, even about delicate matters such as the various sexual positions described at the end of Book 3 (789–92). Always, however, he draws

---

[29] British Library Additional MS 10309, fo. 104.

a distinction between the chaste Greek Muses and his own Muse, whose store of knowledge includes sexual matters.

Rather than hiding behind the modesty of his Muse, Davies of Hereford chides his 'Dull Muse' for being unable adequately to describe his mistress's body. He goes on to describe his mistress's 'Centrique part' (Donne, 'Love's Progress', l. 36) as the dwelling place of the Muses:

> Just at the foote of this my Muses Mount,
> There lies, but what! that doth my Muse surmount,
> T'expresse It as It is, without offence,
> Such is this Secrets unknowne Excellence!
> But, at *Olimpus* Foote runns *Helicon*;
> Then thinke what makes good my Comparison
> (With purest Thought) and so perhapps ye shall
> Neere gesse from whence Loves *Helicon* doth fall. (1605)

At the end of his poem, *The Metamorphosis of Pygmalion's Image*, John Marston teases and then scolds the reader as well as his Muse: 'O pardon me | Yee gaping eares that swallow up my lines | Expect no more. Peace idle Poesie, | Be not obsceane though wanton in thy rhimes' (1961: 61).

Sonnet 70 of *Astrophil and Stella* contains an 'eager Muse' who is yet silenced by the poet. In this poem, where Astrophil exults in Stella's long-awaited bestowal of her favour, the Muse is clearly in the service of the poet who controls the direction of the poem:

> My Muse may well grudge at my heav'nly joy,
> If still I force her in sad rimes to creepe:
> She oft hath drunke my teares, now hopes to enjoy
> Nectar of Mirth, since I *Jove's* cup do keepe.
> . . .
> Come then my Muse, shew thou height of delight
> In well raisde notes, my pen the best it may
> Shall paint out joy, though but in blacke and white.
> Cease eager Muse, peace pen, for my sake stay,
>     I give you here my hand for truth of this,
>     Wise silence is best musicke unto blisse. (Sidney 1962: 1–4; 9–14)

By Sonnet 77, Astrophil's Muse seems to agree with him 'that Wise silence is best musicke unto blisse', for after describing the beauty, grace, and 'true speech' of Stella, Astrophil concludes, 'Yet ah, my Mayd'n Muse doth blush to tell the best'.

One final poem bridges my discussion of contemporary invoca-
tions/incarnations of the Muse and Donne's own representation of
his relationship with his Muse. Attributed to Donne in editions of
his poems between 1633 and 1669 and included by Simeon and
Grosart in their respective editions of 1856 and 1872, the poem
has been rejected as Donne's in this century, beginning with
Grierson in his 1912 edition. Grierson's arguments based on
textual[30] as well as internal, stylistic evidence that the poem is by
John Roe[31] and not John Donne have never been challenged, and
we need to keep in mind Marotti's conclusion in his study of
*Manuscript, Print, and the English Renaissance Lyric*, that '[m]ore
poems are misattributed to Donne than to any other English
Renaissance poet' (1995: 158). Marotti states in a footnote, but
provides no reference to Grierson's argument, or any further
evidence, that this elegy is by Roe. The poem opens with a conceit
in which the speaker wonders whether to bother writing a seduction poem for his mistress:

> Shall I goe force an Elegie? abuse
> My witt? and breake the Hymen of my muse
> For one poore houres love? Deserves it such
> Which serves not me, to doe on her as much?
>
> (Donne 1912: i. 410, ll. 1–4)

Here, invocation becomes penetration. In many ways, nothing
could sound more like a Donne elegy than these opening lines.
The impetuous questions and shocking conceit; the speaker's
immediate focus on himself rather than on his mistress; his focus
on the implications or effects of their relationship rather than on
the act of love-making itself; the possible pun on Donne's name in
line 6—'Who would be rich, to be soe soone undone?'; all these
elements point to a persona familiar from Donne's elegies, satires,
and love poems: the brash, overconfident male lover. Rather than
definitively ascribing authorship of the poem to Donne or Roe,

---

[30] First, the poem appears with the initials 'J.R.' in three of the manuscripts: MS
TCD (Trinity College, Dublin); Lansdowne MS 740 (British Library); Hawthornden
MS (National Library of Scotland). Second, 'the singular regularity with which [a
group of poems including "Shall I goe force"] adhere to one another. If a manuscript
has one, it generally has the rest in close proximity' (Donne 1912: ii, pp. cxxxi–
cxxxii).

[31] Roe was born in 1581 to a family which had produced several Lord Mayors of
London. He died of the plague in 1608. See Grierson in Donne 1912: ii, p. cxxxiv;
and Jonson's Epigrams 27 and 32, 'On Sir John Roe'.

though, what I want to ask, here, is whether or not the portrayal of the Muse as a raped virgin might help us to decide whether the poem is by Donne or by John Roe. The tone of the poem seems recognizably Donnean, but the conceit with which the poem opens is less in accord with Donne's other, more domestic representations of his Muse, as we shall see.

The speaker's language is at once flippantly casual—will I or won't I?—and violent. He uses the verbs, 'force', 'abuse', 'break', and the common euphemism for sex, 'doe' (and 'undone'), which we saw in Donne's 'Love's Growth' and in Davies's 'Stultus, stulta loquitur'. What is more, in lines 3 and 4 the speaker suggests a parallel rape of the woman to whom the poem is addressed. There are, indeed, poems by Donne which are comparably sexually violent, such as the description of the mistress's sexual parts as a fired gun in 'The Comparison', the comparison of the love-making of the speaker and his mistress to the probing of a wound in the same poem, or the image in the 'Epithalamium [Made at Lincoln's Inn]' of the defloration of the bride in terms of a sacrifice performed by the groom/priest as a disembowellment (see Ch. 3, below). And in 'The Autumnall', the words 'force' and 'rape' are linked as synonyms: 'Yong Beauties force our love, and that's a Rape' (l. 3). Part of the wit lies in Donne's reversal whereby it is the young women who 'rape' their admirers.

The word 'force' appears in two other contemporary poems in which connotations of rape—of Poetry or a Muse—are either very close to the surface or explicit. Thomas Carew's funeral elegy on Donne begins: 'Can we not force from widdowed Poetry, | Now thou art dead (Great DONNE) one Elegie | To crowne thy Hearse?'[32] Metaphorical language notwithstanding, it would seem more than a little indecorous for Carew to use 'force' in this way; after all, Carew is thus asking whether or not it is possible to rape the widow of his dead friend. Yet a few lines later he describes Donne as having 'Committed holy Rapes upon our Will' (l. 17). By formulating the inexpressibility topos as a need to force/rape 'widdowed Poetry', perhaps Carew is recalling 'Shall I goe force an Elegie?' The invulnerable Muses of Ovid's *Metamorphoses* had long

---

[32] 'An Elegie upon the Death of the Deane of Pauls, Dr. John Donne' *Elegies Upon the Author* in Donne 1978: p. 88, ll. 1–3. Hereafter, references to any of these elegies on Donne are taken from this edition, unless otherwise indicated, and referred to by line number.

since been unable to fend off their attackers. In Carew's poem and the Donne/Roe poem, however, the rape of the Muse is far more casual, not a critique of indecorousness but a calculation as to whether writing a poem is worth the poet's effort or, in Carew's poem, even possible.

Ben Jonson's 'An Epigram on the Court Pucelle' contains the most vitriolic use of the conceit of a raped Muse and appears to have extra-textual links with 'Shall I goe force an Elegie?':

> Do's the Court-Pucell then so censure me,
>   And thinkes I dare not her? let the world see
> . . .
> What though with Tribade lust she force a Muse,
>   And in an Epicoene fury can write newes
> Equall with that, which for the best newes goes,
>   As aërie light, and as like wit as those?
>
>     (Jonson 1925–52: viii. 222: ll. 1–2, 7–10)

The subject of Jonson's venomous epigram is Cecilia Bulstrode. In the Hawthornden manuscript, 'Shall I goe force an Elegie?' is signed 'J.R.' (as it is in two other manuscripts) and has the title, 'An Elegy 1602. To M^rs Boulstrede'.[33] Cecilia Bulstrode was a woman who seems to have provoked strong feelings in men. One of Queen Anne's ladies-in-waiting and a close friend and kinswoman of Lucy, Countess of Bedford, she was herself a writer. Her brief prose invention based on a courtly parlour game called 'Newes' (see l. 8 of Jonson's poem) survives in the 1614 edition of *Sir Thomas Overbury his Wife*.[34] Based on a letter Donne wrote to Roe's cousin, George Garrard, it is possible that at the time of Cecilia's death in August, 1609, her lover may well have been John's brother and Donne's friend, Thomas Roe (Donne 1977: 39). John Roe had died in 1608. Donne and Jonson both wrote funeral elegies for Cecilia (Donne wrote two, apparently his first did not please the Countess of Bedford), so the fact that Cecilia is indicated as the recipient of 'Shall I goe force an Elegie?' still leaves both Donne and Roe as possible authors. However, Barbara DeLuna notes that the elegy turns up, barely paraphrased, in Jonson's 1629

---

[33] If one's interpretation of Donne's poetry accords with the hagiographic or evolutionary models of Walton and Gardner, then the date 1602—after Donne's marriage to Anne More—would, in itself, preclude Donne's writing such a poem.

[34] See L. Schleiner 1994: 113–14, for the text of Bulstrode's piece, and ch. 5, *passim*, for Schleiner's discussion of its context.

play, *The New Inn* (1967: 169). The poem's appearance in Jonson's drama, DeLuna surmises, argues against Donne's authorship since he was still alive in 1629, whereas Roe had been dead for two decades and so his poem was more easily pilfered.

In contrast to the Muse in 'Shall I goe force an Elegie?' who is imagined as a virgin, and the act of poetic creation as a deflowering, Jonson's misogynistic invective portrays Bulstrode as the aggressor, indeed as a lesbian writer forcing a muse, but most of the poem concerns her apparently loose morals in sleeping with a 'sermoneer' or priest. Thus, she is metaphorically lesbian, invading the body of the Muse which was the sole property of male poets (and could obviously not be envisioned as male, rather than female), and literally heterosexual: the epitome of the sexually voracious woman. In conclusion then, while in this context I can neither fully consider 'Shall I goe force an Elegie?' in the context of the other poems by Roe, nor compare it fully to both Donne and Jonson's poetry, I have suggested that the treatment of the Muse figure situates the poem firmly within the context of the poetry of London and Inns of Court wits, but leaves uncertain the question as to whether the poem might, indeed, be Donne's. If its tone, structure, and many of its imaginative matrices (not all of which can be discussed here) seem recognizably Donnean, its Muse figure is unlike that in any of Donne's poetry, as we will see next.

### III. DONNE'S EARLY VERSE LETTERS

The verse letter was a form new to English poetry in the 1590s, grafted onto an already existing convention, the complimentary poem (Palmer 1970). Its content and form almost unrestricted as long as an address to some person is included, the verse epistle is more of a 'rhetorical mode of address' than a 'fixed genre' (Cameron 1976: 373; Milgate in Donne 1967*b*: p. xxxiv; Palmer 1970: 73–9). Indeed, the name which Horace gave to his epistles—'*sermones*' (2.1.250; 'conversations' or 'discourses')— indicates that in a verse epistle, one was to write as one speaks. But we need to stress the word 'rhetorical', as Lisa Jardine reminds us in her book on Erasmus. The notion of an author speaking with his 'own' voice is a complex one. At least originally, the Muse's aid was invoked in public genres such as epic, in which the poet calls upon the Muse to inspire him with knowledge, authority, and ability equal to the poetic task at hand. Therefore, we might not expect to find the Muse assisting in the private mode of the verse letters, which were intended for a coterie environment. A poet should have no need for a Muse to tell him of his own experiences or thoughts, although she might still provide him with the ability to express himself. She seems to appear in Donne's verse letters, at least formally, because a central concern of the genre is poetry itself. The verse letters engage in a far more self-conscious consideration of the workings of poetry and hence, for Donne, a more self-conscious interaction with the feminine origin of his voice. As Marotti, Jardine, and others have remarked, we need to read cautiously the forms of one-to-one communication whereby letters, whether prose or verse, are written 'in a consciously familiar style' (see e.g. Love 1993: 200). They are not to be read as transparent, factual, or narrative documents, but as controlled, constructed identities presented in accordance with the models Erasmus provided in his *De conscribendis epistolis*. Thus, while one purpose of a verse letter is, as Donne writes to Henry Wotton, to make 'friends absent speake' (see Jardine 1993: 150), that presence is not necessarily identical with the writer of the letter. The Muse, then, still has a role to play in the cultivation of wit and the construction of a persona.

While Thomas Lodge could claim priority when he published a barely developed form of the verse epistle in his *A Fig for Momus* (1595),[35] Donne was already writing verse epistles to his Inns of Court friends, according to Bald, as early as 1592 (1951/2: 283–9), although none of these were published until the posthumous *Poems* (1633). In other words, Donne was among the first to experiment with this form, revived from the classical examples of Horace and Seneca (Levine 1962: 669–77) and as part of the humanist tradition of familiar letters perfected in prose by Erasmus in his *De conscribendis epistolis* (see Jardine 1993: *passim*). William Drummond reports that Ben Jonson '[a]ffirmeth Donne to have written all his best pieces err he was twenty-five years old' (Jonson 1925–52: i. 135). This remark is one of the less sanctified and

---

[35] See Lodge's address, 'To the Gentlemen Readers whatsoever': 'For my *Epistles*, they are in that kind, wherein no Englishman of our time hath publiquely written' (A3–4).

religiously quoted of Jonson's comments on Donne for obvious reasons. Yet Jonson's statement, however fruitlessly engaged in (the phallocentric practice of) ranking poems, suggests that the same young man who produced the elegies, satires, and epigrams was also writing most of the verse letters which will be examined in this chapter. Two of Donne's best modern critics note that his 'collected verse letters are rightly considered the first major achievement in that mode in English' (Pebworth and Summers 1984: 361).

Yet Donne's early verse letters and hence most of his rep-resentations of his Muse have tended to go unremarked until very recently. Of the three books wholly devoted to studies of Donne's poetry which were published in the 1980s, Docherty's does not mention any of the early verse letters, Carey's contains a single reference to one poem, and Marotti's summarizes the early verse letters in three paragraphs to support his thesis that Donne wrote poetry avocationally and for a coterie of equals (1986: 36–7). A. B. Cameron remarks upon the 'deeply ingrained and disabling preju-dice' against the verse letters and he also makes an intriguing but undeveloped observation in passing that '[a]s in the familiar [prose] letters, Donne characteristically describes his relationship to poetry in terms of sexual imagery. The poet is the masculine, active principle—the lover who has been betrayed by the feminine, passive principle, his lover-muse, into the 'vaine" use of his love' (1976: 369, 395). Kitty Datta refers to Donne's 'small literary game with his friends of the Inns of Court involving them and their Muses' and its 'triviality' (1977: 10, 12). Donne may be engaged in a 'literary game' but the implications of such joking can still be of import. Some of Datta's observations concur with my own but she does not develop her analysis from a specifically feminist point of view and pursues her observations in different directions.

Only in the last five years has there been any interest shown in Donne and his Muse from a feminist or gender-focused per-spective. Three articles include brief discussions of the Muse in the early verse letters as a corollary to their main argument. Janet Halley argues in 'Textual Intercourse' that 'the representations of Anne Donne that we have inherited from her husband [in his prose letters] function no differently in the context of male textual exchange than do Donne's representations of that quintessentially fictional female, the Muse' (1989: 199). Likewise, Elizabeth Harvey concurs with this view when she asserts 'the muse forms the basis of poetic transaction between [Donne] and his (male) correspondents' (1992: 134). Halley and Harvey include Thomas Woodward's response to one of Donne's verse letters, but Harvey does not explore the Martial allusion (reading 'base' for 'Bassa') (1992: 135), and Halley does not take into consideration contemporary theories of orgasm and procreation. George Klawitter is the first to identify in print Woodward's reference to Martial's Bassa and argues there is evidence of a homoerotic undercurrent in the poems (1992). Klawitter's argument, while important in that it urges Donne's readers to heed gender issues in the poems more closely, does not wholly convince. Klawitter is as biographically speculative as earlier twentieth-century critics have been, and with as little hard evidence. Arguments of relative autobiography or privacy do not in themselves provide solid ground to make generalizations about Donne's own life, especially in an age of 'self-fashioning'. Mark Fortier recognizes that the Muses 'are not so devoid of meaning as they have often been taken to be' (1991: 90) and suggests a larger analysis of both Donne and Jonson's Muse is needed which 'would require a full account of each man's times, psyche, and history' (93). While I disagree with some of Fortier's analysis, we both read the Muse in the early verse letters as a domesticated figure.

My discussion begins with a group of poems Donne wrote to Thomas and Rowland Woodward,[36] brothers who were part of the same circle as Donne at Lincoln's Inn. My discussion includes T[homas] W[oodward]'s reply to Donne, featuring a lesbian muse. Such a representation might be considered the most exotic of any we have seen so far, but I will show that even a lesbian Muse who would seem to co-opt both the creative and the procreative functions still figures as a token within masculine exchange, however many different 'positions' the sexualization of textual production assumes. In Donne's verse letters where the Muse is domesticated—either married or widowed—what looks like a kind of Protestant valorization of marriage still maintains the supremacy

---

[36] The identity of 'T.W.' has remained somewhat less certain than that of 'R.W.', to both of whom Donne wrote nine verse letters in total. See 1967b: 211, 214. However, I refer to 'Thomas' and 'Rowland' which, although somewhat incongruous with 'Donne', avoids confusion about which 'Woodward' I am referring to.

of male friendship over the love of women because these male poets 'marry' a Muse whose task as 'the Other of the Same', is to bring forth poems for exchange between male friends.

One of Donne's poems, 'To Mr. T.W.', begins by combining invocation with address so that like Tibullus, Donne invokes his friend rather than the Muse:

> All haile sweet Poët, more full of more strong fire,
> Then hath or shall enkindle any spirit,
> I lov'd what nature gave thee, but this merit
> Of Wit and Art I love not but admire;
> Who have before or shall write after thee,
> Their workes, though toughly laboured, will bee
> Like infancie or age to mans firme stay,
> Or earely and late twilights to mid-day. (1–8)

The amplitude of Donne's compliment to Thomas Woodward, so full of 'strong fire' his poetry supposedly represents the pinnacle of achievement for all time, is grotesquely hyperbolical. Yet critics have complained about the indecorously excessive nature of Donne's compliments to his patronesses in the later verse letters, and especially about Elizabeth Drury's apotheosis in the *Anniversaries*, far more often than about the 'warm applauding' (R. C. Bald's understatement) in these early verse letters. One could interpret such epideictic as the masculine psyche's need for the poet to be, not just one of a number of excellent poets, but to obliterate all other poetic achievement in being the best, the only 'man' amongst infants and geriatrics—the same impulse which resulted in the nine Muses gradually 'crusht into one forme', in Jonson's phrase, substituted with one private muse, and then eclipsed altogether by the poet towering alone. The most dramatic illustration of this mentality is the first stanza of Donne's 'A Valediction: of the Booke', where the male speaker instructs his mistress 'How thine may out-endure | Sybills glory, and obscure | Her who from *Pindar* could allure, | And her, through whose helpe *Lucan* is not lame, | And her, whose booke (they say) *Homer* did finde, and name' (1965: 5–9). The speaker obscures the identity of these women competitors by referring to the male poets whom they were reputed to have aided or surpassed in their poetic endeavours: Corinna, who competed against Pindar and won; Polla Argentaria, the wife of Lucan who helped him complete his *Pharsalia*; and Phantasia, whose tales Homer 'found' and claimed as his own *Iliad* and *Odyssey*. But Donne's speaker also eclipses his mistress in the very act he instructs her to undertake in a competition with unnamed female writers (see Harvey 1992: 116–17).

Klawitter's gendered reading of the (potentially) universal 'man' of line 7 of Donne's verse letter as 'male' demonstrates how quickly this 'universal' term slides into gendered meanings (1994: 82). Donne's image of 'man's firme stay' is, in context, one of the vigour and potency associated with masculinity. Donne uses the same double metaphor of time measured in hours and generations in his *Metempsychosis*, where his speaker declares that 'From infant morne, through manly noone I draw' (6). Yet there are also instances in which Donne describes a woman in similar, even more extreme terms. The Countess of Huntingdon is described in Donne's verse letter beginning 'That unripe side of earth', as rising from the clouds of mere mortals: 'our noone-ray | But a foule shadow, not your breake of day' (79–80). Donne also uses words like 'firm' to describe the love between a man and woman, for example in 'The Extasie': 'Our hands were firmely cimented | With a fast balme' (5–6); or 'A Valediction: of my Name in the Window': 'Our firme substantiall love' (62). Most famously, Donne ends his 'Valediction: forbidding Mourning' with the conceit of his beloved as the 'fixt foot' (27) of a compass, and it is her 'firmnes' or fidelity which will enable the speaker to complete his journey and come home. 'A Lecture upon the Shadow' argues that the lovers' 'infant loves' have grown to perfect candidness and therefore must 'at this noone stay' for 'Love is a growing, or full constant light; | And his first minute, after noone, is night' (25–6). It is thus not always illuminating to 'fix' the connotations of words and apply them across the boundaries of the individual poem, for the gender positions associated with certain binarisms are not always predictable in Donne's poetry.

In 'All haile sweet Poët', Donne's reference to the Muses appears in the second stanza, in which he compares himself unfavourably to his friend:

> Men say, and truly, that they better be
>     Which be envy'd then pittied: therefore I,
>     Because I wish thee best, doe thee envie:
> O wouldst thou, by like reason, pitty mee!

> But care not for mee: I, that ever was
> In Natures, and in Fortunes gifts, (alas,
>   Before thy grace got in the Muses Schoole)
>   A monster and a begger, am now a foole. (9–16)

Unnatural or ugly, as well as perhaps both unlucky and im-
pecunious, Donne declares he is also a fool attempting to imitate
Thomas's poetic 'grace got in the Muses Schoole'. Klawitter
suggests that the word 'got' is in this instance 'sexually charged'
(89); in other words, Thomas begets poetry by (pro)creating with
the Muses. Donne frequently uses the word 'beget' or 'get' and
their variants as a sexual metaphor, meaning 'to procreate, to
generate, usually said of the father, but sometimes of both parents'
(*OED* 2). Donne uses 'get' less often in its primary sense of 'to get,
to acquire'. Here, however, Donne describes himself in both
generative and acquisitive terms--born a monster, and denied the
gifts of fortune—so that we cannot tell how much weight to give
the 'got' which describes 'how' Thomas receives his gifts in the
Muses School. Indeed, to present the Muses as bestowing their
gifts or teaching the poet his craft is one of the oldest conventions,
beginning with Hesiod.

In the third stanza of 'All haile' Donne asserts only Thomas can
do justice to himself:

> Oh how I grieve, that late borne modesty
>   Hath got such root in easie waxen hearts,
>   That men may not themselves, their owne good parts
> Extoll, without suspect of surquedrie,
> For, but thy selfe, no subject can be found
> Worthy thy quill, nor any quill resound
>   Thy worth but thine: how good it were to see
>   A Poëm in thy praise, and writ by thee. (17–24)

This rather conventional compliment constitutes a crux in readings of Donne's 'Sapho to Philaenis', as we saw above, where it is
Philaenis' beauty which can be likened only to itself. The difference between Philaenis' incomparable beauty and Thomas's
incomparable character and poetic skill is that Thomas *could* be
worthily 'extoll[ed]' were it not for 'suspect of surquedrie', or
suspicion of arrogance; it is a matter of decorum. Such praise
would be difficult, but not impossible. In other words, Donne
calls for Thomas's autobiography (not, as Klawitter suggests, the

donning of a rhetorical codpiece in praising his 'owne good parts' and 'quill').[37] Still, there is a narcissistic circularity to Donne's encomium, which threatens to turn compliment into absurdity. Izaak Walton's use of the convention is less heavy-handed in his funeral elegy on Donne. Walton laments he can no more break his vows of gratitude than could *'Donnes* vertues [be] spoke | By any but himselfe'. All attempts at *'Encomium'*, Walton asserts, are *'Elegie'* (in Donne 1978: p. 88, see ll. 80–2).

Here is the final stanza of Donne's verse letter:

> Now if this song be too'harsh for rime, yet, as
>     The Painters bad god made a good devill,
>     'Twill be good prose, although the verse be evill,
> If thou forget the rime as thou dost passe.
> Then write, that I may follow, and so bee
> Thy debter, thy'eccho, thy foyle, thy zanee.
>     I shall be thought, if mine like thine I shape,
>     All the worlds Lyon, though I be thy Ape. (25–32)

Donne adopts the subordinate position, as Thomas's 'debter', 'eccho', 'foyle', and 'zanee', yet there is that aspect of epideictic working here as in all these poems of compliment, albeit rather clumsily at this point, in which the magnitude of the compliment reflects backward upon the poet, so that we notice Donne's rhetorical ability rather than the outstanding qualities of the addressee, especially since the former is exemplified while the latter is still at one remove. Donne uses the word 'echo' only one other time, in a verse letter to Thomas's brother, Rowland (see below), with the same implication of his relative inferiority as a poet, so that Donne positions himself as the feminine Echo to the Woodward brothers' Narcissus. Donne's willingness to adopt the feminine position occurs again, most (in)famously and highly fraught, in the *Holy Sonnets* ('Batter my heart') and so we need to reassess critical assumptions of Donne's unabated masculinity within his poems, rather than speculating on his sexuality. Echo will not be the last classical female figure to appear in Donne's poems, if she does so only at a distance and for a brief moment. Donne did not exile 'the goodly . . . traine | of gods and goddesses' quite as quickly as his readers, beginning with Thomas Carew, have suggested. If at some

[37] 'It is difficult to read 'owne good parts'' without understanding a reference to sexual organs. The speaker thus puns when he singles out Woodward's 'quill'' for special praise' (1994: 89).

distance from the centre of these verse letters, there is a network of female figures from classical literature still weaving through the communication between Donne and his friends, pointing up the different ways in which the voice and body of each gender is related to each other. Echo, the Sphinx, the Sirens, woman as lesbian and of course the Muse are all mentioned in these early verse letters. Yet none of these female figures are represented in possession of both a voice and a female body existing in untroubled relation to one another.

Thomas's response to Donne continues the game of self-deprecation and compliment in 'All haile sweet Poët' with a poem in which 'man's firm stay', or phallocentrism, is both disrupted and reinscribed:

> Have mercy on me & my sinfull Muse
> W$^c$ rub'd & tickled w$^{th}$ thyne could not chuse
> But spend some of her pithe & yeild to bee
> One in y$^t$ chaste & mistique tribadree.
> Bassaes adultery no fruit did leave,
> Nor theirs w$^c$ their swolne thighs did nimbly weave,
> And w$^t$ new armes & mouthes embrace & kis
> Though they had issue was not like to this.
> Thy Muse, Oh strange & holy Lecheree
> Beeing a Mayd still, gott this Song on mee.

(1967b: p. 212, ll. 11–20)[38]

Thomas's Muse is 'rub'd & tickled' with Donne's Muse, brought to orgasm by Donne's more accomplished Muse so that she cannot help but 'spend some of her pithe'. Thomas describes what we would call 'lesbian' activity, but Renaissance writers used different terms for 'lesbian': either a 'tribade'—hence, Thomas's 'triba-dree'—or a 'fricatrice', from the Greek and Latin for 'women who rub each other'. Janet Halley suggests that Thomas 'cannot resist assimilating that image [of lesbianism] to one of erection and ejaculation' (1989: 200), but given that a common Renaissance theory of orgasm followed Galen's assertion that women ejaculated a thinner semen that was also necessary for conception, the refer-ence to 'pithe' is more straightforward than Halley suggests (see Maclean 1988: 30, 35–7, 105 n. 54; Rousselle 1988: 27–32).

I suggest that Thomas might be parodying Mary Sidney's dedic-

---

[38] The poem is also printed in Donne 1912: ii. 166–7.

atory poem in memory of her brother, Sir Philip, appended to their translation of the Psalms which she completed after his death in 1586. The Sidneian Psalms were widely known in manuscript and almost surely preceded these verse letters. 'To the Angel Spirit of the Most Excellent Sir Philip Sidney' begins:

> To thee, pure spirit, to thee alone's addressed
> This coupled work, by double interest thine:
> First raised by thy bless'd hand, and what is mine
> Inspired by thee, thy secret power impressed.
> So dared my Muse with thine itself combine,
> as mortal stuff with that which is divine.
>
> (L. Schleiner 1994: p. 77, ll. 1–6)

If one is reading wickedly, there is a kind of intermingling of identity here which borders on incest between sister Muses, upon which Thomas seems to play in his verse letter to Donne.[39] Other Renaissance poets had warmed to the idea of collaborative Muses. Jonson refers to 'those ambling visits that passed twixt thy Muse and mine' in a poem to Drayton; Sir John Davies in a more erotic metaphor asks Sir Richard Martin, 'O would you yet my Muse some Honny lend | From your mellifluous tongue' (1975: 89, ll. 5–6).

In his own poem, Thomas Woodward proceeds to discuss the results of this intense bonding of Muses by alluding to Bassa. Of course, whatever Renaissance theories about female ejaculate were, two women could not conceive and procreate, so that 'Bassaes adultery no fruit did leave'. Bassa is a tiny, yet telling, piece of the puzzle of the representation of lesbian sexuality. Here is Martial's epigram on Bassa:

> Quod numquam maribus iunctam te, Bassa, videbam
>   quodque tibi moechum fabula nulla dabat,
> omne sed officium circa te semper obibat
>   turba tui sexus, non adeunte viro,
> esse videbaris, fateor, Lucretia nobis:
>   at tu, pro facinus, Bassa, fututor eras.

---

[39] I am not suggesting that the metaphor has any bearing on the relationship between the Countess and her brother. One of Donne's last poems is 'Upon the translation of the Psalmes by Sir Philip Sydney, and the Countess of Pembroke his Sister'. His image of 'heavens high holy Muse' (31) subjects the classical Muse to a traditional Christian syncretism.

inter se geminos audes committere cunnos
  mentiturque virum prodigiosa Venus.
commenta es dignum Thebano aenigmate monstrum,
  hic ubi vir non est, ut sit adulterium.

[I never saw you close to men, Bassa, and no rumor gave you a lover. You were always surrounded by a crowd of your own sex, performing every office, with no man coming near you. So I confess I thought you a Lucretia; but Bassa, for shame, you were a fornicator. You dare to join two cunts and your monstrous organ feigns masculinity. You have invented a portent worthy of the Theban riddle: where no man is, there is adultery.] (I.90)

The verb *futuo* was the basic Latin obscenity for the male/active role in sexual intercourse with a woman and hence Martial is mocking Bassa's usurpation of the male role.[40] In using this particular word, Martial illustrates one of the two ways in which male constructions of female homosexuality precisely assume a sexual (in)difference so that female homoeroticism is never an act which takes place outside or independently of the male, scopic, phallic, hierarchical economy. Bassa is 'mentitur virum', a 'fictitious man', imitating him with a monstrous 'Venus', a term usually applied to the penis (Adams 1982: 98), and so here signifying a 'monstrous clitoris'. If two women in sexual congress is, for Martial, scandalous, we have seen most explicitly, above, in Thomas's verse letter that it is the very putting together of 'twin cunts' ('geminos cunnos') which enables Donne and his friends to speak to each another. Shackleton Bailey's translation flattens out the implications of 'geminos', here, by rendering it as 'two' rather than 'twin'. Martial's 'geminos' suggests a lack of differentiation between women or the kind of dereliction which results in the dangerous fusion of identities between women who become part of 'the infinite series of one plus one plus one . . . parts of a broken whole' (Irigaray 1993*a*: 61).

[40] See Adams 1982: 118–22. I am indebted to Mr. Peter C. Brown of Trinity College, Oxford, for aiding me with my translation before Shackleton Bailey's became available in 1993. Martial's first Loeb translator, Walter Ker, who leaves Martial's more obscene epigrams either untranslated or rewrites them, translates 'fututor eras', literally, 'you were a fucker of women', as 'you are a nondescript' or 'a person or thing that is not easily described, or is of no particular class or kind' (*OED*). Hence, Ker ironically perpetuated the apparent inability of the male imagination to describe women's sexuality without reference to the male, a different strategy from Martial's use of a masculine term—*futuo*—for Bassa's activity, but accomplishing the same end.

An epigram by Donne suggests he was scornful and suspicious of the censorship of obscenity. It concerns the Jesuit Matthew Rader's 1602 expurgated edition of Martial intended for use in grammar schools. In the Westmoreland manuscript it is accompanied by the title 'Martial: castratus':

> Why this Man gelded Martial I muse;
> Except himselfe alone his tricks would use
> As Katherine for the Coarts sake put downe Stews. (1995b: 9)[41]

Donne makes this point several times, in his satire of the Jesuits, *Ignatius His Conclave,* as well as in his *Sermons*, that those who censor texts 'reserve to themselves the divers formes, and the secrets and mysteries in this matter, which they finde in the *Authors* whom they geld' (1969: 67). Here, Donne uses the verb 'geld' in its figurative sense of 'to mutilate (a book, quotation, etc.) by excising certain portions, esp. objectionable or obscene passages; to expurgate' (*OED* 2.b). Those who geld texts thus engage in a kind of erotics of censorship, hypocritically keeping the 'good bits' for themselves. More importantly, as we have seen, they obscure those aspects of female sexuality which are most troubling to the patriarchal desire for self-referentiality in all things. Hester points to the epigram of Martial (I.35), left out of Raderus's edition, which addresses another objector and which lies behind Donne's own epigram. In it, Martial draws an analogy between husbands and (these kind of 'jocular') poems, neither of whom can please their wives/readers 'sine mentula [without the penis]' (l. 5), and so he begs 'nec castrare velis meos libellos [do not seek to castrate my poems]' (l. 14). The more usual alignment between woman/text and man/reader is reversed here, although Martial's epigram also draws an analogy between prostitutes and poems.

Martial declares that Bassa has 'invented a portent worthy of the Theban riddle: where no man is, there is adultery'. This is the line to which Thomas refers in his letter to Donne: 'Bassaes adultery no fruit did leave' (15). At first, Bassa seems to comply with the aphorism voiced in countless classical and Renaissance writings: it is not enough to be virtuous, women must seem virtuous also. But Bassa's sexual activities pose a riddle: at least according to the

---

[41] See Milgate's discussion in Donne 1967b: 202; and Hester 1985 who notes that whether the reference to 'Katherine' is to Catherine de Medici or one of Henry VIII's wives (Catherine of Aragon or Catherine Parr) is not clear.

masculine paradigm of it, lesbian sex is paradoxically both non-representable (because no man is involved), therefore a negligible threat to the order of things, and monstrous (because a 'phallus' is involved). Martial calls Bassa another Lucretia, who functions as one pole or end of the spectrum along which Bassa slides in her seeming virtue and actual vice. Unlike Lucretia, Bassa's body is no passive prize suspended between the desires of men; she exercises total agency over her body, so much so that she steps outside of its prescribed boundaries and usurps, according to Martial, the male, active role in sexual intercourse with other women. All her seeming virtue which accords her the reputation of a Lucretia hides something monstrous. Hence the third female figure of the epigram: the Sphinx. Bassa's riddle, like the Sphinx's, also concerns 'man' for she manages to commit adultery without one. 'Here, where no man is, should be adultery'. Bassa as riddle is thus placed on a scale between the anomalous, a chaste woman, and the monstrous, a woman who dares to act like a man; between the thing which all women are expected to be and the thing which all women are, hence their deceptive appearance; between what must remain unspoken and the 'unspeakable'. Woman is doomed to paradox, not posing a riddle, but constructed as such.

The ending of Thomas's poem is curious on several counts. The relationship suddenly becomes heterosexual, between Donne's Muse and Thomas, but gender roles are reversed. Rather than the male in the active role begetting 'on' the passive female Muse, she, he says, 'gott this Song on mee', almost as though Thomas was returning the agency traditionally accorded the Muse. What's more, she is 'a Mayd still', a virgin. That Donne's Muse should be engaged in sexual activity with another 'female' and yet be a virgin suggests either Thomas's complicity in the phallocentric view of 'sex' being unable to occur without penetration of the phallus, or else his ironic awareness of the 'phallacy'. Beyond perhaps parodying the Countess of Pembroke's poem, Thomas's use of the phrases '*chaste* & mistique', 'strange & *holy*' are suspect then, for they suggest that the two lesbian Muses commit no sexual crimes, nor do they engage in sex at all because penetration does not occur, only 'rubbing'. Klawitter's assignation of the phrase, 'chaste and mistique tribadree' as 'an oxymoron of the most striking variety' (91) is not quite accurate. It was no oxymoron in the eyes of these Renaissance poets to view this female homosexual activity as

'chaste', for nothing sexual could happen without a male. With all
the confusion of sexual roles and identities it is difficult to know
whether Thomas has entangled himself in his own 'riddle of
woman', or whether he is intentionally con-fusing as part of the
playful tone of his poems. Thomas's poem is evidence that he and
Donne 'spent' at least some of their imaginative hours on the
implications of lesbian or 'tribade' sexuality.

The phrase in Thomas Woodward's poem, 'chaste & mistique
tribadree', is an echo too close to be coincidental of a phrase in
Donne's epistle to Rowland Woodward, which also incorporates
lesbian imagery. Here is the poem:

> Zealously my Muse doth salute all thee,
> Enquiring of that mistique trinitee
> Wherof thou'and all to whom heavens do infuse
> Like fyer, are made; thy body, mind, and Muse.
> Dost thou recover sicknes, or prevent?
> Or is thy Mind travail'd with discontent?
> Or art thou parted from the world and mee
> In a good skorn of the worlds vanitee?
> Or is thy devout Muse retyr'd to sing
> Upon her tender Elegiaque string?
> Our Minds part not, joyne then thy Muse with myne,
> For myne is barren thus devorc'd from thyne. (1–12)

Donne quizzes his friend on possible excuses for not writing, and
his description of Rowland's devout Muse, 'retyr'd to sing | Upon
her tender Elegiaque string', almost certainly is an allusion to the
opening of Ovid's *Heroides*, 15, 'Sappho to Phaon'. Donne also
substitutes the Muse for the soul in the traditional tripartite
composition of humankind, and in another poem to Rowland,
refers to the Muse as 'the Soules Soule | Of Poets' ('Muse not that
by thy mind thy body'is led'). In these verse letters exchanged
between Donne and the Woodward brothers, the Muse thus
undergoes the most extreme disembodiment or incorporation and
is yet sexualized or incarnated. Donne's letter to Rowland concludes with another assertion of the close identity of the two men
by invoking a fertile joining of their Muses for Donne's Muse is
'barren' when 'devorc'd' from Woodward's. Elizabeth Harvey
asserts that 'for Donne, poetry is only produced by a chaste muse'
(1992: 112), a statement which, when read after this group of
verse letters, seems not to follow. Yet if we recall the 'chaste &

mistique tribadree' which Thomas Woodward envisions, a rubbing together of Muses rather than the penetration which Martial accuses Bassa of performing, the phallocentric view of lesbian sex as not sex at all thus allows Donne and his friends' muses to be both chaste and (pro)creative.

Obviously Donne and his friends had read and were reading classical works—Martial and Ovid at least, and probably Lucian (see Ch. 2)—which alluded to or explored lesbianism. However, in contrast to the intense misogyny of the classical sources, Donne and his friends explore lesbianism in new, less misogynistic, if still phallocentric, ways, by exploring its metaphoric possibilities rather than its actual practice. Woodward's allusion to Bassa is not morally motivated but referential and comparative (Klawitter 1992: 92). It is worth repeating Turner's observation that 'Renaissance discourses on sexuality and gender cultivated a dissociation between ostensible meaning and performative occasion'. If these representations are less misogynistic, however, they are still caught within the confines of 'homotextual' exchange.[42] The anxiety which results in misogyny seems to have disappeared, but it may be at the cost of an increasing '*internal exile*' of the figure of the feminine.

One of the characteristics of Donne's early verse epistles is the intensity with which male friendship is represented. However much they postulate a vertical relationship of merit between themselves as poets, as friends theirs is a horizontal relationship of equals, indeed one in which identities merge and separate. For example, Donne begins 'The Storme' by addressing his close friend Christopher Brooke as 'Thou which art I, ('tis nothing to be soe) | Thou which art still thy selfe' (1–2). What might seem to be veiled homosexual sentiments projected onto the safer territory of a sexualized Muse, are, I would argue, both the effect of masculinist constructions of woman and the sixteenth-century ethos of male friendship. There are at least half a dozen condemnatory references to male homosexuality in Donne's poetry, including one in the verse letter I discuss next, 'To Mr. B.B.'[43] Bruce Smith

---

[42] Defined by Sheila Fisher and Janet Halley as an activity 'in which male writings referred to, responded to, manipulated, and projected desire upon other men and other men's writings as much, if not more, than they claimed to represent the extraliterary world and the women in it' (1989: 4).

[43] See below, Ch. 2, for Donne's references to male homosexuality.

explains the narrow conception of male homosexuality in the Renaissance and alludes to the difficulties presented by poems such as Donne's verse letters:

Sodomy, for Donne . . . as for all satirists, is a man lusting after a boy. On the sexual potentiality in male bonding, so difficult to see because so pervasive and so undefined, they all remain silent. . . . Instructed by their own culture's prejudices about women, they can imagine sodomy only in male-female terms, in terms of 'agent' and 'consentient'. . . . In same-sex relations, someone *had* to be the weaker partner. (1991: 186)

A short poem by Thomas Pestell praising a verse letter written by both Donne and Henry Goodyer in alternate stanzas to two unidentified women ('A Letter written by Sir H.G. and J.D. *alternis vicibus*') illustrates the extent to which language which we would classify as erotic or sexual was not read literally as such in the Renaissance:

> Here two rich ravisht spirits kisse & twyne;
> Advanc'd, & wedlockt in each others lyne.
> Gooderes rare match with only him was blest,
> Who haes out donne, & quite undonne the rest.[44]

Donne's verse letter, 'To Mr. C[hristopher] B[rooke]', distinguishes between 'this love' between male friends and 'that love' of one's mistress:

> Thy friend, whom thy deserts to thee enchaine,
>   Urg'd by this inexcusable occasion,
>   Thee and the Saint of his affection
> Leaving behinde, doth of both wants complaine;
> And let the love I beare to both sustaine
>   No blott nor maime by this division,
>   Strong is this love which ties our hearts in one,
> And strong that love pursu'd with amorous paine; (1–8)

Indeed it is the love between male friends which Donne describes using the language of the marriage ceremony as that 'which ties our hearts in one', and it is a theme which Donne returns to again and again in the verse letters, as in the opening of his letter to Henry Wotton, 'Sir, *more* then kisses, letters mingle Soules; | For, thus friends absent speake' (emphasis added). Male friendship is presented here as more deeply spiritual than romantic love.

---

[44] 'On the Interlinearie poeme begott twixt S^r H. Goo: & D^r Donne', Bodleian Library MS Malone 14, p. 28. Milgate quotes Pestell's poem in Donne 1967*b*: 235.

Donne's verse letter, 'To Mr. B.B.',[45] contains perhaps the most complex rendering of a domesticated Muse and poetic family:

> If thou unto thy Muse be marryed,
>   Embrace her ever, ever multiply,
>   Be far from me that strange Adulterie
> To tempt thee and procure her widowhed.
> My Muse, (for I had one,) because I'am cold,
>   Divorc'd her selfe: the cause being in me,
>   That I can take no new in Bigamye,
> Not my will only but power doth withhold.
> Hence comes it, that these Rymes which never had
>   Mother, want matter, and they only have
>   A little forme, the which their Father gave;
> They are prophane, imperfect, oh, too bad
>   To be counted Children of Poetry
>   Except confirm'd and Bishoped by thee.

Here there is no sudden divine visitation or frenzy. Donne quietly encourages B.B. to remain faithful to his wifely Muse and propagate children/poems. Still, there is a sense of competition: Donne vying with the Muse for B.B.'s attention. That 'strange Adulterie' should 'procure' the Muse's 'widowhed' suggests, perhaps, B.B.'s sexual, even literal death, were he tempted to engage in a (figurative) homosexual relationship with Donne. The sexual connotations of the word 'procure' are played with here ironically, for taboo sexual congress between Donne and B.B. would bring about the Muse's widowhood, rather than the prostitution often associated with the word. Donne also juxtaposes divorce and death in the stanza on virginity in 'A Litanie': 'Divorce thou sinne in us, or bid it die, | And call chast widowhead Virginitie' (107–8).

I want to compare Donne's poem with the image of marriage to a Muse which opens Shakespeare's Sonnet 82:

> I grant thou wert not married to my muse,
> And therefore mayst without attaint o'erlook
> The dedicated words which writers use
> Of their fair subject, blessing every book.
> Thou art as fair in knowledge as in hue,
> Finding thy worth a limit past my praise,

[45] See Milgate in Donne 1967*b*: 220–1, on the probable identity of 'B.B.' as Beaupré Bell, who was at Cambridge and then at Lincoln's Inn in London at the same time as Donne.

And therefore art enforced to seek anew
Some fresher stamp of these time-bettering days. (1–8)

The speaker admits that the addressee is not married to his (the speaker's) Muse, and uses the relationship of marriage as a metaphor for a union—poet and addressee—in which they have vowed to forsake all others. The addressee has clearly had other 'words' dedicated to him, and the speaker is jealous, begrudging 'their gross painting' (13) and comparing it to his own 'true plain words'. Shakespeare and Donne use the metaphor of marriage to a Muse for opposite purposes, then, Shakespeare to free his addressee (on a technicality), Donne to remind B.B. of his poetic responsibilities. Donne goes on in his poem (which is in sonnet form) to talk about his relationship to his Muse in ways that are similar to the reasons Shakespeare gives as to why his addressee should need to 'seek anew | Some fresher stamp'. Donne, like Shakespeare, is 'cold' and unable to write or praise as he should. In Donne's verse letter to Rowland Woodward (see below) he asserts what Shakespeare grudgingly admits to his young man: 'Though to use, and love Poëtrie, to mee, | Betroth'd to no'one Art, be no'adulterie' (7–8). Still, it is impossible to determine whether one poet influenced another because of the difficulty of determining the circulation in manuscript of both poets' work.

In his poem, 'To B.B.', Donne's own Muse initiates a divorce on the legitimate grounds of her husband's impotency. Rather than the poet importuning the Muse to aid him in poetic creation, Donne's Muse is eager to (pro)create but the poet is 'cold'. Since he is the one who is impotent, he cannot 'take' another Muse in 'Bigamye'. Divorce in Renaissance society was *mensa et thoro*, from bed and board, and not absolute. Furthermore, Donne suggests he does not 'will' or desire a second marriage. From this relatively promising representation of female agency, Donne then proceeds to describe what in effect constitutes an act of male parthenogenesis: using the Pythagorean formulation of male/female as form/matter, Donne manages to create this child/poem all on his own, a poem which 'want[s] matter'; that is, it is essentially about nothing except the making of the poem. If B.B. will 'confirm' (L., *con + firmare*, strengthen) or 'Bishop' the poems, or administer the rite of confirmation to, they will be 'legitimate', i.e. not bastards, although here it is Donne who 'gives birth' to poems without a mother. In another sonnet to B.B., Donne asks his friend to join him in London at the Inns of Court: 'weane thy selfe at last, and thee withdraw | From Cambridge thy old nurse, and as the rest, | Here toughly chew, and sturdily digest | Th'immense vast volumes of our common law' ('Is not thy sacred hunger of science', 5–8). Clearly, there is a strong coterie mentality operating in which the Muse as mother, and Cambridge as nurse are eventually outgrown. Ironically, the one time the Muse is explicitly called a mother, she is absent.

Although I do not intend to suggest an actual chronology for the poems in my discussion of them, in another poem 'To Mr. R.W.', Donne's Muse who has been wife and ex-wife in the verse letters is compared to a widow:

> Like one who'in her third widdowhood doth professe
> Her selfe a Nunne, ty'd to retirednesse,
> So'affects my muse now, a chast fallownesse;
>
> Since shee to few, yet to too many'hath showne
> How love-song weeds, and Satyrique thornes are growne
> Where seeds of better Arts, were early sown.
>
> Though to use, and love Poëtrie, to mee,
> Betroth'd to no'one Art, be no'adulterie;
> Omissions of good, ill, as ill deeds bee. (1–9)

Donne appears to be denying a request from Rowland Woodward for some of his satires and Ovidian elegies, and perhaps some of his love poems. He will again use the Muse to excuse his unwillingness to write an epithalamium for Frances Howard and the Duke of Somerset in a prose letter to Sir Robert Ker (see below). His tone is playfully mocking and Donne distracts the disappointment of his petitioner by deflecting agency onto his Muse. She 'affects' the retired life of a Nun so she will not agree to 'show' herself, that is, 'her' poems; yet she has been widowed not once but three times, and here Donne plays on the representation of widows as 'unregenerately lecherous', a reaction to their independent status and to the uncomfortable perception that their remarriage was 'posthumous cuckoldry' (Woodbridge 1986: 177–8). Donne's Muse thrice married (suggesting lustiness? avarice? desirability?) is presented as more autonomous—dangerously so—than the Muses which are 'bought and sold' in the theatre in Hall's satire, but she is nevertheless a mediating figure between Donne and his friends and still 'must play and sing when, and what he would have'.

Affecting 'a chast fallownesse', the Muse's body is the site 'where seeds of better Arts, were early sown', yet 'weeds' and 'thornes' have sprung up instead. Donne's husbandry has not been fruitful, indeed he implies his Muse is an exhibitionist, given half a chance. She must be carefully husbanded and so for the time being, lies 'fallow'. But Donne himself 'affects' an attitude of indifference and promiscuity: he is not adulterous in 'us[ing] and lov[ing] Poëtrie' because he is 'Betroth'd to no'one Art'; but, he admits, he ought to be getting down to more serious work: 'Omissions of good, ill, as ill deeds bee'. The image of the promiscuous woman is used most controversially in Donne's Holy Sonnet, 'Show me deare Christ, thy spouse, so bright and cleare'. In his closing lines, the speaker begs Christ as 'kind husband' to 'Betray . . . thy spouse to our sights, | And let myne amorous soule court thy mild Dove, | Who is most trew, and pleasing to thee, then | When she'is embrac'd and open to most men' (11–14).[46] Once Donne has excused his unwillingness to part with his poems in the first three stanzas of his verse letter to Rowland, the Muse disappears and Donne embarks on a discussion of virtue, encouraging his friend, 'Seeke wee then our selves in our selves' (19) and declaring masculine solidarity: 'know, that I love thee'and would be lov'd' (36). Despite, indeed because of, his Muse's 'fallownesse', Donne has created a poem and reaffirmed his friendship, just as the present absence of the Mother Muse in 'To Mr. B.B.' enabled the exchange of a poem between male friends.

In the verse letter to Rowland Woodward which begins, 'Kindly'I envy thy Songs perfection', Donne again looks to his friend rather than the Muse for inspiration yet (pro)creation still takes place in vaguely sexual language:

> Kindly'I envy thy Songs perfection
>   Built of all th'elements as our bodyes are:
>   That litle of earth that'is in it, is a faire
> Delicious garden where all Sweetes are sowne.

---

[46] See Anthony Low's astute reading of Donne's sonnet in which he recognizes 'that we have on our hands a *ménage à trois*, if not worse. Christ and the speaker have essentially been transformed into rivals for the lady's affections' (1993: 76–7). See also Sabine 1992: 108.

In it is cherishing fyer which dryes in mee
Griefe which did drowne me: and halfe quench'd by it
  Are Satirique fyres which urg'd me to have writt
In skorne of all: for now I admyre thee.
  And as Ayre doth fullfill the hollownes
  Of rotten walls; so it myne emptines,
Wher tost and mov'd it did begett this sound
Which as a lame Eccho of thyne doth rebound.
  Oh, I was dead: but since thy song new life did give,
  I recreated, even by thy creature, live.

Donne's conceit is based on pre-Socratic ontological categories
whereby all living things were composed of some combination of
the four elements—earth, water, air, fire. Although all bodies
contain all four elements and qualities, males as more perfect
creatures were considered to be hotter and drier than females.
Thus, women are characterized by 'cold and moist [earth and
water] dominant humours and a desire for completion by intercourse with the male' whereas men are characterized by hot and
dry (fire and air) dominant humours (Maclean 1988: 30–42).

   Rowland's poem has but 'a litle of earth', one of the 'feminine'
elements. Donne's description of Rowland's poem as 'a faire |
Delicious garden where all Sweetes are sowne' combines the
farming metaphor with words denoting pleasure of the senses,
such as 'faire', 'Delicious', and 'Sweetes', a word which for the
Elizabethans often connoted sexual pleasures (G. Williams 1994).
The word Donne uses to describe the nature of Rowland's 'fyer'—
'cherishing'—is found only one other time in Donne's poetry and
with sexual connotations. In his infamous elegy, 'The Comparison', Donne favourably compares the 'cherishing heat' of his own
mistress's 'best lov'd part' to the genitals of his rival's mistress,
which are 'like the dread mouth of a fired gunne | Or like hot
liquid metall newly runne | Into clay moulds, or like to that Aetna
| Where round about the grasse is burnt away' (39–42). Here,
Donne does not follow convention in deferring to the shyness of
his Muse so as to avoid describing the women's sexual parts,
although he still employs analogies. It is he who supplies the
'cherishing heat' to his own mistress's body, however, as is clear
from the alchemical metaphor used to describe their love-making:

   Then like the Chymicks masculine equall fire,
   Which in the Lymbecks warme wombe doth inspire

> Into th'earths worthlesse durt a soule of gold,
> Such cherishing heat her best lov'd part doth hold. (35–8)

The masculine transforming figure penetrates the receptive body of his mistress. We are reminded by the feminine associations in this elegy why Rowland has only a 'litle of earth' in his poem/body.

Rowland's poetic 'fyer' dries a 'Griefe' in Donne, perhaps an allusion to a failed *amour*, and the watery element of his poem/ body quenches Donne's own 'Satirique fyres'. Donne thus accounts for three of four elements in the octet of his sonnet. While not strictly Petrarchan, Spenserian, or Shakespearean with its rhyme scheme of abbacddceeffgg, the distribution of rhymes argues for a fairly strong division of lines into octet and sestet as in a Petrarchan sonnet. This organization privileges the final element of Rowland's song, air, which is given a full four lines before Donne's concluding couplet. Donne describes his own vacuum of creativity, his dejected state prior to receiving Woodward's inspiring song, indeed he 'was dead'. He uses an image of concoction which is very close to contemporary descriptions of the process of conception during copulation.[47] Rowland's air fills the emptiness of Donne, 'Where tost and mov'd it did begett this sound', a conceit similar to lines in 'The Storme', where the wind first 'kist' and then 'swole' the sails, so that Donne and the rest of the company sailing with Essex 'joy'd, as *Sara*'her swelling joy'd to see' (21–2). And in 'To Mr. S.B.' Donne encourages his friend, Samuel Brooke, with a similar elemental image to that in 'Kindly'I envy', although he gives himself a more active role:

> But seeing in you bright sparkes of Poëtry,
> I, though I brought no fuell, had desire
> With these Articulate blasts to blow the fire. (12–14)

Indeed, Donne almost casts himself in the role of Brooke's muse, 'blow[ing] the fire' that is already within him. But Donne disassociates himself from feminine figures explicitly when he asserts his intention has not been to seduce or recruit his friend

---

[47] See Laqueur 1990: 3, 43–52. Laqueur quotes various authoritative descriptions of orgasm and conception, including Tertullian's, as a 'shiver' or epileptic fit (Hippocrates), or an 'inner turbulence'. For contemporary accounts of the tossing and moving required for conception, see Thomas Cogan, *The Haven of Health* (1589): 240–1; Helkiah Crooke, *Microcosmographia: A Description of the Body of Man* (1618): 200.

away from his other studies: 'I sing not, Siren-like, to tempt' (9).[48]
Donne's poem is still but a 'lame Eccho' of Rowland's because his
own contributing element is mere 'emptiness', 'rotten walls' which
act as the locus, the feminine vessel, of conception. Donne cast
himself as Thomas Woodward's 'eccho' in 'All haile sweet Poët', as
we saw, above. Echo is the precise opposite of the Muse, for in
contrast to the Muse's powers of inspiration and her vast store of
knowledge and wisdom, Echo can express no thoughts of her own
but only mimic the last phrase of whoever speaks first.

The opening lines of 'To Mr. E.G.' set up a similar relationship
as that between Donne, his 'lame' poems, and Rowland Woodward:

> Even as lame things thirst their perfection, so
> The slimy rimes bred in our vale below,
> Bearing with them much of my love and hart,
> Fly unto that Parnassus, wher thou art. (1–4)

Like Woodward, Everard Guilpin represents 'perfection', and is
living in the 'Parnassus' of Suffolk. Donne represents himself as
the feminized 'hollownes | Of rotten walls' in one poem, and the
source of 'slimy rimes bred in our vale below' in the other. The
same image occurs in a poem to the Earl of Dorset which accompanied six of Donne's Holy Sonnets:

> See Sir, how as the Suns hot Masculine flame
>     Begets strange creatures on Niles durty slime,
>         In me, your fatherly yet lusty Ryme
> (For, these songs are their fruits) have wrought the same. (1–4)

Drawing on Pliny's *Natural History* (9.84) for his simile, Donne
again aligns himself with the feminine Nile's 'durty slime'.[49]
Dorset's own 'fatherly yet lusty Ryme' was 'the ingendring force'
(5) behind Donne's own poems, the seventh of which 'hath still

---

[48] It should be noted that Apollonius of Rhodes alludes in his *Argonautica* (4.896) to
a tradition wherein the Sirens were daughters of the Muse, Terpsichore, but no one
seems to have developed this (albeit) negative maternal genealogy until Milton
telescopes the two in *The Reason of Church Government*. Milton hints at his Christian
epic still to be written in which, he says, he will decline to invoke 'Dame Memory and
her Siren daughters' but rather pray to the Holy Spirit for Christian divine inspiration.

[49] Compare the same association with the feminine in Donne's *Elegie upon . . . the
Ladie* MARCKAM': 'But as the tyde doth wash the slymie beach, | And leaves em-
broidered workes upon the sand, | Soe is her fleash refin'de by Deathes cold hand'
(1995a: 18–20). See also Spenser's *Faerie Queene*, 1.1.21.

some maime' (8). It seems odd that Donne would use such a metaphor for divine poems, rather than a biblical or otherwise Christian model of creation. Furthermore, if 'E. of D.' is Richard Sackville, third Earl of Dorset (b.1589), then Donne refers to the 'fatherly rhyme' of someone who is seventeen years his junior. Sackville would be 20, and just married to Anne Clifford, while Donne was 37 in 1609 when the poem was likely written. But if addressed to a possible patron, perhaps no awkwardness was perceived. I mention this later verse letter to show that the early poems were not mere squibs or 'sample[s] of undergraduate wit' (Bald 1986: 75) but set down imaginative resources on which Donne drew throughout his life. In the process of complimenting his male friends, Donne tends to adopt the weaker or more passive (and hence feminine) position and he represents his efforts as maimed or imperfect children in deferring to the poetic virility of his friends. The verse letters thus function not as competition, at least not overtly, but as encouragement to Donne's friends. They are poems which demand that we reassess the entrenched view of Donne's unabashed and unabated masculinity (see Carr 1988: 97), because he is so often willing to take up a feminine gender role in relation to his male friends. However, Donne's feminization, his Echo to his friends' Narcissus, is adopted only in order to cement male homosocial relations.

More mundane images of pregnancy can be found in Donne's verse letters. In his poem to Guilpin, Donne describes London as a woman who has just given birth using language as brilliantly evocative of the atmosphere of London streets as it is sensitively observant of the woman:

> Now pleasures dearth our City doth posses,
> Our Theaters are fill'd with emptines;
> As lancke and thin is every Street and way
> As a Woman deliver'd yesterday. (7–10)

In yet another verse letter 'To Mr. T.W.', Donne uses the word 'pregnant' unusually for his time. Until well into the seventeenth century, 'pregnant' referred primarily to mental capacities, to metaphorical fecundity rather than the state of a woman with child, but Donne's use clearly includes both meanings:

> Pregnant again with th'old twins Hope, and Feare,
> Oft have I askt for thee, both how and where
> Thou wert, and what my hopes of letters were;

As in our streets sly beggers narrowly
Watch motions of the givers hand and eye,
And evermore conceive some hope thereby. (1–6)

Like his description of London streets in 'To Mr. E.G.', these lines
are some of Donne's most brilliant in the early verse letters in that
they show his exquisite genius for observation, an element often
considered lacking in his poetry. As in 'The Storme', Donne
switches from a generative to a digestive metaphor in the rest of
the poem, so that Thomas's 'Almes', or poem, is given to Donne
the hopeful beggar and he is restored to life: 'The body risen
againe, the which was dead, | And thy poore starveling bountifully
fed' (8–9). This poem to Thomas, and the sestet of Donne's poem
to Rowland relates, as in 'To Mr. B.B.', a kind of male
parthenogenesis.

What we see in these poems, then, are variations on the scenario
with which, according to Irigaray's strategic reading in *Speculum*,
Plato leaves us (and Western culture) in his myth of the cavern: the
illusion of male parthenogenesis. 'Of the two elements involved in
reproduction, the seed of the Father (the Idea) and the womb of
the Mother (the cavern itself), only the paternal element remains
in the final scene. . . . the paternal Idea has incorporated both
elements, and engenders, alone, copies, replicas, and shadows
without any material aid'.[50] Whitford explains,

The fact that the woman also engenders has been obliterated from the
scene of representation by cutting off the Sensible from the Intelligible.
The effect is that the male function takes over and incorporates all the
female function, leaving women outside the scene, but supporting it, a
condition of representation. The picture of the cavern *represents*, while
concealing, the process. (1991: 106; Whitford's italics)

A similar process occurs, I would argue, in the whole tradition
of invocation as it is set up by classical tradition. The Muses would
appear to be foundational and indeed integral to the act of '*poiein*',
of making or fiction, for we see them invoked endlessly in classical
poetry. Yet the male poet speaks/writes to other male poets, struc-
turing his language so that 'the male function takes over and

---

[50] Whitford 1991: 109. I use Whitford here to summarize Irigaray's extremely
dense and difficult reading of Plato which does not accommodate the excision of
short passages from it. There are instances of female parthenogenesis, for example, in
Hesiod's *Theogony* (131–2, 213–14, 217), but these births are 'fruitless' or monstrous.

incorporates all the female function, leaving women outside the scene, but supporting it, a condition of representation'. Katharine Maus's interpretation of the first sonnet of Sidney's *Astrophil and Stella* leads her to draw similar conclusions about the 'necessary female absence' of the Muse. Here are some of the most quoted lines yet once more:

> Thus great with child to speake, and helplesse in my throwes,
> Biting my trewand pen, beating my selfe for spite,
> 'Foole,' said my Muse to me, 'looke in thy heart and write.'
>
> (1962: 12–14)

Maus writes:

this is pregnancy without impregnation. . . . Astrophil's pregnancy is revealed to be essentially self-generated: something comes out, but nothing came in. He becomes able to give birth when he recognizes his own self-sufficiency, stops relying upon externals, and looks within his own heart. The Muse gives him advice, but she does not give him the poem: she is a midwife, not an origin or even a co-begetter. (1993: 275)

Harold Love discusses the related metaphor of 'sex-as-printing' in similar terms: 'the aspect of the printing press that most vividly imposed itself on the Renaissance masculine imagination was its ability to produce an endless succession of identical copies of the type-page. . . . The characteristic form of the topos is one which presents the woman as a means whereby a man is able to produce an exact simulacrum of himself' (1993: 151–2). With printed texts allowing greater control and thus suggesting fidelity, and scribal texts more vulnerable to 'promiscuous' multiple inscriptions, 'the modes of reproduction characteristic of print and script pointed, at the level of metaphor, towards a socially approved and a socially disapproved mode of procreation' (153), depending, I would add, on how close the text is situated, in its mode of production, to the body itself. Once again, however, as Love relates, Donne reverses the valuation in some Latin verses he writes to Richard Andrewes whereby the productions of the press, imagined as a woman in labour, are 'offspring . . . destined for death'—moths and ashes—but that which is written by hand with the pen 'reverenter habetur | Involat et veterum scrinia summa Patrum [is held in reverence and flies to the privileged shelf reserved for the ancient fathers]' (1993: 152–3).

IV. DONNE'S MUSE INTERRED

It is Donne's Muse who is destined for death, however, as Donne's incarnation of his Muse comes to its own logical terminus when the silencing of a voice is accompanied by the burial of a body. Donne phrases his valediction to poetry in a 1614 funeral elegy for the 22-year-old John Harrington, brother to Lucy, Countess of Bedford, in which he figures his valediction as the burial of his Muse:

> Doe not, fayre Soule, this sacrifice refuse
> That in thy Grave I do interre my Muse
>  Which by my greefe, greate as thy worth, beeing cast
>  Behind hand; yet hath spoke, and spoke her last. (1995*a*: 255–8)

Only a Muse with a body can be buried. Donne figuratively 'interre[s]' an entity traditionally perceived to be deathless. The text is ambiguous as to whether his Muse has died 'naturally' of grief or whether Donne buries her alive with the corpse of John Harrington. The Muse is 'cast | Behind hand' or discarded like a mistress,[51] and indeed Donne refers in a letter to 'Poetry, the Mistress of my youth, and Divinity, the wife of mine age' (see Bald 1986: 446) in another instance of his construction of the myth of two irreconcilable Donnes. Leaving behind the feminized discourse of poetry and his role as the Muse's priest/ husband, Donne as priest is now sufficiently inspired by the Word so as to leave us with ten volumes of sermons, the ultimate masculine exchange, as we will see in Chapter 3; in Carew's words, he is 'Apollo's first, at last, the true Gods Priest'.

   Donne obviously liked the metaphor for he uses it again in a letter to Robert Ker, in a graceful refusal to write an epithalamium for the scandalous marriage of Frances Howard to James's favourite, also named Robert Carr, Earl of Somerset: 'If my Muse were onely out of fashion, and but wounded and maimed like Free will in the *Roman Church*, I should adventure to put her to an Epithalamion. But since she is dead, like Free-will in our Church, I have not so much Muse left as to lament her losse' (1977: 270). Donne's Muse is not left to rest in peace, however. The bulk of David Novarr's book-length study, *The Disinterred Muse* (1980) a

---

[51] For this connotation of 'cast', see G. Williams 1994.

title which Novarr seems to have chosen without irony, concerns the fourteen poems which Donne wrote after his ordination and the 'death' of his Muse,[52] precisely because the figural feminine can be resurrected whenever necessary.

While we saw one other example of a dead Muse in Davies's irreverent epigram, above, most poets are content either to lament their own abandonment by their Muse (as a result of overwhelming grief, usually) or to dismiss her, like Ben Jonson in his epigram, 'To My Muse':

> Away, and leave me, thou thing most abhorred,
>     That hast betrayed me to a worthless lord,
> Made me commit most fierce idolatry
>     To a great image through thy luxury.
> Be thy next master's more unlucky muse,
>     And, as thou hast mine, his hours and youth abuse.
> . . .
> With me thou leav'st a happier muse than thee,
>     And which thou brought'st me, welcome poverty;
> She shall instruct my after-thoughts to write
>     Things manly, and not smelling parasite.
> But I repent me: stay. Whoe'er is raised
>     For worth he has not, he is taxed, not praised. (1–6; 11–16)

Jonson performs a kind of reverse invocation, in contrast to Donne's disposal of his Muse once and for all.[53] Jonson does not kill his Muse but dismisses her from his employ, to be hired by another 'master'. More affectionately in 'The Farewell to his Muse', Sir John Harington 'bequeaths' his 'Sweet wanton Muse' to his 'sonn and heire', for 'Now to more serious thoughts my soule aspyers, | This age, this minde, a Muse awsteare requiers'. Barnabe Barnes is content with conversion and in his *A Divine Centurie of Spirituall Sonnets* (1595) asks the Holy Ghost to 'consecrate my Muse to sacred verse'.

Jonson's poem admittedly illustrates the kind of insecurity Marotti argues was rife among gentlemen waiting on the court in late Elizabethan, early Jacobean England, for he first commands his Muse to leave him and thus appears to control her, then blames

---

[52] Likewise, Dennis Kay uses without comment 'The Disinterred Muse: 1614–1625' as a subtitle for a chapter in his book (1990: 116).

[53] For a historical contextualization of Jonson's poem and its relation to Cecil, see DeLuna 1967 and Wiltenburg 1988.

her for 'betray[ing]' him, for 'making' him commit idolatry and for 'abus[ing]' his time, and then repents and asks her to 'stay' while he turns his bitterness on Cecil. He blames her 'luxury' (i.e. lechery) and looks forward to writing 'Things manly' once his Muse is gone, yet he immediately takes the feminized 'poverty' into his service. He cannot do without his Muse for even a single poem as he admits again in 1633 in his 'Elegy on My Muse, the Truly Honoured Lady, the Lady Venetia Digby' (*Underwood*, 84.9) 'What's left a poet, when his muse is gone?'

Donne's reconfiguration of the poet/Muse dynamic was clearly one aspect of his poetics which left an impression on his contemporary readers. Fully half of the sixteen elegies included in Grierson's 1912 edition contain explicit references to the Muse[s] or Poetry in which gender is active rather than 'latent'. In his elegy, Carew portrays Donne as having been married to Poetry Herself, not just a small-'m' muse, so to speak. Donne left his fellow poets with no chance of finding their own poetic 'mate'; he had cornered the market by marrying Poetry herself, now 'widdowed'. Michael Parker identifies the second stanza of Donne's verse letter, 'To Mr. Rowland Woodward', as the source of Carew's image of the 'Muses garden with Pedantique weedes | O'rspred' (25–6) later in his elegy (1986: 194), but Carew clearly drew his domestic image of the 'widdowed' Muse/Poetry from this poem of Donne's as well. Henry King's elegy which Parker persuasively argues is 'a testy refutation of Carew's assessment' (195) uses the same variation of the inexpressibility topos at greater length and less violently; indeed more like Donne's images of a domesticated Muse:

> Widow'd invention justly doth forbeare
> To come abroad, knowing Thou art not here,
> Late her great Patron; Whose Prerogative
> Maintain'd, and cloth'd her so, as none alive
> Must now presume, to keepe her at thy rate,
> Though he the Indies for her dowre estate. (13–18)

To conclude, I want to briefly address William Hazlitt͘ tions to Donne's poetics which I use as an epigraph for this for Hazlitt uses precisely the two conventions with which ͘ne plays in establishing his poetic voice in the early verse letters. Moreover, the incarnation and interment of Donne's Muse is neatly figured in Hazlitt's formulation, found in his *Lectures on the*

*Comic Writers* (1819) where he largely concurs with Samuel Johnson's well-known criticisms of 'metaphysical' poetry (1903: viii.
51). Donne and his Muse have engaged in poetic 'intercourse' and
the resultant 'offspring', Donne's 'thought', insist on being born.
In contrast to Sidney's Astrophil himself being 'Great with child to
speak', in Hazlitt's formulation it is Donne's Muse who suffers
prolonged, indeed perpetual labour pains, and who is relieved of
the burden of 'His thoughts' only by having her body cut open in a
'Cæsarean operation'. Any 'unnaturalness' in the conventional
childbirth metaphor (because males cannot give birth) is buried
beneath Hazlitt's assertions of Donne's own tortuous creative
process. Indeed the female body's natural function returns to
the Muse (bodily function—parturition—and femaleness correspond), but in dire circumstances which require the intervention
of a third party; for a Cæsarean operation, this third party, rather
than a midwife, would be a male surgeon who would step in in
order to try to save the child. In other words, Hazlitt reverses the
usual relationship so that Donne's Muse depends on the male poet
and male surgeon to give birth, rather than that Donne depends on
the Muse to create a poem.

Thus, in his description of Donne's poetics, Hazlitt argues that
what should be a 'spontaneous impulse'—the birth process—
becomes the interventionist practice of 'the Cæsarean operation'.
He continues: '[t]he sentiments, profound and tender as they
often are, are stifled in the expression; and, "heaved pantingly
forth", are "buried quick again" under the ruins and rubbish of
analytical distinctions' (51). Cæsarean sections performed before
the twentieth century were not able to save the lives of both
mother and child, and the mother was regularly sacrificed in order
to save the child, who was cut out of the mother's body as soon
as possible after she died.[54] Therefore, in Hazlitt's formulation,
Donne sacrifices his Muse in the violent delivery of his thoughts,
rather like the bride/mother in the 'Epithalamium [Made at Lincoln's Inn]' who is sacrificed to the patriarchy, 'put to the knife' by
the bridegroom/priest. The female body is cut to pieces in the

---

[54] Renate Blumenfeld-Kosinski examines a late sixteenth-century treatise by
François Rousset, who advocates performing Cæsareans on living women, but 'Only
now, in the twentieth century, has medicine fulfilled what Rousset hoped for: routine
Cæsareans in which both mother and child survive' (1990: 4). See also Alison Weir's
refutation of the rumour that Jane Seymour was cut open to allow Edward VI to be
born safely (1991: 367).

metaphysical poetic process and in phallocentric discourse. The body of woman is used not only as the site of creation, it is unnaturally delivered upon her death of what is identified not as her 'progeny', her inspired work, but Donne's thoughts. Hazlitt implies an unnatural relationship between Donne and his Muse, but in criticizing Donne for not 'being *conversant*' (my emphasis) with the 'face' of (female) Nature (50), Hazlitt manipulates the childbirth metaphor with the effect that the feminine-Nature-mother is denied twice over: she is 'incarnated' as Muse only to be sacrificed for the child-poem.

The Muse, separated from her ancient religious origins, is clearly one manifestation of the imaginative importance of the feminine to male writers. The Muse never achieves the individuality of a Medea, Wife of Bath, or Lady Macbeth, yet 'she' is always there, 'from cover to cover'. Michael Parker asserts 'the figure of Donne himself now presides in place of the pagan muses he has exiled' (1986: 194). But even Donne's phallic 'phansie' is never able to banish entirely the feminine Muse from his masculine exchanges. Despite the avowed self-sufficiency of, and identification between, male friends, the feminine—as incarnated and embodied Muse or as an abstract gender position occupied by one male poet or the other (for example in 'Kindly'I envy')—is still indispensable to poetic creativity and the perpetuation of hom(m)osexual culture; 'she' is both there and not there, dead or alive, consigned to '*internal exile*'.

# 2

# 'The Desire for the Proximate': Lesbian 'Likenesse' in 'Sapho to Philaenis'

Difference of sex no more wee knew,
Then our Guardian Angells doe.

('The Relique')

So, to one neutrall thing both sexes fit.

('The Canonization')

And if some lover, such as wee,
  Have heard this dialogue of one,
Let him still marke us, he shall see
  Small change, when we'are to bodies gone.

('The Exstasie')

Likenesse begets such strange selfe flatterie
That touching my selfe, all seemes done to thee.

('Sapho to Philaenis')

## I. INTRODUCTION

From a consideration of the function of the feminine as figured by the Muse in a number of early verse letters Donne exchanged with male friends, we move in this chapter to the consideration of one poem's representation of feminine erotics. This chapter will focus on Donne's lesbian love poem, 'Sapho to Philaenis', in an effort to understand its place in Donne's philosophy (or philosophies) of love. Donne writes in a letter of 1612 to Sir Henry Wotton: 'You (I think) and I am much of one sect in the Philosophy of love; which though it be directed upon the minde, doth inhere in the body, and find piety entertainment there.'[1] Donne reiterates the notion in

---

[1] Donne 1977: 121. I would suggest 'piety' is probably a printing error for 'prety'.

'The Exstasie' and 'Love's Growth', for example, from which I quoted in Chapter 1: his conviction that only when the body participates in love along with the soul or 'minde' is the fullness of love experienced. How does this philosophy of love operate in 'Sapho to Philaenis'? In what way does love 'inhere in the body' when the lover and the beloved are both women? There can be no procreative cause for such physical love, so does 'Sapho to Philaenis' thus expand the repertoire of love? Does Donne's poem suggest that sexual pleasure is more than functional[2] or accidental, and that sexuality has a 'life of its own' apart from procreation? Is the poem even about love? Sex? Neither?

Like the speaker of 'A Lecture upon the Shadow', I offer in this chapter on 'Sapho to Philaenis' but 'A Lecture . . . in loves philosophy'; an examination of Donne's articulation of female bodies and desire as it accords with or disturbs the constructs of femininity established through literary exchange between men within patriarchal culture. I will argue that 'Sapho to Philaenis', whether as a consequence of Donne's aspiring and contentious wit or as an issue or project in and of itself, goes further than anything prior to it in suggesting (a) that there is such a thing as a female subject defined in relation to herself rather than as a 'negative' male 'reduced to being a womb or a seductive mask'; and (b) of what that female subjectivity might consist, other than woman as 'the means of conception, growth, birth, and rebirth of *forms* for the other' (Irigaray 1993c: 180). My qualification that 'Sapho to Philaenis' goes further than previous representations of female homoeroticism is important. Donne's poem is not by any means wholly successful, indeed its complexities and tensions have caused some readers to argue that it is an indictment of female self-determination and an affirmation of phallogocentrism. Regardless of one's final interpretation, 'Sapho to Philaenis' demands that we question the fundamentals of human relationship in ways unlike any other poem of its time.

As a lesbian love poem 'Sapho to Philaenis' would seem the perfect work to illustrate the impossibility of comprehensive neatness when reading Donne,[3] and thus the need for critical agility

---

[2] According to some Renaissance anatomists, both male and female orgasm were believed necessary for procreation to take place. See Laqueur 1990: 2–3; 43 ff.

[3] See Kerrigan 1987; Carey 1990: 76–7; Herz 1986: 5; Guibbory 1993: 124.

and flexibility; indeed, the need for wonder. If we cannot altogether dispense with our propensity to find unity and coherence (even in this postmodern age), we must at least be sensitive to the ways in which this instinct affects our horizons of interpretation. 'Sapho to Philaenis' is especially valuable in this regard. This poem teaches the need to 'doubt wisely' (*Satire III*, l. 77) and that formulation of the right sorts of questions is as important as, perhaps more import-ant than, finding 'an' answer. Like Donne at the end of *The First Anniversary*, we seem undeterred (or else terrified) by incompre-hensibleness, and so we sometimes 'emprison' Donne and ourselves in a reductive analysis that does not even allow certain questions to be raised. 'Sapho to Philaenis' has suffered ostracization from dis-cussions of Donne and 'right enquiry' in part because it would seem to frustrate or embarrass all attempts at incorporation within a Donnean orthodoxy, even when this orthodoxy recognizes the range of Donne's attitudes towards love. Helen Gardner's relega-tion of the poem to Donne's 'Dubia' has been the most influential dismissal despite (on her own admission) strong textual evidence of its authenticity. Yet scholars are trained not to disregard loose ends. 'Sapho to Philaenis' is, I think, a loose end that until the last decade of the twentieth century has seemed incomprehensible to Donne scholars, and so it has been politely ignored.

The structure of this chapter will be as follows. Several points of comparison and contrast will be established between the previous chapter and this one in part to suggest a possible date for 'Sapho to Philaenis'. Possible reasons for and implications of the poem's near invisibility and its relegation beyond the margins of Donne's canon will emerge as the chapter unfolds. Next, a summary of the criti-cism to date will serve to situate my own method and questions. Any reading of a poem traditionally regarded as an apparent anom-aly such as 'Sapho to Philaenis' must take into consideration at least three contextual environments: classical models of lesbian sexuality which may have influenced Donne, Renaissance repres-entations of lesbianism, some sense of the ideology underlying constructions of human sexuality throughout Western patriarchal phallocentric discourse. Furthermore, in reading 'Sapho to Philaenis' as a 'lesbian' love poem, we must be careful to distin-guish historical differences in the terms and concepts relating to sexual dynamics. Perhaps the most important question to answer in this regard is the extent to which Donne's 'scandalous' poem is really about sex at all. Certainly it provides an arena in which Donne can work out his rivalry with Ovid, and perhaps Sappho. The final section of the chapter will consist of my close reading of 'Sapho to Philaenis'. I want to ask, how might we compare the 'I' and the 'you' of Donne's early verse letters—'Thou which art I, ('tis nothing to be soe)'—and the 'I' and the 'you' of 'Sapho to Philaenis'—'Likenesse begets such strange self-flattery'? Is Sapho's identification with Philaenis different from the 'likenesse' Donne celebrates in his verse letters, or, for that matter, the identity between lovers in the love poetry? My own conclusions to some extent concur with Janel Mueller's assertion that Donne's representation of lesbian love arises out of a desire to synthesize the 'unitive perfections' of the marriage relationship and 'the Renaissance ideal of friendship between equals'.[4] I hope to show that while Donne's representation of lesbian love makes 'Sapho to Philaenis' astonishingly anomalous within classical and Renaissance literature generally, on another level it can be seen to be continuous with some of Donne's most famous love poetry insofar as it is another attempt, albeit unique, to work out the fundamental dynamics of love relationships—the causes and effects of two becoming one.

II. THE MUSES' TENTH SISTER

'Sapho to Philaenis' is a heroical epistle, modelled on the fifteenth poem of Ovid's *Heroides*, a group of letters written by mythical heroines to the lovers who have abandoned them. Donne uses the epistolary genre again here, particularly suited as it is to the themes of absence and separation, and the nature of friendship and love. There are links other than generic ones between the verse epistles explored in Chapter 1 and Donne's heroical epistle, 'Sapho to Philaenis'. From a consideration of the nine Greek Muses, gradually 'crusht into one forme' to become a more personal attendant of Renaissance poets, we turn to the Greek poet whom Plato hailed as 'the Tenth Muse'. Like the Muses, Sappho has been no less subject to customization beneath the pens of male writers. In *Fictions of Sappho*, Joan DeJean identifies the bifurcation of Sappho in the

---

[4] J. Mueller 1992: 103–24, simultaneously published in Summers 1992: 103–34. A longer version of this article appears in J. Turner 1993*b*: 182–207.

various fictionalizations of her life, especially in France but also throughout Western discourse: the attempt to separate her troublingly sexualized body from her indisputably divine poetic voice. We saw in Heywood's *Gunaikeion* that while the Muses were female figures, their relationship to language was perceived as wholly different from that of their flesh-and-blood counterparts. I argued that while Donne gives his Muse a body which is more 'active' in the creation of his poems than is her inspiring voice, she remains an enabling figure of exchange between Donne and his friends. From mythical female figures given actively sexual bodies by Donne within a gestational paradigm so that the male poet 'thinks through' (that is, using) the female body or adopts a feminine position within a gendered relationship so as to manage male parthenogenesis, we move to a historical woman poet, whose voice (that is, its perpetuation) depended at various historical moments on *not* having a (sexual) body, and whose voice had earlier been ventriloquized by various male poets and writers. Does Donne empathetically reunite Sappho's lesbian voice and body which had been 'bifurcated' by her poetic heirs or does Donne use Sappho's body and voice for his own coterie-driven purposes?

If the Muses were traditionally only 'latently' female, all voice and no body, Donne's Sapho declares herself to be all body and no voice. In the early verse letters, Donne insists on the Muse's body, yet only insofar as it aids the male poet in 'conceiving' a poem. In 'Sapho to Philaenis', reproduction as a metaphor for poetic production is absent, and literal reproduction is rejected as the telos of sexual pleasure in Sapho's rehearsal of a lesbian erotics. However, like many Renaissance poets in their sonnet sequences, Sapho invokes her beloved Philaenis as her Muse. Grief-stricken at Philaenis' abandonment, Sapho has lost her poetic gift, and she writes to Philaenis begging her to return. Sapho's lover must bestow her inspiring body on the poet in order to enable her to create poetry. In Donne's verse letters he asserted the need to marry one's Muse (or marry them to each other) but also that he could create poetry with no 'Mother' or matter.

While we do not know exactly when Donne wrote 'Sapho to Philaenis', a provisional argument can be made by comparing it with the early verse letters to show that it might have some chronological proximity with them. Beginning with Grierson in 1912, this single heroical epistle with its elegiac couplets has been grouped with Donne's Ovidian love elegies. The poem appears in some manuscripts with the title, 'Eleg: 18th' or 'An Elegy'. In other manuscripts the poem appears untitled or with the title, 'Sapho to Philaenis'. Carey suggests a possible date as late as 1601 (in Donne 1990: 434). Editors and critics have pointed both to the unlikelihood of Donne composing such a poem after his marriage in late 1601, as well as to the craze for Ovidian imitation in 1590s England, as reasons for dating 'Sapho to Philaenis' some time during this decade. Yet J. Mueller raises the possibility that the poem could be as late as 1612, citing as evidence the absence of astronomical terms such as 'galaxy' (see l. 60 of the poem, below) in Donne's writings before 1612 (1993: 204–5 n. 10). Positive lexical evidence seems more convincing, however. For example, Donne uses the same simile in a verse letter to Henry Wotton, 'Sir, more than kisses', as in 'Sapho to Philaenis', when Sapho argues for the naturalness of lesbian love (see below, pp. 130–1, for a full comparison). Pebworth and Summers identify 'Sir, more than kisses' as one of three verse letters written between Donne and Wotton in the summer of 1598 (1984: 361–77). It is possible then, that Donne, having recently written one or the other poem, had the simile still floating in his imagination and decided it was a useful vehicle for a surprisingly different notion of human relations.

No one thus far has argued that 'Sapho to Philaenis' might be a more in-depth consideration of lesbian erotics triggered by the speculation upon lesbian Muses in Donne and Thomas Woodward's verse letters. It seems plausible that in the midst of the Ovidian vogue occurring in England, while writing both the elegies and the early verse letters, Donne's imagination would be especially ripe for a typically Donnean challenge: outdoing Ovid and his fellow Inns of Court wits with one stroke by writing a lesbian epilogue to Ovid's heterosexual love poem between Sappho and Phaon, the ferryman. But from the male bonding mediated by their muses in the verse letters, sometimes threatened by business or the demands of a wife, we move to more complex 'love' triangles: in one triangle, two male poets, Ovid and Donne, give voice to a woman considered to be one of the greatest poets in history and at the same time vie, as one critic suggests, for 'property rights' to Sappho's name and fame; in a second triangle, there are two female figures, Sapho and Philaenis, 'Before, behind, between, above, below' whom lies (in all its meanings?) Donne; in the third triangle, which constitutes the 'plot' of the poem, Sapho competes with a man for Philaenis' love. Perhaps a more confident Donne, having written the early verse letters, felt ready to take on the challenge of responding more directly to his poetic predecessors.

## III. THEORETICAL PERSPECTIVES

The readings of James Holstun (1987), Elizabeth Harvey (1989; 1992), and Janel Mueller (1992; 1993), considered chronologically, move in a progressively favourable direction as they assess Donne's possible motives for choosing such a subject, his rewriting of Ovid's portrayal of Sappho, his success or failure in representing female homoeroticism. Holstun occupies a position on the interpretive spectrum furthest to the left. He argues that in a poem which is intentionally 'bad', Donne 'periodizes' lesbianism in two ways: by relegating lesbian love to a regressive, irrecoverable past, and by rendering lesbian language impossible. Holstun asserts, '[a]fter trying and failing to construct a private, self-signifying autocosm cut off from the public worlds of men, hierarchy, and domination, Sappho tries and fails to construct a timeless erotic moment cut off from mutability' (841). Holstun reads 'Sapho to Philaenis' as a doomed attempt to separate oneself from the social body by forming a self-contained community which is female-centred, and thus different from the strategies of the male speakers in 'The Good-morrow' and 'The Sunne Rising' who seem to do the same thing with their mistresses, but in fact reproduce the social, political hierarchies they seem to reject. It is here that I want to make the careful distinction between Holstun's assertion that Donne intentionally consigns Sapho's lesbian love to an irrecoverable past, that he works unquestioningly within the patriarchal system, and my own assertion that we must at least consider whether Donne explores what is *already* the dereliction of woman (who is always subjected to 'the mediating domination of man') from the symbolic, and hence points to the need for a new paradigm of relationship, an assertion which is closer to the positions of Paula Blank and Mueller. Holstun's interpretation begs the question of why Donne would be the first to tackle lesbian erotics, only to relegate it to an irrecoverable past. Why bring the subject up at all? Surely Ovid had already confined lesbianism to the past in his 'Sappho to Phaon' when he presents Sappho as having 'progressed' from homo- to heterosexuality, or, to put it another way, from foreplay to the sexual act.[5] As Blank also notices, Holstun equates Sapho's autoeroticism with lesbianism and then locates the failure of the poem in her sexuality, rather than in the very 'patriarchal scheme' which demands identity with the other rather than allowing for what Irigaray calls a 'fertile couple' engaged 'in a collective process of self-definition'.

J. Mueller's interpretation of 'Sapho to Philaenis' stands as Holstun's polar opposite. Her conclusions are based on an impressive and thorough consideration of Sappho's representation in the writings of Donne's Renaissance humanist forebears. Rather than as an incarceration of lesbian love in the past, she sees Donne's poem as a 'positive figuration' which 'projects . . . lesbianism . . . into a fully utopian moment for human possibility' (1992: 125). However, as Donne was fond of pointing out,[6] opposites are not as exclusive of one another as they seem. If Holstun views the poem as a calculated failure to affirm a female-centred erotics 'by subordinating it to a patriarchal scheme of nature, history, and language' (838) and Mueller views it as a *sui generis* celebration of female-centred erotics, both see Donne's lesbian erotics as suspended either in an irrecoverable past or in an unattained future. Mueller is troubled by the fact that 'no present exists for Sapho's and Philaenis' perfect mutuality: all hangs in suspension between Sapho's memories of the past and anticipations of the future' (1993: 32).

On the critical spectrum I have set up, Elizabeth Harvey's reading of the poem can be located slightly to the right of Holstun's but considerably to the left of Mueller's. In contrast to Holstun, Harvey

---

[5] Valerie Traub, in an essay entitled, 'The (In)Significance of "Lesbian" Desire in Early Modern England' (1994), concurs with Holstun's analysis of lesbian love as elegaic, although she does not discuss Donne's poem (only citing Holstun and Harvey's articles in her notes). Traub limits her proofs to the dramas of Shakespeare, and then contrasts these elegaic instances of female homoeroticism with later plays by Thomas Heywood and James Shirley which, she argues, present such desire in the present tense and as explicitly erotic. Traub suggests that 'symmetrical, "feminine" homoerotic desire was granted signification only *after* it was rendered insignificant' (72; author's italics) by relegating it to girlhood or sexual immaturity.

[6] See 'Upon the Annunciation and Passion': '(As in plaine Maps, the furthest West is East)' (21), and 'Hymne to God my God, in my sicknesse': 'As West and East | In all flatt Maps (and I am one) are one' (13–14).

argues that Sapho's body is not negligible, but negotiable. Mueller takes issue with the 'categorical neatness' of what she considers to be Holstun and Harvey's absolute regard for gender difference 'whereby a male poet cannot do other than assimilate, dominate, and silence the self-expression of a female predecessor or a female character whom he incorporates in his work' (1993: 204). While she is right, I think, in identifying such a hermeneutics to be generally active in their readings, Mueller fails to recognize a pivotal qualification Harvey makes in emphasizing that her reading is not essentialist but rather seeks to expose an essentialist construction: 'the fabricated . . . connection' 'between female physiology and the feminine voice'; 'the way male authors create a feminine voice that seems to be—but is not—linked to a whole set of feminine characteristics (a sexualized body, an emotional make-up, an imagination)' (1992: 4–5). In other words, Harvey's suspicions lie not in Donne's ability to speak with a feminine voice, whatever that is, but in his claim to be doing so. Holstun also seems to point to the very constructedness of Sapho's voice (or rather, silence) in Donne's poem, rather than to the prior assumption of an 'authentic' Sapphic voice. The question of whether Donne as a male poet presents an authentic image of lesbian love and of women's speech is, as Mueller notes, a *reductio ad absurdum*. To ask such a question is to miss the point. But I disagree with Mueller's assertion that Holstun's and Harvey's approaches imply inane questions such as 'Is the sole proper domain of a male dramatist or novelist the portrayal of male characters? Can love lyrics and verse epistles adopt only the gender perspective that matches that of the poet writing?' (1993: 204). I do not think any of these three critics suggest that the polyphonies of Donne's poem can be reduced to a 'single monological experiential truth' (DeJean 1989: 65), a truth which is 'male' or 'female'. Stella Revard is concerned not so much with the question of voice as masculine or feminine, but with whether Donne indicates he has read Sappho's poetry directly. She argues that as much as with Ovid, Donne 'initiates a dialogue' with Sappho, and attempts to speak with her voice, having read her 'Phainetai moi' and other fragments, probably in a 1567 edition of Greek lyric poets (with a parallel Latin translation) by Henri Estienne (1993: 68). But Revard argues that 'this dialogue breaks down into a Donnean monologue' (76) and her conclusion implies a need for 'categorical neatness': 'Donne began his elegy with the serious motive of looking through Sappho's eyes. We must not blame him that he only succeeded in looking over her shoulder' (1993: 76).

Paula Blank suggests Donne is exploring the limits of poetic power to 're-create the other as the self and the self as another', regardless of gender differences (1995: 364). But if Sapho fails, it is the failure not of homoeroticism but of homopoetics, also apparent in the heterosexual love poetry, 'in which a subject attempts to possess its object by blurring the distinction between them' (359). In contrast to Blank's assertion, in 'Sexual Transgression in Donne's Elegies', Diana Treviño Benet discusses how Donne uses lesbian love and the bisexual natures of Sapho and Philaenis to understand 'the basic question of sexual difference: What differentiates her loving from his?' (1994: 22). Benet concludes that Donne is 'surprisingly sensitive' in his imaginings and that the poem suggests 'female lovers . . . have a better chance than their heterosexual counterparts of achieving the stasis of desire and desirability that is love's ideal' (24). In 'Symbolic Economies and Zero-Sum Erotics: Donne's "Sapho to Philaenis"', Barbara Correll argues that for Donne's masculine speakers in the elegies and other love poetry, an erotic economy operates in which 'the amatory poem reanimates the guilty member in language' (1995: 488). The male speaker can assuage the loss (of an erection) with poetic production (497). Using the same logic, in 'Sapho to Philaenis', because there is no loss, neither is there a poem. The crisis of signification ('self-referential collapse') in 'Sapho to Philaenis' results in a poem 'in which nothing happens, in which, because there is no difference, there's no loss' (495). '[N]o friend of women', Donne writes a poem that 'is both utterly characteristic and thus continuous with the other *Elegies*; a different way of addressing the kind of failure that marks the success of the heteroerotic poems' (490).

★

In response to Ovid's heroical epistle in which Sappho writes to the male lover, Phaon, who has abandoned her, Donne portrays Sapho loving a woman again, Phaon having already come and gone. Yet now Philaenis has come and gone, and from Sapho's argument, it looks as though she has been seduced by a man. Determining the significance of Donne's lesbian 'epilogue' to Ovid's heterosexual story is crucial, and I think it is more than what Alan Armstrong, discussing Donne's 'apprenticeship' to Ovid in the Elegies, describes as Donne's almost unfailing tendency, unlike his contemporaries, to regard 'such a poetic model, not as an opportunity for pedestrian borrowing, but as an example to be outdone' (1977: 423). At the climax, or, one might argue, the anti-climax of 'Sapho to Philaenis', Sapho declares, 'Likenesse begets such strange selfe flatterie, | That touching my selfe, all seemes done to thee'. Sapho has argued eloquently for the naturalness of lesbian love in a letter to the absent Philaenis, the status of whom remains ambiguous. Possibly she is lost to the clutches of a heterosexual lover, or perhaps she will return to Sapho. Only in the lines following Sapho's declaration do we realize that Sapho is standing in front of her mirror, embracing, kissing, talking to herself, intensely longing for Philaenis. She has earlier demonstrated her poetic skill in a series of crescendoing praises of her absent lover, which culminates in the assertion that Philaenis is in the end incomparable to anyone or anything except her own beautiful self: 'thy right hand, and cheek, and eye, only | Are like thy other hand, and cheek, and eye' (23–4). These escalating compliments are a complex example of what Joel Fineman identifies as an underlying motive of epideictic: 'an objective showing that is essentially subjective showing off' (1986: 6). Sapho has thus enjoined herself linguistically with Philaenis by means of praise which, paradoxically, puts Philaenis in a category by herself, a category which, I have suggested, insofar as Philaenis (or Sapho) is a woman, and on the most fundamental cultural level, is that of dereliction, outside the symbolic order. Then, in front of her mirror, having declared Philaenis' right half to be as beautiful as her 'other' half, Sapho argues for their physical union on the grounds that the two women's bodies are alike; indeed, like the right and left sides of a single body. Two women making love is in fact less strange, less foreign, less a site of difference, than heterosexual love-making. Homoeroticism is the 'naturall Paradise' (35); heterosexuality, the fallen condition of a move towards the supposed civilization of cultivation and private property, as indicated in Donne's metaphors of tillage and theft. Sapho defends both her own personal physical desire for Philaenis, and lesbian love itself:

> My two lips, eyes, thighs, differ from thy two,
>   But so, as thine from one another doe;

> And, oh, no more; the likenesse being such,
>    Why should they not alike in all parts touch?
> Hand to strange hand, lippe to lippe none denies;
>    Why should they brest to brest, or thighs to thighs? (45–50)

Sapho herself is so convinced of her argument that as she caresses herself, for a moment the illusion of Philaenis' presence is sustained: 'Likenesse begets such strange selfe flatterie, | That touching my selfe, all seemes done to thee'.

It would seem particularly perceptive for Donne to place this argument in the mouth of Sapho: this kind of naturalness, symmetry, and a sameness *which is yet multiple and thus contains difference* cannot be claimed by a male lover and his female beloved because of the singular phallus which the woman 'lacks'. Complementarity (opposites attract) rather than symmetry are the terms in which heterosexual union was often described in Donne's time as part of that paradox which Laqueur and Maclean recognize: 'pairs of ordered contrarieties played off a single flesh in which they did not themselves inhere' (Laqueur 1990: 61). Does the complementarity of heterosexual lovers constitute the sole paradigm within which love can generate itself, as implied in 'Love's Deitie'?:

> [Love's] office was indulgently to fit
> Actives to passives: Correspondencie
> Only his subject was. It cannot bee
> Love, till I love her, that loves mee. (11–14)

Is the bliss which results from the fitting of 'Actives to passives', or men to women in their biological roles as inseminator and incubator (as is evident in the tenor of every metaphor for sexual congress[7]), the same bliss that is generated by the 'mutuall feeling' which Sapho argues makes woman-centred love superior to this active/passive love? I think the relationship which Sapho articulates in Donne's poem is different from heterosexual and male homosexual relationships, insofar as both of these are constituted by an active partner dominating a submissive or passive partner. Still, as Paula Blank argues, Sappho's vision is 'humanly impossible to achieve, no matter who attempts to achieve it', precisely because it is a homopoetics 'in which a subject attempts to possess its object by blurring the distinction between them', so as to rewrite

---

[7] A perusal of Eric Partridge 1990 or Aretino's *Dialogues* (1971: 43–4) will show the ubiquity of 'nut and bolt' metaphors.

'two terms as one' (1995: 359). What is so extraordinary is how close Donne presses against 'the limits of the thinkable' in demonstrating the need for an altogether new paradigm of sexual ethics. One might argue that Donne, in 'Sapho to Philaenis', is an exception to the following observation of Irigaray's in which she posits via strategic essentialism that: 'Man . . . might have had some trouble in saying what constitutes the particularity of the female sexual world: a different energy, a different morphology, a special relation to mucus and to the threshold that goes from inside to outside the body, from the inside to the outside of the skin (and the universe?) without leaving a wound' (1993*c*: 179–80). What is impossible to determine in the end is on which side of the 'thinkable' Donne stands. For example, Sapho uses the verb, 'begets', a word which is strongly associated not just with reproduction but with the male (active) role in reproduction. 'Likenesse', as it refers here to two bodies of the same sex, cannot 'beget'. Reproduction can only occur between male and female. Does Donne use 'beget' to point up the 'strange' physiological sterility of such a relationship or to point towards a love or 'fecundity' irreducible 'to the reproduction of bodies and flesh' (Irigaray 1993*a*: 5), but rather one which enables movement between self and other continuously? Does Sapho use her mirror as a kind of threshold, stepping 'through the looking-glass' to an 'other' logic, but also stepping back out to reaffirm her subjectivity? Does she get caught in her mirror, like Narcissus gazing at his image in a pool of water? Does her mirror continue to reflect the inevitability of patriarchal constructions of gender?

Sapho also speaks of what Irigaray calls in her well-known essay and book, 'this sex which is not one' (1985*b*: 23–33). Irigaray plays with the bias of Freudian discourse which asserts 'that *the feminine occurs only within models and laws devised by male subjects.* Which implies that there are not really two sexes, but only one' (1985*b*: 86). Thus, females 'lack' a penis, they do not have 'one', nor do they have something different, something of their own.[8] Teresa de Lauretis extrapolates from Irigaray's analysis: 'That a woman might desire a woman "like" herself, someone of the "same" sex, that she

---

[8] Elizabeth Grosz makes an important point: 'this sociolinguistic inscription of women's bodies [as castrated] must be seen as the unspoken condition of the attribution of men's phallic status: it is only if women's bodies *lack* that men's bodies can be seen to *have*' (1994: 337).

might also have auto- and homosexual appetites, is simply *incomprehensible* in the phallic regime of an asserted sexual difference between man and woman which is predicated on the contrary, on a complete indifference for the "other" sex, woman's' (1988: 156; my emphasis); hence, male constructions of female homosexuality assume a sexual (in)difference so that female homoeroticism is always perceived in relation to a male paradigm: the female homosexual acts either as a man in desiring a woman, or engages in a kind of immature dress rehearsal before graduating to the ultimately fulfilling and mature heterosexual Act, a dress rehearsal which is practised and performed for the benefit of the male gaze.

Irigaray questions this conception of female sexuality which derives its meaning only in relation to a single (male) libido: 'Why should the desire for likeness, for a female likeness, be forbidden to, or impossible for, the woman?' (1985*b*: 65). In a famously controversial passage she asks,

So woman does not have a sex organ? She has at least two of them, but they are not identifiable as ones. Indeed, she has many more. Her sexuality, always at least double, goes even further: it is *plural*. . . . 'She' is indefinitely other in herself. . . . [W]oman's autoeroticism is very different from man's. In order to touch himself, man needs an instrument: his hand, a woman's body, language. . . . And this self-caressing requires at least a minimum of activity. As for woman, she touches herself in and of herself without any need for mediation, and before there is any way to distinguish activity from passivity. Woman 'touches herself' all the time, and moreover no one can forbid her to do so, for her genitals are formed of two lips in continuous contact. Thus, within herself, she is already two—but not divisible into one(s)—that caress each other. (1985*b*: 28; 24; 3rd ellipsis is Irigaray's)

Obviously Irigaray is not suggesting that men and women can be reduced to their genitals and a pattern of behaviour assigned to each; she posits a possible morphological model for language and relationship different from that model (of oneness and identity) which is based on the male body. 'One should keep in mind as a horizon that the sexual difference [whatever that difference turns out to be] has to be rearticulated *within the symbolic* for any radical change to take place; this would be true whether one is homosexual or heterosexual' (Whitford 1991: 154; my emphasis). She shows, rather, that links between gender and sex have been naturalized and constructed as originary. Nevertheless, the strategies Irigaray suggests for questioning such fundamentals can be confusing. In calling for an enquiry into 'who the female is in relation to herself', Irigaray is not calling for female homosexuality as necessarily a sexual practice but as a provisional strategy. The 'amorous exchange' she envisions need no more be an exchange between a biological male and a biological female than between two individuals of the same biological sex. Rather, her 'amorous exchange' would take place between 'the fertile couple: fertile according to the spirit'. But again, 'for exchange to take place between the two terms of sexual difference, there must first *be* two terms' (Whitford 1991: 154). Irigaray thus uses gender defined as 'I' and 'you' to establish two terms of 'irreducible difference'. Therefore, 'love between women (a female homosexual economy) . . . is the matrix which can generate change' (48). Love between women generates change by providing 'a homosexuality that is both auto-erotic and 'other'-directed. It provides a model of homosexuality not as a *substitute* for heterosexuality but as its disavowed prerequisite' (Grosz 1989: 338). By using an argument of 'likenesse', indeed double 'likenesse' as a means for Sapho to draw Philaenis back to her while she engages in autoerotic activity, is Donne celebrating, perhaps even vicariously desiring the plenitude, the multiple and autonomous pleasures which the female body allows itself? Is it not beyond the 'limits of the thinkable' for Donne to recognize the possibility of moving through female homosexuality to a fuller experience of love between human beings? Does Donne's sexual (in)difference reduce Sapho's 'likenesse', as James Holstun suggests, to the literal insignificance of feminine identity, which 'without the mediating domination of man . . . liquefies' (1987: 843), and so leave 'hom-(m)osexuality' intact?

In addition to the phallocentric logic of the 'One', Irigaray also addresses the predominance of the visual in Western culture and posits an alternative eroticism based on touch: 'Woman takes pleasure more from touching than from looking, and her entry into a dominant scopic economy signifies, again, her consignment to passivity: she is to be the beautiful object of contemplation' (1985*b*: 26). In this regard, Sapho figures as a typical lover who loses herself in the beloved:

> Me, in my glasse, I call thee; But, alas,
>     When I would kisse, teares dimme mine eyes, and glasse.
> O cure this loving madnesse, and restore
>     Me to mee; thee, my halfe, my all, my more. (55–8)

Sapho, when she leans forward to kiss her 'other' realizes she is still in the mode of 'semblance', of the visual. Real proximity is still somewhere on the other side of the mirror, wherever Philaenis, the true 'other of the other' is. By placing Sapho in front of a mirror while she caresses herself, Donne incorporates both the visual and the tactile bases of male and female eroticism as defined by Irigaray but her 'I' which displaces the usual Donnean male speaker as both lover and poet, a female subject who names herself and her desires, is still caught in the 'I'/eye of a patriarchal grammar of discourse.

Many critics have pointed to Donne's lack of interest in representing female physical beauty, especially in the *Songs and Sonets*. So, what is it that Donne hears or envisions Sapho as articulating through the female body with which he either wants to identify or neutralize? Perhaps Donne's motivation for writing such a poem is the need, at least metaphorically, to escape from that universal malady, 'postcoital sadness', the phrase by which Christopher Ricks refers to Donne's 'dislike of having come' (1988: 33; see Correll 1995). In other words, Donne uses lesbianism vicariously, to compensate for the anticlimax of detumescence, fetishizing lesbianism within an economy of the male gaze so that it becomes the 'erotic signifier of a referent [the erect penis] whose absence [through orgasm] the lover refuses to acknowledge' (Freccero 1975: 39). In such a reading he is guilty of a kind of mental onanism, the desire not for *coitus interruptus* but *coitus in æternum* or, more technically, *coitus reservatus*, in which orgasm is delayed or avoided. The paradox lies in that Donne can only use love between two women to compensate for the 'unevennesse' ('Sapho to Philaenis', l. 33) of the phallus.

IV. SAPPHO AND PHILAENIS: CLASSICAL AND
RENAISSANCE REFERENCES

Who were Sappho and Philaenis, or more specifically, who were they for Donne? What facts or fictions had been established in connection with these two names which may have influenced Donne's writing of the first English lesbian love poem? There were a number of texts available to Renaissance scholars in which Donne could have encountered surviving fragments of Sappho's poetry. The extent of Donne's knowledge of Greek in his earlier life is difficult to determine. 'Sapho to Philaenis' would long since have been written by the time Donne applied himself, in Walton's careful phrasing, to 'a greater perfection in the learned Languages, *Greek* and *Hebrew*', in 1613 or 1614.[9] Donne could have found Sappho's most famous poetic fragment (four stanzas survive), *'Phainetai moi'*, either in the treatise ascribed to Longinus, *On the Sublime*, or in Plutarch's dialogue, *The Lover*, found in his *Moralia*. Both authors include Sappho's poem as an example of consummate dramatic intensity and both authors were widely read in the late sixteenth century, some editions including parallel Latin translations.[10] Whether or not he knew Greek, we can be almost certain that Donne knew at least Catullus' Latin version of Sappho's poem. The first English translation of Sappho's most famous odes was not made until 1748 by Ambrose Philips who renders fragment 1, the 'Ode to Aphrodite', and fragment 31, *'Phainetai moi'*, in rhymed quatrains. Ovid's *Heroides*, 15, as it was edited, translated, and commented upon, was clearly the most influential of Sapphic fictions, but Ovid's epistle is just one example in a series of determined attempts by classical writers and humanist scholars either to distinguish Sappho's name, poetry, and sexual proclivities from one another, or to render them compatible with one another. Ovid's representation of Sappho will be discussed in the final section of this chapter. A consideration of commentaries or treatises on poetry which discuss Sappho and/or Philaenis is in order here.

Sappho could not be forgotten, or her reputation altogether dismantled, since she had such powerful advocates in Plato, Horace, Catullus, Ovid, and so many other classical writers. To make Sappho respectable, various techniques were used depending on whether the writer was relating her biography or translating fragments of her poetry. Catullus' substitution of a male speaker for the female of Sappho's *'Phainetai moi'* in his *Carmen*, 51 is the most well-known freedom taken with Sappho's own works. J. Mueller cites another important pattern in the transmission of Sappho. In

---

[9] Walton 1927: 46. Also quoted in Bald 1986: 280. Don Cameron Allen suggests that Donne, who 'had more classical learning than he cared to reveal' (1964: 189), would have known Catullus' Latin translation of one of Sappho's poems and possibly the original. Yet Bald cites another article of Allen's in his assertion that Donne's early training involved 'little or no Greek' (40), in which Allen concludes that even much later in Donne's life, his Greek 'scholarship was far below that of the average preacher of the age' (1943a: 208–29).

[10] See DeJean 1989: 30–3; Mueller 1993: 185 for other possible sources.

Ovid's 'Sappho to Phaon', Sappho's reference in line 19 to her former female lovers was variously rendered as either defiantly unrepentant or self-incriminating, depending on the editor's opinion of Sappho's morality: 'The earliest editions give the reading of a majority of the manuscripts that contain this poem: "quas hic sine crimine amavi" ("them"—feminine plural—"have I loved without blame in this"). But textual scholars in the later Renaissance emend line 19 to accord with a variant reading from a different manuscript source: "quas non sine crimine amavi" ("them have I loved, not without blame")' (Mueller 1993: 187). The 1594 London edition of the *Heroides* adopts the self-condemnatory reading and, if this was indeed the volume which Donne knew, it is part of the tradition which Donne rejects in 'Sapho to Philaenis', since his Sappho returns to lesbian love after her affair with Phaon.

If we consider the milieu in which Donne wrote—of hom(m)osexual culture and 'homotextual exchange' within his coterie—the following is one hypothesis as to Donne's sources: having inevitably read Ovid's poem which recasts Sappho as a repentant ex-lesbian in love with a male, and Catullus' 'translation' of Sappho's *Phainetai moi*, in which Catullus changes the speaker's gender from female to male—again like Ovid insisting on a heterosexual dynamic but changing the other side of the equation—there was only one thing left for Donne to do in order to align himself but also to compete with this illustrious group, and that was to revert to the original situation of two female lovers. In other words, we must consider whether Donne decided to champion female homoeroticism having learned about Sappho, and then looked about for an appropriate vehicle with which to do so, or whether the Sappho-Ovid-Catullus gender-bending tug-of-war presented Donne with one last permutation—coming full circle—with which to outdo his poetic competitors, classical and contemporary.

Philaenis enjoyed a much less glorified reputation than Sappho as a poet but suffered similar complications (and multiplications) due to her sexuality, unacceptable both in its intensity and its object. A virtuous Philaenis is the subject (and the voice from beyond the grave) in two sepulchral epigrams in *The Greek Anthology* (vii. 345, 450). This Philaenis defends her chastity and objects to her misrepresentation as another Philaenis. A second Philaenis was a heterosexual courtesan famous for writing a book of poetry about sexual positions and practices, described for us by none other than

Thomas Heywood in *Gunaikeion*: '*Philenis* was a strumpet of Leucadia, her Verses were as impurely wanton as her life was immodest and unchast. . . . Shee was the first that devised*katachresis* in the Veneriall Trade, and left certaine bookes behind her of Veneriall Copulation' (1624: 395). A third Philaenis is found in two of Martial's epigrams. Martial portrays a tribade named Philaenis who sodomizes boys, lifts weights, wrestles, and is both a glutton and a drunk (7.67).[11] Her tribade activities are described as follows: 'tentigine saevior mariti | undenas dolat in die puellas; [with an erection more savage than a husband you split eleven girls a day]' (2–3). After vomiting up her wine and food, she feels the onset of sexual desire but disdains fellatio because it is not masculine enough. Instead, she devours girls at their 'medias [middles]'. Martial ends with 'di mentem tibi dent tuam, Philaeni, | cunnum lingere quae putas virile; [May the gods give you what you would like to have, Philaenis, you who think it manly to lick a cunt]' (16–17). A second epigram runs as follows: 'Ipsarum tribadum tribas, Philaeni, recte, quam futuis, vocas amicam ['Tribade of tribades, Philaenis, rightly do you call she whom you fuck your girl-friend]' (7.70). Martial's most recent translator for the Loeb Classical Library series renders 'tribadum tribas' as 'Lesbia of the very Lesbians' but in doing so obscures a subtle tension.[12] The word, 'tribade', literally means a 'woman who rubs', yet Martial uses, as he does in the previous epigram, the verb, 'futuo', which denotes the male penetrative role in sexual intercourse, to describe this tribade's transgression. Like Bassa, she uses some kind of dildo to penetrate her 'amicam'. Martial writes several more of his most stinging epigrams about a 'one-eyed' Philaenis, her ugliness and bad odour (4.65; 9.62), and in one epigram compares her to a phallus: 'Cur non basio te, Philaeni?', asks the speaker, 'Why don't I kiss you, Philaenis?' Because she is bald (*calva*), ruddy (*rufa*), and one-eyed (*lusca*), and 'haec qui basiat, o Philaeni, fellat [he who kisses these things, Philaenis, sucks] (2.33).

There is one further epigram by Martial which does not bode well for a reading of Donne's 'Sapho to Philaenis' as a complete

---

[11] I am grateful to Mr Peter C. Brown for assisting me with the unusual vocabulary of Epigram 67.

[12] D. R. Shackleton Bailey does the same again at 7.67, rendering 'tribas Philaenis' as 'Lesbian Philaenis'. His choice illustrates our modern association of female homoeroticism with Lesbos and Lesbians, a connection which does not seem to have been made until the 4th century AD by Pseudo-Lucian.

rejection of negative representations of lesbian activity and a positive figuration of female homoeroticism. At 12.22, Martial's language seems too close to lines in Donne's poem to be coincidental: 'Quam sit lusca Philaenis indecenter | vis dicam breviter tibi, Fabulle? | esset caeca decentior Philaenis. [Do you want me to tell you in a nutshell how uncomely Philaenis is with her one eye, Fabullus? Philaenis would be more comely if she were blind.]' Compare Donne's Sapho as she praises her Philaenis' beauty:

> Thou art so faire,
> As, gods, when *gods* to thee I doe compare,
> Are grac'd thereby; And to make blinde men see,
> What things gods are, I say they'are like to thee. (15–18)

That both Martial and Donne refer to blindness in order to describe Philaenis—either insultingly as in Martial, or, it seems, favourably, if proverbially, in Donne—suggests that Donne intended his readers to recollect Martial's epigram, but whether to identify or contrast Martial's tribade with his own Philaenis is more difficult to determine. Martial was so well-known and so frequently emulated in Renaissance epigram collections that his Philaenis rather than the two of *The Greek Anthology* would, I think, more likely have been the woman conjured up by Donne's use of the name.

There is a reference to Philaenis, later than the period in which 'Sapho to Philaenis' could have been written, which suggests that the name was indelibly associated with Martial's depraved lesbian. Two manuscripts in the Bodleian Library contain a poem which appears with the title, 'Uppon y$^e$ L$^d$ Audleys Convictio[n]'. The poem is dated 'Aprill 1631', and is signed 'Jo:R:'. Mervyn, Lord Audley, second earl of Castlehaven (1592?–1631) was convicted of various sexual crimes including rape and sodomy, for which he was executed.[13] The text of MS Ashmole 47 opens as follows:

> Romes worst Philenis, and Pasiphaes dust
> Are now chast ffictions and noe longer lust
> This wilder age hath monstred out a sinne
> That vertues them, and saints and [*sic*] Aretine. (88$^v$)[14]

---

[13] Castlehaven's second wife was Lady Anne Stanley, the sister of Elizabeth Stanley, the Countess of Huntingdon for whom Donne wrote two verse letters.
[14] See also MS Eng.poet.e.97.

It seems then, that 'Philenis' was a generic term for someone sexually depraved, for the phrase is comparative—'Romes *worst* Philenis'—as though there were more than one (as Martial's epigrams might be taken to imply). Philaenis and Pasiphae, an oft-cited negative exemplum whose lust drove her to sexual congress with a bull resulting in the minotaur, are cited as epitomes of lust in order to show the surpassing bestiality of Castlehaven. Holt R. Parker's exploration of ancient erotic handbooks sheds further light on Philaenis as negative exemplum:

> the most famous author of these sex manuals is said to be a woman named Philaenis, but it is clear that her name is later used as a cover term for writers of sex manuals for prostitutes, for whatever the user of her name considers to be sexually depraved. . . . Where works are attributed to women, we cannot be sure of the truth of the attribution, which may have been made as an attack, a distortion, or a misunderstanding. (1992: 93)

In his satire, *Affairs of the Heart,* Pseudo-Lucian refers to 'wanton Lesbianism' and 'Sapphic amours'; perhaps the first time the place, Lesbos, and the person, Sappho, have been used to describe a specifically lesbian activity rather than heterosexual wantonness. More importantly for Donne's poems, as Elizabeth Harvey was the first to point out, Sappho and Philaenis are also linked in a 'defense' of lesbianism by the character, Charicles:

> If males find intercourse with males acceptable, henceforth let women too love each other. . . . Let them strap to themselves cunningly contrived instruments of lechery, those mysterious monstrosities devoid of seed, and let woman lie with woman as does a man. Let wanton Lesbianism—that word seldom heard, which I feel ashamed even to utter—freely parade itself, and let our women's chambers emulate Philaenis, disgracing themselves with Sapphic amours. And how much better that a woman should invade the provinces of male wantonness than that the nobility of the male sex should become effeminate and play the part of a woman! (Lucian 1979: 194–5)[15]

The way in which the male presence is both written in and out of Lucian's accounts of lesbianism here is telling. Because they are not there, they cannot say what it is women do, but because they

---

[15] Once attributed to Lucian, it is now thought to have been written by an imitator some time around the 4th century AD. Note Charicles' concept of effeminacy. See also his *Dialogues of the Courtesans.*

cannot bear not to be there, they assume female homoeroticism can only be a parodic re-enactment of (male) heterosexual behaviour. 'The question remains: in what way does he see what goes on between women? In other words: *do women who are "among-themselves-under-his-watchful-eye" behave as they do among themselves?* (Irigaray 1985*b*: 200). Those listening to Charicles obviously think so because he is complimented on his phallic speculation and eloquence: 'For hardly even those among them thought pre-eminent for wisdom could, if given full authority to speak, have spoken about themselves with such zeal, no, not even . . . Sappho, the honey-sweet pride of Lesbos' (197).

*

A survey of lesbianism in early modern England will inevitably be brief. My concern here is with what Janel Mueller qualifies as 'cognizant' female homoerotic attraction, that is, a woman who knowingly desires another woman. Those relationships which involve transvestite disguise and mistaken sexual identity in so many Renaissance works, or sex-changes, as in Ovid's tale in the *Metamorphoses* of Iphis and Ianthe or Montaigne's anecdotes in his *Essais*, ultimately reinforce heterosexual norms.[16] The potential corruption of such homoerotic relationships is shown to be falsely present, or else the mere absurdity of such relationships is presented as an opportunity for salacious humour. Realizing they have fallen in love with a woman the heroines despair until the 'imbalance' is put right with the help of the gods.

Judith Brown notes 'an almost active willingness to *dis*believe' on the part of theologians, lawmakers, physicians and other writers, for 'in a period of roughly fifteen hundred years, [any documentation of female homosexuality] amounts to no more than a dozen or so scattered references' (1986: 9). Lillian Faderman's survey of the Renaissance is completed in a dozen pages where she identifies one aspect of the operative ideology behind the relative lack of concern

---

[16] See Ariosto's *Orlando Furioso*; Spenser's *Faerie Queene*; Sidney's *Arcadia*; Shakespeare's *Twelfth Night* and *As You Like It*; *A Midsummer Night's Dream*; *Two Noble Kinsmen*. The *Hic Mulier/Haec Vir* pamphlet war in 1620, attacking cross-dressing, and the Swetnam controversy of 1615–20 are well-known examples of the turbulence surrounding gender construction in late Renaissance society, of which the 'nature of woman' question was a part. For thorough discussions of these debates, see Woodbridge 1986; Henderson and McManus 1985; Shepherd 1985; C. Jordan 1990.

about lesbians: 'It seems then that a narrower interpretation of what constitutes eroticism permitted a broader expression of erotic behavior since it was not considered inconsistent with virtue' (1985: 33); however, 'the closer [such behaviour] approximated intercourse, the more significant it became' (37) and required containment. Valerie Traub comes at the problem from a different direction: 'As critics and historians, the difficulty we face is not necessarily the lack of erotically desiring women, but our inability to crack the code organizing the conceptual categories of an earlier culture' (1994: 65).

Pierre de Bourdeille, Seigneur de Brantôme (1540–1614), in his *Lives of Fair and Gallant Ladies* dwells salaciously on sexual relations between women at the court of Henri II, two of whom, he says, were observed through a crack in the wall of their cabinet. Brantôme cites Martial and Lucian and says he has heard there are Lesbian women in France, Italy, Spain, Turkey, and Greece, who are cloistered and do not have free access to men. He clearly conceives of female homoeroticism as heterosexual foreplay in the following passage:

This little exercise, as I have heard, is only an apprenticeship so as to come to the greater one [love] of men; because after they have overheated themselves and greatly excited one another, their heat does not diminish unless they bathe in a livelier and more active current, which refreshes much better than stagnant water; for as I have heard from good surgeons and seen myself, he who wants to bandage and heal a wound must not play at treating and cleaning around it or on the edges, but he must probe it to its deepest point. How many of these Lesbians I have seen, who despite all their frications and inter-rubbings, don't stop going to men; did not even Sappho, who was their Mistress, come to love her good friend Faon, for whom she was dying? Because in the end, as I have heard several ladies say, there is nothing like a man; and all they take from other women are enticements to go and satisfy their hunger with men. (1666: 205–6)[17]

Donne indicates in his Satires, his letters, and in *Ignatius His Conclave* that he has read Continental authors such as Dante, Rabelais, and Aretino.[18] If he was reading Rabelais and Aretino, Donne may

---

[17] I am grateful to Ms Hélène Tronc for assisting me with this translation.
[18] See e.g. *Satire IV*, ll. 59, 70, 158; See David O. Frantz's argument that 'the Italian tradition of pornography which the English knew at least by reputation' was also known first-hand (1989).

have sought out what soft-pornographic writing was available in Europe and England, most probably in the 1590s, and so he may have read Brantôme. Donne suggests in *Ignatius His Conclave* that even Aretino was mild stuff compared to what one could find in Greek and Latin literature:

I was sory to see [Lucifer, the Devil] use *Peter Aretine* so ill as he did. For though *Ignatius* told him true when he boasted of his licentious pictures, that because he was not much learned, hee had left out many things of that kind, with which the ancient histories & poëmes abound; and therefore *Aretine* had not onely not added any new invention, but had also taken away all courage and spurres from youth, which would rashly trust, and relie upon his diligence, and seeke no further, & so lose that infinite & precious treasure of Antiquitie. (1969: 64–7)

In any case, the infamous Aretino, unlike Brantôme, was not interested in lesbianism, although he wrote frequently about women using dildos as a form of masturbation rather than in a sexual act with another woman. Further slight evidence for Donne's familiarity with Aretino and perhaps Brantôme lies in the way they use the conventional image of women's vaginas as wounds. Brantôme uses an image of a wound being probed to describe the sexual act in the passage I quoted above. Aretino uses the image of a probe searching a wound as a euphemism for sex in his *Dialogues* (1971: 61), and Donne uses the same image rather infamously at the end of his elegy, 'The Comparison'. Whereas the rival lover's mistress's genitals are described as 'an invenom'd sore', the speaker boasts of his and his mistress' sensitivity and tenderness with the couplet: 'And such in searching wounds the Surgeon is | As wee, when wee embrace, or touch, or kisse' (51–2). All three authors describe not rapes, as one might expect, but 'healthy' fulfilling sexual encounters.

One cultural institution with which Sappho did not have to cope was the Christian Church, which likewise did not seem threatened by Sapphism. Dante does not include female homosexuality in any circle of hell, although male sodomites and the lustful merit their own circles. The Church's relative silence on the matter of female homosexuality can perhaps be explained by its determination to link sexual activity with procreation rather than pleasure, for male homosexuality received harsh censure indeed. J. Mueller explains the theological interpretation of female versus male homosexuality: 'the former involved relatively venial pollution . . . whereas the latter incurred the mortal sin of disposing what was held to be the most vital element in human reproduction, the semen, in what were claimed to be unnatural ways' (1992: 114–15). The (in)difference towards what could occur sexually between two women also hinges on the classical active/passive sexual dynamic which we saw in 'Love's Deitie' and which David Halperin describes:

sexual objects came in two different kinds—not male and female but active and passive, aggressive and submissive. The relevant features of a sexual object were not so much determined by a physiological typology of genders as by the social articulation of power. . . . a cultural formation [of] . . . a single, undifferentiated phallic sexuality of penetration and domination, a socio-sexual discourse whose basic terms are phallus and non-phallus. (1986: 39–40)

This construction of sexuality enabled Aphra Behn's speaker at the end of the seventeenth century to assert in 'To the fair Clarinda, who made Love to me, imagined more than Woman':

> In pity to our sex sure thou wert sent,
> That we might love, and yet be innocent:
> For sure no crime with thee we can commit;
> Or if we should—thy form excuses it. (1992: 343)

## V. DONNE WRITES BACK: HIS DIALOGUE WITH OVID AND SAPPHO

That imitations and translations of Ovid in the sixteenth century constituted a large part of literary endeavour hardly needs stating. Ovid's *Epistulae heroidum* or his *Heroides* were translated into English by George Turberville in 1567, the same year that Arthur Golding's translation of the *Metamorphoses* appeared. Turberville, John Lyly, whose drama *Sapho and Phao* was first performed in 1584 before the Queen, and Michael Drayton, who in 1597 wrote

---

[19] Turberville takes much licence in shifting the emphasis of Ovid's epistles to his own Tudor culture's concerns and expectations. Contemporary advice on women's conduct which demanded a woman's silence in exchange for her chaste reputation provides the lexicon of Turberville's moralized renditions. Lyly chose the fictionalization of Sappho which remembered her as a virtuous princess, not as a poet nor a lover of other women, nor a courtesan; in fact, the only choice

*England's Heroicall Epistles*, had their own agendas in responding to Ovid and were not interested in the question of lesbian 'likenesse'.[19] I mention them here to set in relief the uniqueness of Donne's focus. Recent critical discussion of Ovid's relationship to Sappho centres around the motivation behind his 'invention' of a discourse of female desire: empathy (Jacobson 1974); or the knowledge that his portrayal of Sappho would forever link his name with hers and her literary authority (DeJean 1989: 75); or the display of his own wit, resulting in a 'duplicitous glance', malevolent and compassionate, which suggests he is primarily concerned with the display of his own wit (Verducci 1985: 136).[20]

Donne responds to or departs from several episodes in Ovid by foregrounding the question of Sappho's sexual orientation rather than engaging as intensely as does Ovid with the questions of authorship and literary property. In Ovid's poem, Sappho renounces the female community which she loves and for whom she wrote, to love a single youth whose attentions or lack thereof have become the source of her poetic genius: 'ingenio vires ille dat, ille rapit; [My genius had its powers from him; with him they were swept away]' (206). Ovid exaggerates the number of women Sappho refers to in her own poetry to emphasize the power of a single man and perhaps to portray something of the prodigious lust lesbians were perceived to exercise. Donne's Sapho has recovered from Phaon's desertion and now loves Philaenis. Are we to read Donne's lesbian epilogue as a correction of Sappho's inconstancy or promiscuity, which Ovid emphasizes, or is Donne subtly perpetuating the belief that women were fickle?

Both poems open with laments. Here is Ovid's Sappho:

> Ecquid, ut adspecta est studiosae littera dextrae,
> Protinus est oculis cognita nostra tuis—

open to him in a presentation before Her Majesty. While sharing the Renaissance preoccupation with the proper relations of those on various levels of the world hierarchy, Lyly chooses to represent the threat to and restoration of this order in a social rather than sexual context. But see Philippa Berry's discussion of Lyly (1989: 120–4) in which she suggests Lyly's presentation of Elizabeth as Sappho is more ambiguous in its exploration of the relations between power and sexuality. Drayton's poems (1961: ii. 129–308) constitute a sophisticated and complex response to Ovid, but the epistles are written by women from English history and so Sappho does not appear.

[20] Verducci refers to 'Sapho to Philaenis' which she suggests is wholly a reaction to *Heroides*, 15, a portrayal of Sappho 'as macabre and anachronistic as Ovid's', yet perfectly faithful to the central tenet of Ovid's poem: the claims of art and life on the poet (1985: 143).

an, nisi legisses auctoris nomina Sapphus,
    hoc breve nescires unde movetur opus?
Forsitan et quare mea sint alterna requiras
    carmina, cum lyricis sim magis apta modis.
flendus amor meus est—elegiae flebile carmen;
    non facit ad lacrimas barbitos ulla meas.

[Tell me, when you looked upon the characters from my eager right
hand, did your eye know forthwith whose they were—or, unless you
had read their author's name, Sappho, would you fail to know whence
these brief words come? Perhaps, too, you may ask why my verses
alternate, when I am better suited to the lyric mode. I must weep, for
my love—and elegy is the weeping strain; no lyre is suited to my
tears.] (1–8)

The opening of Donne's 'Sapho to Philaenis' gestures towards
Ovid's poem with some important differences in emphasis, primarily the less self-conscious state of Sapho. She does not complain
about the generic implications of her mood, but more generally
laments her lack of inspiration:

Where is that holy fire, which Verse is said
    To have, is that inchanting force decai'd?
Verse that drawes Natures workes, from Natures law,
    Thee, her best worke, to her worke cannot draw.
Have my teares quench'd my old Poetique fire;
    Why quench'd they not as well, that of desire? (1–6)

Sapho's declaration of loss suggests confusion and instability by
using an undirected interrogative, unlike the assertive question
Ovid's Sappho puts to Phaon. So bereft is Donne's Sapho, she can
only state that verse 'is said' to be inspired by 'holy fire'. Moreover,
she refers to 'that' holy fire and 'that' inchanting force, again suggesting some disorientation and a sense that what was hers is no
longer. Yet in both Ovid and Donne's poems, Sappho/Sapho's first
concern is for her poetry rather than for her beloved, whether
Phaon or Philaenis. This prioritization could be an aspect of the
topos of inexpressibility, or part of the self-consciousness of letter-
writing which we saw in Chapter 1. Many of Ovid's other
heroines in the *Heroides*, perhaps conventionally, immediately draw
attention to the physical fact of the letter they are writing or the
words written on it, but they are not as concerned about their own

writing ability as is Sappho. As a poet and as a woman in love, she has two losses to lament.

In the first two lines, Sapho refers to the inspiration which fuels verse as 'holy fire' and as 'that inchanting force'. While we must keep in mind that the poem is written in the voice of an ancient Greek and not a Christian one, there is still and would have been, I think, in the minds of Donne and his readers, a tension between the different associations of 'holy' and 'inchanting'. The first word suggests the divine inspiration of the Muses, or heaven-sanctioned utterance, while the second suggests that the source of 'inspiration' is a darker one. Donne's only other use of the word 'inchant' (L. , *cantare*, to sing) or its cognates occurs in 'The Dampe', a poem atypically filled with Spenserian 'Gyants' and 'Witches'. The speaker projects his death as a result of the coldness of his mistress, and suggests a more challenging murder: 'But if you dare be brave, | And pleasure in your conquest have, | First kill th'enormous Gyant, your *Disdaine*, | And let th'enchantresse *Honor*, next be slaine' (9–12). Donne's language recalls Spenser's fairy world of bewitched heroes and heroines, spells and magic mirrors; a world of illusion, rather than the special access to knowledge granted to poets filled with 'holy fire'.

The tension between Nature and Art becomes overt in lines 3 and 4, and is sustained throughout the poem to a point where Sapho appears to resolve it. Repetition, rhyme, and more subtle aural effects are introduced here as well, and produce incantatory effects so that we already realize that Sapho's 'inchanting force' has not 'decai'd'. We are constantly being asked to assess 'likenesse' and difference, both in terms of sound and of sense. The allusion to Orpheus' powers to draw 'Natures workes, from Natures law' is, I think, of central importance to the poem, both in terms of the poem as a response to prior poets, Ovid and Sappho, and in terms of Orpheus' own experiences of love and sexuality. Sappho, like Orpheus, is a bisexual poet for Ovid and Donne. Here is the opening of *Metamorphoses*, 11, to which Donne's lines refer:

> Carmine dum tali silvas animosque ferarum
> Threicius vates et saxa sequentia ducit,
> ecce nurus Ciconum tectae lymphata ferinis
> pectora velleribus tumuli de vertice cernunt
> Orphea percussis sociantem carmina nervis.

[While with such songs the bard of Thrace drew the trees, held beasts enthralled and constrained stones to follow him, behold, the crazed women of the Cicones, with skins flung over their breasts, saw Orpheus from a hill-top, fitting songs to the music of his lyre.] (1–5)

Orpheus is then dismembered by the Maenads whose love he repulsed in favour of 'tender boys' after losing his wife Eurydice. For both Orpheus and Sappho, their sexual 'transgression' seems to be of as great or greater import than their poetic gift. Orpheus' head floats with his lyre down the river Hebrus. His unacceptably (homo)sexual body is literally separated from the bodily site of his poetic gift, his mouth and tongue, and his instrument, the lyre. Head and lyre float out to sea and wash up on the shore of Lesbos, the island on which Sappho was born. Like Orpheus, Sappho's promiscuous and/or 'depraved' sexual body is often separated from her voice, 'literarily' rather than literally. Orpheus is reunited with his beloved Eurydice in Hades. Sappho, in Ovid's version, is a repentant lesbian now aching with longing for Phaon. Ovid makes sure both poets end up heterosexual, although neither's desire is fulfilled since Orpheus and Eurydice are bodiless shades and Sappho threatens to jump off the Leucadian cliff. And yet Sappho does get her Phaon, for in his *Amores*, Ovid writes that the lovers were reunited in the epistles his fellow poet, Sabinus Aulus, wrote as replies to the *Heroides*: 'det votam Phoebo Lesbis amata lyram [the daughter of Lesbos, her love returned, may offer to Phoebus the lyre she vowed]' (2.18.34). Again, Donne departs from the tradition following Ovid in leaving his readers in suspense as to Philaenis' response to Sapho's letter.[21]

The allusion to Orpheus' powers to draw 'Natures workes, from Natures law' is also a way of representing Sapho's lesbianism,

---

[21] The ambiguous ending of Ovid's poem and this allusion to a happy ending for Sappho in Sabinus, was and is usually rejected or ignored in favour of Sappho's suicide. In Ovid's poem, the naiad who appears to Sappho in the forest tells her not that her leap from the Leucadian cliff will kill her, but that it will cure her passion for Phaon (163–72). Sappho makes up her mind to follow the nymph's advice and prays, 'tu quoque, mollis Amor, pennas suppone cadenti, | ne sim Leucadiae mortua crimen aquae! [Do thou too, tender Love, place thy pinions beneath me, lest I die and bring reproach on the Leucadian wave!]' (179–80). She pledges her lyre to Phoebus if she survives her attempt to free herself of her passion for Phaon, and this is the vow to which Ovid refers at *Amores*, 2.18.34. Certainly Sappho worries that her leap from the Leucadian cliff will be fatal, but she seems in part to be indulging in a little calculated rhetorical posturing in order to sway Phaon (see ll. 187–90).

which draws woman (Philaenis), Nature's 'best worke', from the 'Natural law' of heterosexuality to what Sapho argues is a *more* 'naturall Paradise', the body of a woman untouched ('unmanur'd', as she says, punning on *manus*/hand) by man. Implicit in this first reference to 'Natures law', however, is an indictment of lesbianism, for it draws women away from one of their primary functions: reproduction. The same feminine pronoun, 'her', refers first to Nature, traditionally personified as female, but then to Verse, also personified as female: 'Thee, her best worke, to her worke cannot draw'. Identities already begin to melt and merge here in a fourfold totality of femaleness: Verse, Nature, Sapho, Philaenis. Does Donne intend his reader to become entangled in pronouns and repeated words, setting up tensions, paradoxically through the use of identical words—'her', 'drawe', 'worke',—which mimic the tension between Sapho and Philaenis, and the tension between Verse or Art, and Nature? Is this the singing of a Siren or an Angel, an Enchantress or a Muse?

Sapho describes the unhappy state in which Philaenis' abandonment has left her using standard Petrarchan imagery:

> Thoughts, my mindes creatures, often are with thee,
>     But I, their maker, want their libertie.
> Onely thine image, in my heart, doth sit,
>     But that is waxe, and fires environ it.
> My fires have driven, thine have drawne it hence;
>     And I am rob'd of Picture, Heart, and Sense.
> Dwells with me still mine irksome Memory,
>     Which, both to keepe, and lose, grieves equally.
> That tells me'how faire thou art. (7–15)

As many critics have argued, most recently Heather Dubrow in *Echoes of Desire*, Donne enjoyed turning Petrarchan conventions upside down as much as he often dispensed with them altogether or, indeed, participated in them. There is a curious passage in *Metempsychosis* in which Donne mocks the suffering of the Petrarchan lover and yet warns against deviant forms of sexual desire with a reference to sodomy. When we read both passages together, we are once again unsettled as to Donne's tone in 'Sapho to Philaenis'. If we recall that Carey suggests 1601 as a possible date for 'Sapho to Philaenis', the year we know Donne wrote *Metempsychosis*, there is a possibility that these two passages are variations on a theme in Donne's mind at the time. Donne describes an Ape into whom the 'Soule' enters soon after the creation of the world, one whose 'organs now so like theirs hee doth finde, | That why he cannot laugh, and speake his minde, | He wonders' (1967*b*: 454–6). The Ape assumes a 'likeness' between himself and the children of Adam and Eve. Is there an echo here of Sapho's 'Likenesse begets such strange selfe flatterie, | That touching myselfe, all seems done to thee'? We hope not, but following a description of the Ape's desperate Petrarchan antics as 'the first true lover' who desires the daughter named Siphatecia—his 'love faces', 'sombersalts' and 'hoiting gambolls'—the speaker rather abruptly warns: 'Sinnes against kinde | They easily doe, that can let feed their minde | With outward beauty; beauty they in boyes and beasts do find'. How does Sapho's beautiful apology for the 'naturall *Paradise*' of lesbian love sound next to this post-Edenic warning about the dangers of feeding one's mind with outward beauty?

Against the Law of Nature, Siphatecia gives in to the Ape's seduction in a graphic scene in which Siphatecia's bodily sensations are described. Since the Ape is having no success with mere flirting, 'likelier meanes he tries':

> And up lifts subtly with his russet pawe
> Her kidskinne apron without feare or awe
> Of nature; nature hath no gaole, though shee have law.

> First she was silly'and knew not what he ment:
> That vertue, by his touches, chaft and spent,
> Succeeds an itchie warmth, that melts her quite;
> She knew not first, now cares not what he doth,
> And willing halfe and more, more then halfe loth,
> She neither puls nor pushes, but outright
> Now cries, and now repents. (478–87)

Like Sapho's Orphic verse which 'drawes *Natures* workes, from *Natures* law', the Ape sets about to commit a sin 'against kinde', or against what Donne implies is a law of nature if the Ape will nevertheless suffer no punishment ('gaole') for breaking it. The adoption of a law governing sexual congress once there were enough of Adam and Eve's descendants to make incest unnecessary is an issue to which Donne frequently alludes in his poetry, indeed he does so earlier in *Metempsychosis*: 'Men, till they tooke laws which made freedome lesse, | Their daughters, and their sisters did ingresse; |

Till now unlawfull, therefore ill, 'twas not' (201–3). Donne, fascinated as he is by words which enact and denote an intermingling,
uses 'ingress' here (from the Latin, *in* + *gradi*, to step in or enter)
uniquely, according to the *OED*, as a synonym for intercourse.
The libertine speakers of Donne's Elegies 'Change' (10–14) and
'Variety' (48–9), and the female speaker of 'Confined Love' all
begrudge the existence of a law which states, 'One should but one
man know' (6). On the other hand, the lover in 'The Relique'
boasts: 'Our hands ne'r toucht the seales, | Which nature, injur'd
by late law, sets free' (29–30). But one of the main cultural attitudes,
at least in England, towards the kind of female homoeroticism
which Donne describes in 'Sapho to Philaenis' was that it did not
break any man-made laws.[22] Only when a woman 'supplemented'
her own natural body, as Valerie Traub states, with either natural
(an enlarged clitoris) or artificial (a dildo) implements of penetration (1994: 66) was the serious charge of sodomy levelled against
her. Thus, the condemnation of 'Sinnes of kinde' in the *Metempsychosis* may serve to contrast, rather than mirror, the relatively
innocent behaviour of Sapho and Philaenis. Except that Donne
presents Sapho envisioning this mode of relating as permanent,
and not as an immature prelude to heterosexuality.

  In the passage from *Metempsychosis*, above, the Ape lifts the girl's
apron, and 'touches' her. In 'Sapho to Philaenis', it is the sense of
touch which is emphasized, as Sapho touches herself in front of
her mirror and argues for the coming together of her body and
Philaenis' not through penetration but in the touching of 'brest to
brest' and 'thighs to thighs'. It is the girl's pleasure which is focused
on, indeed mocked, for Donne states that Siphatecia 'Now cries'
out against the Ape and 'now repents' at the cessation of pleasurable
sensation. Siphatecia, being 'silly' or ignorant of the meaning of
the Ape's advances, 'melts' in confusion and pleasure. The language
of abandonment and loss of self-awareness is again uncomfortably
like that of Sapho near the end of her epistle. There is the same
'addition problem' for Siphatecia, who is 'willing halfe and more,
more then halfe loth', and for Sapho who cries, 'O cure this loving
madnesse, and restore | Me to mee; thee, my halfe, my all, my
*more*' (57–8), although such language is conventional enough.
Donne was fond of such mathematical paradoxes elsewhere when it

[22] But see Crompton 1980/1 for a correction of the notion that lesbianism was
not legislated against in Continental Europe in the Middle Ages and Renaissance.

came to sorting out the ones and twos of love, however. One plus one could equal zero, one, two, three, or 'all'. There are enough similarities between 'Sapho to Philaenis' and Donne's anecdote of the Ape and Siphatecia in *Metempsychosis*, the primary ones being the congruity of a parody of Petrarchisms and a warning against 'Sinnes against kinde', to make 'Sapho to Philaenis' sound less like a championing of Sappho's *Phainetai moi* and more like an extremely subtle if still voyeuristic exploration of female homoeroticism for wholly self-interested purposes.

Certainly Donne's references to male homosexuality or bestiality as we would categorize them today are, without exception, unambiguously negative. In *Satire I*, the speaker asks his decadent companion,

> Why should'st thou (that dost not onely approve,
> But in ranke itchie lust, desire, and love
> The nakednesse and barenesse to enjoy,
> Of thy plumpe muddy whore, or prostitute boy)
> Hate vertue, though shee be naked, and bare? (37–41)

Here is an example of Donne's assertion which I quoted in my Introduction, that 'lesse particles then words have busied the whole Church' (*Sermons*, ix. 71). If it be not a 'great thing', the discrepancy among manuscripts and editions in the spelling of the word, 'barenesse' in line 39 is nevertheless pertinent here. Is the word 'bareness' or 'barrenness'? The syllogism which the speaker is employing would suggest that it is 'bareness', an emphatic synonym for 'nakednesse', as Grierson points out (Donne 1912: ii. 107). As he admits, however, 'barrennesse' is also appropriate to the context in that sexual activity between the libertine and his 'plump muddy whore, or prostitute boy' would be barren, the purpose being physical pleasure rather than reproduction. This reading would support Sapho's argument that the female body (and the female in her social role) neither needs, nor benefits from, insemination by a male, and what I will argue is possibly an oblique reference to dildos at line 44, which, in the soft pornography of the time, were celebrated or condemned (depending on whether a woman or a man was speaking) as being better than a penis because its use would not result in pregnancy. In *Satire II*, Donne makes reference to the endemic 'Symonie'and Sodomy in Churchmens lives' (75), and in *Satire IV*, to the corrupt courtier who notices 'Who loves

Whores, who boyes, and who goats' (128) so as to blackmail them. Except for his epigram, 'The Jughler', then, Donne's condemnation of sodomy and other 'deviant' sexualities are contained in his satires.

We have not yet looked at the whole of 'Sapho to Philaenis', however. It is the centre of Donne's poem which startles most, and complicates the poem's allusiveness. Sapho is finally distracted from her misery by her memory of Philaenis' beauty:

> Thou art so faire,
> As, gods, when gods to thee I doe compare,
> Are grac'd thereby; And to make blinde men see,
> What things gods are, I say they'are like to thee.
> For, if we justly call each silly man
> A litle world, What shall we call thee then?
> Thou art not soft, and cleare, and strait, and faire,
> As Down, as Stars, Cedars, and Lillies are,
> But thy right hand, and cheek, and eye, only
> Are like thy other hand, and cheek, and eye.
> Such was my *Phao* awhile, but shall be never,
> As thou, wast, art, and, oh, maist thou be ever. (15–26)

Sapho compares the gods to Philaenis and it is they who benefit from such a comparison. Donne rejects the entire natural world and moves, blasphemously, right to the supernatural. J. Mueller, as do Allen and Revard, suggests that by comparing Philaenis to the gods, Donne takes the first line of *Phainetai moi*, 'He seems to me equal to the gods', and 'wittily translates [it] from the male rival to the female beloved—outsapphizing, at this juncture, Sappho herself' (1993: 186). This point seems to me to be Mueller's and Revard's strongest in arguing for Donne's familiarity with Sappho's poem, especially since Donne, as usual, goes one step further and rather than making Philaenis 'equal to the gods', he has Sapho blaspheme that Philaenis surpasses them.

The blasphemy of the first simile is surpassed by the evangelism of the second. If read literally, Sapho's simile is absurd, for if blind men cannot see the gods, neither can they see Philaenis to enable the comparison. But the idea of something so striking it allows blind men to 'see' was conventional in Donne's time. Juan Luis Vives's *Instruction of a Christen woman* (1541) criticizes the current fad in women's fashion of exposing one's breasts: 'howe foule a thynge is that, as the commen sayeng is, a blynde man may espy, whan those that se it, some abhorre the abhominablenes: and some wanton menne seyng the parte of the bodye, nat used to be sene, are set on fyre therewith' (39ᵛ). Donne is perhaps also using the words 'blinde' and 'see' in their theological senses, the notion that atheists are spiritually blind, for in a sermon, Donne describes the Church as 'A place where the *blind* might recover sight; that is, Men borne in *Paganisme*, or *Superstition*, might see the true God, truly worshipped' (v. 125).

As I set out in my Introduction, Sapho's defence of her 'blasphemy' can be read on several levels, one of which is the way Donne uncannily points, through his mimicry of a convention, to the dereliction of woman from the symbolic order, the 'world', but also to her '*disruptive excess*', beyond patriarchal prescriptions. The micro/macrocosm comparison is a favourite device of Donne's and is worth looking at in a few poems as well as in a sermon, for purposes of comparison and contrast. In his Holy Sonnet which begins 'I am a little world made cunningly | Of Elements, and an Angelike spright', Donne does not play with gender but his imagination pushes against another frontier when he addresses the astronomers and discoverers who were stretching the limits of the known world and universe: 'You which beyond that heaven which was most high | Have found new sphears, and of new lands can write, | Powre new seas in mine eyes' (5–7). In 'The Goodmorrow', the speaker uses the convention as if the statement, 'man is a little world', includes the woman: 'Let sea-discoverers to new worlds have gone, | Let Maps to others, worlds on worlds have showne, | Let us possesse our world, each hath one, and is one' (12–14). Likewise in 'The Sunne Rising', 'the world's contracted thus' (26) in the lovers, although the arrangement between them betrays a significant imbalance of power: 'She'is all States, and all Princes, I, | Nothing else is' (21). Trying to outdo himself in finding one more permutation for the metaphor and extend the limits of epideictic, Donne reverses the comparison in *The First Anniversary* when he describes Elizabeth Drury as 'She to whom this world must it selfe refer, / As Suburbs, or the Microcosme of her' (235–6). In a sermon on Psalm 62: 9 Donne embarks on a dazzling defence of 'man's' divinity. I include this sermon passage to set in relief the gender-inflected use in 'Sapho to Philaenis':

[A]s though one God were not enough for the administration of this world, God hath multiplied gods here upon Earth, and imparted, communicated, not onely his power to every Magistrate, but the Divine nature to every sanctified man. . . . [S]ince God is so mindfull of him, since God hath set his minde upon him, What is not man? Man is all. . . . Absolutely, unconditionally we cannot annihilate man, not evacuate, not evaporate, not extenuate man to the levity, to the vanity, to the nullity of this Text. . . . For, man is not onely a contributary Creature, but a totall Creature; He does not onely make one, but he is all; He is not a piece of the world, but the world it selfe; and next to the glory of God, the reason why there is a world. (vi. 297–8)

In this astounding affirmation of both 'man's' divinity, his share in the immortal not just in 'the next world' but 'here on earth', and of the impossibility of his 'annihilation', woman is once again subject to '*internal exile*', both there and not there, her difference assumed to be participating in the relationship between God and man. But 'if we justly call each silly man | A litle world, What shall we call' woman? Man is 'all; He is not a piece of the world, but the world it selfe'. The phrase, 'Partaker of the divine Nature', also reminds us that part of the debate on the nature of women was the very question (usually asked in jest to show off one's rhetorical skills) of whether women partook of the divine nature (Maclean 1988: 13–14), hence Donne's Problem, 'Why hath the common opinion affoorded woemen Soules?' (1980: 28–9).

Holstun uses the gender-inflected use of the macro/microcosm metaphor in 'The Good-morrow' to argue that 'Because sapphic love cannot participate in this political and erotic play of domination . . . it cannot employ this trope' (1987: 840). But Sapho does employ the trope, wittily playing with its gender inflections, and then she rejects it because of its inadequacy. As the speaker of 'Negative Love' professes, 'If that be simply perfectest | Which can by no way be exprest | But *Negatives*, my love is so' (10–12). Likewise, in a sermon Donne states, 'we can expresse God himselfe in no clearer termes, nor in termes expressing more Dignity, then in saying we cannot expresse him' (viii. 105). Sapho realizes that neither gods nor anything in the natural world can do justice to Philaenis and so she is forced to resort to praise by negative comparison. In her lyrical essay, 'When Our Lips Speak Together', Irigaray explains to her female interlocutor why she has been insisting on negatives in her evocation of love between women:

And if I have so often insisted on negatives: *not, nor, without* . . . it has
been to remind you, to remind us, that we only touch each other
naked. And that, to find ourselves once again in that state, we have a lot
to take off. So many representations, so many appearances separate us
from each other. They have wrapped us for so long in their desires, we
have adorned ourselves so often to please them, that we have come to
forget the feel of our own skin. (1985*b*: 217–18; Irigaray's ellipsis)

That Donne's Sapho should insist on negatives therefore might be
interpreted as a sloughing off, as it were, the trappings of a specular,
possessive claim to the other. Sapho insists on the nakedness of
woman that is both 'her destitution in language' (1985*a*: 143), and
the starting point for a different language. There is no way of
articulating woman or her desire apart from the 'words as the
*wrappings* with which the "subject," modestly, clothes the "female"'
(142; my emphasis). But what about Irigaray's 'metaphor' of the
two lips, which I quoted above? Is she not just substituting one
metaphor, one series of metaphors, for another in her exploration of
what a 'speaking (as) woman' might be? Diana Fuss clarifies the
difference in Irigaray's mimicry of the operation of substitution in
phallogocentrism: 'what is important about Irigaray's conception
of this particular figure is that the "two lips" operate as a metaphor
*for* metonymy' (1989: 66). I will return to the implications of what
Fuss identifies as Irigaray's proposed metonymic relationship between language and the body.
    Anachronistic a reference though it may be for Sapho, in her
rejection of Petrarchisms there is almost certainly an allusion to
the imagery the lover uses in the Song of Solomon, or Canticles.
Sapho says of Philaenis:

> Thou art not soft, and cleare, and strait, and faire,
>     As Down, as Stars, Cedars, and Lillies are. (21–2)

While 'Down' has the most textual support, Grierson notes the
'Dowves' (i.e. doves) of the Phillips manuscript gives the plural as
in the other nouns, and a closer parallel in poetic vividness. 'We get
a series of pictures—doves, stars, cedars, lilies' (Donne 1912: ii.
91). Grierson cites *The Winter's Tale*, in which Florizel describes
Perdita's hand: 'As soft as dove's down, and as white as it' (4.4.364).
Doves, cedars, and lilies appear frequently in the Canticles and all

three occur in the blazon the woman sings of her male beloved, here in the Geneva Bible's translation:

His eyes are like dooves upon the rivers of waters, which are washt with milke, & remaine by the ful *vessels*. His chekes *are* as a bed of spices, *and as* swete flowres, & his lippes *like* lilies dropping downe pure myrrhe. . . . His mouth *is as* swete things, and he is wholy delectable: this is my welbeloved, & this is my lover. (vv. 12–13, 16)

Both male and female sing each other's praises and both are compared to doves and lilies. The woman yearns for her beloved: 'In my bed by night I soght him that my soule loved: I soght him, but I founde him not' (3: 1). Both the erotic blazons and the lovers' separation and desired union in the Canticles seem to echo in Donne's poem. Sapho's words are part of a negative comparison, however. Again, there is an ambiguity as to whether Sapho and Philaenis' love is nothing like the love expressed in the Canticles or is one which defies all (current) categories. None of the comparatives in line 22, with the exception of stars, are frequent in Donne's poetry. 'Sapho to Philaenis' contains the only reference to lilies. Only Donne's 'Upon the Annunciation and Passion' makes reference to 'a Cedar' (8) which plants itself and falls, an allusion to Christ and the cross on which he is crucified. A dove or doves figure in 'The Canonization' ('And wee in us finde the'Eagle and the Dove', line 22). In the epithalamium Donne wrote for Princess Elizabeth's marriage to Frederick ('the grave whispering Dove', line 6), 'Holy Sonnet XVIII' ('And let myne amorous soule court thy mild Dove', line 12), and 'His Parting From Her', in which the speaker refers to his 'Dove-like friend' (line 30), the dove obviously symbolized the tenderness which Donne felt was integral to such a relationship. If we are to read 'Down', rather than 'Doves', 'Sapho to Philaenis' is the only instance of it as a substantive noun.

Considered as a group, I suggest Donne's 'insignificant' metaphors could also point towards the kind of ineffability we see in Dante's *Paradiso* as Dante attempts to describe his union with God in the thirty-third Canto, 'the end of all desires': 'O how scant is speech and how feeble to my conception! and this, to what I saw, is such that it is not enough to call it little. O Light Eternal, that alone abidest in Thyself, alone knowest Thyself, and, known to Thyself and knowing, lovest and smilest on Thyself!' (1961: 33.46–7, her strange blazon, Sapho admits that the best praise she can bestow upon Philaenis is that her right side 'only' is like her left. Likewise in Donne's 'The Dreame', the speaker says of his beloved:

> Thou art so true, that thoughts of thee suffice,
> To make dreames truth; and fables histories
> . . .
> I doe confesse, it could not chuse but bee
> Prophane, to thinke thee any thing but thee. (7–8; 19–20)

In the epithalamium Thomas Heywood wrote for the 1612 marriage of Princess Elizabeth and Frederick, he obviously intends it as the highest compliment that 'Unto your selves, your selves, then we must say, | We onely may compare' (1613: $C^v$). Finally, compare the sonnet Henry Constable writes 'To the Countesses of Cumberland and Warwick, Sisters':

> Yow sister Muses doe not ye repine,
> That I two sisters doe with nyne compare
> For eyther of these sacred two more rare
> In vertue is, then all the heavenly nyne.
>
> But if ye aske which one is more devine?
> I say like to theyre owne twin eyes they are
> . . .
> How should I yow commend, when eyther one
> All things in heaven and earth so far excell.
> The highest prayse that I can give is this,
> That one of yow like to the other is. (1960: 146–7)

Outside the context of lesbian love, this compliment of incomparability is both politic and conventional (as we saw in 'All haile sweet Poët'); it is the context of Sapho's compliment which is, to indulge in a colloquialism, earth-shattering.

There would seem to be at least two ways of interpreting this group of metaphors in 'Sapho to Philaenis', both of which cast radically different lights on the issue of lesbian 'likenesse' and the Nature versus Art tension. Is Sapho expressing defeat or wonder? Is her epideictic which begins with comparisons to the gods and ends with a comparison of the self to the self a blasphemous parody or a pointing to the dwelling of the immortal in the mortal? On the one hand, critics argue that Donne buries the possibility of lesbian expression in an unmarked grave, so to speak; that Philaenis inhabits a 'self-contained signifying system' (Holstun 1987: 840).

On the other hand, several critics responding to Holstun argue that Donne suggests a 'remedy' for the intertextual rivalries so much more apparent in Ovid's text (Harvey 1989: 128) and moves closer to Sappho (whether he'd read her or not) in whose lyrics 'love is a forgetfulness of self, a delight in mutuality, in mirroring, in giving pleasure to the beloved' (Kauffman 1986: 55). On one side of language, we have the realm Holstun asserts Philaenis inhabits, a 'realm of preverbal monstrosity'; and on the other side of language we have that phenomenon so appealing for Donne: 'reaching beyond language and thought into wonder' (Carey 1990: 111) and hence, towards the divine. Both interpretations bring to mind the 'limit of the thinkable'.

I suggest that one reading of Sapho's epideictic is to see it as wonderment at the uniqueness rather than the 'monstrosity' of Philaenis. A sense of wonder which renders the speaker speechless is expressed in a number of *Songs and Sonets*. For example, the speaker of 'The Relique' admits to the inability of language to express the perfection of his beloved: 'All measure, and all language, I should passe, | Should I tell what a miracle shee was' (32–3). Wonder in the *Songs and Sonets*, however, is often complicated by the speaker's need to assert that his love relationship is unique in the world and thus in need of safeguarding from contamination. The speaker of 'The Undertaking' boasts: 'I have done one braver thing | Then all the *Worthies* did, | Yet a braver thence doth spring, | Which is, to keepe that hid' (1–4). The need to hide their superior love from 'prophane men' is urged on the beloved in 'A Valediction: forbidding Mourning': ''Twere prophanation of our joyes | To tell the layetie our love' (7–8). Likewise, the woman in 'A Valediction: of the Booke' is urged to collect the love letters passed between herself and the speaker, but 'This Booke', 'this all-graved tome, | In cypher write, or new made Idiome; | Wee for love's clergie only' are instruments' (19–21). There is in each of these excerpts what Anthony Low and others identify as Donne's desire for a private world which is manifestly superior to the world of 'dull sublunary lovers'. Such exclusivity demands a code of expression in order to protect it from 'inundat[ions]' of the uninitiated, so that the wonder of love is not necessarily inexpressible, it just cannot be shared, or will not be shared, with the outside world. If Sapho's epideictic acknowledges the uniqueness of Philaenis, the confusion of Sapho with Philaenis later in the poem as she stands in front of her mirror—'touching my selfe, all seems done to thee'—is her attempt to identify completely with the other, which she ultimately recognizes is impossible. But between the unhappy extremes of fusion and unknowability lies the 'neere[ness]' which Sapho calls for in the final line of the poem.

There are problems, however, with such a positive reading of Sapho's 'all or nothing' epideictic. After manipulating the topos of inexpressibility and incomparability with dazzling virtuosity, Sapho is suddenly reminded of her old lover, Phaon, and says he was like her, for 'awhile'. Sapho has breached one of the laws of love: never bring up former lovers. Our imaginations have been taken to the edge of the universe and back, only to find Philaenis compared to someone in Sapho's own backyard: her former male lover. So far, critics have noted that Philaenis comes out ahead of Phaon in this comparison, but the deflatory effect of the comparison has not registered. Phaon appears, moreover, so as to allow us to compare Donne to Ovid, to Sappho. What exactly is being compared in this couplet?:

> Such was my *Phao* 'awhile, but shall be never,
> As thou, wast, art, and, oh, maist thou be ever. (25–6)

The end of Sapho's radical epideictic is the first indication that Sapho and Philaenis are post-Phaon. Phaon is no longer what Philaenis was, is and ever shall be: smooth, symmetrical, and 'indefinitely other in herself'. Donne perhaps alludes to Sappho's declaration in Ovid's *Heroides*, 15, 'o nec adhuc iuvenis, nec iam puer, utilis aetas; [O neither yet man nor still boy—meet age for charm]' (93). But both males and females change at puberty; indeed women continue to experience time cyclically rather than linearly because of menstruation. Renaissance women were considered to be lustier and naturally more changeable in temperament. So in what way is Philaenis as a woman the same in past, present, and future time? Donne's lines hint that his experimentation with the nature of lesbian love arises out of male performance anxiety. Only a man suffering from such anxiety would look at a woman and view her as unchanging relative to a man, if only in the arena of physical love. The unfavourable comparison of Phaon to Philaenis would suggest that Donne was especially attracted by the imaginative opportunities for stability and constancy which a certain perception of lesbian love presented to his mind. Holstun's assertion that 'lesbian sexuality becomes a phenomenon of the past which can only be discussed in retrospect', is one which seems to stem from a careless reading of the present tense in Donne's poem, and of the tentativeness with which Sapho frames her argument against heterosexuality. While Ovid's Sappho waxes elegiac about the good times she and Phaon shared, Donne's Sapho engages in an eloquent argument which she still obviously believes can persuade Philaenis to come to her senses (all of them) and return to Sapho. Donne's Sapho, unlike Ovid's, is not about to jump from the Leucadian cliff to 'seek her fate'; she is not suspended in a literal cliff-hanger that is resolved beyond the margins of *Heroides*, 15 in Ovid's *Amores* where, it turns out, Phaon wises up.

Ovid's Sappho had also compared her beloved Phaon to the gods, Apollo and Bacchus. She argues that if these two gods could love Daphne and Ariadne, neither of whom were poets, Phaon ought to love her: 'si mihi difficilis formam natura negavit, | ingenio formae damna repende meo. | sim brevis, at nomen, quod terras inpleat omnes, | est mihi; mensuram nominis ipsa fero. [If nature, malign to me, has denied the charm of beauty, weigh in the stead of beauty the genius that is mine. If I am slight of stature, yet I have a name fills every land; the measure of my name is my real height]' (31–4). Sappho's defence is both a cheap shot on Ovid's part—referring as he is to the tradition that Sappho was ugly—and rather extraordinary in that a woman argues her literary skills more than 'make up' for the physical attributes which usually make or break a woman's fortunes. Moreover, a woman's name, although it was better if no one heard of her, was usually made famous or infamous because of her sexual 'reputation', chaste or unchaste, not her poetry.

In what is probably another nod to Ovid, Donne's Sapho also refers to her own beauty briefly so that her far-reaching praise of Philaenis seems further eroded after her reminiscence of Phaon.

> Here lovers sweare in their Idolatrie,
>    That I am such; but Griefe discolors me.
> And yet I grieve the lesse, least Griefe remove
>    My beauty, and make me'unworthy of thy love. (27–30)

Mueller suggests Donne draws from Sappho's *Phainetai moi* here, but the tone seems to be that of parody. From references outside of time and space, Sapho brings us back to her immediate situation with 'Here'. To whom does 'lovers' refer? Is Sapho loved by others? If so, does she scorn them all for Philaenis or does the promiscuity Ovid exaggerated ('atque aliae centum, quas *hic* sine crimine amavi'; my emphasis) continue? Finally, the soaring, visionary language with which Sapho describes Philaenis comes crashing down, like Icarus with his melted wings, into a sea of bathos. Sapho's final lines of this passage can be rudely paraphrased thus: 'My distress over your absence mars my face, but I am crying less for you so that I do not look so bad that you cannot love me'. Such interludes as lines 25 to 30 make it difficult to assert Donne has a single agenda in 'Sapho to Philaenis'. It is as if he tries to entertain a male coterie, deflate the reputations of Sappho and Ovid so as to inflate his own, and yet find an answer for his own imaginative problem with which he is so obsessed in his love poetry: the impossibility, the mystery, of two becoming one.

Sapho's argument begins in earnest in the following lines, for the threat of a male supplanting Sapho in Philaenis' affections is real.

> Plaies some soft boy with thee, oh there wants yet
> A mutuall feeling which should sweeten it.
> His chinne, a thorny hairy'unevennesse
> Doth threaten, and some daily change possesse.
> Thy body is a naturall Paradise,
> In whose selfe, unmanur'd, all pleasure lies,
> Nor needs perfection; why shouldst thou than
> Admit the tillage of a harsh, rough man?
> Men leave behinde them that which their sin showes,
> And are as theeves trac'd, which rob when it snows.
> But of our dallyance no more signes there are,
> Then fishes leave in streames, or Birds in aire. (31–42)

Against Holstun's argument of periodization, I would suggest that Sapho's epistle constitutes a wooing of Philaenis, the promise of a second honeymoon, as it were. First, however, she must dismiss the competition, and she does so on purely physical grounds. The word 'play' is a common euphemism for sexual intercourse. The words, 'chinne', 'thorn' and 'hair' are all used by Shakespeare as euphemisms for the penis or pubic hair (G. Williams 1994). Celia and Rosalind in *As You Like It* pun on 'chin' in the same way (3.2.201–6). Sapho's argument is thus based on primary and secondary sex characteristics, and the unevennesse of (de)tumescence is augmented by the threat of pregnancy. Sapho thus answers Shakespeare's question in his third Sonnet: 'For where is she so fair whose uneared womb | Disdains the tillage of thy husbandry?' (5–6).

Before discussing Sapho's radical reappraisal of woman's reproductive capacity as measure of her worth, I want to address the 'mutuall feeling' which heterosexual 'playing' lacks. The OED defines 'mutual' as 'reciprocal' (A.1.a). Its essence is qualitative as opposed to 'equal', a word more objectively quantifiable, at least according to Milton who describes Adam and Eve in Paradise Lost: 'both | Not equal, as thir sex not equal seem'd' (4.295–6). Consider Donne's use of the word in 'The Exstasie': 'As 'twixt two equall Armies, Fate | Suspends uncertaine victorie, | Our soules, (which to advance their state, | Were gone out,) hung 'twixt her, and mee' (13–16). Elsewhere in his poetry, Donne uses 'mutuall' to connote the absolute unity of heterosexual lovers. In 'The Dissolution', the speaker says, 'wee were mutuall Elements to us, | And made of one another' (3–4); in the epithalamium Donne wrote for Princess Elizabeth and the Elector Palatine, they are 'Two Phænixes whose joyned brests | Are unto one another mutuall nests' (23–4). At least ideally, there is 'a mutuall feeling' in these relationships which sweetens it and is part of what Low recognizes as Donne's reinvention of love in terms of the communal rather than the social (1993: 33).

Donne's Sapho compares the mutuality of lesbian 'likenesse' with the ownership implied in heterosexuality. Philaenis lacks nothing whatsoever, there is nothing wanting in the natural Paradise of her body, 'In whose selfe, unmanur'd, all pleasure lies'. The use of the word, 'unmanur'd', is an unusual one to our ears. The verb 'to manure' was used as it is today, according to the OED, as early as 1599, but its primary meaning in Donne's time was 'To hold, occupy (land, property); to have the tenure of, to administer, manage'. It also meant 'to inhabit' (1.b) and 'to till' or 'cultivate' (2), and was used figuratively of the body or mind (2.d). Donne uses it in his verse letter to Rowland Woodward, 'Like one who'in her third widdowhood', in its primary, secondary, and figurative senses, to recommend the retired life to Woodward: 'Manure thy selfe then, to thy selfe be'approv'd' (34). Self-sufficiency and discretion—literally possession of one's self—are the ideals Donne holds up. In 'Sapho to Philaenis', Donne uses 'unmanur'd' to suggest the same kind of self-possession, not so much in the moral sense, but the physical one, and not just in terms of the individual but a single sex. His puns on 'man' and the Latin, *manus* / 'hand', thus contracts several connotations in one word: Philaenis need not be touched by man, sexually or any other way which tries to appropriate her as his property. In both instances, the economic connotations of holding one's property or 'place' in the world and of being independent thus have radically different implications for the speakers and their addressees, because of their gender differences. Janel Mueller states, 'that economic aspects of lesbianism are addressed at all remains for me a compelling index to the seriousness and rigor of Donne's "what if" in "Sapho to Philaenis"—the attempt to imagine friendship and marriage as a conjoint relation of equality' (1993: 202).

According to Sapho, Philaenis is in no need of the perfection women were considered to achieve upon marriage and subsequent motherhood, nor must she capitulate to becoming the possession or property of her husband, a commodity to be exchanged between men, father and husband. The natural Paradise of Philaenis evokes a world both antithetical and analogous to Marvell's assertion in 'The Garden' that 'Two paradises 'twere in one | To live in Paradise alone' (63–4). Paradise for Sapho is a body which refuses to 'Admit the tillage of a harsh rough man'. Ian Maclean concludes that 'matrimony was a divine, natural and social institution in the eyes of Renaissance thinkers: any alternative is theologically contentious, and requires a new vision of the mental and physical predispositions of the sexes' (1980: 84). Humanists such as Erasmus in his *Praise of Matrimony* and Thomas More in his *Utopia* actively promoted marriage as centrally important to their ideal societies, actively reviving classical metaphors such as David Halperin quotes from the Athenian betrothal ceremony 'in which the father of the bride says to her future husband, "I give you this woman for the plowing of legitimate children"' (1990: 141). Renaissance thinkers were, for the most part, of the same mind as the Greeks: 'in the absence of men, women's sexual functioning is aimless and unproductive, merely a form of rottenness and decay, but by the application of male pharmacy it becomes at once orderly and fruitful' (141). Irigaray observes: 'Thus, the idea has been introduced in

women's imagination that their pleasure lies in "producing" children: which amounts to bending them to the values of production,
even before they have had an occasion to examine their pleasure'
(1990: 85). Here, Irigaray points to the operation of the Oedipal
complex which constructs woman as castrated and therefore desir-
ous of the phallus, which she obtains indirectly through the production of (boy) children, and thus acquires value in the eyes of the
Father.

What is astounding is that Donne argues against the opinions of
his time when Sapho compares the consequences of hetero- and
homosexuality for women:

> Men leave behinde them that which their sin showes,
>     And are as theeves trac'd, which rob when it snowes.
> But of our dallyance no more signes there are,
>     Then fishes leave in streames, or Birds in aire.

Two women making love are as creatures in their natural element,
they belong together and they leave the world as they found it.
Donne uses the same metaphor in a verse letter to Henry Wotton,
'Sir, more than kisses, letters mingle soules'. In his argument that
life is a voyage which requires self-disciplined navigation, Donne
counsels his friend:

> And in the worlds sea, do not like corke sleepe
> Upon the waters face; nor in the deepe
> Sinke like a lead without a line: but as
> Fishes glide, leaving no print where they passe,
> Nor making sound, so, closely thy course goe;
> Let men dispute, whether thou breathe, or no. (53–8)

The balance here between presence and absence is a delicate one.
Donne's image is so subtle it would seem he almost counsels invisibility and silence, anonymity rather than discretion, but the
notions of moderation and assimilation to effect the mutual benefit
of individual and community or surroundings are present as well.
The image in 'Sapho to Philaenis' is perhaps vulnerable to the same
set of readings but in its antithetical position to the description of
men's sexual activity, it functions primarily to continue the argument of naturalness and mutuality. Donne is not talking about
non-signification here, a lack of difference—fishes are different
from water, birds are different from air—but they exist in a non-
hierarchical relationship, something which is impossible on patri-

archal terms. In addition to avoiding pregnancy, Sapho and Philaenis' 'dallyance' is not an example of the performative, display-oriented male conception of sexual activity. Sapho's ideal, like the advice Donne gives to Wotton about discretion, is decidedly different from the crowing male lovers in the *Elegies* and the *Songs and Sonets* or even the ideal lovers of 'The Canonization', who will be 'invoke[d]' and begged for 'A patterne of [their] love'. J. Mueller points out the third party observing the lovers in 'The Extasie' and that that third party is male (1985: 39–42). Yet another viewpoint is expressed in 'A Lecture upon the Shadow', however, whereby disguises or secrets have no part in true love and lovers are indifferent to opinion: 'That love hath not attain'd the high'st degree, | Which is still diligent lest others see' (12–13).

Donne's analogy of men to thieves is perhaps not as straight-forward as it appears. Sapho's meaning seems obvious enough: that men who make love to women often leave behind a child which 'showes' the 'sin' of fornication. But the analogy to thieves who steal in winter and can thus be traced by their footprints betrays the collective and individual male anxiety of fixing paternity absolutely. The man who loves and leaves, indeed any man, can never be sure of tracing the children his mistress/wife gives birth to, back to his own seed. It is in fact women who could potentially rob men if their children are conceived extramaritally. Family inheritances could be diverted into impure bloodlines and hence, anyone who could be proven a bastard could be cut out of any inheritance. Again here, Sapho's argument in part betrays a male perspective, in which it is males, illegitimate sons, who steal from other males, their supposed fathers. Those men who 'trespass' on the property of other men, their wives, are also thieves and cause for anxiety. Donne uses the lover/thief analogy in the same way but more overtly, to begin 'The Perfume'. The man as lover/thief is betrayed by his 'traiterous' perfume. And it is the woman's father, not the woman, who is compared to one who has been robbed. As Anthony Low points out, the most intense relationship is not that of the lover and his mistress but rather the lover and his mistress's father (1993: 38). The woman is the loot, even as the speaker implies she is promiscuous:

> Once, and but once found in thy company,
> All thy suppos'd escapes are laid on mee;

And as a thiefe at barre, is question'd there
By all the men, that have beene rob'd that yeare,
So am I, (by this traiterous meanes surpriz'd)
By thy Hydroptique father catechiz'd. (1–6)

Donne's Sapho holds out the best of both worlds to Philaenis: 'betweene us all sweetnesse may be had; | All, all that Nature yields, or Art can adde' (43–4). The Nature versus Art argument, most famously articulated by Sidney in his *Defence of Poetry*, has been one of the tensions underlying Sapho's entire epistle. Sidney argues that 'Nature never set forth the earth in so rich a tapestry as divers poets have done; . . . Her world is brazen, the poets only deliver a golden' (78). The poet is both *poiein*/maker and *vates*/ prophet, and embellishes the world in which he/she lives. Sapho, despite her protestations of inability, has been employing her considerable Art in wooing Philaenis, convincing her of her own desirability as a woman, over any man. But the sudden surfacing of this 'Art' in line 44, after an extensive agricultural, Paradisal paean does not seem logical. If Philaenis' body is a 'naturall Paradise' what need is there of Art? Perhaps I employ a 'hermeneutics of suspicion' (Janel Mueller's term) here, but I cannot but suspect Donne could not resist a joke about dildos. Sapho and Philaenis as two women can enjoy each other naturally as well as use artificial penises and thus make men utterly superfluous. We have just heard Sapho argue that one of the greatest merits of lesbian love is that there is no risk of pregnancy, and she does so without even remotely implying that she and Philaenis use a dildo. Yet not having to fear pregnancy along with never 'detumescing' are the two properties of the dildo which women—such as Nashe's Francis in *The Choise of Valentines*—celebrate in the soft-core pornography of the Renaissance. Donne refers to dildos twice, in 'The Anagram' and *Satire II*. While one cannot say for sure that these four words, 'or Art can adde', added to the end of an argument for natural love have a deflatory effect, it is just the kind of subtle jab Donne could make to amuse his friends and yet not take away from the sincerity of the argument Sapho makes.

Donne, through the voice of Lesbian Sappho, the Tenth Muse, seems to want to construct a world through poetry which holds out the possibility of a world devoid of 'change' and 'sicknesse', a world symbolized by the naturalness of lesbian love as Sapho argues for it, even as she draws 'Natures workes, from Natures law'. If

Donne's motivation for portraying lesbian love is not simply to rescue it and Sapho from the dismemberments of his poetic predecessors, or to present it as a viable choice for 'real' women, his imagination seems attracted to the lesbian woman because she represents through a sexuality which is not frustrated by the changes and 'unevennesse' of ejaculation, detumescence, even pregnancy, the perfect union and constancy which proves so elusive in heterosexual relationships, both real and imagined. Sapho speaks for Donne, mediating this union through the sexuality she expressed in her poetry, and while Donne uses her as a kind of Muse figure here, a mutual redemption takes place: Donne represents the 'honey-sweet pride of Lesbos' instead of the butch of Martial; Sapho redeems Donne from a fallen world of, to use Ricks's term, 'post-coital sadness'.

Finally then, we are back where we began: looking at Sapho looking in the mirror as she touches herself. Now that I have discussed what precedes this scene both inside Donne's poem and outside it, are we any closer to determining Donne's construction of lesbian 'likenesse'? Sapho has just concluded her articulation of a female pleasure which is other than the procreation of children as male property, and her argument sounds very much like what Judith Butler calls the 'antipenetrative eros of surfaces' which appears in some of Irigaray's writing: '[t]he refusal of an eroticism of entry and containment seems linked for Irigaray with an opposition to appropriation and possession as forms of erotic exchange' (Butler 1994: 158; see Irigaray 1993*c*: 179–80). Sapho asks of Philaenis, 'Hand to strange hand, lippe to lippe none denies; | Why should they brest to brest, or thighs to thighs?' She suggests that 'the likenesse being such | Why should they not alike in all parts touch?' Nowhere does Sapho espouse the bee-line approach to the 'Centrique part' which the speaker of 'Love's Progress' asserts is the 'desir'd place', the *telos* of love. Donne thus seems to pass the 'test' Irigaray imposes:

even the motifs of 'self-touching,' of 'proximity,' isolated as such or reduced to utterances, could effectively pass for an attempt to appropriate the feminine to discourse. [*sic*] We would still have to ascertain whether 'touching oneself,' that (self)touching, *the desire for the proximate rather than for (the) proper(ty)*, and so on, might not imply a mode of exchange irreducible to any *centering*, any *centrism*, given the way the 'self-touching' of female 'self-affection' comes into play as a rebounding from one to the other without any possibility of interruption, and given that, in this interplay, proximity confounds any adequation, any appropriation. (1985*b*: 79; first emphasis mine)

There is a startling example of what seems to be an eros of 'the fecundity of the caress' (see Irigaray 1993*a*: 185 ff.) in Ben Jonson's translation of Petronius: 'Doing, a filthy pleasure is, and short; | And done, we straight repent us of the sport: | Let us not then rush blindly on unto it, | Like lustful beasts, that onely know to doe it'. Rather, 'Let us together closely lie, and kisse, | There is no labour, nor no shame in this; | This hath pleas'd, doth please, and long will please; never | Can this decay, but is beginning ever' (1925–52: viii. 294). Jonson's male performance anxiety registers here in the shame and disgust he expresses for the wholly inadequate sexual act. Jonson was obviously attracted to a 'becoming' which avoided postcoital sadness, the 'disappointment of having come', and thus his privileging of touch over penetration is at least in part substitutive for intercourse rather than an altogether independent mode of relating. Moreover, we saw the rage with which he expressed Cecilia Bulstrode's 'rubbing' and writing in his 'Epigram on the Court Pucelle'.

In her essay, 'Love of Self', Irigaray points to the dangers of love between women in which Sapho appears to get caught up in front of her mirror:

The female has always served the self-love of man, obviously. But there is also the fact that the female does not have the same relation to exteriority as the male. . . . She herself cannot watch herself desiring (except through another woman? Who is not herself? One of the dangers of love between women is the confusion in their identities, the lack of respect for or of perception of differences). (1993*a*: 63)

It takes Sapho some time to distinguish her image in the mirror from Philaenis, even as she touches her own body, but she does, crucially, return to her own body from the 'other side' of the mirror. Unlike the opinion of the speaker in 'Communitie' and 'Variety', one woman is not just like another. Irigaray articulates the likeness and difference in the love between women she enacts with her female interlocutor in 'When Our Lips Speak Together': 'We live by twos beyond all mirages, images, and mirrors. . . . Our resemblance does without semblances: for in our bodies, we are already the same. Touch yourself, touch me, you'll "see"' (1985*b*: 216).

There is a corresponding moment to Sapho's mirror scene in which Ovid's Sappho describes her dreams of Phaon:

> illic te invenio, quamvis regionibus absis;
> . . .
> oscula cognosco, quae tu committere linguae
>   aptaque consueras accipere, apta dare.
> blandior interdum verisque simillima verba
>   eloquor, et vigilant sensibus ora meis.
> ulteriora pudet narrare, sed omnia fiunt,
>   et iuvat, et siccae non licet esse mihi.

[In them I find you, though in space you are far away; . . . I recognize the kisses—close caresses of the tongue—which you were wont to take and wont to give. At times I fondle you, and utter words that seem almost the waking truth, and my lips keep vigil for my senses. Further I blush to tell, but all takes place; I feel the delight, and cannot rule myself]. (125, 129–34)

Sappho has switched from the past tense to the present in this passage in order to convey the illusion of Phaon's presence as she dreams. She describes the physical sensations of her fantasy as if they were real, she touches Phaon, she utters 'words that seem almost the waking truth', and if Ovid's Latin is more literally translated, she brings herself to orgasm. In Sappho's dream, her words function in the same way to make Phaon, a man, 'present', as Sapho's words and body do in Donne's poem to make Philaenis, a woman, 'present'. The likeness of their bodies is such that the required suspension of disbelief is something less than in the case of a woman and a man. When compared to the scene in Ovid then, Sapho's autoerotic mirror-gazing is less troublingly narcissistic than it is coincidentally useful to Donne's argument for perfect union. The danger of narcissistic everlastingness is in fact dissolved as Sapho moves to kiss her image in the glass and recognizes it is she and not Philaenis. Likewise in Ovid, Sappho wakes up with only her memories of Phaon's presence, symbolized by the pressed-down grass of the forest.

In her final lines, Sapho resumes her wooing through epideictic and again attempts to surpass stale Petrarchisms. Philaenis once again is thrust into the outer reaches of the galaxy, encompassing or 'outwear[ing]' time itself. The final image of the poem is of Philaenis 'comming neere' and thus keeping 'change' and 'sickness' from Sapho. The undecidability of the whole poem does not let up in the final line, for here is both a desire for the absolute, for mastery over time and space which constitutes a phallogocentric economy, and an evocation of the proximate which Irigaray advocates in 'This Sex Which Is Not One':

Woman always remains several, but she is kept from dispersion because the other is already within her and is autoerotically familiar to her. Which is not to say that she appropriates the other for herself, that she reduces it to her own property. Ownership and property are doubtless quite foreign to the feminine. At least sexually. But not *nearness*. Nearness so pronounced that it makes all discrimination of identity, and thus all forms of property, impossible. Woman derives pleasure from what is *so near that she cannot have it, nor have herself.* She herself enters into a ceaseless exchange of herself with the other without any possibility of identifying either. (1985*b*: 31)

Donne's Sapho seems to practice an exchange, a love of self and other through the other once she has '*cross[ed] back through the mirror that subtends all speculation*' (1985*b*: 77; Irigaray's italics). Sapho and Philaenis seem to relate as do the lovers in 'The Good-morrow' where the speaker says, 'Let us possesse our world, each hath one, and is one' (14). But the same thing occurs at the end of both poems: a sudden desire to 'freeze' the becoming and exchange between lovers. 'Sapho to Philaenis' ends with only the wished-for return of Philaenis; she and Sapho have yet to come 'neere', and when they do Sapho anticipates *no* change rather than *ex*-change. 'Love's Infiniteness' is another poem which expresses the split within Donne's imagination between a desire for an unchanging 'All' and the wonder of love which 'doth every day admit | New growth' (25–6). 'The Good-morrow' ends with a supposition: 'If our two loves be one, or, thou and I | Love so alike, that none doe slacken, none can die'. Catherine Belsey recognizes in her discussion of the crux at the end of 'The Good-morrow' that there is a direct conflict between desire's two imperatives: sustained intensity and fulfillment (1994: 143–6); the same conflict is carried over in Donne's exploration of homoerotics, because here Donne is unable, finally, to step across the threshold of the thinkable and comprehend that difference can bring us together in wonder as much as it always—inevitably yet creatively—separates us.

While Donne's homopoetics, to use Paula Blank's term, are still caught in the mirror of the Same and the Other of the Same, still frustrated rather than invigorated by the difference between Sapho and Philaenis, and if he still to some degree exploits lesbianism and the body of woman, Donne represents homoerotics in a way which Irigaray suggests can be useful in establishing an ethics of sexual difference, regardless of actual practices; that is, as a morphological model, one step in the process of realizing the gender relationship as intersubjective; hence, the possibility of an 'I, you' mode of relating rather than an 'I, not-I' 'dialogue of one'. It is precisely that we cannot 'forget the Hee and Shee' ('The Undertaking'), insofar as they signal the irreducible difference between subjectivities, if we wish to enter into fully creative dialogue with one another. In this sense, the poem is not 'about' sex at all, as Paula Blank argues in her discussion of the way sameness and difference ultimately transcend gender (1995). 'Sapho to Philaenis' shows that there is something 'other' to the feminine (and hence, to the masculine) besides its patriarchal status as merely Other of the Same; that it remains 'somewhere else', a 'residue' or excess which insists on troubling the borders of masculine amplitude. Donne criticism has assumed familiarity with the 'scene of representation' (see Irigaray 1985*b*: 68–85) with which phallogocentrism, Donne's 'masculine perswasive force' has obscured the entire landscape, so that if a poem like 'Sapho to Philaenis' does not fit, we remove it from our sights. I suggest that 'Sapho to Philaenis' points to another 'place' entirely unmapped, a 'new love . . . so far ahead of its time culturally that it is questionable whether even Donne himself could have understood all its potential implications' (Low 1993: 3). Anthony Low and I disagree as to the precise characterization of Donne's 'reinvention of love' as well as to the orientation of 'Sapho to Philaenis', but we agree that Donne did, almost, reinvent love. Low suggests Donne's 'private love' is 'idealized, Romantic, mutual, and transcendent in feeling', whereas I would point to Donne's rejection in at least some poems of 'either/or' modes for the 'both/and' modality of flesh and spirit, in something which comes closer to Irigaray's 'sensible transcendental' or what Kerrigan suggests 'we might term, thinking of early Heidegger, a "fundamental ontology" of love, a revelation of being-in-love through the charted voyage of its temporal possibilities' (1987: 13). Donne's efforts to 'forget the hee and shee' when he employs an image of neutrality between lovers in love poems such as 'The Canonization', are to erase an aspect of human relating which he elsewhere insists upon, but they might also be read as what Irigaray calls 'crossing through the neuter—the space-time of remission of the polemic' so as to 'set up the return or reappearance of God or of the other' (1993*a*: 147); a means of reconfiguring the self and other in a relationship which is horizontal rather than hierarchical. One senses that in writing 'Sapho to Philaenis' and so many of his love poems, Donne comes very close to recognizing that the 'mystery of relations between lovers is more terrible but infinitely less deadly than the destruction of submitting to sameness' (Irigaray 1993*a*: 191).

# 3

# 'The Mother in the Hungry Grave': Marriage, Murder, and the Maternal

> Therefore shall a man leave his father and his mother, and shall cleave unto his wife: and they shall be one flesh.
>
> (Genesis 2: 24)

> The whole of our western culture is based upon the murder of the mother.
>
> (Luce Irigaray)

## I. INTRODUCTION

From a startling if ultimately ambiguous poem which shows Donne at his most 'original', we move to texts which reveal Donne at his most conservative. This chapter explores Donne's articulation of the maternal feminine or 'woman-for-man' in some of his writings on marriage. I will consider Donne's answers to the questions, 'Why was woman made?' (in the first place), and 'How is woman made?' (within the ritual of consummation on the wedding night). My texts are Donne's references in his sermons to the marriage 'model' in Genesis (Gen.) 2: 24 and his wedding sermon on Gen. 2: 18, the verse which begins the story of Eve's creation: 'And the Lord God said, It is not good that the man should be alone; I will make him an help meet for him.'[1] I will then offer a close reading of Donne's 'Epithalamium [Made at Lincoln's Inn]'. How does Donne construct the feminine in his interpretation of the creation of the first woman, Eve, 'Mother of all Living', and in his representation of the subsequent

---

[1] Unless otherwise indicated, scripture quotations are taken from the King James Authorized Version (1611), hereafter cited as (AV).

transformation and engendering of Eve's daughters, crystallized in the Lincoln's Inn refrain: 'To night put on perfection and a Womans name'?[2] In her recent book, *The Renaissance Bible*, Deborah Shuger observes that the Bible in the English Renaissance was the central cultural text, which meant not just that everyone read or listened to it in church, but that it was 'reshaped according to self-conscious exegetic and mythopoeic/literary procedures. . . . In such gentile *midrashim*, the ancient stories served as a primary locus for synthetic, speculative, and symbolic production' (1994: 2–3). We have seen how Donne 'reshaped' the Muse and Sappho. Let us now turn to Donne's articulation of Eve, the archetypal woman for Donne's Christian audience, and to the function of the feminine in Christian marriage. Donne's strategies, I suggest, can be illuminated by Irigaray's statement that the 'whole of our western culture is based upon the murder of the mother';[3] that is, the maternal feminine or 'woman-for-man' is both the only identity prescribed for women, and yet, at the same time, even this identity and the debt owed to it is buried in and by discourse and consigned to '*internal exile*'.

There is nothing particularly interesting in pointing out exclusionary and misogynistic language in seventeenth-century sermons; I am concerned in this chapter not to show the obvious —that Donne participated in the perpetuation of patriarchal culture—so much as I am to show how he does so, how he erases the cultural debt to the maternal feminine even as he articulates the purpose of woman's creation as being, precisely, a wife and mother. As James Turner observes, the 'need to make women "naturally" inferior simply hangs in isolation, beyond logic and beyond even the Logos, as a pure ideological imperative' (1993*a*:

---

[2] Donne 1995*b*: p. 88, l. 60. Hereafter all quotations of epithalamiums are taken from this edition and referred to by line number. The order I follow in this chapter is that of 'historical' chronicity pertaining to the creation of woman, rather than the order in which Donne wrote his works. Donne wrote the epithalamium long before any of his sermons.

[3] 'Women-Mothers, the Silent Substratum of the Social Order', trans. David Macey in Irigaray 1991*a*: 47; first published as an interview in *Le Corps-à-corps avec la mère* (Montreal: Editions de la pleine lune, 1981). Irigaray's essay, 'Le Corps-à-corps avec la mère', has been translated by David Macey in Irigaray 1991*a*: 34–46; and by Gillian C. Gill in Irigaray 1993*c*: 9–21. In the essay Irigaray explores the implications and metaphorical applications of a matricide more ancient than the patricide Freud identifies in the Oedipal story: Clytemnestra's murder by her son, Orestes, in Aeschylus' *Oresteia*.

100). Understanding the degree of illogic in the operation of patriarchal discourse at various historical moments in Western culture allows us to go beyond recognizing misogynist attitudes. Feminist literary criticism of male-authored texts has for the most part focused on the 'presence' in the 'present absence' which is 'woman'—that is, the various types of the feminine which have been constructed, often misogynistically, for use by the patriarchy—with the aim of recovering a more authentic feminine. Once the misogynistic constructs are removed, however, there is still only an 'absence' waiting to be symbolized and come into its own. Donne describes God in a sermon as 'like us', i.e. human beings, in that 'he takes it worse to be slighted, to be neglected, to be left out, then to be actually injur'd' (i. 195). Likewise, it is worse for women to be 'neglected' and without access to the symbolic order, than to be 'injur'd' by misogyny.

In my exploration of Donne's representations of woman as wife and mother, this chapter will examine two distinct genres, the sermon and the epithalamium, which originate in divergent traditions and which are directed to different audiences, but both of which nevertheless serve, as public forms of discourse, to re-inscribe patriarchal gender constructs.[4] The 'Epithalamium [Made at Lincoln's Inn]' was written much earlier than Donne's other two epithalamia for Princess Elizabeth's marriage to Frederick, Count Palatine, in February 1613, and for the scandal-ridden marriage of the Earl of Somerset to Frances Howard in December 1613. It is somewhat unique in that it does not seem to have been written for an actual wedding, and is, at least in part, a parody of Spenser's *Epithalamion* (1595).[5] Almost certainly directed towards a male coterie rather than a larger public, the libertine 'Epithalamium [Made at Lincoln's Inn]' offers us a unique opportunity to examine anxieties inherent in the genre but which are more easily buried beneath layers of rhetorical convention and decorum when a real couple is the subject of the poem. Implicit in my argument which follows then, is that the epithalamium and the sermon are

---

[4] The authority of the sermon as an instrument of patriarchal culture is obvious. See n. 24, below. Virginia Tufte states of the epithalamium as a generic type that it 'deals with marriage as an institution and as an ideal' (1970: 30). Likewise, Heather Dubrow notes that in epithalamia, sexuality is 'constructed not as a self-indulgent, uncontrollable pleasure but rather as a socially sanctioned and even mandated responsibility' (1990: 25).

[5] See my discussion of Novarr and Dubrow on these issues, below.

not the work of two separate 'minds'—Jack Donne the rakish poet
and John Donne the priest—as is often implicit or explicit in the
separation of Donne's religious and secular writing in the discussions of Donne scholars, a tendency which in recent years has
become less frequent.[6] Rather, epithalamium and sermon function
as two registers of one patriarchal discourse; they are two means to
a single end. In a discussion of an epithalamium and a sermon, I
will show that the libertine's and the divine's constructions of the
feminine stem from the same root: whether revelling in sexual
relations, circumscribing, or condemning them, patriarchy seeks
to contain sexuality and the feminine in order to perpetuate its
own hegemony.

A comparison of Donne's representation of marriage in different genres reveals another tension which, however, cannot be
fully explored here. Catherine Belsey observes that marriage in
the sixteenth and seventeenth centuries becomes 'the site of a
paradoxical struggle to create a private realm and to take control of
it in the interests of the public good' (1993: 130). Belsey's general
summation is, I will show, applicable to the particulars of Donne's
writings on marriage. Donne's particular 'paradoxical struggle'
seems especially to lie between his use of marriage as metaphor in
the love poems and his prescription of Christian marriage in his
sermons, despite his recognition in a sermon that 'God is *Love*,
and the *Holy Ghost* is amorous in his *Metaphors*; everie where his
*Scriptures* abound with the notions of *Love*, of *Spouse*, and *Husband*,
and *Marriadge Songs*, and *Marriadge Supper*, and *Marriadge-Bedde*'
(vii. 87). We see far more often the essence of marriage as defined
in Gen. 2: 24—two becoming one—as a liberating force in the
poetry or in the sermons where marriage is used as allegory or
metaphor to describe our relationship as humans with the
divine.[7] In contrast, the reality of marriage presented in all three of

---

[6] Annabel Patterson notes that the two 'personae' in Donne's famous letter (Donne
1977: 21–2) have each 'attracted different schools of criticism' (1983: 39). The split
is still resonating even as it is being resisted; for example, P. M. Oliver's introduction
to his book, *Donne's Religious Writing*, is titled 'The Two Donnes' (1997). Scholars
who discuss both the poetry and prose are Kremen 1972; Carey 1990; Mann 1985/6
and 1992; Low 1993.

[7] But see Low's assertion that Donne's 'naturally aggressive, masculine personality
made it hard for him to accept the feminine role the trope demanded in loving God'
(1993: 87). 'Donne simply cannot submit to the woman's passive role' (81), unless it
is as a woman who must be violently subdued, as in 'Batter my heart'.

Donne's wedding sermons is one of necessary constriction, a confining of desires. Donne's sermon on Gen. 2: 18 is about the giving up of 'private respects' for 'publique good', whereas the recognition of his desire in the love poems to create a private space, a 'little room' for the lovers, has long been a critical commonplace.[8] The middle ground where this struggle between private and public is most apparent is in the epithalamia.

The tendency of Donne scholars to isolate Donne's religious and secular works from each other is not a unique phenomenon. Shuger notes a related tendency in discussions of religious texts in general: the curious 'disciplinary segregation' in 'modern Renaissance scholarship, which, for complex political, ideological, and institutional reasons, brackets off religious materials from cultural analysis and vice versa' (1994: 2; see also her introduction). While she notes that there has been much work 'devoted to the religious backgrounds of English Renaissance literature', this work 'usually conceived of religion as a circumscribed category unrelated to the constructions of gender, subjectivity, sexuality, power, nationalism, and so forth' (205).[9] In her excellent corrective to the indiscriminate quotation of sermon passages out of context, Jeanne Shami makes a similar point, that Donne's sermons are used as straightforward 'reference texts' to provide glosses on Donne's poetry and other writings, and are considered themselves to be 'less valuable as cultural performances' (1995: 384). Shami and Shuger remind us of what might seem an obvious point: that sacred texts not only influenced culture, but that their interpretation was influenced by culture. Of Genesis in particular, Arnold Williams recognizes the tendency to 'misread' extrapolations—what he calls the 'Genesis material'—rather than the few pages of actual text (1948: 3). Donne himself alludes to the 'infinite' commentary on Genesis in a sermon (ix. 48). J. Turner uses the term 'eisegesis', or 'the process of reading

---

[8] Lindsay Mann, always a careful reader of Donne's poetry and prose, differs from my reading of Donne in that he finds greater 'consistency of principles' in Donne's views on marriage from the early love poems to the sermons (1992: 111–32).

[9] Obviously there has been an enormous amount of work done on the religious background of Donne's poetry, and on the political circumstances and implications of his early Catholicism and conversion to Anglicanism. The construction of gender in Donne's religious works beyond his Holy Sonnets, 'Batter my heart, three person'd God', 'Show me deare Christ', and the *Anniversaries*, is garnering more attention. See Sabine 1992: 1–110.

meanings *into* a text' (1993*a*: p. v) to describe responses to the 'indeterminacy' of Genesis. In my exploration of Donne's eisegesis of Gen. 2: 18, I will show that this process of 'reading into' results in a writing out or erasing; a particularly clear example of the 'pretermission' of woman from the narrative of her very creation.

Donne uses the word 'pretermit' five times in his marriage sermon. Its denotations and connotations illuminate both my specific argument and Irigaray's larger critique of the dereliction of the feminine in discourse. From the Latin, *praetermittere*, 'to let pass, omit, overlook', the applications of 'pretermit' range widely as to the magnitude of the omission. For example, the *OED* lists the primary meaning as follows: 'To leave out of a narrative; not to notice, mention, insert or include'. Depending on what was left out, this use suggests something like an oversight, unlike the theological sense which means 'to pass over in electing to salvation' (*OED* 1.b). The term also denotes serious legal and economic consequences: 'To omit mention of (a descendant or natural heir) in a will'. A further definition also suggests wilful omission and hence, fault: 'To allow to pass without notice or regard; to overlook intentionally' (*OED* 2). I have defined 'pretermit' in such detail because we will see how Donne uses it so deliberately in a sermon which yet epitomizes patriarchal contra-diction: he explains the reason why God created a female, and yet subscribes to the exclusion or pretermission of that female from full participation in her own creation and creativity, despite the different story told in the original Hebrew text of Genesis. Again, none of this is surprising, but the 'what', the misogyny of patriarchy, has been extraordinarily successful in distracting us from the 'how' and thus the real 'limits of the thinkable' for the Renaissance. We must go back to the misogynist texts, dig deeper and examine 'the *operation of the "grammar"* of each figure of discourse, its syntactic laws or requirements, its imaginary configurations, its metaphoric networks, and also, of course, what it does not articulate at the level of utterance: *its silences*' (Irigaray 1985*b*: 75).

The first section of this chapter will establish a brief contemporary context for Donne's writings on marriage. I will then briefly outline exegetical issues relevant to Donne's reading of the 'marriage model' in Gen. 2: 24 and his wedding sermon on Gen. 2: 18. What was his knowledge of Hebrew and how closely did he scrutinize the original text? Whether Donne in his study of biblical exegesis and ancient languages was aware of the interpretive bias applied to the original text is an important question. I draw on Mieke Bal's brilliant analysis of St Paul's precedent-setting inter-pretation of the creation myth in 1 Timothy 2: 11–14 (1986: 317–37). Closely reading the original Hebrew text and building on Phyllis Trible's ground-breaking feminist hermeneutics in *God and the Rhetoric of Sexuality* (1978), Bal argues that St Paul attributes an erroneous priority to maleness and then attaches a superior value to this male priority. According to Paul, even before Adam and Eve eat the apple and subvert God's original order, a hierarchical relationship is established in pre-lapsarian Eden as 'natural' and divinely ordained between men and women. Bal thus identifies what she calls the 'retrospective fallacy' in Paul's reading of Genesis: the projection of 'the accomplished characters Adam and Eve . . . onto their previous stages of particularization' (319); in other words, gender is projected onto a being which initially is not even sexualized and then onto two beings who attain sexual identity at the same time upon their simultaneous emergence from the undifferentiated creature, and to whom, only later in the story, are gender roles assigned. The creature which God forms from the dust of the earth is 'as yet only a species, not an individual' and furthermore, 'it' is not even androgynous or bisexual (as in Aristophanes' myth in Plato's *Symposium*) 'since sexuality is still to be created' (Bal 1986: 321). Thus, according to Bal, when Paul declares, 'I suffer not a woman to teach, not to usurp authority over the man; but to be in silence', and gives as his reason, 'For Adam was first formed, then Eve', he is wrong in his facts, his logic, and his value judgements (317).

Bal's argument would be irrelevant to Donne's seventeenth-century sermon except that Donne seems to indicate an awareness of these discrepancies in the Hebrew, and yet he is able to capital-ize on the ambiguities in the original text itself as well as those which arise in translation so as to perpetuate traditional interpreta-tions. The whole premise of Donne's reading of Gen. 2: 18, as we shall see, depends on the application of St Paul's retrospective fallacy whereby when the text says, 'It is not good, that man should be alone', Donne exploits the original Hebrew and the Vulgate Latin and reads 'male' for 'man' or 'creature'. Donne's use of a term denoting a sexed being is made despite his apparent knowledge that the Hebrew original of Genesis denotes either a sexually undifferentiated creature (at 2: 18) or an androgynous creature (at 5: 2), although it is used in other parts of the Hebrew text to indicate the male creature who is eventually named 'Adam'. If we use Alastair Fowler's classification of the logical phases of criticism—construction, interpretation, evaluation (1982: 256)— it is with Donne's construction of the original text (recognizing that he is following a tradition of over a thousand years) that I take issue, for while we cannot expect Donne to situate himself in relation to the text as we are situated in the twentieth century, we can hold him to standards of accurate (as opposed to selective) translation. In a passage on the dangers of controversy, Donne states, 'It is the Text that saves us; the interlineary glosses, and the marginal notes, and the *variae lectiones*, controversies and perplexities, undo us. . . . It is the hand of man that induces obscurities' (*Sermons*, iii. 208). Why does Donne not give the close attention to the discrepancies between *hā'ādām/hominem*/man which he gives to other words in those same verses, and to other Hebrew words in the early Genesis chapters?

It is important to reiterate both Bal's caution that the point of establishing the practice of a 'retrospective fallacy' is not to assert 'anachronistically a "feminist" content of the Bible' (318), and my paraphrase of Irigaray on Freud: 'It is not a matter of naively accusing [Donne] as if he were a "bastard"'. Ancient Hebrew society was pervasively misogynist. Jacobean England was pervasively misogynist. But Bal observes that 'the confrontation between the extant mythical text and the documents of its later use, like "Paul's" version, and the subsequent innumerable ones which [through eisegesis] produce the myth as it still functions, displays a chronological evolution of patriarchy which contains a paradox' (318): the supposed evolution of Western society towards less sexist practices and attitudes when in fact the opposite is true, thus providing, says Bal, 'insight into the dynamic nature of myth, into the actual state of sexual ideology, and into the necessity of *reversal* as a political move' (1986: 318; see Irigaray 1985*b*: 79–80). Donne occupies his own unique position in this 'evolutionary' myth reading and myth construction and it is worth exploring. As J. Turner suggests, 'exegesis of the creation of Eve depends on, and helps to determine, the politics of gender, and . . . the ideological inscription of "Eve" into "woman" was different in kind from that of Adam into man' (1993*a*: 97).

Just as Bal observes that 'it seems rather discouraging that we have to appeal to ancient Jewish Patriarchs to defend our [female] character against today's progressive atheists', so might students of Donne be disheartened to discover in his Nethersole[10] wedding sermon such an intensely misogynistic version of the creation of woman. Even in the anti-feminist tradition of patristics such as Jerome and Tertullian upon which Donne obviously draws (rather than Puritan companionate formulations), his sermon is relentless in its demolition of Eve and the feminine. If Donne's imagination gave rise to a poem like 'Sapho to Philaenis', which, among other things, separates love and sexuality quite deliberately from the procreative function, why did Donne not apply his powers of original thinking and of revision to Genesis? 'Far from being unthinkable . . . the fundamental equality of woman could certainly be conceived as part of the legacy of Genesis' (Turner 1993*a*: 108). Jeanne Shami explains that the main goal of Renaissance biblical exegesis is 'the ethical and moral reform of the listener. Its aim is what Donne calls "nearness," the recognition by the audience that the preacher "speaks to my conscience, as though he had been behinde the hangings when I sinned, and as though he had read the book of the day of Judgement already"' (Shami 1995: 391; see *Sermons*, iii. 142). A more accurate reading of Genesis seems to be 'unthinkable', then—even to the priest who invokes the 'nearness' of congregation and preacher and to the poet who evoked the 'neere[ness]' of Sapho and Philaenis—in the sense of being politically inexpedient and/or culturally undesirable; as Protestant preacher and then Dean of Paul's, Donne was a servant of the state speaking publicly and officially.

In the last part of the chapter I will suggest that the 'Epithalamium [Made at Lincoln's Inn]' enacts the same paradox as does Donne's sermon, whereby at the very moment 'woman' comes into being (*'To night put on perfection, and a womans name'*), she is symbolically murdered. Read psychoanalytically, the poem dramatizes the 'trial of intercourse' which is the man's encounter with the mother and with death, especially in his devirgination of

---

[10] I am aware that by following the critical convention of referring to the sermon preached at the wedding of Frances Nethersole and Lucy Goodyer as 'the Nethersole sermon' I appear to be perpetuating woman's absence from the inscription of what is supposedly her very 'becoming', but in drawing attention to her absence, which is real, this note hopefully shifts the balance of her 'present absence'.

the bride. The 'perfecting' or making whole of the bride involves a man's confrontation of the 'hole' or 'wound' of the (castrated) woman/mother; by surviving 'the horror of closeness to that absence of sex/penis, that mortification of sex that is evoked by woman' (Irigaray 1985*a*: 27), man achieves mastery. In patriarchal modes of discourse, representing the union of male and female bodies thus constitutes the most dangerous moment in which the contradictions and aporias upon which patriarchal discourse are built regarding masculine and feminine identity most threaten to expose their own failure of logic. In other words, the most crucial moment of definition is also the moment at which the desired definition is most precarious. The writings of the Renaissance and specifically the works of Donne seem to me examples in which this phenomenon is particularly apparent: the paradoxical desire to have access to and yet be protected from the feminine in all its phantasized manifestations.

## II. MARRIAGE IN RENAISSANCE ENGLAND: A BRIEF CONTEXT

There has been much debate over whether or not Renaissance Protestant formulations of the 'companionate marriage' improved the lives of real women.[11] My concern is not with the marriage debate, past or present, but with that aspect on which there could be no debate: that on the basis of biblical authority, the only role prescribed for an English Renaissance woman was as wife and mother. Maclean concludes that religious doctrine was the greatest obstacle to any tolerance of roles for women outside marriage (1988: 84–5). The contemporary paradigm maid/wife/widow, plus whore, defined a woman solely in relation to men according to her marital or sexual status. Conspicuously absent from this paradigm is 'mother', a term which implies much greater female power. The author 'I.S.' in a poem praising Thomas Overbury's 'A Wife' (see below) writes: 'For woman (in the abstract) hath no more | Than hath the wife, the widow, maiden, whore' (Overbury 1968: A3). In the sympathetic treatise, *The Lawes Resolutions*

---

[11] The amount of critical literature exploring marriage in the Renaissance is vast. See e.g. Joan Kelly 1977; Fitz [Woodbridge] 1980: 1–22; Dubrow 1986; Valerie Wayne's introduction in Tilney 1992: 13–38.

*of Womens Rights; or, The Lawes* Provision for Woemen (1632), the
anonymous author states of women: 'All of them are understood
either married or to be maried and their desires or [*sic*] subject to
their husband, I know no remedy though some women can shift it
well enough' (B3ᵛ). As we saw in the Introduction, sexual difference as it has been constructed participates in the binary fallacy
that one term of a pair is not only the negation of the other, rather
than something in and of itself, but subordinate to it. Hence 'a
married Woman perhaps may doubt whether shee bee either none
or no more than halfe a person' (*Lawes Resolution*: B4ʳ). Marriage is
thus a union of men and 'not-men' for the purpose of (pro)creat-
ing more men to supply a culture of 'men-amongst-themselves'
(Irigaray 1994: 110). Irigaray's terms make clear the paradox:
women have no identity outside of their marital status, but even
so, they do not even enter into the equation.

    Another example of the assimilation of woman from the work
of a contemporary, indeed a friend, of Donne's, is Thomas Overbury's extraordinarily popular poem, *A Wife*. The final lines of
Overbury's poem read:

> My *Wife* is my *Adopted-Selfe*, and Shee
> As Mee, so what I love, to Love must frame.
> For when by Marriage both in one concurre,
> Woman converts to Man, not Man to her. (1968: 61)

Even as the language of his final line lets slip an identity prior to
'Wife', Overbury's unequivocal 'dialogue of one' makes explicit
the operation of two becoming one in a patriarchal society, a
process which Donne formulates more idealistically, for example,
in 'The Canonization'. Notably, marriage is nowhere mentioned
as the bond between lovers in Donne's poem where 'we two being
one . . . | So, to one neutrall thing both sexes fit'. Overbury's 'one'
is 'Man': Donne's 'one' is a third, 'neutral thing'. But Donne,
unlike Overbury, is not prescribing a relationship constrained by
social roles. Indeed, he is explicitly rejecting the imposition of the
social on the relationship between himself and his beloved, although he asserts, as the central paradox of the poem, the sacred
nature of their profane love. Donne in the love poems is sometimes willing to 'forget the Hee and Shee' ('The Undertaking',
l. 20) in his quest for unity. Whether this forgetting of both the
'Hee and Shee' is another Neoplatonic elision of the feminine or

the use of the neuter as an 'alchemical site of the sublimation of "genitality"' (Irigaray 1993*a*: 14) is a question I can only raise in this context. Far less ambiguous, Overbury insists in *A Wife* that 'Shee' be forgotten or 'convert[ed]'. At the end of his 'Character of a Good Woman', he again concludes, 'her chiefest vertue is a good husband. For *Shee* is *Hee*' (65).

The 'both in one' mystical union which is marriage becomes in Overbury's formulation a conversion or assimilation of woman into the Lacanian 'Name-of-the-Father': as mother, she 'converts' her body into sons to ensure the continuance of the patronym and its property. This is why there can be no return to the mother, the first home, '[e]xcept in the father's name' (Irigaray 1985*a*: 353). Overbury writes:

> *God* to *each Man a private Woman* gave,
> That in that *Center* his *desires* might stint,
> That he a *comfort like himselfe* might have,
> And that on her *his like* he might *imprint*.
>     *Double* is Womans *use*, part of their end
>     Doth on *this Age*, part on the *next* depend.

Overbury alludes to the three doctrinally sanctioned purposes of post-lapsarian marriage: as a remedy for lust, for companionship, and for procreation, and he makes explicit an implicit andro-centrism. Woman's 'use' is for man's desire, to be a comfort 'like himself', and to perpetuate 'his like'. In Overbury's formulation then, one might say 'Likenesse begets . . . strange selfe flatterie'. Overbury's 'wife' is 'that Center' whose 'Centrique part' (Donne 'Love's Progress', line 36) is appropriated to the exclusion of her subjectivity. Yet that 'Center' is also de-centred through the syntax of the last two lines, so that we hear that 'Womans *use*' depends on '*this Age*' and 'the *next*', rather than that male posterity is, in fact, indebted to the maternal body. Aemilia Lanyer points out this indebtedness in her address to the reader in *Salve deus rex Judæorum* when she upbraids 'evill disposed men, who forgetting they were borne of women, nourished of women, and that if it were not by the means of women, they would be quite extinguished out of the world, and a finall ende of them all, doe like Vipers deface the wombes wherein they were bred' (1993: 48).

If Overbury's works exemplify an oppressive attitude towards woman, her primary function was, even in some of the more progressive writings of the Renaissance, asserted to be that of procreation. Two influential works are worth mentioning here: Cornelius Agrippa's 1531 treatise, *Of the Nobilitie and excellencye of woman kynde* (translated into English in 1542 by David Clapham) and Baldassare Castiglione's *The Courtier* (translated into English by Thomas Hoby and published in 1561). Agrippa's treatise contains assertions about the nature of woman which are, as Woodbridge notes, almost uniquely revolutionary (1986: 38–45): primarily his recognition that woman's subordination is a result of custom rather than nature; in other words, that woman's subordination is constructed (see Aughterson 1995: 265). Erasmus's Fabulla also asserts woman's oppressor is 'custom' rather than any natural inferiority in his colloquy, 'The New Mother' (1965: 270). But Agrippa's and Erasmus's proto-feminist declarations are expressed in the service of sophistry. Woodbridge observes that while Agrippa as 'a realist in the study of sexual politics' was 'capable of laying philosophic foundations for modern feminism', 'in the early Tudor controversy, we are not in the presence of Renaissance Attitudes Toward Women. We are in the presence of Art' (1986: 45).[12]

Agrippa also declares, 'the greattest & chiefest offyce and duetye of woman, is to conceyve' (1542: Sig. C). The misogynist, Gaspar, in Baldassare Castiglione's *The Courtier* makes the same argument: 'the world hath no profit by women, but for gettinge of children. But the like is not of men, whiche governe Cities, armies, and doe so manye other waightye matters, the whiche (sins you will so have it) I will not dispute, how women coulde do, yt sufficeth they do it not' (1994: 248).[13] Gaspar has just listened to Julian's catalogue of *exempla*, in which he cites female queens, warriors, poets, and teachers, yet Gaspar acknowledges no contradiction in his response, which, in the final two phrases, contains an admission that women's function is a matter of custom rather than nature. Cesar postpones his response to Gaspar in women's defence: 'I will not nowe speake of the profit that the worlde hath by

---

[12] Woodbridge's analysis of Agrippa and the formal controversy is thus more qualified in its assertions of 'feminist' intent than is Constance Jordan's, who considers Agrippa's to be 'the most explicitly feminist text to be published in England in the first half of the century', an anthropological 'critique of patriarchy' and its legal, economic and linguistic oppression of women (1990: 122–33).

[13] Woodbridge suggests Castiglione and Agrippa might have been directly familiar with one another's work (1986: 71 n. 5).

women beeside the bearinge of children, for it is well inoughe declared howe necessarye they be, not onlye to oure beeinge, but also to oure well beeinge (249–50). Cesar does proceed later on to provide a long list of the ways in which the world 'profits' by women, just as Julian had done earlier, but at this point in the dialogue, the effect is one whereby both detractor and defender leave women—aside from their role as mother—unsymbolized, and thus together affirm the primary purpose of women in bearing children.

Thomas Overbury's language makes the same distinction between being and well-being as does Cesar, but with different conclusions:

> *Man* did but the *well being* of his life
> From *Woman* take, her *Being* she from *Man*,
> And therefore *Eve* created was a Wife,
> And at the end of all, her *Sex* began:
>     *Mariage* their object is; their *Being* then,
>     And now *Perfection*, they receive from *Men*.

Overbury alludes here to God's declaration at Gen. 2: 18 but denies woman's maternal role by using Eve's creation from Adam (part of Paul's retrospective fallacy) as the model for all women in his final couplet. Despite the temporal indicator, 'then', Overbury's syntax—'then, | And now'—implies that women still receive their Being and their 'Perfection' from men. Ironically, Overbury (unconsciously) transmits the original Hebrew correctly in the line, 'at the end of all, her *Sex* began'—the very last thing to occur was the gender assignation of the two creatures—but of course Overbury is referring to the fact that Eve was the last of the creatures to be created by God.

To conclude this very brief consideration of Renaissance marriage ideology and its simultaneous circumscription and erasure of woman in her role as mother, I want to point out that the occasional proto-feminist assertions regarding women which humanist writers such as Agrippa and Castiglione made within their texts were not taken up by male writers of Donne's generation. And works by women writers such as Aemilia Lanyer's *Salve deus rex Judæorum* (1611), or Elizabeth Cary's *The Tragedy of Mariam* (1613), while unquestionably revolutionary in other aspects, were more ambiguous about the authority of husbands in marriage.[14] This phenomenon suggests that the cultural strategy whereby unorthodox views were contained within the dominant ideology—as rhetorical devices rather than political statements stemming from a fully developed ideology—was, on the whole, successful.[15] What is in the story of Eve's creation and the first marriage in Genesis that requires containment and how does Donne do so?

### III. DONNE'S KNOWLEDGE OF HEBREW

A brief review of translation differences in the Bibles Donne quotes from, as well as an understanding of Donne's grasp of Hebrew must precede my analysis of his references to Gen. 2: 24 and the sermon on Gen. 2: 18. My argument concerns three Hebrew words used in the Gen. 2 account of the creation of Adam and Eve. The Hebrew words are *hā-'ādām* ('the earth creature'[16]), *'îš* ('man') and *'iššâ* ('woman'). For now, I want to establish only that *hā-'ādām*, composed of the definite article, *hā-*, and the common noun, *ādām*, denotes a creature of unspecified gender in the verses I will be considering. The nouns, *'îš*, and *'iššâ*, refer to the sexualized human beings who emerge from the *hā-'ādām* in Gen. 2: 22–3, and who are then assigned gender roles later in Gen. 3. I want to determine whether Donne was aware of these distinctions made in Hebrew—between a being whose sex is not signified, and the sexualized humans who were later named Adam and Eve—and whether he then distinguished the Hebrew from the Latin and English translations which he used. Is Donne's interpretation of Gen. 2: 18 and his construction of gender based on it an effect of his imperfect grasp of Hebrew? An unconscious inevitability which the semantic structure of English allows (indeed encourages)? A pretermission or deliberate omission of woman?

Potter and Simpson tally Donne's references to Hebrew words

---

[14] See 'Eves Apologie', spoken by Pilate's wife (Lanyer 1993: ll. 759–60, 809–10, 825–30). For an assessment of Elizabeth Cary's ideal of submissiveness, see L. Schleiner 1994: 178.

[15] See Valerie Wayne's discussion of one of the unsuccessful containments of 'emergent' views of marriage by the dominant ideology in Edmund Tilney's 1568 dialogue, *The Flower of Friendship* (Tilney 1992: 69–92).

[16] I follow Mieke Bal in using Phyllis Trible's translation of *hā'ādām* throughout.

in his sermons at about 140 passages and conclude, 'Donne took much more interest in Hebrew studies than in Greek, and his knowledge of the language was more extensive' (*Sermons*, x. 307). They include a list of Hebrew words on which Donne commented in an Appendix (x. 329–44), *Adam* and *ish* (*'îš*)[17] among them. Don Cameron Allen suggests relativity is key, however. Allen's analysis leads him to conclude that while most of Donne's Hebrew references seem to have come from the Hebrew Bible, and that there are even instances where Donne corrects the Latin Vulgate using the Hebrew original, 'Donne had "small Hebrew and less Greek."'[18] Certainly when one compares Donne's biblical scholarship to that of someone like Lancelot Andrewes, who was a principal in translating the Pentateuch for the 1611 Authorized Version, or that of Joseph Hall, Donne is clearly less than an expert Hebraist. However, in a recent article, Eugene Hill suggests Donne thought carefully, even originally, about the Hebrew language, so much so that 'it was Donne who first attributed [moral] significance' to an otherwise commonplace observation: the lack of a present tense in Biblical Hebrew.[19]

Donne's interest in Hebrew rather than Greek, such as it was, was in accord with the greater interest in Hebrew shown in the sixteenth and early seventeenth centuries (at least by theologians and linguists). Deborah Shuger notes that 'the largest number of entries in Renaissance biblical commentaries discuss philological matters' (1994: 29). Rediscovered Jewish commentaries such as the Targums (Aramaic paraphrases of the Old Testament) and the Midrash (rabbinic commentaries on the Old Testament) were responsible for this new wealth of information: 'Access to these

[17] As Potter and Simpson note, 'Donne's system of transliteration is not quite the same as that used by modern scholars' (*Sermons*, x. 309). When discussing these Hebrew words, I will use the modern transliteration in my own textual discussion and include the modern transliteration in brackets following Donne's transliteration when I refer to his text.

[18] Allen 1943a: 213–14, 223. Allen suggests that 'we should be more cautious in applying the words *scholarly* or *learned* to Donne the divine' (229), for Donne is unsystematic at best: 'he selects his texts as he pleases, . . . he is governed by no particular preferences, and . . . he does not seem to make the slightest attempt to secure the best reading' (228). See Ch. 2, n. 9, for further comment.

[19] Hill notices that Donne finds '*unity in difference*: he assumes that he lives in the same world as the Psalmist, and that the Biblical language is structured in such a way as to point up the unity of the two men's experience' (1987: 197; my emphasis). For Donne on Hebrew grammar, see *Sermons*, vii. 62; 252; ix. 335.

texts marks the critical rupture between Renaissance biblical scholarship and patristic exegesis. After the mid-sixteenth century
the Church Fathers, still principal authorities for Erasmus, were
gradually replaced by Hebraic texts as sources for . . . philological
and cultural interpretation. . . . The majority of Renaissance exegetes were professors of Hebrew or Oriental philology'
(32–3).[20] Translated with extensive marginal commentary by
Marian exiles on the Continent just prior to Elizabeth's reign, the
Geneva Bible alludes to the new resources in its address to the
reader. Donne would have used several aids in his interpretation
of scripture: the polyglot Bibles printed in the sixteenth-century
(with parallel texts in Hebrew, Greek, Chaldaic, and Latin); Tre-
mellius's sixteenth-century Latin translation of the Old Testament
canonical books; some of the sixteenth century Latin grammars of
the Hebrew language; rabbinical and other biblical commentaries
such as the popular commentaries by Pareus and Pererius. Thus, a
century of biblical exegesis which eagerly made use of the new
knowledge of Hebrew and other Semitic languages preceded
Donne, so that one might expect close attention to be given to the
original text of the early chapters of Genesis, and that Donne
would be equally concerned with accuracy.

Potter and Simpson summarize Donne's usual method of biblical exegesis: 'It was always to the Latin text that Donne first
turned, and where the Authorized Version differed from the Vulgate he examined the Hebrew to see whether there was justification there for the difference' (x. 311).[21] Interpreting Gen. 2:
18, Donne turns to the Vulgate to support the Authorized Version.
The *AV* reads,

And the Lord God said, It is not good that the man should be alone; I will
make him an help meet for him.

The Vulgate reads,

Dixit quoque Dominus Deus: Non est bonum esse hominem solum:
faciamus ei adiutorium simile sibi.

While the *AV* remains ambiguous at best, the Vulgate translates the Hebrew term, *hā'ādām*, which in this verse is sexually

---

[20] See her first chapter on New Testament scholarship in the Renaissance, which
lists the emergence of exegetical tools which were no less relevant to Old Testament
hermeneutics, esp. pp. 33–4.

[21] But see Allen's opinion of Donne's haphazardness, n. 18, above.

undifferentiated (Trible 1978: 98), as the 'neutral' or 'comprehensive' *hominem*. If the Vulgate had wanted to denote a specifically male human being here, it could have used *virem*. Donne does not, however, take into account the distinctions between 'man', and either the Latin *hominem* or the Hebrew *hā'ādām*. Yet Donne is scrupulous on another point in this same verse: the discrepancy between plural and singular forms of the verb, 'to make', in the original Hebrew and its translations:

> in this remedy of Gods provision, the woman, God proceeded not, as he did in the making of man; it is not *Faciamus*, with such a counsell, such a deliberation as was used in that case [Gen. 1: 26]. . . . for though the first Translation of the Bible that ever were and the Translation of the Roman Church have it in the plurall, yet it is not so in the Originall; it is but *faciam*. (*Sermons* ii. 344)

Donne has gone back to the original Hebrew text, then, and selected its singular verb form over the Vulgate's plural, but he does not heed the Hebrew *hā'ādām* and instead translates the Vulgate *hominem* as the English 'man', which he then reads as 'male'. We will see what Donne makes of this selective reading.

## IV. GENESIS 2: 24: THE MARRIAGE MODEL

In his sermons Donne refers specifically to Gen. 2: 24 three times, two instances of which are especially relevant to my discussion. The Book of Genesis presents something of a special case for several reasons, such as its position as the first book of the Scriptures; its content, which tells of the origins of the world and the first human beings; the presence of two accounts of the creation of man and woman: simultaneously in Gen. 1, which was written after Gen. 2 in which, as it is traditionally interpreted, the creation of man and woman takes place sequentially and in much greater detail. Harmonizing the two seemingly contradictory accounts in Gen. 1 and 2 was a necessary challenge for Renaissance commentators. While many reformed theologians abandoned the patristic tenet of 'total recuperation' whereby no biblical text could contradict any other part but had to form a seamless whole, the crucial opening chapters of Genesis were still subject to total recuperation. Thus, yet another potential avenue for different constructions of gender roles was not pursued (Maclean 1988: 26), nor was it recognized that the two accounts were not necessarily in any need of tinkering so as to form a seamless whole.[22] The two creation stories in Gen. 1 and 2 were 'reconciled' so that the version in Gen. 1: 26–7 was considered to be a summary of the more detailed account in Gen. 2: 7–8; 18–24. But without question, the account in Gen. 2 was almost exclusively the focus of interpretation, as it could be used to support cultural definitions of male and female already in place (E. Clark 1983: 15).

Donne, like most commentators, silently accords more authority to the account in Gen. 2. Indeed, in his sermons, Donne never explicitly refers to Gen. 1: 27: 'So God created man in his *own* image, in the image of God created he him; male and female created he them', although he writes two complete sermons on the previous verse 26. He refers only once to the reiteration of Gen. 1: 27 at Gen. 5: 1b–2: 'In the day that God created man, in the likeness of God made he him; Male and female created he them; and blessed them, and called their name Adam, in the day when they were created'. It is this single reference to the creation of male and female in Gen. 5 which raises questions about Donne's reading of Gen. 2, for we will see that this reference suggests he, along with the tradition which he follows, was aware that the Hebrew distinguishes the non-gendered being which God created initially out of the dust of the earth from the sexuate beings which this 'earth creature' becomes only at the point when a second creature is formed from the first. After this point, the non-gendered $h\bar{a}'\bar{a}d\bar{a}m$ is then used 'frequently, though not exclusively for the male' (Trible 1978: 98) and becomes a proper name only after Eve has been named at Gen. 3: 20. If there is some ambiguity in the use of the Hebrew term, $h\bar{a}'\bar{a}d\bar{a}m$, after the two sexuate creatures are formed at 2: 20, there is none in 2: 18 or 1: 27, to which 5: 2 refers. As in the selective abandonment of total recuperation by reformed theologians, Maclean concludes that '[t]extual criticism based on improved language skills and the study of manuscripts, although influential in causing changes in other domains, seems in [the sphere of notions of woman] to offer few possibilities in the way of reassessment' (26). What we find again and again—and Donne is no exception—is that Gen. 2 is made to bear the weight of authority for doctrinal beliefs which the text itself cannot support.[23]

[22] See Bal 1986: 321, 326, esp. n. 9 on the 'one coherent creation story' in Gen. 1–2.

[23] See J. Turner 1993a: 23–4. See also Phyllis Trible's list of specifics cited in

Donne first refers to Gen. 2: 24 in an early sermon on Prov. 22: 11: 'He that loveth pureness of heart, for the grace of his lips, the king shall be his friend'. I want to pause for a moment to consider the biographical circumstances of this sermon because in it, Donne preaches at length about women (although space permits only a very small portion of it to be addressed here). The occasion was Donne's first appearance in the outdoor pulpit next to St Paul's Cathedral, called Paul's Cross, on 24 March 1616/17, the anniversary of James's accession to the throne. Donne's wife, Anne, was still alive at this time, pregnant with their twelfth child who would be stillborn in August, her own death to follow a few days later. She was perhaps part of the large crowd gathered on this occasion to hear her husband's first sermon from Paul's Cross.[24] One of John Chamberlain's letters indicates some of those in attendance:

I had almost forgotten, that on Monday the 24th of this moneth beeing the Kings day, the archbishop of Caunterburie, the Lord Keper, Lord Privie-seale, the earle of Arundell, the earle of Southampton, the Lord Hayes, the controller, Secretarie Winwood, the Master of the Rolles, with divers other great men, were at Paules Crosse, and heard Dr. Donne who made there a daintie sermon, upon the eleventh verse of the 22th of Proverbs; and was excedingly well liked generally, the rather for that he did Quene Elizabeth great right, and held himself close to the text without flattering the time too much. (1939: ii. 67)

Chamberlain tells us only that Donne's sermon was 'excedingly well liked generally', so we can assume that nothing in it—including Donne's comments on the nature of women—struck his audience as untoward, and that perhaps people's concerns were of a more mundane nature in any case, for they were relieved Donne did not preach for too long. Sir Francis Bacon had

canonical readings of Genesis, 'not one of [which] is altogether accurate and most of [which] are simply not present in the story itself' (1978: 73). I discuss some of these in my reading of Donne's sermon, below.

[24] On the popularity and publication of the Paul's Cross sermons, see Maclure 1958; Bald 1986: 322. Arnold Williams suggests that the sermon was 'the center of the religious experience of multitudes and often their strongest link with the world of the mind as well as with that of the spirit. Many an humble layman must have got his notions about the creation and fall, about Cain and Noah, about Abraham and Joseph from the sermon he heard in his parish church' (1948: 37). Regarding less spiritual matters, Thomas Wilson alludes to the prevalence of pick-pocketing among the crowds gathered at Paul's (1994: 169).

just been created Lord Keeper by James, and Bald suggests that Donne's sermon was probably Bacon's first public appearance since his appointment (1986: 323). Donne's chosen text and several passages in the sermon suggest he was preaching with Bacon's presence and new duties in mind.[25] It also seems significant that Donne should choose to speak at length on the nature of women in such an especially public sermon. Considering James's and Bacon's misogynistic attitudes towards women, was Donne perhaps gearing this part of his sermon to their particular sensibilities, especially considering the text concerned 'friendship' between (male) king and (male) public servant?[26]

Donne cites Gen. 2: 24 in the following passage:

The highest degree of other love, is the love of woman: Which love, when it is rightly placed upon one woman, it is dignified by the Apostle with the highest comparison, *Husbands love your wives, as Christ loved his Church*: And God himself forbad not that this love should be great enough to change natural affection, *Relinquet patrem*, (for this, a man shall leave his Father) yea, to change nature it self, *caro una*, two shall be one. Accordingly *David* expresses himself so, in commemoration of *Jonathan*, *Thy love to me was wonderful, passing the love of women*: A love above that love, is wonderful. (i. 199)

At this point in his sermon Donne is concerned to show that as strong and divinely sanctioned as is the love of woman, so much more is the love of pureness of heart from the Holy Ghost, for 'All love which is placed upon lower things, admits satiety; but this love of this pureness, always grows, always proceeds' (199). We must keep in mind that Donne's overt intention is not to denigrate women but to show that they are more worthy of men's love than any other 'lower thing', even if the effect of his comparison is the dereliction of women, as I will show. Right away, Donne limits this 'other love' of woman to within the boundaries of marriage and lists three biblical 'witnesses' to the intensity of marital love: St Paul, God, and David. Is the order of these three references significant? Donne appears to think of St Paul's text before God Himself which suggests that Genesis was read almost automatically through the lens of Paul's interpretation. Donne notes that Paul 'dignifies' marriage by alluding to Christ, the Bridegroom,

[25] See *Sermons*, i. 213–17, esp. ll. 1242–5.
[26] See *Sermons*, iv. 241 for another example of masculine-inflected language used when preaching before James.

a metaphor which has its roots in God's own language of love for his people in the Old Testament. Donne then continues to a higher authority, 'God himself', using a negative construction—'God himself forbad not'—which introduces a syntactically registered resistance to full approbation of the love of woman, that 'other love' which changes 'natural affection' and 'nature itself'. So far, we have heard that St Paul 'dignified' marriage and God 'forbad it not'. Donne cites Gen. 2: 24 in the margin here and quotes from the Latin Vulgate as well, giving his translation in a parenthesis. He quotes only the first two words of the Latin—'Relinquet patrem'—and then skips to the end of the verse—'caro una, two shall be one'. References to the man's mother and his wife or woman in verse 24 are not mentioned. Is the way in which Donne cites his scriptural text significant? To conclude that it is may seem an instance of (the wrong kind of) 'overreading' what is merely a kind of shorthand; a tag which would identify the verse for Donne's auditors. The same shorthand occurs in his second citation of Gen. 2: 24 which I discuss below. But a passage from Thomas Wilson's *The Arte of Rhetorique* demonstrates the inevitability of women being left out. In an explanation of 'Order' Wilson says,

Order is of twoo sortes, the one is, when the worthier is preferred and set before. As a man is sette before a woman. The seconde is, when in amplificacion the weightiest wordes are sette last, and in diminishyng the same are sette formoste. 'With what looke, with what face, with what harte dare thou do soche a dede?' . . . [I]n speakinge at the leaste let us kepe a *natural order,* and set the man before the woman for manners sake. . . . Who is so folyshe as to saye the counsayle and the kyng, but rather the Kynge and his counsayle, the father and the sonne, and not contrary. And so likewise in al other, *as they are in degree firste,* evermore to set them formost. (1560: fo. 106)

The significance of Wilson's argument, as Dale Spender notices, is not that he asserts the superiority of males 'but that this superiority should be reflected *in the structure of the language*' (1985: 147; my emphasis). The 'natural order'—this logic of first and second inherent in the 'chain of being' notion by which Renaissance society assigned a place to every creature along a vertical axis of degrees of perfection—drew its authority in part from Paul's letter to Timothy in which Bal identifies the 'retrospective fallacy' as he interprets Gen. 2: 18: 'Let the woman learn in silence with all subjection. But I suffer not a woman to teach, nor to usurp authority over the man, but to be in silence. *For Adam was first formed, then Eve.* And Adam was not deceived, but the woman being deceived was in the transgression. Notwithstanding she shall be saved in childbearing, if they continue in faith and charity and holiness with sobriety' (1 Tim. 2: 11–15; emphasis added). But as Wilson's explanation of 'Order' shows, the reverse can also occur. In defences of women, one encounters the argument that because Eve was created last, she is the epitome of God's creation and thus superior to man. Yet both arguments are based on the same incorrect reading of Gen. 2 whereby it is argued that the sexes are created sequentially rather than simultaneously as the Hebrew indicates.

Donne's third illustration of the highest degree of other love achieves the opposite effect of its apparent intention. The reference to the 'wonderful' love of Jonathan for his friend David (2 Sam. 1: 26)—the bond of male friendship—undermines the supremacy of the 'other' love of woman which is yet divinely ordained and apostolically dignified. A marginal note in the Geneva Bible suggests that this elegaic statement of David's—'thy love to me was wonderful, passing the love of women'—was read in at least one other way. Donne reads the 'of' in 'the love of women' as 'for', i.e. the love [of men] for women. The editors of the Geneva Bible read it as a possessive whereby the love of women, 'Ether [*sic*] towardse their housbandes, or their children' is surpassed by Jonathan's love for David. Yet whether woman is subject or object, the love 'of' woman is inferior to that 'of' men. Mary Beth Rose's observation of Donne's marriage sermons applies here as well to his supposed celebration of 'the highest form of other love, the love of woman': 'It is not that Donne finds nothing positive to say about marriage [or women]. It is rather that he subverts any arguments he makes about the importance of the institution by developing them in unpredictably negative ways, by undermining his praise with contradictions, or by changing the subject entirely (1988: 99).

Donne cites Gen. 2: 24 a second time in a sermon preached while he was Divinity Reader at Lincoln's Inn from 1616 to 1621.[27] The reference occurs in a passage on the names for 'man',

---

[27] Potter and Simpson suggest a probable date of spring/summer 1618, so it was likely preached about a year after his first Paul's Cross sermon. (ii. 14).

a subject on which Donne was fond of reflecting in his sermons. First, however, Donne explains the significance of 'Adam':

In all those names that the Holy Ghost hath given man, he hath declared him miserable, for, *Adam*, (by which name God calls him, and *Eve* too) signifies but *Redness*, but a *Blushing*: . . . *both* may be *Adam*, both may *blush*. So God called that pair, our first Parents, man in that root,*Adam*. (ii. 78–9)

Here then, is a statement which could be read as an indication that Donne knew the Hebrew original, *hā'ādām*, referred to the 'earth creature'—here in 5.2 interpreted as androgynous rather than sexless—from whom emerged two beings, male and female, in Gen. 2: Donne cites Gen. 5: 2 in the margin. Gen. 5: 1b–2 reads: 'In the day that God created man, in the likeness of God made he him; Male and female created he them; and blessed them, and called *their name Adam, in the day when they were created*' (AV; my emphasis). At the name, 'Adam', which is not the proper name here but more like 'human being', the Geneva Bible's marginal note for Gen. 5: 2 reads: 'By giving them bothe one name, he noteth the inseparable conjunction of man and wife'. This seems to be an explanation of the relationship between Adam and Eve after they have been joined in marriage by God as 'man and wife' rather than an explanation of the Hebrew as it applies to the one sexless or androgynous creature.

Donne's exegesis of 'Adam' likely took its precedent from Augustine in *The City of God* (15.17):

ipsum enim [Adam] interpretatur Homo, sed commune perhibetur esse in illa lingua, id est hebraea, masculo et feminae. Nam sic de illo scriptum est. *Masculum et feminam fecit illos, et benedixit illos, et cognominavit nomen eorum Adam* (Id.v.2). Unde non ambigitur, sic appellatam fuisse feminam Evam proprio nomine, ut tamen Adam, quod interpretatur Homo, nomen esset amborum.

[although Adam means 'man', we are told that in Hebrew it is common to male and female; thus Scripture says, 'He created them male and female, and blessed them, and named them Adam' [Gen. 5: 2] This makes it clear that although the woman was called Eve, and that was her personal name, the name Adam, which means 'man', belonged to them both.] (*CSEL* 40/2.96; 1984: 626)

The narrative which Bal follows so carefully through the series of differentiations which the 'earth creature' undergoes at its creation from earth itself (Gen. 2: 7), through to assuming a proper name and character (at the very earliest, 2: 23 and more certainly at 3: 20 when Eve is named) is compressed into a single moment by Augustine. Even if Augustine argued that the time span from the creation of Adam and Eve to their expulsion was only about six hours, there was time for a narrative to unfold nonetheless (*CSEL* 28/1.272–3). Jerome also argues that 'In hominem, et vir et femina continetur. . . . Legamus principium Geneseos, et inveniemus Adam, hoc est hominem, tam virum quam feminam nunc par; [the word *man* comprehends both male and female. . . . Let us read the beginning of Genesis, and we shall find Adam, that is *man*, called both male and female] (*PL*, xxiii. p. 251; 1893: 368).

   Donne refers to the man, whose proper name is also Adam, and the woman, Eve, by the same Hebrew word which derives from *ᵃdāmâ* (see Trible 1978: 79) or 'earth', which allows Donne to make his point about the sinfulness of Adam and Eve, and the resultant shedding of Christ's blood which it necessitated. Donne repeatedly uses the plural pronoun 'they' and 'their' to refer to both Adam and Eve, and concludes that in its original signification, 'Adam' is an apt term for 'both' because they both sinned. Donne's purpose in including Eve in 'Adam' then, is to point to her part in the 'misery' inflicted on 'man' because of 'their' transgression. In the passage in Donne's Paul's Cross sermon on the love of woman, from which I quoted, above, the partnership between Eve and Adam is not so equitably distributed. Donne warns against drawing a typological parallel between Eve and Mary as is done in the New Testament between Adam and Christ, the Second Adam:

I know the Fathers are frequent in comparing and paralleling *Eve*, the Mother of Man, and *Mary* the Mother of God. But, God forbid any should say, That the Virgin *Mary* concurred to our good, so, as *Eve* did to our ruine. It is said truly, *That as by one man sin entred, and death* [Rom. 5: 12], so by one man entred life. It may be said, *That by one woman sin entred, and death,* (and that rather then by the man; for, *Adam was not deceived, but the woman being deceived, was in the transgression.* [1. Tim. 2: 14]) But it cannot be said, in that sense, or that manner, that by one woman innocence entred, and life: The Virgin *Mary* had not the same interest in our salvation, as *Eve* had in our destruction; nothing that she did entred into that treasure, that ransom that redeemed us. (i. 200)

Here is one of Donne's most severe pretermissions of motherhood. Compare the Protestant divine's harsh 'disowning' of the

Virgin with the (crypto-Catholic?) poet's praise of the Virgin in 'A Litanie':

> For that faire blessed Mother-maid,
>    Whose flesh redeem'd us; That she-Cherubin,
>    Which unlock'd Paradise, and made
> One claime for innocence, and disseiz'd sinne,
>       Whose wombe was a strange heav'n, for there
>       God cloath'd himselfe, and grew,
> Our zealous thankes wee poure. As her deeds were
> Our helpes, so are her prayers; nor can she sue
> In vaine, who hath such titles unto you. (37–45)[28]

The parallel here is between Mary and Christ, the Redeemer and Second Adam. And rather than being unable to escape from the shadow of Eve, Mary is both a 'strange heav'n' and a 'she-Cherubin' (suggesting angels do know 'Difference of sex', contra 'The Relique'), whose flesh 'redeem'd us', a truly astounding claim. The same unambiguously Catholic terms can be found in 'Good-friday, 1613. Riding Westward' (a poem written only four years prior to the sermon Donne preached at Paul's Cross), where Christ's 'miserable mother' was 'Gods partner here, and furnish'd thus | Halfe of that Sacrifice, which ransom'd us' (30–2). Preaching before the crowd assembled at Paul's Cross, Donne seems to have wanted to quell any doubts as to the thoroughness of his conversion.

To return to the Lincoln's Inn sermon in which Donne cites Gen. 2: 24, having explained the signification of Adam, Donne moves to the next name for 'man', *Ish* ['*îš*]'. Here, the Geneva Bible cites correctly that in verse 23, sexually distinct creatures are named, and the punning that occurs in both English and Hebrew is noted. Adam says in verse 23, 'She shalbe called woman, because she was taken out of man', and, says the Geneva, 'in *Ebr [Hebrew]*, *Ish* ['*îš*] is man, and *Ishah* ['*iššâ*] the woman'. Bal notes a possible problem in the use of the sexually marked noun '*îš*, here, rather than *hā'ādām*, but suggests two reasons for it: (1) 'the man retrospectively assumes that he always had this sexual identity. He

---

[28] Gardner suggests a date of 1608, in Donne 1982: 81. See Sabine 1992: 1–110, where she traces what she sees as Donne's increasingly covert (as he conformed more and more outwardly to Protestantism) grappling with the significance of the Virgin Mary and her sacred Motherhood for his own faith and psyche.

focalizes his earlier version from his actual state'; (2) 'The phrase "taken from" does not mean "made out of" but "taken away from" in the sense of "differentiated from"' (1986: 324–5). Donne distinguishes between *Adam* and *Ish* however, by saying that *Ish,* which signifies the male of the species only, is 'the first name, by which God called man in generall, *mankinde*'. He then cites Gen. 2: 24—again quoting only the 'tag', 'Therefore shall a man leave his Father'—and the Hebrew for 'man' here is *'Ish'* [*'iš*] as well. But verse 24 is told from a male's (or *'iš*'s) perspective. He 'cleaves unto his wife', or woman, and therefore Donne's synonym, 'mankind', cannot in this case include man and woman. Donne gives 'mankinde' as a synonym for 'man in general' yet he refers to a Hebrew word for 'male'. The female is not included in the term which is supposedly a universal, 'mankinde'. Is woman in or out? Clearly, the ambiguities which arise as a result of translation allow Donne and his fellow exegetes to use the scripture as a means of enforcing gender constructions favourable to patriarchal society.

### V. DONNE'S WEDDING SERMON ON GENESIS 2:18

The three wedding sermons which we have among Donne's surviving sermons form a fascinating triad on marriage as institution and as metaphor, on the practical dimensions or 'duties', as well as the mystical symbolism of marriage, indeed on these two elements as they are presented in Gen. 2: 24: 'Therefore shall a man leave his father and his mother, and shall cleave unto his wife: and they shall be one flesh.' The scriptural texts on which Donne preached at these weddings treat of marriage from the beginning to the end of time. They are taken from Genesis, on the first marriage between Adam and Eve; from the prophet, Hosea, on God's promise to marry his people, Israel; from Jesus' own words in the Gospel of Matthew on marriage as earthly institution made obsolete by our mystical marriage, our eternal union with God in heaven. The earliest of these wedding sermons, written in February 1619/20, presents to us Donne's interpretation of what has traditionally been regarded as the founding moment of gender construction in Christian myth: the creation of 'woman', which begins with God's recognition of the necessity of woman at Gen. 2: 18, just prior to her creation from Adam's side.

That Donne should choose to focus on marriage as a means of procreation at the wedding of Francis Nethersole and Lucy Goodyer, both of whom he knew personally, is somewhat disappointingly conventional. Donne takes a subject which he so imaginatively handled elsewhere, as metaphor in both the poetry and other sermons, and delivers an uninspired, crabbed vision of the potentialities of human bodies for loving union. Where is the Donne who celebrates marriage—'God is *Love*, and the *Holy Ghost* is amorous in his *Metaphors*' (vii. 87)—and observes 'The union of Christ to the whole Church is not expressed by any metaphore, by any figure, so oft in the Scripture, as by this of *Mariage*, (*Sermons*, vi. 82)? Even if we allow for the assertion in Donne's time of the 'natural' inferiority of actual women, in the case of his sermon on Gen. 2: 18, as his editors remark, 'it seems clear that Donne for some reason or reasons could not at the time express his best or deepest feelings. To guess at the reasons is probably futile' (*Sermons*, ii. 44–5). However, Lindsay Mann reminds us that right at the time of Donne's sermon, the Bishop of London had delivered an 'express commaundment' from King James to the clergy instructing them to 'inveigh vehemently and bitterly . . . against the insolencie of our women' (quoted in Mann 1992: 113), as part of the popular misogyny circulating at the time against women who were taking too many freedoms.

Who were the bride and groom to whom Donne preached? Lucy Goodyer was the eldest daughter of Donne's closest friend, Sir Henry Goodyer, and at the time of her marriage in 1619/20 was about 25 years old (b.1594, d.1652). Lucy and her sisters were close friends of Donne's eldest daughter, Constance, as is evidenced in one of Donne's letters to Sir Henry (1977: 158–9). Lucy Goodyer was also a favourite godchild of the Countess of Bedford and a member of her household. John Chamberlain mentions the wedding and the countess's largesse in a letter to Dudley Carleton: 'I forgat in my last [letter of 12 February] that Sir Fra: Nethersole was then newly maried to Mistris Goodyeare that served the Lady of Bedford who gave her 500$^{li}$ or 700$^{li}$, besides 500$^{li}$ she bestowed upon them in gloves, which brought in a great contribution of plate to make up a portion which her father Sir Henry could not geve' (1939: ii. 291). R. C. Bald doubts that the countess could have been quite so generous, but there is no doubt Sir Henry's estate was deeply in debt as a result of a lawsuit and his own love of extravagant and generous living so that he was unable to provide for his children.[29] Lucy's three younger sisters remained unmarried because of their father's inability to provide them with dowries and they staved off disaster only by obtaining a renewal of the royal protection against the creditors of their father, who died in 1627.

Sir Francis, therefore, cannot have married Lucy Goodyer for her money. There wasn't any. Sir Francis, about age 32 at the time of his marriage, had been knighted while acting as secretary to Lord Doncaster in Germany only a few months prior to his wedding.[30] Donne himself was sent as King's chaplain on the mission and so would have come to know Nethersole in some capacity during the seven months they were in the service of Doncaster. 'Donne's friendship with both bride and groom made it natural that he should be the one to perform the ceremony and preach the sermon' (Bald 1986: 366). Certainly Sir Henry Goodyer and probably the Countess of Bedford were in the congregation listening to Donne's sermon. These were two of Donne's most intimate friends, both of whom would have known Anne Donne, and both of whom are known to have exchanged poetry with Donne and who would have been familiar with at least some of his poetry. Knowing the circumstances surrounding this particular sermon would lead us to expect Donne to be at his most eloquent and joyful best, as Potter and Simpson suggest, but instead we find a dour and pedantic Donne.

Donne begins his sermon with a distinction between that general blessing which God bestowed upon all his creatures, a desire to 'conserve, and propagate their kinde by way of *Generation*', and that 'proper and peculiar blessing, in contracting, and limiting that naturall desire' (ii. 335) among humans so that 'this desire of propagation, though it be naturall in man, as in other creatures, by his creation, yet it is limited by God himselfe, to be exercised onely between such persons, as God hath brought together in mariage, according to his Institution, and Ordinance' (ii. 336). Donne is careful to stress that the very first blessing which

[29] On Goodyer's financial difficulties, see Bald 1986: 63–6.

[30] Doncaster had been sent as James's ambassador to Germany in order to assist James's son-in-law, Frederick, in resolving the religious tensions between Protestants and Catholics in Bohemia, and to act as secretary to James's daughter, Princess Elizabeth, who lived with her husband as Queen of Bohemia, although they were soon forced into exile.

God bestowed on Creation in Gen.1: 22 and 28 is that of an 'ability and a desire of propagating their kinde'. Following August-ine's radical departure from Jerome and Ambrose who read the Fall as a fall into sexual knowledge, Donne does not condemn sex itself, for it is 'naturall' to both pre- as well as post-lapsarian worlds (if differing in its mechanics), but points to the parameters God has established for it. So far, then, Donne is relatively posit-ive: sex is good, indeed a blessing, providing it occurs for the purpose of procreation within marriage.

Next, Donne reiterates a commonplace formulation of English Protestant society in order to establish that marriage constitutes both a formal model and a literal source for the larger bodies of society:

Though then societies of men doe grow up, and spread themselves into Townes, and into Cities, and into Kingdomes, yet the root of all societies is in families, in the relation between man and wife, parents and children, masters and servants: . . . both of *Civill* and of *Spirituall* societies, the first roote is a *family*; and of families, the first roote is *Mariage*; and of mariage, the first roote, that growes out into words, is in this Text; *And the Lord God said, It is not good etc.* (ii. 336)

Marriage as a formal model for all '*Civill*' and '*Spirituall*' relation-ships is a construction we see so often in Elizabeth I and James I's manipulation of the familial metaphor to describe their relation-ship to their subjects,[31] as well as in the familial relationship between two persons of the Trinity: God the Father and God the Son. Donne leaves the metaphorical applications of marriage to another sermon (iii. 241–55) and focuses on one of the three purposes of marriage (almost as if it were the only one), the reproductive necessity of the female and the 'fit help' she provides in assisting in the propagation of 'Townes . . . Cities . . . King-domes'. Donne's singular focus derives from Augustine's discus-sion of Gen. 2: 18 in *De Genesi ad Litteram* (9.5): 'Qua propter non invenio ad quod adjutorium facta sit mulier viro, si pariendi causa subtrahitur. [I cannot think of any reason for woman's being made as man's helper, if we dismiss the reason of procreation]' (*CSEL* 28/1.273; *ACW* 42, p. 75). Donne makes the same claim in much earlier works. For example, in his Paradox, 'That Virginity is a

---

[31] In Elizabeth's case, so successfully as to avoid marriage itself. On James, see Goldberg 1986: 3–33.

Vertue', Donne declares: 'For surely nothing is more unprofitable in the Commonwealth of Nature then they that dy old maids, because they refuse to be used to that end for which they were only made' (1980: 56).[32] In *Ignatius His Conclave* (1611), Queen Elizabeth is described as 'but a little a woman' because she 'put off all affections of woemen', the 'principall Dignity of which sex, (which is, to be a *Mother*)' (1969: 85, 87).

There is a passage relevant to my discussion, here, in a christening sermon, the text of which Donne takes from Paul's instructions to married couples in Eph. 5: 25–7, 'Husbands, love your wives.' In it, we find an explanation of the dynamic of the three fundamental societal relations which Donne lists in the Nethersole wedding sermon. I quote it at length because it further illustrates the ways in which patriarchy's debt to the mother remains unacknowledged:

Almighty God ever loved *unity*, but he never loved *singularity*; God was always *alone* in heaven, there were no *other Gods*, but he; but he was never *singular*, there was never any time, when there were not *three persons* in heaven. . . . As then God seemes to have been eternally delighted, with this eternall generation, (with persons that had ever a relation to one another, *Father*, and *Sonne*) so when he came to the Creation of this lower world, he came presently to those three relations, of which the whole frame of this world consists; . . . the third relation was between *parents* and *children*, when *Eve* said, that she *had obtained a Man by the Lord*, that by the plentifull favour of God, she had conceived and borne a sonne: . . . from that beginning to the end of the world, these three relations, of *Master* and *Servant, Man* and *Wife, Father* and *Children*, have been, and ever shall be the materialls, and the elements of all society, of families, and of Cities, and of Kingdomes. . . . The generall duty, that goes through all these three relations, is expressed, *Subditi estote invicem, Submit yourselves to one another, in the feare of God*; for God hath given no Master such imperiousnesse, no husband such a superiority, no father such a soverainty, but that there lies a burden upon them too, to consider with a compassionate sensiblenesse, the grievances, that oppresse the other part, which is coupled to them. For if the servant, the wife, the sonne be oppressed, worne out, annihilated, there is no such thing left as a Master, or a husband, or a father; They depend upon one another, and therefore he that hath not care of his fellow, destroys himselfe. (*Sermons*, v. 113–14)

---

[32] Donne's editor, Helen Peters, suggests the Paradoxes were written in the early 1590s (1980: p. xv). She places this Paradox in Donne's *Dubia*, as it appears only in the 1652 edition of Donne's poems.

Here Donne establishes being in relationship as one of the givens of existence, based on nothing less than the model of 'eternall generation' with which God was 'eternally delighted'. Along with his oft-quoted assertion that 'No Man is an *Iland*', Donne in his *Devotions* observes, '*Solitude* is a torment, which is not threatned [*sic*] in *hell* it selfe' (1987: 87, 25). We will see that Donne does not feel quite so averse to solitude in the Nethersole sermon.

The definitive relationship on which the others are patterned in the passage quoted above is that between Father and Son, the relationship by which the plurality of the Godhead is expressed. After his one allusion to the parent/child relationship between Eve and her first-born, Donne always subsumes the mother within a parental partnership and refers to 'Father and children'.[33] However, Donne's exposition of societal relations stresses that without the subjected term, the dominant term cannot exist: 'They depend on one another', yet the ultimate goal seems to be self-preservation on the part of the dominant term. On the hierarchical chain of being, from inanimate stones to plants to animals to the various categories for human status, mutual responsibility is understood but does not guarantee or imply equal status. The qualities or attributes which Donne cites for each dominant partner reveal the inequity in the relationship: 'imperiousnesse' or absolute command of the Master over the Servant, the power to enforce obedience based on higher rank which also describes the husband's 'superiority', and the 'soverainty' or 'supremacy in respect of power, domination or rank' (*OED*) of the father over his children. Yet in the first sermon Donne preached at Paul's Cross from which I have already quoted, he also stresses mutual dependence inferred from the Godhead:

The greatest Mystery in Earth, or Heaven, which is *the Trinity*, is conveyed to our understanding, no other way, then so, as they have reference to one another *by Relation*, as we say in the Schools; for, God could not be a father without a Son, nor the Holy Ghost *Spiratus sine spirante*. As in Divinity, so in Humanity too, *Relations* constitute one another, King and subject come at once together into consideration. Neither is it so pertinent a consideration, which of them was made for others sake, as that

---

[33] See Belsey 1993: 155–8. In her discussion of seventeenth-century political discourse, Belsey notes the 'extremely common' 'silent slide . . . between "parents" and "men"' (156) as a result of the 'unease about women which places them as simultaneously present in and absent from the discourse of patriarchalism' (158).

they were both made for Gods sake, and equally bound to advance his glory. (i. 184)

Remember Donne is preaching here before King James and Sir Francis Bacon. Donne can go so far as to assert mutuality between king and subject, but it seems when he returns to the Garden and confronts the founding moment of gender construction, 'relations' become chains. Eve was created only as 'helper' (another word not translated correctly, as we will see), and only to help procreate not just children, we will see, but male children. Yet Donne's statement of correlation above, '*Relations* constitute one another', is exactly what the narrative of Gen. 2 implies if one reads the Hebrew correctly, and is another expression of Irigaray's 'I' and 'you', self and other as two subjectivities. Donne seems to assert here that difference is the very condition of relationship. Indeed in Gen. 2's story of the creation of male and female, the emphasis is on intimacy and distinction, not superiority and inferiority. Donne expresses this contiguity only negatively when he makes the following astonishing observation at the end of the Bridgewater marriage sermon:

when I consider, that even he that said *Ego & pater unum sumus, I and the Father are one*, yet had a time to say, *utquid dereliquisti? My God, my God why hast thou forsaken me?* I consider thereby, that no two can be so made one in this world, but that that unity may be, though not *Dissolved*, no nor *Rent*, no nor *Endangered*, yet *shaked* sometimes by domestique occasions, by Matrimoniall encumbrances. (viii. 109)

Let us return to Donne's marriage sermon on Gen. 2: 18. Thus far, Donne has established that marriage is the root of society and the very means by which God achieves his purpose for Creation which Donne explains next as he considers the precise nature of the man's aloneness, which God declares is 'not good':

in regard of the *publique* good, God pretermits *private*, and particular respects; for, God doth not say, *Non bonum homini*, it is not good for man to be alone, man might have done well enough so; nor God does not say, *non bonum hunc hominem*, it is not good for *this*, or that *particular* man to be alone; but *non bonum, Hominem*, it is not good in the *generall*, for the *whole frame of the world*, that *man should be alone*, because then both Gods purposes had been frustrated, of being glorified by man here, in this world, and of glorifying man, in the world to come; for neither of these could have been done, without a succession, and propagation of man. (ii. 336–7)

Donne's first task is to show 'that in regard of the *publique good*, God pretermits *private* . . . respects'. There are two issues I want to address here: (1) Donne's choice of the word, 'pretermit', both as he applies it and as it might be read from a feminist perspective; (2) Donne's privileging of the 'public good' over 'private respects'. The analogies Donne draws from nature and from God's own actions suggest he uses 'pretermit' as it denotes sacrifice and abandonment. Donne notes that water and air 'will depart from their owne Nature' and, respectively, go so far as to 'clamber up hills' and 'sinke downe into vaults, rather then admit Vacuity' (337). This notion of doing what is against one's own nature, when applied to pretermitting private respects for public good, suggests that men go against their own nature when they marry. In other words, Donne places a higher priority on man's *bonum* than on God's purpose for his whole creation. Donne says as much in the sermon on Eph. 5: 25–7:

> It is true, this contracting of our affections is a *burden*, it is a submitting of our selves; All States that made Lawes, and proposed *rewards* for *maried Men*, conceived it so; that naturally they would be loth to doe it. . . . For, by being a husband, I become subject, to that sex which is naturally subject to Man, though this subjection be no more in this place, but to *love* that one woman. (v. 116–17)

Indeed, Donne warns Lucy Goodyer that if she be anything other than a Helper, her husband 'will ever returne, to the *bonum esse solum*, it had been better for him, to have been alone, then in the likenesse of a Helper, to have had a wife unfit for him' (ii. 337).

Donne's next example of pretermitting private respects for public good unquestionably implies sacrifice, both on the part of God the Father, who pretermits, and God the Son, who is pretermitted. Donne urges his listeners,  'But take the example nearer, in Gods bosome, and there we see, that for the publique, for the *redemption* of the whole world, God hath (shall we say, pretermitted?) derelicted, forsaken, abandoned, his own, and onely Sonne. Do you so too?' (ii. 337).   This time, 'pretermit' appears in a parenthesis which neatly figures the meaning of the word. The first two synonyms which follow the parenthesis, 'derelicted, forsaken', inevitably recall Christ's words on the cross in both the Vulgate and the Authorized Version at Matt. 27: 46 and Mark 15: 34: '*Quid dereliquisti mei* | My God, my God, why has thou forsaken me?'[34] Donne uses God's example to ask, if God can 'pretermit' his only Son, can we not even give up ambition, pride, greed, and lust?[35] Donne thus concludes the initial paragraph of his first partition with an exhortation to follow God's example, 'for the publique to pretermit the private, for the larger, and better, to leave the narrower, and worser respects'.

Donne proceeds with his exploration of how God pretermits private for public good with reference to the man's aloneness: 'we noted, that God did not say, *non bonum Homini, It was not good for man to be alone;* man might have done well enough in that state, so, as his *solitarinesse* might have been supplied with a farther creation of more men' (ii. 338–9). Whereas when Donne first made this point an ambiguity remained as to the precise meaning of man, here Donne reads *hominem* as 'male'. He also alludes to Augustine's question in *De Genesi ad litteram* when Donne asks 'how much more conveniently might two friends live together, then a man and a woman?'[36] One of the things which must be 'pretermitted', it is implied, then, are the friendships which Donne and his friends celebrated in the verse letters, the 'private' preferences as opposed to one's public duties, one of which is to procreate. Donne continues to examine 'man's' aloneness from every angle: 'God doth not then say, *non bonum homini,* man got not so much by the bargaine, (especially if we consider how that wife carried her selfe towards him) but that for his particular, he had been better alone' (ii. 339).[37] Donne's use of a parenthesis here suggests that he uses it for emphasis, or to shift the balance of the sentiment: what is 'contained' by the parenthesis turns inside out and contains or, to use a different metaphor, colours, the rest of the sentence. If the brackets of the parenthesis are supposed to say, 'You can ignore this if you prefer', what they do instead is highlight the statement. Furthermore, when we consider that Donne would have delivered this sermon orally, we realize that his audience, unless singularly attuned to changes in tone, pauses, and so on, would not hear this

[34] See my Introduction, n. 27; Donne 1987: 27.

[35] And as Donne urges elsewhere, God only appears to have abandoned Christ, whose final words on the cross are 'Father, into thy hands I commend my spirit' (Luke 23: 46); see *Sermons*, ii. 161.

[36] 'Quanto enim congruentius ad convivendum et colloquendum duo amici pariter quam vir et mulier habitarent?' *PL*, xxxiv. 395.

[37] See Donne's *Devotions* (1987: 110) for a similar complaint.

clause as a parenthesis but as an elaboration.[38] Man's aloneness cannot be remedied except by woman, with whom he can carry out the 'publique good' which he summarizes later in the sermon:

That God might not be frustrated of this great, and gracious, and glorious purpose of his, *non bonum*, it was not good that man should be alone; for without man God could not give this glory, and without woman there could be no propagation of man. And so, though it might have been *Bonum homini*, man might have done well enough alone; and *Bonum hunc hominem, some* men may doe better alone, yet God, who ever, for our example, prefers the publique before the private, because it conduced not to his *generall* end, of Having, and of Giving glory, saw, and said, *Non bonum hominem*, it was not good that man should be alone. (ii. 342–3)

Woman is the fulcrum on which the whole operation rests. It could be argued that Donne's use of 'man' in this double parallelism, its second occurrence in the sermon, is non-gendered; indeed, that 'woman' is the very foundation on which all depends. But the syntax which presents the relationship, 'man is to God as woman is to man', seems to force woman into the role of mere facilitator for something being exchanged between God and man.[39] As Donne's sermon progresses, any ambiguities dissolve, as we shall see.

Donne takes a moment to address the debate between the relative goodness of marriage and virginity which is still, after a long paragraph of proofs of the goodness of marriage, 'that, which justly seemes the best state' (341), following St Paul again. I want to quote his more vivid defence of marriage in the sermon he preached at the wedding of Margaret Washington in 1621 in which he argues against the Roman Catholic privileging of virginity: 'When God had made *Adam* and *Eve* in Paradise, though there were foure rivers in Paradise, God did not place *Adam* in a Monastery on one side, and *Eve* in a Nunnery on the other, and so a River between them. They that build wals and cloysters to frustrate Gods institution of mariage, advance the Doctrine of Devils in forbidding mariage' (iii. 242). Surprisingly, Donne goes on in this sermon to insist that the groom, as well as the bride, be a

[38] For the 'exploitation' of parentheses, see my discussion of John Lennard's book in Ch. 4.
[39] See Donne's verse letter to the Countess of Huntingdon which begins, 'Man to Gods image, *Eve*, to mans was made, | Nor finde wee that God breath'd a soule in her', and Donne's rather half-hearted refutation of this idea at *Sermons*, iv. 241.

virgin on his wedding night: 'The body is the temple of the Holy Ghost; and when two bodies, by mariage are to be made one temple, the wife is not as the Chancell, reserv'd and shut up, and the man as the walks below, indifferent and at liberty for every passenger. God in his Temple looks for first fruits from both' (iii. 248). Donne implies the same virginal state of both man and woman in his much earlier Paradox, 'That Virginity Is a Virtue', when he advises 'female *Virgins*' to practise the Paracelsian principle of 'curing like by like':

By this Rule, female *Virgins* by a discreet marriage should swallow down into their *Virginity* another *Virginity*, and devour such a life and spirit into their womb, that it might make them, as it were, immortall here on earth, besides their perfect immortality in heaven: And that *Vertue* which otherwise would putrifie and corrupt ['by exceeding a limited time'], shall then be compleat; and shall be recorded in Heaven, and enrolled here on Earth; and the name of *Virgin* shall be exchanged for a farre more honorable name, *A Wife*. (1980: 58)[40]

The female virgin is to 'swallow' and 'devour' into her womb 'another *Virginity*': the man's. The voracious maiden, the *vagina dentata*, the notion of a man's semen reducing his lifespan and increasing the woman's are conventional motifs in a patriarchal culture which fears and desires the mother. We will see in the 'Epithalamium [Made at Lincoln's Inn]', however, that the 'female *Virgin*' is not a succubus this time but the mirror opposite, a sacrificial lamb.

Donne concludes his comparison of marriage and virginity in the Nethersole sermon thus, where the dereliction of woman begins in earnest: 'If we could consider merit in man, the merit of *Abraham*, the father of nations, and the merit of *John*, who was no father at all, is equall. But that wherein we consider the goodnesse of [marriage/propagation] here, is, that God proposed this way, to receive glory from the sonnes of men here upon earth, and to give glory to the sonnes of men in heaven' (ii. 341). Woman is nowhere to be seen or heard. She is saved through childbearing according to St Paul (1 Tim. 2: 15), and a woman's virginity is her most precious 'jewel', yet Donne resolves the issue only with regard to men for whom it makes no difference

[40] The unusual implication of male virginity is perhaps an argument for its authenticity considering Donne's tendency to push the 'limits of the thinkable'.

whether they propagate or not; they are still deserving of equal merit. Donne gives poetic voice to this same construct in his late poem, 'To Mr. Tilman after he had taken orders', describing the role of priests who 'keepe heavens doore' and 'Bring man to heaven, and heaven againe to man' (ll. 40, 48).

In the Nethersole sermon, Donne spends considerably less time on the second part of his text, how woman is a 'helpe, meete for man', but he manages to make himself very clear nonetheless. Donne had told his listeners earlier in the sermon that   'even the workes of God, are not equally excellent; this is but *faciam*, it is not *faciamus*; in the creation of man, there is intimated a Consultation, a Deliberation of the whole *Trinity*; in the making of *women*, it is not expressed so; it is but *faciam*. And then, that that is made here, is but *Adjutorium*, but an accessory, not a principall; but a *Helper*' (337).   Donne's appeal to the Hebrew original, *'ēzer*, over the Vulgate regarding *faciam/faciamus* is selective, for he does not or will not notice the way in which *'ēzer* is used elsewhere in the Old Testament, especially in Psalms, which was his favourite book of scripture.[41] Trible argues that the English translation (and the Vulgate *adiutorium* I would add) is 'totally misleading' because it suggests subordination and inferiority. In contrast, *'ēzer* 'often describes God as the superior who creates and saves Israel. In [Gen. 2: 18] the accompanying phrase, "corresponding to it" *(kᵉnegdô)*, tempers this connotation of superiority to specify identity, mutuality, and equality. According to Yahweh God, what the earth creature needs is a companion, one who is neither subordinate nor superior; one who alleviates isolation through identity' (1978: 90; see E. Clark 1983: 15–16). Donne comes so much closer in 'Sapho to Philaenis' to recognizing the 'like-opposite' God creates for the earth creature in Gen. 2 than he does in his sermon on this very text: according to Donne, woman 'is but *Adjutorium*, but a Help: and no body values his staffe, as he does his legges' (345).[42]

Briefly digressing to criticize the use of cosmetics by even 'honest women': 'they take the pencill out of Gods hand, who goe about to mend any thing of his making'. Donne then returns to the discrepancy between verb forms of *facere*:

[41] For *'ēzer*/helper, see Exod. 18: 4; Deut. 33: 7, 26, 29; Pss. 33: 20, 115: 9–11, 121: 2, 124: 8, 146: 5.

[42] Compare the imagery in Thomas Gataker's *A Good Wife Gods Gift: And, A Wife Indeed* (1623: Sig. F) and Karen Newman's discussion of Gataker (1991: 7–9).

I presse no more upon this, but one lesson to our selves, That . . . if God
come not altogether in his *faciamus*, to powre down with both hands
abundance of his worldly treasures, or of his spirituall light and clearnesse,
let us content our selves with one hand from him. . . . And then one
lesson also to the other sexe, That they will be content, even by this form
and change of phrase, to be remembred, that *they are the weaker vessell*, and
*that Adam was not deceived* but *the woman was*. (ii. 344)

Significantly, Donne indicates with the phrase, 'our selves', above,
that he has been addressing the men in the congregation. Donne
continues to address women 'as the other sexe' to the end of the
paragraph, where he puts her in her place: 'That as she is not a
servant, but a Mother in the house, so she is but a Daughter, and
not a Mother of the Church' (345). She is 'but a Mother in the
house', contained within the patriarchal domicile for the purpose
of breeding future patriarchs and placed there through the operation of language. On another level, Donne seems to be going out
of his way to deny the Catholic belief that Mary was Mother of the
Church (Sabine 1992: 5). Donne appears to 'presse no more'
when in fact he brings down all the authority he can muster to
make clear the role of 'the other sexe', quoting or alluding to St
Paul (twice), Theodoret, Chrysostom, Oecumenius, and Ambrose.

Donne's misogyny continues to gather force in the next paragraph: 'It is not an ordinary disease now, to be *too uxorious*;
that needs no great disswasion'.[43] Donne quotes the ever severe
Jerome: discretion, rather than affection is key: '[t]here is not a
more uncomely, a poorer thing, then to love a Wife like a Mis-
tresse' (345); in other words, do your duty with your wife and
make love with your mistress. To make the comparison is to
acknowledge the double standard. Donne reminds his congregation in Pauline terms and by quoting Gen. 3: 12 that marriage
exists to 'pay a debt, not to satisfie appetite; lest otherwise she
prove *in Ruinam*, who was given *in Adjutorium*, and he be put to the
first mans plea, *Mulier quam dedisti, The woman whom thou gavest me,
gave me my death*' (ii. 345). Here at last, yet inevitably and on
biblical authority, woman and death are brought together, even
in a sermon preached at a marriage, about the creation of
Eve, 'Mother of all Living', for the purposes of procreation.

[43] It should be noted that there is no equivalent term to 'uxorious' that would
denote loving one's husband 'too much'.

In *Metempsychosis* (1601) and *The First Anniversary* (1611) Donne glosses the fall of humanity in almost identical terms as those he uses in this sermon. In *The First Anniversary*, woman 'sent | For mans reliefe, [is] cause of his languishment. | They were to good ends, and thy are so still, | But accessory, and principall in ill' (101–4). Here is the tenth stanza from *Metempsychosis*:

> Man all at once was there by woman slaine,
> And one by one we'are here slaine o'er againe
> By them. The mother poison'd the well-head,
> The daughters here corrupt us, Rivulets;
> No smalnesse scapes, no greatnesse breaks their nets;
> She thrust us out, and by them we are led
> Astray, from turning, to whence we are fled.
> Were prisoners Judges, 'twould seeme rigorous,
> Shee sinn'd, we beare; part of our paine is, thus
>   To love them, whose fault to this painfull love yoak'd us. (91–100)

Donne takes Ecclus. 25: 24 ('Of the woman came the beginning of sin, and through her we all die') as his scriptural authority (and 1 Tim. 2: 14 less directly) for the view that Eve was to blame for the fall, against the orthodox view that Adam's sin resulted in the Fall (see Rom. 5: 12; 1 Cor. 15: 21–2). Ecclesiasticus is a book which the Protestant Churches assigned to the Apocrypha but which the Roman Catholic Church fully accepted as part of the biblical canon. It is as though, taught by Jesuits in his boyhood and at that point still presented with two models of femininity—Eve and the Virgin Mary—Donne went on to profess the Protestant faith in which the Virgin Mary plays an almost invisible role, but he retained the especially negative view of Eve, proportional to the Catholic faith's positive view of Mary, yet out of all proportion when she is left standing alone in the Protestant landscape.

In this stanza of the *Metempsychosis* is a mirror image of Irigaray's 'psychoanalysis' of Western culture, a perfect example of the phallic speculation of woman. Rather than Irigaray's 'murder' of the mother, man is 'poison'd' by 'The mother'. Rather than the absence of a maternal genealogy between mothers and daughters, who are separated when daughters are exchanged between father and husband, daughters here learn from their mother's poisoning and 'corrupt' the sons of Adam. Rather than the *'internal exile'* and dereliction suffered by woman, 'She thrust us out' and has made men 'prisoners'. Donne exacerbates his tenuous theology with his near blasphemy in questioning God's divine plan. The last line and a half of the stanza seems to suggest that wit is the foremost concern rather than hermeneutics, but I would not go so far as Arthur Marotti who says of Donne's similar gloss on Genesis in *The First Anniversary* that what Donne substitutes is 'comic anti-feminism' for 'genuine evidence' (1986: 239).

Donne is not yet finished with the maternal in his Nethersole sermon. He reminds woman of the various synonyms for marriage which indicate her role, one of which is '*Matrimonium*, and that is derived from a Mother, and that implies a religious education of her children'.[44] But this term only seems to ignite Donne's imagination in one last furious denunciation of woman in an attempt to 'emprison' her 'incomprehensiblenesse' so that he sounds like one of Aemilia Lanyer's 'evill disposed men': 'But she must be no more; If she think her self more then a Helper, she is not so much. He is a miserable creature, whose Creator is his Wife. God did not stay to joyn her in Commission with *Adam*, so far as to give names to the creatures; much lesse to give essence; essence to the man, essence to her husband' (ii. 346). The imaginings in the early verse letters of male parthenogenesis do indeed, in comparison, seem like harmless 'sample[s] of undergraduate wit' (Bald 1986: 75). But it is the same desire to master and contain the feminine, I suggest, which drives Donne to such relentless denunciation. Here is Donne in another sermon: 'I have a Soul, of which God was the Father, he breath'd it into me, and of which no matter can say, I was the Mother, for it proceeded of nothing' (iv. 126). Likewise, in the dedicatory letter to Prince Charles of his *Devotions*, Donne can write:

I *Have had three* Births; *One,* Naturall, *when I came into the* World; *One* Supernatural, *when I entred into the* Ministery; *and now, a* preternaturall Birth, *in returning to* Life, *from this* Sicknes. *In my* second Birth, *your* Highnesse Royall Father *vouchsafed mee his Hand, not onely to sustaine mee in* it, *but to lead mee to it. In this* last Birth, *I my selfe am borne a* Father: *This* Child *of mine, this* Booke, *comes into the world, from mee, and* with *mee. And therefore, I presume (as I did the* Father *to the* Father) *to present the* Sonne *to the* Sonne. (1987: 3)

So, woman participates in neither essence nor language, nor in the very role she is circumscribed within. The male poet is the

---

[44] But see *Sermons*, vii. 418–19, where Donne takes away all roles for the mother except feeding, in a complex passage on God as mother in Isaiah.

mother; the male God, God the Father, is also the mother; King James is the midwife. The male writer can even write himself as child and father, and of course his book is a boy. The Father is thus immortal 'because he has always refused to be born' (Irigaray 1985*a*: 319).

Donne concludes the Nethersole wedding sermon with a comparison of essential virtues for a wife: '*chastity, sobriety, taciturnity, verity*, and such' and 'such vertues as may be had, and yet the possessor not the better for them, as *wit, learning, eloquence, musick, memory, cunning*, and such, these make her never the fitter'. Above all, 'the fitnesse that goes through all, is a *sober continency*; for without that, *Matrimonium jurata fornicatio*, Mariage is but a continuall fornication, sealed with an oath: And mariage was not instituted to prostitute the chastity of the woman to one man, but to preserve her chastity from the tentations of more men' (ii. 346–7). Almost comically anti-climactic is Donne's first reference, in the very last sentence, to the poor couple sitting before him. Lucy and Sir Francis demonstrate both a '*Civill*' and a '*Spirituall fitnesse*', so that 'I am not sorry, if either the houre, or the present occasion call me from speaking any thing at all, because it is a subject too mis-interpretable, and unseasonable to admit an enlarging in at this time. At this time, therefore, this be enough, for the explication and application of these words.' Throughout the sermon, Eve is not referred to with her proper name until the final paragraph, whereas Adam is referred to by name nine times. Donne refers to four other individual biblical women: the Witch of Endor, Adah, Zillah, and Bathsheba; and to twenty-two male figures, biblical or otherwise.[45] Donne's meditation on God's recognition that his creature required a 'like-opposite' results in an exhausting diatribe which constitutes a pretermission of the feminine more relentless than perhaps any other text we have of Donne's. Propagation is the focus of instruction in a marriage sermon based on a text which was read as the story of woman's creation for precisely this purpose—following the 'narrow-Augustinian' (J. Turner 1993*a*: 101) view found in *De Genesi ad Litteram*. Yet propagation is constructed as something which occurs between the masculine principle (God and 'man') and for the masculine principle ('to

---

[45]  God, Adam (9x), Christ, Moses, Habbakkuk, Xenophon, David, Augustine (6x), John the Baptist, Abraham, St Paul, Saul (OT), Jonathan, Asa, Chrysostum (2x), Mahomet, Jerome (4x), Lamech, Theodoret, Oecumenius, Melchisedek, Ambrose.

receive glory from the sonnes of men here upon earth, and to give glory to the sonnes of men in heaven'). Woman is, grudgingly and by necessity, present, but she is brought on stage only to be obscured. The simultaneous 'birth' and 'death' of woman as mother is confidently accomplished by Donne through the authority of the Logos: woman's flesh is made word, and then erased. The Father usurps all creative powers.

### VI. 'EPITHALAMIUM [MADE AT LINCOLN'S INN]'

In the epithalamium I will discuss next, Donne represents the act of sexual consummation as a fearful confrontation at the threshold of the female body: a fight to the death. What is accomplished by the end of the poem, in a passage which has not attracted but which 'deserves sustained attention' (Dubrow 1990: 162), is the bride's willing sacrifice of her body to the patriarchy. Indeed, there is little of the commonplace punning on the 'little death' of orgasm, which in itself conflates sex and death; Donne's language suggests deeper fears of castration or impotence, and of male identity being swallowed by an engulfing mother.

In *The Arte of English Poesie*, George Puttenham narrowly defines the genre (from the Greek, θαλαμος, 'bridal chamber'), sung 'very sweetely by Musitians at the chamber dore of the Bride-groome and Bride . . . and . . . called *Epithalamies* as much to say as ballades at the bedding of the bride: for such as were song at the borde at dinner or supper were other Musickes and not properly *Epithalamies*'(1936: 50–1). Puttenham begs the pardon of 'chaste and honorable eares' both if he 'offend[s] them with licentious speach, or leave[s] them ignorant of the ancient guise in old times used at weddings, in my simple opinion nothing reproveable'. He explains that these songs were 'very loude and shrill, to the intent there might no noise be hard out of the bed chamber by the skreeking and outcry of the young damosell feeling the first forces of her stiffe & rigorous young man, she being as all virgins tender & weake, & unexpert in those maner of affaires' (51). One purpose of the epithalamium, then, is to 'diminish the noise of the laughing lamenting spouse' (51). Puttenham's language betrays a conflict inherent in the genre between celebration and real or imagined danger. He declares the goal of the wedding night: 'the husband to rob his spouse of her maidenhead and save her life, the bride so lustely to satisfie her husbandes love and scape with so litle daunger of her person' (52–3).

Violent imagery was by no means alien to a genre which addressed a liminal state, a 'crossing over' into a different social category especially for the bride, and one which involved the crossing of thresholds for both: the threshold of the woman's body by the man, and the threshold of the man's house by the woman. Heather Dubrow shows that many elements which earlier critics found disturbing about the 'Epithalamium [Made at Lincoln's Inn]', such as the focus on death, the attention given to the bride in proportion to the groom, and the 'fescennine' or obscene elements are in fact part of the epithalamic tradition.[46] The conflation of these elements in marriage poems suggests, then, that Donne's epithalamium is a local example of a more pervasive cultural association between women and death; what in other epithalamia is kept in the wings, so to speak, Donne typically brings centre stage. The poem is an example of Carey's observation of Donne's poems in general, that 'their inner inconsistencies and dubieties of tone make them resistant to summaries of any kind, and that is why they are valuable. They do not take up a "position"' (1990: 176). Donne characteristically views his poetic model—here, Spenser—as a rival, so that imitation and parody contend with one another in the same poem. The resistance of the poem to simple classification is apparent in critical discussions of the poem thus far: Virginia Tufte notes the poem 'has long been an enigma' (1970: 218), David Novarr argues that Donne's poem is a parody of Spenser's 1595 'Epithalamion', while Dubrow and Wesley Milgate suggest elements of both satire and 'straight' celebration are present.[47] The 'unstable combination of awe and

---

[46] For accounts of the epithalamic tradition, see Dubrow 1990: *passim*. Dubrow includes a brief discussion of the poem in her book on Stuart epithalamia because it 'conveniently demonstrates' tensions which continued to challenge Stuart poets (156). See also Tufte 1970: *passim*.

[47] For these discussions and on the date of Donne's poem, see Novarr 1956: 250–63; rpt. in Novarr 1980: ch. 3. Dubrow qualifies the conclusion of her earlier response to Novarr (1976) that the epithalamium is entirely not parodic and suggests it operates along a spectrum of straight and ironic responses (1990: 157–61, esp. nn. 17 and 23). See also Milgate in Donne 1978: pp. xxi–xxii; Gardner in Donne 1982: p. lxxxix, notes the poem is given only the title, 'Epithalamium', in the Westmoreland manuscript (suggesting that at the time it was copied, the other two epithalamia had not been written) and is in the company of poems which antedate 1600.

antagonism' (162) which Dubrow identifies as a generic issue is, as she affirms, an effect of psychic models as well: the tension between fear of and desire for the feminine.

Unlike many other epithalamia, in which invocations of the Muses, Venus, or Hymen, god of marriage, are made, Donne's poem has no presiding figure or deity. The frequency with which intermediary figures were used between the speaker and the couple suggests it was a way of maintaining some distance from events which were, after all, taking place between real people. Indeed, the function of the speaker in the epithalamium as instructor/voyeur/censor of the mysteries of the marital bed is a problematic and unique one. That the bridegroom should conventionally have a lesser part to play in epithalamia perhaps points to the difficult negotiation between private and public realms: it is women as objects of exchange between fathers and husbands in a community of men who had to be marked as no longer the potential property of any man but the property of one man. Competition between men was to occur only up to a point. Lucrece's tragedy demonstrates the crux: how is a man to declare his possession of a valuable commodity and hence increase his status, without displaying (even verbally) this commodity and thus leaving it vulnerable to appropriation? There is always the danger that, whether due to violation by another man or indeed by her own agency/desire, the father might be left with a worthless commodity or the husband might be left with another man's children and the 'horns' of a cuckold (see P. Parker 1987: 104–7, 126–54).

The relentless association of *eros* and *thanatos* begins in the first stanza, where Donne's speaker addresses the bride immediately, and subjects her to the first of a number of 'deaths'. Donne spends one line setting the scene with reference to the natural world before engaging in a conceit which he carefully develops throughout the poem:

> The Sun-beames in the East are spred
> Leave leave fayr bride your solitary bed.
> No more shall you returne to it alone.
> It nourseth sadnes and your bodyes print
> Like to a grave the yielding Downe doth dint. (1995*a*: 1–5)

At least initially, Donne's poem seems to announce itself as a response to Spenser by echoing his description of the sun in the

'Epithalamion': 'His golden beame upon the hils doth spred'.[48]
Donne's bride is urged to awake, however, not in the endearingly
impatient voice of Spenser; rather, she is asked to rise from her
solitary virginal bed, 'Like . . . a graue' in its barrenness so long as
she remains there alone. The bride's solitary bed is a death-bed
from which she will be 'resurrected' only by undergoing another
death or sacrifice on her wedding night. The only word associated
with life in Donne's opening lines is used ironically: the bride's
bed 'nourseth' only 'sadnes', or melancholy.

Donne's speaker will later say

> This bed is only to Virginitee
> A grave, but to a better state a Cradle
> Till now thou wast but able
> To bee, what now thou art: then that by thee
> No more be sayd, I may be, but I ame
> To night put on perfection, and a Womans name. (79–84)

The Protestant assertion in *The Lawes Resolution* that a woman is
'either married or to be married' is articulated both here and in
Donne's opening conceit; a woman has no status, indeed no being
as a 'solitary' virgin, for her *telos*, as we saw in Donne's sermon on
Gen. 2: 18, is procreation. But it was the marriage bed which then
led to childbed that woman had greater cause to fear as a 'grave',
considering the high incidence of death due to infection or other
complications during or immediately after giving birth. Consciously or unconsciously, Donne relocates the danger, just as
Puttenham reassures the woman that she 'scape[s] with so little
daunger of her person' on her wedding night.

Donne's conceit of the bed as grave is complex in other ways. In
his *Devotions* written much later in 1623, Donne refers to his
sickbed logically enough as a grave, but the bed is also a site of
wantonness: 'The bed is not ordinarily thy *Scene*, thy *Climate:
Lord*, dost thou not accuse me, dost thou not reproach to mee, my
former sinns, when thou layest mee upon this bed?' (1987: 16).
Later on, he says, 'I have a *Bed* of *sinne*; *delight* in *Sinne*, is a *Bed*; I
have a *grave* of *sinne*; *senselesnesse* in *sinne*, is a *grave*' (112).[49] And yet

---

[48] Spenser 1989: 'Epithalamion', l. 20. Spenser begins with an invocation of 'Ye
learned sisters' (1) and spends 74 lines setting the scene before addressing his bride.
Dubrow warns 'it is risky to trace sources in a genre that relies so heavily on stock
motifs', but she notes the same echo (1990: 159).

[49] See *Sermons*, vi. 316, where the association works in reverse, since Donne is

in his epithalamium, the bride's bed is a grave even before it is the site of any 'wantonness'. She must be convinced that her own life depends on the production of male heirs; but Donne also associates sex with death—the death of the male self—insofar as the man must come in contact with woman as she represents materiality, death, the absence of the phallus, and so on. Woman is thus caught between death and death in the discourse of patriarchy. Irigaray suggests that as patriarchy has constructed her, woman *qua* woman lacks a penis and possesses a 'hole' which threatens man with his own castration. Therefore man confronts 'that fissure (of) woman, against which/whom he can only defend himself by (re-)making her a mother', the place 'where each (male) *one* comes to seek the means to replenish resemblance to self (as) to same' (1991*a*: 53, 54).

Donne's phrase, 'your bodyes print', is key. The bride as she sleeps alone imprints the shape of her body in her bed. She 'print(s)' her own text or *corpus*—her body—but this imprint is read only as a blank page. Her solitary authority is never acknowledged. In fact the speaker himself writes only her 'dead' body, using a simile to 'bury' her body in a 'grave'. On her wedding night she must leave a different imprint on the bed, the authenticating authority of her virginal status, yet this is written by the male pen(is) with the bride's blood on the sheets of the marriage bed. To leave a 'blank page' on her wedding night is to write herself out of the patriarchal story,[50] yet 'the woman's part' must be articulated by a man. The poem's refrain completes the new imprinting by saying she puts on 'perfection, and a womans name'.

Donne's good friend, Sir Henry Goodyer, wrote an epithalamium in 1612/13 for the marriage of Elizabeth and Frederick in which he makes similar associations between bed and body, sheets and text. The poem was printed for the first time in 1896 (in Robert Case's *English Epithalamies*). Aside from Tufte, who mentions it only to dismiss it as a poor imitation of Donne's metaphysical style (1970: 249–50), Dubrow is, to my knowledge, the

---

contemplating his relationship with God, and the 'consolation' of the Holy Ghost as '*Ille, He*, He the Comforter': 'It makes my death-bed, a mariage-bed, And my Passing-Bell, an Epithalamion'.

[50] For illuminating parallels which cannot be elaborated here, see Isak Dinesen's short story, 'The Blank Page', and Susan Gubar's article, '"The Blank Page" and the Issues of Female Creativity' (1981).

only critic to discuss Goodyer's poem, in which she sees gender relations as well as international relations at work, sexual as well as political imperialism (1990: 67). Here, Elizabeth waits between the sheets of her bed/book for Frederick to come and read (for) her:

> Lift up thy modest head
> Great & faire Bride, & as a well taught soule
> Calls not for death, nor doth controule
> Death when hee comes, come you unto this bed,
> Doe not pursue, nor flie,
> Enter, for when these sheetes
> Open, the Booke of fate thee meetes
>     Study't a while alone but instantly
>     Comes hee that shall reveale it sensybly,
>     And spend in tellinge you, what your fate saies
> This night w$^{ch}$ to this Moneth supplies her twoe lost dayes.[51]

Elizabeth's wedding night involves a death which must be met in the *ars moriendi* tradition of meeting death with Stoicism, as an inevitability, and with requisite grace rather than eagerness or reluctance (see Lamb 1986: 207–26). She is commanded to 'Enter' the bed and 'mete' the 'Booke of fate'. Goodyer suggests she might 'Study't a while alone', which alarming thought is anxiously followed by the 'instant' arrival of Frederick who will 'reveale' Elizabeth's fate 'sensybly'; that is, he not only reads but writes, again with his pen(is), the blank page of Elizabeth's virginal body. Her body is his book.

Goodyer uses a different if conventional metaphor to describe the groom's approach. Frederick is 'the Destenies greate Instrument, | For this important business sent', but still, as Dubrow notes, more subject than object:

> Enter into possession of your Myne,
> There you maye fitly fayne
> These sheetes to bee a sea,
> And you in it an Argosea,
> And shee an Island, whose discoverie Spaine
> (W$^{ch}$ seldome us'd to miss) hath sought in vaine,
> Here end thy voyage then, & therby praise
>     This night, w$^{ch}$ to this Moneth supplies her twoe lost dayes.

---

[51] I use my own transcription of the poem in British Library Additional MS 25707.

Goodyer's stanza conveys his relief that pacifist James in the end cemented Protestant alliances between England and Protestant Germany against the threat of Catholic Spain and the Austrian Hapsburgs (see Akrigg 1962: 141 ff; Willson 1956: 283). Frederick has not only the power to read the 'booke of Fate' to Elizabeth, he can 'fitly fayne' his own myth of political imperialism as a Jason who 'Enter[s] into possession' of the Golden Fleece (Elizabeth) on the island of Colchis (England) and can thus return to and claim his rightful place as ruler. Frederick's 'stamp[ing]' of 'the pure pliant Gold' which is Elizabeth and Protestant England will 'turne [her] to usefull coyne'. In his epithalamium, Donne addresses the 'Daughters of London' in a less imperial, more bourgeois manipulation of the metaphor: 'you which bee | Our golden Mines, and furnish'd Treasurie' (13–14). The initial response of the modern reader that Donne cannot possibly be serious in referring so blatantly to the economic foundation of marriage must therefore be tempered when one reads Goodyer's poem, which was addressed to actual persons.

Donne's description of the same moment of consummation between Elizabeth and Frederick in the epithalamium he wrote for their marriage is different in tone, far more joyous than in his Lincoln's Inn epithalamium, and he expresses the conventional impatience for the wedding night proper to begin. Elizabeth cannot be undressed fast enough by her attendants and there are altogether too many 'Formalitys retarding' (72) the pleasures of the night. 'Yet there are more delayes, for, where is hee?' (80). Frederick seems to be less eager than Donne to embark on his voyage of discovery. At last, 'Hee comes, and passes through Spheare after Spheare | First her Sheetes, then her Armes, then any where' (81–2). Donne's 'mapping' of Frederick's 'voyage' is more ambiguous than Goodyer's, either deferring to an uncharacteristic modesty in becoming increasingly vague as Frederick approaches Elizabeth's 'Centrique part', or perhaps even more imperious in staking his claim to 'any where' and everywhere (another variation on 'Donne the space man'?)[52] like the speaker of Elegy XIX: 'Licence my roving hands, and let them goe | Behind, before, above, between, below' (25–6). In all three epithalamia, the attempt to limit woman's incomprehensibleness is made even as it is acknowledged.

[52] See William Empson's essay with this title (1995: 78–128).

To return to Donne's Lincoln's Inn epithalamium, his bride is not leaving her bed/grave forever, she will just not 'return to it alone'; indeed the speaker thrice more states that she will return to it with her lover:

> You and your other you meete ther anone.
> Put forth, put forth that warme balme-breathing thigh
> Which when next time you in these Sheetes will smother
> Ther it must meet an other
> Which never was, but must be ofte more nigh;
> Come glad from thence, go gladder then you came
> To day put on perfection, and a womans name. (6–12)

The speaker has nearly jumped into bed—'these' sheets—with the bride. Is a voyeuristic impulse exposed here? Goodyer makes the same reference to 'These sheetes' and instructs Frederick, 'Here end thy voyage', but defends his frankness by suggesting that 'silence' about these matters is 'disloyall', perhaps a nod to the unabashedly voyeuristic James I's habit of being the first one into the marriage chamber of his favourites the next morning, insisting that the couple provide full details of their consummation. In Donne's poem, the bride's thigh is of course a bold metonymy for the site of the bride's new 'imprint'. 'Balm' is a positive word in Donne's writing, used to connote the life-giving force or essence which courses through every living thing.[53] But again here, life and death are never very far apart; her balm-breathing thigh will be 'smother[ed]' in line 8's anticipation of consummation.[54] As indicated by the number of words he uses to indicate time ('No more', 'anone', 'next time', and all of line 10), the speaker is highly aware of a 'before' and 'after', the final moment of a particular identity 'imprinted' on the bed, or rather the negative/blank space waiting to be filled up and completed. This 'before and after' structure is also manifested in line 11's caesura.

Stanza 3 ends with a strange description of the bride:

> Lo, in yon path which store of strawd flowers graceth
> The sober Virgin paceth

---

[53] See e.g. Donne's description of Elizabeth Drury as the 'intrinsique Balme' and 'preservative' of the world in *The First Anniversary*, l. 57; 'To the Countesse of Bedford' ('Reason is our Soules left hand'), ll. 21–4; 'The Exstasie', l. 6; 'A Nocturnall upon S. Lucies Day, being the shortest day', l. 6.

[54] See 'The Dissolution', l. 8, for Donne's only other use of the word, in apposition to 'nourish'.

> Except my sight fayle: t'is no other thing.
> Weepe not, nor blush; here is no griefe nor shame
> To day put on perfection and a womans name. (32–6)

We are given few visual details up to this point, only 'strawd flowers' and a 'fayr' bride 'gay as Flora, and as rich as Inde' (22) who is made 'fitt fuell' for love by the 'Daughters of London'. The glint of gold outshines the bride's beauty. There is none of Spenser's rich detailing of the kinds of flowers, the clothing or jewels of the bride or any of her physical characteristics, except the albeit highly sensual 'warme balme-breathing thigh'. Donne is far more descriptive of Princess Elizabeth and Frances Howard in his other two epithalamia. Line 34, above, is a puzzle, either a throw-away line or one which suggests, as Novarr states, that the bride is some-'thing' other than she seems, perhaps an Inns of Court member dressed up as a bride in a mock wedding. 'Thing' was after all a euphemism for both 'penis' and 'vagina' (G. Williams 1994). It is difficult to explain these lines otherwise, and impossible to accept that they could have been presented to a real bride and groom.

The couple now approach the church, which the speaker addresses at the beginning of stanza 4:

> Thy too-leavd gates fayre Temple unfold
> And these two in thy sacred bosome hold
> Till mistically joynd but one they bee:
> Then may thy leane and hunger sterved wombe
> Long time expect their bodyes and ther tombe
> Long after ther owne Parents fatten thee. (37–42)

Two words used in the first line of the stanza hearken back to stanza 1. We have heard 'fayre' used to describe the bride twice before, in line 23 and line 2. Line 2 is also one in which the word 'leave' appears twice, so that these two words occurring in the same line twice seems more than coincidence. Although 'too-leavd' is an adjective and 'leave' in the earlier line a verb, the echo is unavoidable. So, while we hear the poet addressing the 'Temple', asking it to open its doors to the couple, we also hear the bride, or rather, a particular part of the bride's anatomy, being associated with the church through the use of the same words. From this point on we are not witnessing the couple entering the church but a man's encounter with the female body. Donne is clearly parodying Spenser's lines here: 'Open the temple gates unto my love, | Open them wide that she may enter in' (204–5), and it is easy to see how Donne has associated the Church as Bride with the bride and her anatomy in a blasphemous conceit.

Novarr asks, 'And what shall we make of the "two-leav'd gates"? Our minds withdraw, and not into happiness' (1980: 68). Novarr's dismay is not unfounded. 'Book', 'gate', 'door', and hence the adjective 'two-leav'd' were all euphemisms for 'whore' or 'vagina' (G. Williams 1994). For example, in his translation of Ovid's *Amores*, Christopher Marlowe's speaker refers to his mistress opening 'the two leav'd booke' (1987: i. 3.13.44). The metaphor of a woman's legs as a 'two-leaved book' occurs in a poem in an early seventeenth-century miscellany, and the anatomist and physician to James I, Helkiah Crooke, describes the female genitalia in exactly these terms. The first stanza of the anonymous 'A Song against weomen that weare their brests bare' reads:

> Madam be cover'd whye stand yow bare
> it fitts not with your female sexe
> we know yow carry worthy ware
> which may be found without Index
>   These bare signes doe but bid us looke
>   for unknowne stuffe in your twoe leav'd booke.[55]

The woman's tailor is a kind of bawd, for sewing such a dress, 'he would leave ope a wicked dore | That there mens eyes might allwaies enter | and soe descend to loves lowe center' (st. 6). She is 'read in Rhet'ricks schoole' as a synecdoche, that 'shew's but a part for the whole' (st. 8). Goodyer's metaphor in his epithalamium for Elizabeth and Frederick seems that much more indiscrete; even if Goodyer refers to the 'Book of fate', Frederick still 'reads' a volume which is Elizabeth herself.

In *Microcosmographia* Crooke uses the term 'leaf-gate' to describe the hymen, torn in the 'devirgination' of the maid: 'The torne Membranes of this production in their utmost compasse indented, do somtimes hang downe on either hand in the sides by the cleft like unto valves . . . or leaf-gates' (1618: 236). The same terminology is used to describe the external genitalia a few paragraphs later: 'The last dissimilar part of the wombe . . . [is called] in

---

[55] Bodleian Library, MS Rawlinson poet.60, fo. 150ᵛ.

Latine *pudendum muliebre*, that is, the womans modesty, . . . of some *Vulva*, as it were *vallis* a valley, or *Valva* a Flood-gate, because it is divided into two parts by a cleft, which like Flood gates or leafe-doores are easily opened or shut as neede is. We will call it the lappe' (237). Gordon Williams suggests the description of female genitalia as gates or doors is an 'important part of bourgeois imagery. There is an easy transition between the idea of wife as possession, kept behind closed doors, and the need to ensure that she keeps her own door closed' (1994: i. 405).

In Donne's poem the consummation of the marriage, very nearly accomplished with the wrong people in stanza 1—the poet hovering over the bride and 'these Sheetes'—is occurring in the church itself, which Donne personifies and addresses directly. The threshold of the church and its 'too-leavd gates' is that of the female body. The church becomes an organic being, Mother Church and Mother Earth, a living female maw which draws the couple into its 'sacred bosome' and holds them until 'but one they bee'. The spiritual and carnal elements of the marital union are brought together in the Church figured as the mother's body. 'She' will then await their return upon their death for burial in the crypt, her 'leane and hunger sterved wombe', hopefully 'Long after ther owne Parents fatten thee'.[56]

The womb/tomb rhyme (ll. 40–1) is one which is extremely common in poetry of this period, for which several reasons might be posited: the idea that birth and death frame our life on earth, the view that life on earth is a death from which we rise to eternal life, the frequency of infant deaths and women dying in child-birth.[57] Donne's final sermon, 'Deaths Duell', preached only a few weeks before his death in March 1631, is a staggering virtuoso performance on the womb as tomb. I quote it here because it illuminates the way in which the sacrifice of woman as mother underlies the image of the Mother Church and the bride as sacrifice in Donne's epithalamium:

all our *periods* and *transitions* in this life, are so many passages *from death* to *death*. Our very *birth* and entrance into this life is *exitus à morte*, an *issue from death*, for in our mothers *wombe* wee are *dead so*, as that wee doe *not know*

---

[56] See G. E. Wilson 1980: 72–3. Wilson suggests Donne plays on the etymology of a synonym for 'vault' and 'tomb': 'sarcophagus', from the Greek for 'flesh eating'.

[57] The rhyme 'womb'/'loom', as rich in its suggestiveness of creating and weaving life rather than juxtaposing life and death, is almost never used.

wee *live*, not so much as wee doe in our *sleepe*, neither is there any *grave* so close, or so *putrid* a *prison*, as the *wombe* would be unto us, if we stayed in it *beyond* our time, or dyed there *before* our time. . . . There in the wombe wee are fitted for *workes of darkenes*, all the while deprived of light: And there in the *wombe* wee are taught *cruelty*, by being *fed with blood*, and may be *damned*, though we be *never borne*. . . . The *wombe* which should be the *house of life*, becomes *death* it selfe, if God leave us there. . . . Wee have a winding sheete in our Mothers wombe, which grows with us from our conception, and wee come into the world, wound up in that *winding sheet*, for wee come to *seeke a grave*. (x. 231–2, 233)

Donne plays in this sermon on the paradox of the womb as both the 'house of life' and a gateway to the 'death' of this earthly life. In her essay, 'The Bodily Encounter with the Mother' (1991*a*: 34–46; see also 1993*c*: 7–21), Irigaray describes how the patriarchal imaginary (as described by Freud) functions on the basis of a matricide (which Freud fails to acknowledge):

A taboo is in the air. If the father did not sever this over-intimate bond with the primal womb, there might be the danger of fusion, of death, of the sleep of death. Putting the matrix of his language [*langue*] in its place? But the exclusivity of his law forecloses this first body, this first home, this first love. It sacrifices them so as to make them material for the rule of a language [*langue*] which privileges the masculine genre [*le genre masculin*] to such an extent as to confuse it with the human race [*le genre humain*]. . . . The father forbids the bodily encounter with the mother. . . . The imaginary and the symbolic of intra-uterine life and of the first bodily encounter with the mother . . . where are we to find them? In what darkness, what madness, have they been abandoned? (1991*a*: 39; last ellipsis Irigray's)

Donne does imagine our intra-uterine life but it is with the relentlessly morbid and culturally determined imagery of 'darkness', 'cruelty', and damnation. But Donne can only posit the womb as a place of death if he inserts the suppositional 'if' in many of his clauses, although again, the high incidence of stillborn babies and mothers dying in childbirth no doubt also informs these suppositions. There is no recognition that the mother's body provides life, yet Donne celebrates Christian renewal with the body and blood of Christ in the communion feast. Indeed, in *Essays in Divinity*, Donne embarks on an extensive metaphor of God as mother but explicitly diminishes the debt owed to real women-mothers. Donne describes the Church as 'nourced' by God, 'ever more delicately and preciously then any natural children (for they are fed with their Mothers blood in her womb, but we with the blood of our most Blessed Saviour all our lives)' (1952: 48; see Irigaray 1993c: 21).

In *Deaths Duell*, God—specifically 'the *God* of *power*, the *Almighty Father*' (x. 231)—is our deliverer from a disembodied womb. 'Mother' is used as a modifier only twice in the entire sermon, although one could argue that Donne may be trying to dissociate the maternal figure from this locus of death:   'by denying the mother her generative power and by wanting to be the sole creator, the Father, according to our culture, superimposes upon the archaic world of the flesh a universe of language [*langue*] and symbols which cannot take root in it except as in the form of that which makes a hole in the bellies of women and in the site of their identity' (Irigaray 1991a: 41).   Thus, I have taken as the title for this chapter a line from one of Donne's elegies deliberately out of context. In 'The Bracelet' Donne expresses his own distress at having to melt twelve of his own gold coins to make a bracelet as replacement for one of his mistress's which he lost:

> But thou art resolute; Thy will be done.
> Yet with such anguish as her only sonne
> The mother in the hungry grave doth lay,
> Unto the fire these Martyrs I betray. (79–82)

Donne's speaker identifies his mistress with God the Father (see also l. 18) and himself with the Virgin Mary and Christ: 'Thy will be done'. I isolate the line to expose, in the context of my discussion, the masculine fear of the feminine, of the inside of the female body—the mother is a 'hungry grave'—so that a matricide, a forgetting of the mother, forms the foundation of patriarchal culture—the mother is placed in a 'hungry grave':

woman will assume the function of representing death (of sex/organ), castration, and man will be sure as far as possible of achieving mastery, subjugation, by triumphing over the anguish (of death) through intercourse, by sustaining sexual pleasure despite, or thanks to, the horror of closeness to that absence of sex/penis, that mortification of sex that is evoked by woman. (Irigaray 1985a: 27)

At the end of *Deaths Duell*, Donne meditates on Christ's death as that death which delivered us into eternal life: 'as *God breathed a soule into the first Adam, so this second Adam breathed his soule into God, into the hands of God'*. The life cycle from birth to death, the whole of human history—from creation through to salvation—is achieved without the feminine. And yet the final image is one in which we are left 'in that *blessed dependancy*, to *hang* upon *him* that *hangs* upon the *Crosse*, there *bath* in his *teares*, there *suck* at his *woundes*, and *lye downe in peace* in his *grave'* (x. 248); in other words we are left clinging to Christ as Mother.

Donne ends the 'Temple' stanza of his epithalamium with a classical convention: the banishment of any troubles that might plague the newly-weds, usually on the night itself. Yet in banishing these possible marital strifes, he must name them, and they thus invade the celebratory space of the poem:

> All elder claymes and all cold barrennes
> All yielding to new loves, be farr for ever,
> Which might these two dissever.
> All wayes, all th'other may each one possesse
> For the best bride, best worthy of prayer and fame
> To day puts on perfection and a Womans name. (43–8)

The disruption of these possible perils is not as clear-cut in this epithalamium which exploits more than it celebrates, but the contrast is one which Donne appears to be parodying. As the word 'all' is repeated, the sense of an overwhelming number of possible spoilers of wedded bliss is uppermost in one's mind. Moreover, 'all' these evils are only 'farr'; even if they spin on those far boundaries 'for ever', they are still present. 'All elder claymes' suggests that the groom or the bride has perhaps pledged their love to another who might then appear on the scene. As much as the speaker wishes 'all cold barrennes' 'farr for ever', he has just referred to the church's voracious 'hunger sterved wombe'. The third evil is stated almost as an inevitability; that is, the speaker wishes that the 'yielding' to 'new loves' be far, but the new loves, it seems, are going to turn up regardless. The syntax of line 46 is confusing, and considering what has gone before, makes one suspicious that Donne's speaker is making a veiled reference to sexual positions in 'All wayes', perhaps more apparent on the page than when spoken and heard as 'always'. One could also read the line as a wish that 'each one possess all members of the other sex'.

In the sixth stanza, the poet forgets about the bridegroom, or rather becomes the bridegroom. He begins this stanza as he did the first one, spending one line telling us that 'The amorous evening Star is rose' (61), and then moving on to the bride and her bed, this time telling her not to get out of it but to get in: 'Why should not then our amorous Star enclose | Herselfe in her wish'd bed' (62–3). Donne follows the tradition of the maid who cannot wait to become a wife in referring to the bride's 'wish'd bed'. A much copied poem in seventeenth-century miscellanies presents a maiden who dreams of sex. Significantly the speaker is female and she voices her own desire, but her desire is dictated by masculine expectations and titillations. She is eager for sex, and dreams 'as mayds can hardly chuse' of a 'Gallant' who woos her: 'me thought we married were and went to bed'. Her eagerness turns to fear when he 'gote up' (had an erection) so that she awakes from her dream: 'With that for feare I quaked | and trembling laye cry'd out and soe awaked | It would have vex'd a Saint, my blood did burne | to be soe nigh and misse soe good a turne' (MS Rawlinson poet.160, fo. 151). Her desire is thus figured for the delectation of a male reader but it is ultimately denied and deferred until a real man comes along, and her fear is imagined at what is the most vulnerable moment for the man.

Donne does not follow the tradition inverse to that of the eager bride: that of the unwilling and fearful bride, cowering beneath a bridegroom warrior on the battlefield of love, eager to inflict a 'wound';[58] rather, he goes beyond the idea of the willing or hopeful bride in making her a willing and a pleasing sacrifice. The groom need not even fight, she'll lie down and 'die' for him upon his 'wish'd approch':

---

[58] See Claudian, 'Fescennine Verses', 4 (14) in which the groom is urged 'ne cessa, iuvenis, comminus adgredi, | impacata licet saeviat unguibus. . . . crescunt difficili gaudia iurgio. [Hesitate not to be close in thine attacks, young lover, e'en though she oppose thee savagely with cruel finger-nail. . . . The refusals of coyness do but increase the joy]'; Ausonius, 'Nuptial Cento', where the bride's vagina is 'hic specus horrendum [this dreadfull Cave]' (113) and the groom 'haesit virgineumque alte bibit ata cruorem [virgins blood did drink at length]' (118). I quote the translation of Ausonius found in Bodleian Library MS Ashmole 38 (p. 149). See Secundus 1930, 'Epithalamium', which employs the 'love as war' topos so that the narrator encourages the groom to 'Strike hard, strike steady, and strike deep'; Ben Jonson, 'Epithalamion' from *The Masque of Hymen*, 1606 (for the first wedding of Frances Howard): 'Joys, got with strife, increase. | Affect no sleepy peace; | But keep the bride's fair eyes | Awake with her own cries, | Which are but maiden fears: | And kisses dry such tears'. (1925–52: vii. 227).

> Thy Virgins girdle now unty
> And in thy nuptiall bed, Loves Altar, ly
> A pleasing Sacrifice: Now disposses
> Thee of these chaines and robes, which were put on
> To'adorne the day not thee; for thou alone
> Like Vertu and Truthe art best in nakednes. (73–8)

We have heard such arguments elsewhere in Donne's poetry, for example in 'To His Mistress Going to Bed', but I want to suggest that Donne is perhaps parodying not just Spenser's epithalamium but the episode in *The Faerie Queene* in which Serena is captured by a 'salvage nation' of cannibals who prepare to sacrifice her, until Calepine rescues her in the nick of time. However, since this episode occurs in Book 6 (8.31–51), which was not published until early 1596,[59] we would have to posit either a later date for Donne's epithalamium than Novarr's of mid–1595 (1980: 71 ff) or, that Donne saw this part of Spenser's poem in manuscript.[60] Here is the final stanza of Donne's epithalamium in which the actual consummation takes place:

> Even like a faythfull Man content
> That this life for a better should be spent
> So She a Mothers riche Stile doth prefer.
> And at the bridegroomes wish'd approch doth ly
> Like an appointed Lambe, when tenderly
> The Priest comes on his knees to'embowell her.
> Now sleepe or watche with more joye: and O Light
> Of heaven, to morrow rise thou hott and early:
> This Sun will love so dearly
> Her rest, that long, long, we shall want her sight;
> Wonders are wrought, for She which had no maime
> To night puts on perfection and a Womans name. (85–96)

Is Donne aligning himself and his Inns of Court coterie with Spenser's 'salvage nation' who raid 'their neighbours borders' and chance upon Serena, 'like a sheepe astray'?[61] Serena awakes, terrified by their ritual preparations and 'they hands upon her lay',

---

[59] Entered in the Stationer's Register on 20 January.
[60] Spenser indicates in *Amoretti* 80 that he has completed six books of his proposed twelve-book epic. The *Amoretti* and *Epithalamion* were entered in the Stationer's Register on 19 November 1594 and published in early 1595.
[61] Spenser 1995: 6.8.35.2, 4; 36.8. Hereafter references to stanza and line number (all in Book 6, canto 8) are cited in parentheses.

remove her jewels and clothing, and 'view with lustfull fantasyes' 'her bellie white and clere, | Which like an Altar did it selfe uprere, | To offer sacrifice divine thereon' (42.4–6). In the Longman annotated edition of *The Faerie Queene*, the editor A. C. Hamilton provides the following gloss on these lines and indeed cites Donne's epithalamium: 'Since the episode treats the sexual phantasies of a woman in love, the Altar suggests the nuptial bed on which the bride awaits the groom'. Serena is placed on the altar which the cannibals have 'fayned' and

> the Priest with naked armes full net
> Approching nigh, and murdrous knife well whet,
> Gan mutter close a certaine secret charme,
> With other divelish ceremonies met. (45.4–7)

At the whooping of the savages, Calepine (the almost too-late bridegroom?) comes crashing through the underbrush, kills the Priest, and puts the throng to flight or to the sword. Certainly there are similarities—thematic as well as verbal—between Donne's stanza and Spenser's albeit far more complex episode. Spenser's priest 'Approching nigh' seems to be echoed by Donne's bride/lamb who 'at the bridegroomes wish'd approch doth ly', and both 'priests' may be 'on [their] knees' in a sexual position (see Carey 1990: 129), parodying a gesture of reverence. In both poems, 'primitive urges'—hunger and lust—as well as the 'indigenous' need for religious ritual (see Berger 1988: 230) meet over the body of a woman. In Donne's poem, however, she is a willing sacrifice,[62] but the similes of woman/lamb, bridegroom/ priest, also suggests bestiality on the part of the bridegroom, or homosexuality if the bride is really a man, especially since, as Carey points out, the verb 'embowell' suggests something going in, not taken out, and suggests the site of the bowel rather than the vagina. The penultimate line is another which can be read as playing on a man dressed as a bride, for 'Wonders are wrought, for She which had no maime'—or he who does not lack the phallus and so is in no need of perfection—'To night puts on perfection and a Womans name'.

Donne draws a parallelism between heaven and the married

---

[62] And if one agrees with Hamilton that the episode deals with the phantasies of a woman in love, then Serena is a kind of willing maid as well, who 'wakes up' just at the moment the priest approaches with his frightening instrument.

state, at least for the bride, who is 'faythfull' and 'content' in giving up her virginal life 'for a better', the same idea which Goodyer perhaps borrowed in his epithalamium when he describes Elizabeth approaching her wedding night in the manner of dying well. Donne is not above casting himself in the role of sacrificial 'victim', as in his *Devotions* when he prays, 'As thou hast made this *bed*, thine *Altar*, make me thy *Sacrifice*; and as thou makest thy *Sonne Christ Jesus* the *Priest*, so make me his *Deacon*, to minister to him in a chereful surrender of my body, & soule to thy pleasure, by his hands' (1987: 18). But Donne's bride is given no opportunity to voice her desires, nor does her sacrifice bring about her identification with the divine. She is the scapegoat who ensures that the violence which threatens to disrupt the community (of men), because they inevitably experience desire for the same, is directed outside the community (see Girard 1977; Irigaray 1993*c*: 73–88). She 'a Mothers riche Stile doth prefer', an identity she is given just as the Bridegroom approaches 'to'embowell her'. Man puts his thing, his language (the 'rich Stile' of mother) in her empty place. From virgin to mother, the bride's transformation leaves no room for her own subjectivity: 'Woman fulfills man's needs as mother, matrix, body (both living and as a container-sepulchre), nurse. Apparently man wants woman only as mother and virgin, or sometimes, rather ambiguously, as sister—but not as woman, as other gender' (Irigaray 1993*c*: 121). As virgin and as mother, woman is the sacrificial victim, and relations between mother and daughter are also sacrificed, as Ben Jonson makes explicit: 'Help, youths and virgins, help to sing | The prize, which Hymen here doth bring; | And did so lately rap [i.e.rape] | From forth the mother's lap' (1925–52: vii. 226). Numerous paradoxes are enacted on the wedding night: the container is contained within the masculine 'house', that which was waiting *in potentia* 'outside' the structure of society is brought inside it by being penetrated. Puttenham relates that not only were the bride's cries drowned out by the epithalamium, a second song was sung around midnight to encourage the couple to 'persist in all good appetite with an invincible courage to the end' (54). Indeed, procreation was to be aimed at even in this first encounter, hence these 'second assaultes . . . lesse rigorous, but more vigorous and apt to avance the purpose of procreation'.

In conclusion then, I return to the questions I posed at the outset of this chapter. Why is woman made? To produce sons who will inherit the property of their fathers and continue to exchange property, in all its forms, with other men. Yet Donne's Nethersole wedding sermon shows us that 'historically, in Genesis, the feminine has no conception. She is figured as being born from man's envelope, with God as midwife' (Irigaray 1993a: 93). How is woman made in a patriarchal society? Through a man's symbolic encounter with the mother in the act of consummation on the wedding night, whereby the original mother who reminds him of death is 'murdered' and replaced with a substitute mother—the wife—who will enable him to achieve a kind of immortal life through his progeny and thus thwart death a second time. 'Faithless to God, man lays down the law for woman, imprisons her in his conception(s). . . . Woman, who enveloped man before birth, until he could live outside her, finds herself encircled by a language, by places that she cannot conceive of, and from which she cannot escape' (1993a: 93–4). If procreation requires male and female principles, society pretends to require only man and woman as 'not-man'; female never becomes woman as male becomes man, to the impoverishment of both and the denial of true fecundity, that 'eternall generation' in which God so delights.

# 4

# He Sings the Body Electrum:
# Re-membering Elizabeth Drury

> [T]he identity of the human female is unknown or has
> become unknown.
>
> (Luce Irigaray)
>
> [T]he body itself balks account.
>
> (Walt Whitman)

## I. PARENTHESES AND BLANK SPACES: ASSESSING THE NEGLIGIBLE ACHIEVEMENT OF ELIZABETH DRURY

The epitaph, elegy, and *Anniversaries* which Donne wrote on the occasion of Elizabeth Drury's death constitute a body of texts which, when read together, map out the problematics of writing and reading the female body for Donne. In the first section of this chapter I will offer a possible strategy for tackling Donne's difficult poems, the *Anniversaries*. A close reading of over a thousand lines of poetry is impossible to carry out in the space of a single chapter, although I will focus on many smaller portions of the text which have been built around and upon the dead body of Elizabeth Drury. My aim is more to show the potential for a close reading of the poems when we view them as carrying out a textual sexualization of Elizabeth, beginning with her epitaph and ending with *The Second Anniversary*. The second section of this chapter consists of a reading of Elizabeth's epitaph, a return to the grave site, as it were, which offers a fitting reminder of what lies at the centre of Donne's *Anniversaries*: the present absence of the feminine.

Recent criticism of Donne's *Anniversaries* indicates that the problem of decorum is no less of a persistent itch today than it was for those first readers who brought 'many censures' (Donne 1977: 74) against Donne, not least of which was Ben Jonson's famous charge of blasphemy.[1] Who is this Elizabeth Drury to be so extravagantly launched into immortality and the literary stratosphere, we ask? We point to the precise wording of the titles: it is only 'By Occasion of the untimely' and 'religious death' of Elizabeth that the poems have been written (see e.g. Lewalski 1973: 13). Some argue that Elizabeth's death is not even an occasion but rather an opportunity for Donne to impress a prospective patron. We then proceed with our sometimes Procrustean operations to find a perfect fit for the 'shee' of the poems, the subject Donne really had in mind when he defensively claimed, so we have it from Ben Jonson through Drummond of Hawthornden, that he wrote of 'the Idea of a Woman and not as she was'. Thus, 'shee' becomes e.g. Astræa, the Virgin Mary, Queen Elizabeth, St Lucy, Wisdom, or the Logos,[2] 'she allows herself to be consumed again for new speculations, or thrown away as unfit for consumption'.[3] Regardless of whether Donne's motives were mercenary or not, he had to make choices in the representation of Elizabeth Drury, and it is those choices which this chapter seeks to understand and to place in the wider context of Donne's own writing and culture. This is not to deny the importance of Donne's material ties to a patronage system which inevitably influenced his poetry; no doubt opportunistic motives played a part in the writing of these poems, especially considering his straitened circumstances after almost a decade of unemployment, but the net Donne casts in constructing his poems lies beyond (if inclusive of) material considerations, in the network of phallocentric discourse's negotiation of the feminine.

Let us look more closely for a moment at the figure of Elizabeth Drury 'as she was', as one who seems 'imaginatively . . . of the

---

[1] William Drummond reports the following exchange between Jonson and Donne. Jonson charges 'that Dones Anniversarie was profane and full of Blasphemies that he told Mr Donne, if it had been written of ye Virgin Marie it had been something to which he answered that he described the Idea of a Woman and not as she was'. See Jonson 1925–52: i. 133.

[2] For a summary of critical discussions of the 'she' of the poems, see Donne 1995a: 293–317.

[3] Irigaray 1985a: 228. See her whole essay, 'Volume-Fluidity', 227–40, for an uncanny gloss of Donne's re-membering of Elizabeth.

highest significance; [yet] practically she is completely insignificant' (Woolf 1977: 43). On the one hand, we have a young girl
who lived from 1596 until 1610 when she died in London of
unknown causes, but about whom we have no other historical
records (Bald 1959). On the other hand we have an unusually
extensive memorialization of her:[4] a life-size portrait,[5] an elaborate
funeral monument with an epitaph written by Donne; apocryphal
tales,[6] charities for poor women established in her name; and over
a thousand lines of poetry written with encyclopædic virtuosity by
one of the greatest poets of his age, which he then most uncharac-
teristically published. Thus, like the scholastics trying to pile all

---

[4] Leah Marcus (1978) discusses the increasing number of commemorations of
children throughout the seventeenth century, but notes these were still relatively rare
in the early part of the century.
[5] The portrait of Elizabeth Drury has received almost no attention from either the
art or literary world. An engraving of it appears in Cullum's history of Hawstead, in
whose possession the painting then was (Cullum 1784: 146). The portrait was
painted by Paul van Somer, who from 1616 until his death in 1621/2 was a successful
painter at the English court (Campling 1937: 63). Van Somer did not settle in
England until December 1616 so it is difficult to determine the genesis of Elizabeth's
portrait, which was either painted at least six years after her death, or was perhaps
executed from life during the trip she took with her parents to the Continent shortly
before she died. The 'singularity of the attitude' which Cullum mentions is perhaps
the most unusual aspect of the painting, for Elizabeth lies in a semi-recumbent
position which, as Campling points out, is unusual except in paintings of nudes
(1937: 63). The semi-recumbent figure was not, however, altogether unseen in
English portraiture at this time. Roy Strong discusses Nicholas Hilliard's miniature of
Henry Percy, 9th Earl of Northumberland (the 'Wizard Earl'), (painted c.1590–5) and
Isaac Oliver's portrait of Edward, Lord Herbert of Cherbury (c.1610–1614), and
observes that the semi-recumbent posture of both men is an attribute of the 'Ficinian
philosophic melancholic' persona the men wished to present as part of a male
intellectual élite (1983: 180). Elizabeth Drury's similar posture is perhaps intended
to symbolize a melancholy temperament or her bent towards the contemplative,
which would make her portrait even more unusual, she being female. Elizabeth might
best be described as a fully-clothed nude. Her clothes are rich and heavy and hide her
form from us, but an intelligent, thoughtful face meets our gaze. Her monument in
Hawstead Church represents her, if much less skilfully, in the same semi-recumbent
position as the portrait. Philippe Ariès, writing of funeral monuments, notes that 'the
symbolic gesture of the head resting on the hand . . . even in the frescoes of Giotto,
already signified melancholy meditation' (1981: 244). For reproductions of the
painting and the monument, see Bald 1959: facing 68–9. Prof. Janel Mueller tells me
that Elizabeth's portrait now hangs in a Rhode Island museum, but has undergone
extensive 'repair' because of climate damage so that Elizabeth is unrecognizable.
[6] Three stories, none substantiated, circulated after the death of Elizabeth Drury.
The legends revolve around paternal violence, and love and marriage, either ideal
(Prince Henry) or tragic (a stable groom) matches, perhaps no coincidence considering Elizabeth's class and age placed her on the threshold of this rite of passage.
See Cullum 1784: 145–6 and Bald 1959: 68.

those angels on the head of a pin, we try to stack these remembrances of Elizabeth on the hyphen which holds a space for her life between the dates of her birth and death, 1596–1610. But the pressure is too great; the hyphen buckles, the years close together and Elizabeth Drury is parenthesized, abandoned for figures better able to withstand the pressures of time and sublimation. We still only know that she lived; we do not know how, except through, or rather in, the imagination of Donne. Our dismay at Elizabeth's hyperbolic trajectory, our inability to 'sit still' and accept the ambiguity of Donne's extraordinary reconfiguration of the ordinary is a curious, complex phenomenon which has haunted these works since their publication in 1611 and 1612. It constitutes an often crippling weight around the neck of these works and their young female catalyst, a weight with which Dante's Beatrice, Petrarch's Laura, or, on a lesser scale, Jonson's Venetia Digby (see Lebans 1972: 558), and Marvell's Maria Fairfax, are unencumbered.

In this chapter I will argue that there is no 'key' to unlocking the identity of Elizabeth Drury to determine who she 'really' is, as if the poems were allegorical. Rather than the sole subject, focus, or 'end' of these poems (although she begins as their subject in the smaller works), Elizabeth's virtue and her virtuous body become the means by which Donne illustrates the virtuosity of his own powers of language, his ability to 'emprison' incomprehensibleness in a verbal monument. Elizabeth becomes Donne's most complex rendering of the present absence of the feminine. An evolution of purpose and scope can be traced from the epitaph—the text closest to her body—to *The Second Anniversary*, so that the epitaph is the kernel of the funeral elegy which in turn contains the 'germ' (Bald 1986: 240), of some of the motifs of the larger poems.[7] Such a reading highlights only one of many processes

---

[7] The chronology of the poems must be established. In 1611 'A Funerall Elegie' was placed after *The First Anniversary* in a different typeset. In the 1612 reissue of *The First Anniversary* and 'A Funerall Elegie' with *The Second Anniversary*, the elegy was placed first. Grierson, Bald, and Milgate all concur the 1612 arrangement is the chronologically correct one, contra Frank Manley in his edition of the poems (see Donne 1912: ii. 178; Bald 1986: 240; Donne 1978: p. xxix; Manley 1963). Milgate points to the generic requirements of the elegy as 'designed, or imagined, as an epitaph suitable to be pinned on the hearse over Elizabeth Drury's grave', and thus it would have been written soon after her death. It seems to this reader that the generic evidence outweighs the 1611 printed arrangement of the poems. Moreover, if we study the endings of the three poems, we will discover a progression in terms of how

occurring in what are endlessly allusive (and elusive) poems. Both 'virtue' and 'virtuoso' derive from the same Latin root, *virtus -tutis*, which literally means 'manliness, manly excellence' or more generally, 'excellence, capacity, worth'. Elizabeth's feminine virtues—her chastity and silence—are celebrated in the epitaph and elegy. But it is Elizabeth's virtuous virginity, her 'sexlessness'—she is 'sine sexu' in the epitaph—and her position on the threshold of womanhood, which paradoxically allows Donne poetically to transform her e.g. as the 'Father' who inseminates Donne's 'chast' Muse 'to bring forth such a child as this', *The Second Anniversary*. Why should he need to do this? Philippa Berry compares the function of the feminine in Dante and Petrarch:

> whereas Dante's conception of Beatrice in the *Divina Commedia* had been as guide to the universe of medieval Christianity, in which all things were related to each other and simultaneously to God, in the *Rime Sparse* the idealized woman becomes a means for man to know and affirm himself in his material environment rather than in relation to a transcendent order. [Laura] is the key to an androcentric rather than a theocentric universe. . . . Petrarch attempts to assimilate and redefine [a pre-Renaissance tradition of mystical and religious] symbolism in terms of a self-referential system. (1989: 22)

Donne occupies a different world again from Dante and Petrarch, a post-Reformation world in which there is a division not only between God and man but a choice between which God and which man; the virginal feminine is not only mediator between man and God as well as mirror of man to himself, but, with a newly sanctioned yet carefully contained sexuality, a mediator between man and man, as we saw in the Nethersole wedding sermon. Donne's figuration of the feminine is correspondingly complicated, no longer the 'unequivocally chaste' virgin of Dante or Petrarch (Berry 1989: 18) but one which, I suggest, masterfully manipulates a Catholic valorization of virginity so as to capitulate to a Protestant ideal of womanhood as wife and mother.

One reason for Donne's particular figuration of Elizabeth Drury may be the psychic scars of what Carey calls his apostasy (1990: 1–22). In *Feminine Engendered Faith*, Maureen Sabine suggests that

---

Donne viewed the roles of speaker and subject within the works, their relationship to the reader, and, as it turns out rather importantly, to God. There is no means of dating the epitaph exactly, and in placing it 'first', I am, as stated, beginning with the text closest to Elizabeth's body and moving away from it. See Sparrow 1949: 208.

Donne's 'subliminal reflex to honour the Blessed Virgin' under whose spiritual care he was raised as a child, and his 'conscious resolve to refrain forever more' in the growing knowledge that his destiny lay in the Anglican Church, are mutually exclusive inclinations which 'generate much of the stress in the *Anniversary* poems' (1992: 79). Sabine suggests 'A Funerall Elegie' is Donne's consolation of the Drurys in the thought that womanhood and motherhood was not the ideal, and 'that their daughter had been spared through death the "infirmities" (l. 77) associated with the loss of virginity' (92). I suggest that while Donne's epitaph and elegy are more 'Catholic' in their praise of the virginal Elizabeth Drury, they set up the conditions for Elizabeth's sexual textualization in *The Anniversaries* that will allow Donne to satisfy the Protestant readership of these more public poems. Elizabeth was a virgin, but one on the brink of womanhood and the attendant duties of wife and mother; she was also an heiress. Sabine argues that in *The Anniversaries*, 'adverse comparison between the unfinished life of a church-going virgin and maternal fulfillment of God's will was carefully avoided' (107), whereas I suggest Donne holds both roles before us: what should be incompatible states (the exception being the Virgin Mary) would be, except that Elizabeth Drury is dead, and, through elegy, her virginal body can be transformed by and into (Protestant) text or Word. In *The Second Anniversary* Elizabeth is described as possessing a soul of 'Gold' (241) and a body of 'Electrum' (242). Electrum is described by Pliny as an amalgam of four parts gold to one part silver (*Nat. Hist* 33.23) and by Paracelsus as 'a substance midway between ore and metal, neither perfect nor imperfect, but moving towards perfection'.[8] In suggesting that Donne sings the body Electrum of Elizabeth, then, I offer one way of reading the poems which sees Elizabeth as both *in potentia* as a Protestant virgin and a Catholic virgin *in perpetua* and hence closest to 'perfection'.

The parenthesis and blank space I will be considering also serve, respectively, to focus both Catholic (closed) and Protestant (dilatory) conceptions of the female body. Donne makes use of Eliza-

---

[8] Both Pliny and Paracelsus are quoted by Milgate in Donne 1978: 164. See also *Sermons*, iii. 300 in which Donne argues Christ is not, as Tertullian suggested, like Electrum, because he is not a third metal made of two others, gold and silver, but rather 'a person so made of God and Man, as that, in that person, God and Man, are in their natures still distinguished'.

beth's paradoxically chaste and fertile body which aligns her with the Virgin Mary to arrive finally at a fully Protestant position from which to preach: that of mediator between heaven and earth. Elizabeth is his first sermon, in other words. But a tension results from the public telling of Elizabeth's private virtue which is problematic. A woman's body always spoke for her—its beauty or ugliness, its fecundity or barrenness, its chastity or looseness—but patriarchal culture asserted that it spoke loudest of her virtue when it remained out of sight. Donne must keep Elizabeth's virtuous reputation intact while somehow making her accessible as a Christian example to be emulated (see P. Parker 1987: 138). The distinction between inside and outside must remain clear on one level and made irrelevant on another.

In a sermon preached on Psalm 6: 8–10 in 1623, Donne indirectly offers us an insight into approaching his poems via their endings. Donne explains that David leaves his 'primary duty'— thankfulness—to the end of the psalm because 'it leaves the best impression in the memory. And therefore it is easie to observe, that in all Metricall compositions, of which kinde the booke of Psalmes is, the force of the whole piece, is for the most part left to the shutting up; the whole frame of the Poem is a beating out of a piece of gold, but the last clause is as the impression of the stamp, and that is it that makes it currant' (vi. 41). Irigaray argues that if we reverse the kind of teleological closure which Donne suggests is the 'stamp' of meaning, we will discover other meanings and begin to clear a space in language for the feminine: 'we need to proceed in such a way that linear reading is no longer possible: that is, the retroactive impact of the end of each word, utterance, or sentence upon its beginning must be taken into consideration in order to undo the power of its teleological effect' (1985*b*: 80). What happens when we apply Donne's observations to the endings of 'A Funerall Elegie' and both *Anniversaries*, and then reverse the direction of meaning, so to speak, as Irigaray urges, so as to read both ways? The endings of the *Anniversaries*, I suggest, offer a possible reading of the poems as a whole as well as of the role Donne plays, ostensibly as mediator between Elizabeth Drury and the reader.

As we consider these relationships it is vital to remember that these are almost the only works Donne published during his lifetime, and that Donne supervised the preparation for printing of the 1611 and 1612 editions. Donne expresses in two letters his embarrassment and regret at having published verse but defends the extravagance of his praise for Elizabeth:

for no body can imagine, that I who never saw her, could have any other purpose in that, then that when I had received so very good testimony of her worthinesse, and was gone down to print verses, it became me to say, not what I was sure was just truth, but the best that I could conceive; for that had been a new weaknesse in me, to have praised any body in printed verses, that had not been capable of the best praise that I could give. (1977: 75)[9]

The regret expressed in his letters has tended to overshadow what the endings of these poems at least make problematic: the poems were either written with publication in mind and intended for a public audience, or, the ending of *The Second Anniversary* is a self-justification in response to the objections voiced after *The First Anniversary* was published. At the end of *The First Anniversary*, Donne seems to anticipate the objections when he rather defensively identifies himself with Moses:

> if you
> In reverence to her, doe thinke it due,
> That no one should her prayses thus reherse,
> As matter fit for Chronicle, not verse,
> Vouchsafe to call to minde, that God did make
> A last, and lastingst peece, a song. He spake
> To *Moses*, to deliver unto all,
> That song: because he knew they would let fall,
> The Law, the Prophets, and the History,
> But keepe the song still in their memory.
> Such an opinion (in due measure) made
> Me this great Office boldly to invade. (457–68)

In Deuteronomy 31–3, just before the Israelites enter the Promised Land with Joshua, Moses is charged by God with delivering a

---

[9] Donne's sister, Ann, lived in Hawstead in close contact with the Drurys from 1598 to 1603, the year her husband, William Lyly, a close friend of Sir Robert Drury, died. She would have thus known Elizabeth Drury as an infant and young child, and perhaps even longer, since it remains unknown whether she continued in Hawstead after her husband's death or moved elsewhere. The second person who could have provided Donne with protestations of Elizabeth Drury's singularity is Joseph Hall, author of *Virgidemiarum,* discussed in Ch. 1, who became the rector at Hawstead Church and knew Elizabeth from age 6 to 13. See Donne's letters to George Garrard (1977: 238–9, 255).

song to bear witness to God's fulfillment of His promise. Hence, Donne defends his poetic mode as a privileged, rather masculine invasion, for it was used by God when he wanted his people to remember Him and His laws the most (see *Sermons*, ii. 170–1). Dennis Kay observes that 'it is important to retain a sense of the biblical context of these remarks. Donne is claiming kinship with writings that are more than merely generically various and memorable: they are also, axiomatically, divinely inspired and as such exemplary' (1990: 106).

At the end of *The Second Anniversary*, Donne declares,

> Since his will is, that to posteritee,
> Thou shouldst for life, and death, a patterne bee,
> And that the world should notice have of this,
> The purpose, and th'Autority is his;
> Thou art the Proclamation; and I ame
> The Trumpet, at whose voice the people came. (523–8)[10]

At the end of both poems Donne aligns himself with biblical precedents so as to imply divine endorsement of his role. In positioning himself between God and 'the people', with Elizabeth as his 'song' and 'Proclamation', Donne seems to anticipate his preacherly role in the pulpit which he was to assume in just a few years (see W. Mueller 1962: 19–22); hence, there is the question of whether *The Anniversaries* are to be read as preliminary to his career as preacher or as Donne's last attempt to impress his abilities upon a secular imagination in the hope of a patronage appointment, or perhaps both.

The endings of *The Anniversaries* present Elizabeth Drury as a difficult scriptural text, the compression which Donne must expand upon, a point to which I shall return.[11] The ending of 'A Funerall Elegie', however, presents her as a blank, no text at all:

> He which not knowing her sad History,
>     Should come to read the booke of destiny,
>
>     . . .

---

[10] Lewalski provides the fullest gloss on these lines as signifying through allusion to various biblical trumpets Donne's status as 'poet-prophet/priest/preacher' (1973: 277–80). See Judg. 6: 34; Ezek. 33: 3–5, 32; Rev.; and Donne's sermon on Ezek. 33: 32, *Sermons*, ii. 166–70.

[11] See Donne's verse letter 'To the Countess of Bedford' ('You have refin'd mee') in which he explains, 'as darke texts need notes: there some must bee | To usher vertue, and say, *This is shee*' (11–12). See Aers and Kress 1978: *passim*.

> Should turne the leafe to reade, and read no more,
> Would thinke that eyther destiny mistooke,
>    Or that some leafes were torne out of the booke.
>                       . . . if after her
>    Any shall live, which dare true good prefer,
> Every such person is her delegate,
>    T'accomplish that which should have beene her fate.
> They shall make up that booke, and shall have thankes
>    Of fate and her, for filling up their blanks.
> For future vertuous deeds are Legacies,
>    Which from the gift of her example rise.
> And 'tis in heav'n part of spirituall mirth,
>    To see how well, the good play her, on earth.
>
>                    (83–4, 88–90, 97–106)

Donne refers in line 83 to 'He' who 'come[s] to reade the booke of destiny' and uses a plural pronoun, 'their' in line 102 to modify 'blanks', which suggests both 'that booke' (101) and 'her' (102) contain 'blanks' which need to be filled. 'He' is arguably the 'universal' pronoun but Donne could have referred to the Book of Fate and 'its' blanks, instead of 'their blanks'. I am not suggesting that Donne consciously constructs the reader as male and Elizabeth as a 'blank' text to be 'filled' sexually; this would be to posit her as a whore, like the Spouse of 'Show me deare Christ', ready for every male (reader) who comes along; however, I think such a reading is possible.[12] Obviously Donne's different class, his position of deference in relation to this girl whom he 'never saw' and to her family would hardly allow such an explicit representation. But earlier in 'A Funerall Elegie' Donne presents Elizabeth as 'desir'd' by male suitors. She is

> One, whose cleare body was so pure, and thin,
>    Because it neede disguise no thought within.
> T'was but a through-light scarfe, her minde t'enroule,
>    Or exhalation breath'd out from her soule.
> One, whom all men who durst no more, admir'd;
>    And whom, who ere had worth enough, desir'd. (59–64)

---

[12] See the implicit notion in Overbury's *A Wife* that men desire virgins: 'shee that in the act's afraid | Every night's another maide'. 'Of the choyce of a wife' in Overbury 1968: 29. For the reader as male and the text as female, recall Davies's 'Paper's Complaint'; woman as a 'two-leav'd booke' (p. 190, above); Halley 1989: 193; P. Parker 1987: 11, 128 ff.; Ricks 1988: 50; Gilbert and Gubar 1979: ch. 1; Irigaray 1993*b*: 42–3; Love 1993: 148 ff.

In a passage from his *Devotions* in which he finds 'conspiracies' or whisperings amongst men in society and an impenetrable natural world which constantly amazes one, Donne asserts 'that which is most *secret,* is most *dangerous*' (52). Woman is, of course, one such dangerous secret, a 'mystique booke' ('To his Mistris Going to Bed', l. 41). In the passage above, Elizabeth contains no secrets. In Donne's description there is no perilous encounter with the mother's body, as in the Lincoln's Inn epithalamium; no one waiting to castrate the potential bridegrooms, in fact nothing at all. There is no longer an inside and outside, no need to risk entering that dark 'hole' which threatens the wholeness of the masculine subject in order to possess the female body. I will return to Donne's image of Elizabeth as transparent, but I want to continue tracing the evidence for an implicit or explicit male reader in the texts of Elizabeth's commemoration. In *The First Anniversary* Donne uses an us[males]/they[females] construction in his misogynistic account of Eve's legacy:

> For that first mariage was our funerall:
> One woman at one blow, then kill'd us all,
> And, singly, one by one, they kill us now.
> We doe delightfully our selves allow
> To that consumption; and profusely blinde,
> We kill our selves, to propagate our kinde.
> And yet we doe not that; we are not men. (105–11)

In *The Second Anniversary*, Elizabeth is described as one who 'tooke, | (Taking herselfe) our best, and worthiest booke' (319–20), one of two extended conceits of Elizabeth as text, to which I will return.

In *Literary Fat Ladies: Rhetoric, Gender, Property*, Patricia Parker elucidates the rhetorical figure of *dilatio* or amplification and its use as a technique for deferring closure. Its roots can be found in the story of Rahab (whose Hebrew name means 'broad, wide'), the redeemed harlot of Jericho who, as Parker says, 'turns from letting in men to letting in men', and who becomes a principal Old Testament figure for the Church. Alluding to Donne's Holy Sonnet, Parker notes that in early Christian writings, the dilation or expansion of the Church 'involves symbolically two orifices: expansion to take in a multiplicity of members (as in Donne's sexual pun in the Sonnet on the Church as she who is—he is addressing Christ her Master—"most trew, and pleasing to thee, then | When she's embrac'd and open to most men"); and the propagation through the mouth, of the Word' (1987: 9). In the writings of the Church Fathers, 'that crucial meantime or threshold period before Apocalypse became known technically as the "dilation of Christendome", a phrase used repeatedly by St Thomas More and others in the Renaissance for the period of spreading or widening through the "dilation of the Word"' (ibid.). Another context for dilation which involves the literal rather than the metaphorical female body is that of propagation, the 'postponement of death through natural increase, *one of the principal arguments against the premature closure of virginity*' (15; my emphasis) made in Protestant writings. Parker notes that the divine command given to Adam and Eve to 'increase and multiply' lies behind this aspect of dilation. God's command applies not just to the generational process but to the rhetorical and the hermeneutic one as well. I suggest both 'expansion' and 'propagation' occur in *The Anniversaries* on and through the virtuous body of Elizabeth Drury, 'T'accomplish that, which should have beene her fate' (FE 100), marriage and procreation. It is the rhetorical dilation of the discourse about Elizabeth's body which Donne enacts in *The Anniversaries* so that while the command 'increase and multiply' may not have been obeyed by Elizabeth's virginal body, it is fulfilled in making her example fruitful, increasing and multiplying the number of good Christians on earth.

Parker's discussion of *dilatio* and *partitio* centres on romance narrative where dilation is associated with 'the figure or body of a female enchantress' (Circe, Calypso, Alcina, Acrasia) who could corrupt or lead astray the will, 'making it into a kind of Prodigal Son who might never return to his father' (10). *The Anniversaries'* explicit purpose as we saw from their endings is to counter this kind of 'error' for they posit a return to the Father, indeed through the remembrance of a virtuous female who is also a 'Father' to Donne's Muse, and yet they enact their own delay. Donne creates a further dilatory space with his poems between the time when the world is so sick that 'thou hast lost thy sense and memory | . . . thou art speechlesse growne' (FA 28, 30) and the time when, in response to his poem, they have remembered their Christian calling. The speaker of 'At the round earths imagin'd corners' makes the same dilatory plea. We have not the voluptuous body of a female enchantress, one of Parker's 'fat ladies', but the equally seductive prospect of a young virgin who possesses a slender, see-through body, both a blank space waiting to be filled and a text waiting to be read, with no risk of being engulfed by the castrated mother.

Parker quotes Donne the preacher[13] as an authority on the dilatory method of preaching who sums up the entire tradition of the *ars praedicandi*: 'The Word of God is made a Sermon, that is, a Text is dilated, diffused into a Sermon' (*Sermons*, v. 56; see Chamberlin 1976: ch. 5). The expansion of a scriptural, or any other kind of text must nevertheless be controlled; dilation must not lose sight of its end or move beyond the formal guidelines and boundaries set for it. One of these guidelines is the use of *partitio* and Parker cites Cicero's *Topics* where 'a discussion of physical "walls" is juxtaposed with a definition of oratorical "partition", [and] involves the dividing of a discourse, like a body, into "members"' (14). The virginal hymen of Elizabeth can be seen to function as a dividing wall or partition between her and all the 'Saints' in 'A Funerall Elegie' who 'emulate | To which of them, [the 'Temple' of her body] shall be consecrate' (65–6), but as I mentioned, the anxiety over encountering the female body is avoided because they can all see (through) Elizabeth. Her liminal position foregrounds the question of 'the degree to which possession of a gender is held to invade the whole person', an issue which is problematic in the epitaph, as I will show. As Denise Riley observes in asking this question, 'the critical gender is female; again, it is the difficulties of the woman-to-human transition' (1988: 18) which need to be untangled and understood. In Elizabeth's case, the difficulties lie in both her sexual human-to-woman transition—the markers of which hover between the lines of Donne's texts as veiled desire—and in her textual human-to-Woman transition.

The premature closure of Elizabeth's body as a result of her death, however, can itself be read as a form of dilation and partition which Parker describes as 'the erotics of prolongation', 'the putting off of coitus or consummation as e.g. Eve's 'sweet reluctant amorous delay' in Book IV of Milton's *Paradise Lost*. It is described by Andreas Capellanus in *The Art of Courtly Love* as a particularly

---

[13] These quotations are the extent of Parker's use of Donne. Her discussion, as mentioned, focuses on romance narrative.

feminine strategy, a lengthening of the time of courtship (1960: 200 ff.). Elizabeth's virginity is the site of a struggle, then, a conveniently empty space for masculine self-reproduction but also 'the sign . . . of a body and an identity which ha[s] somehow eluded successful appropriation by the masculine'. Philippa Berry observes this phenomenon in representations of the virginal Queen Elizabeth, who obviously wielded much more power and hence was that much more of a paradox than was Elizabeth Drury (1989: 6–7). In the patriarchy, according to Irigaray, 'a virgin is one as yet unmarked by them, for them. One who is not yet made woman by and for them. Not yet imprinted with their sex, their language. Not yet penetrated, possessed by them. . . . A virgin is the future of their exchanges, transactions, transports. A kind of reserve for their explorations, consummations, exploitations. The advent of their desire, Not of ours' (1985b: 211–12). Elizabeth is the object of one kind of dilatory process, in need of textual perfecting like the bride in Donne's 'Epithalamium [Made at Lincoln's Inn]', because she has been the agent of another dilatory process—the erotics of prolongation—in choosing, Donne implies, to die.[14] Here is Elizabeth's 'strategy' described in 'A Funerall Elegie':

> But as when Heav'n lookes on us with new eyes,
>     Those new starres ev'ry Artist exercise,
> What place they should assigne to them they doubt,
>     Argue, and agree not, till those starres go out:
> So the world studied whose this peece should be,
>     Till she can be no bodies else, nor she:
> . . .
> To scape th'infirmities which waite upone
> Woman, shee went away, before sh'was one.
> . . .
>                  . . . Fate did but usher her
> To yeares of Reasons use, and then infer
> Her destiny to her selfe; which liberty
> She tooke but for thus much, thus much to die.
>                       (67–72, 77–8, 91–4)

Frustration is implied by Elizabeth having got away, as it were,

[14] See Donne's anecdote in *Biathanatos* (1984b: 100) of the Virgins of Miletus who preferred death to the loss of virginity until threatened with public exposure of their dead bodies, quoted below.

while the suitors squabble over her in the marriage marketplace. In the image of 'Heav'n look[ing] on us with new eyes'—i.e. Elizabeth was a star looking at them—Donne deflects the fact that 'the world', and some more than others 'studied' Elizabeth. The study of Elizabeth's virtue is presented as not just worthwhile, but a matter of life and death at the beginning of *The First Anniversary* (28–32), but here in the funeral elegy, the study of Elizabeth's male admirers has the potential to become 'an eroticized, even potentially prurient and voyeuristic, looking' (P. Parker 1987: 129), especially when we bear in mind the lines just prior to these which I have already quoted, describing Elizabeth's 'cleare', thin body. We need only recall Marston's 'prostitution' of his Muse—'Reade all, view all, even with my full consent'—the chaste 'glance[s]' which Joseph Hall approves of, or the speaker of 'Shall I goe force an Elegie?' who says it matters not to him, 'both for delight and view, | I'le have a Succuba, as good as you' (23–4) to recognize not only the ease with which an enquiring mind or an admiring glance can turn lustful, but the phenomenon which William Kerrigan and Gordon Braden, among others, have observed: 'during the late sixteenth century the psychic transaction by which the image becomes preferable to the woman herself emerges into the open' (1989: 181).

Sir Francis Bacon states in his *Essayes* (1597) that 'a way to amplifie anything, is to breake it, and to make an anatomie of it in severall parts' (F4r). Donne literalizes the rhetorical figure of partition throughout his sermons,[15] and this rhetorical strategy is explicit in Donne's *First Anniversary, An Anatomy of the World* where he dissects the decaying world as it languishes in the wake of Elizabeth's death. Anatomies of various bodies, literal and figurative, are a major trope in Donne's *Anniversaries*. Devon Hodges in her book, *Renaissance Fictions of Anatomy*, observes that anatomies were 'a fad in sixteenth-century England', a fad which nevertheless signalled an important transitional moment between a medieval discourse of 'patterning' or 'resemblance' and the newer, scientific, analytical discourse, which sought to strip away false appearances and expose the truth, about the body itself, or any other body of knowledge (1985: 1–19). Hodges notes that the word 'anatomy' began appearing frequently in the Tudor period, according to the

---

[15] See e.g. v. 231; vi. 40; x. 230, the opening of *Deaths Duell*.

*OED* around 1540, signifying the dissected body itself, then in 1541 the process of dissection and the science of bodily structure (also used in this way as early as 1391), and eventually it was first used as a trope in 1569. One purpose of an anatomy, whether of the medical or literary kind, is to break down a whole into its parts, to determine the relationship of each part to the whole and its role in the life (or death) of that whole. Hence, it is a kind of articulation. Hodges notes the 'conflict within an anatomy between its desires and methods' (2), its 'paradoxical doubleness' as a method for revealing a unified truth which fragments its object (6; see also Hirsch 1991). I suggest that the conflict of desires and methods which Hodges identifies in anatomies is absent in the anatomization of woman in Renaissance culture; in fact, desire and method are one and the same. The desire to name and know woman is a desire to articulate her, divide her up into 'peece[s]' (FE 28, 71), dissipate and dissolve her power while at the same time preserving the wholeness, the identity of the male, an 'operation' which occurs on the body of Elizabeth Drury even though it is already made transparent in 'A Funerall Elegie'. The following passage from Irigaray's essay on woman as 'Volume-Fluidity' illuminates Donne's articulation of Elizabeth into

Fragments: of women, of discourse, of silences, *of blanks that are still immaculate* (?) . . . Everything thrust aside wherever the 'subject' seeks to escape from his emprisonment. But even as he struggles to fracture that specular matrix, that enveloping discursivity, that body of the text in which he has made himself a prisoner, it is Nature he finds, Nature who, unknown to him, has nourished his project, his production. It is Nature who now fuses for him with that glass enclosure, that spangled sepulcher, from which—imaginary and therefore absent—she is unable to articulate her difference. . . . her function henceforward will be as *hole*. And for her, metaphor will continue to work as violation and separation, except if, *empty of all meaning that is already appropriate(d)*, she keeps open the indefinite possibilities of her jouissance—that is, God.[16]

As R. L. Kesler asserts of *The First Anniversary*, 'the attribution of the disintegration of the world to the death of the woman is doubly strategic, since it not only appears to elevate or praise the woman it destroys, but inverts or obscures the very process through which it destroys her' (1990: 120). Donne describes

[16] Irigaray 1985*a*: 228, 231. The first emphasis is mine. The first ellipsis is Irigaray's.

Elizabeth early in 'A Funerall Elegie' as 'those fine spirits, which doe tune and set | This Organ, . . . those peeces which beget | Wonder and love' (27–9) and later as 'this peece' (71) over whom her suitor-Saints argue. Kesler's point is clearly demonstrated in Donne's use of the word 'peece', for in the first instance, Donne suggests (as he will again in *The First Anniversary*) that Elizabeth is that which holds the world together, the body politic of 'Princes', 'Counsailors', 'Lawyers', 'Divines', and 'Officers', none of which occupations she would be allowed to pursue as a female. In *The First Anniversary* Elizabeth is again described as the 'cyment' (49) and '[i]intrinsique Balme' (57) of the world, its 'Magnetique force' (221) and 'Harmony' (312). But Donne's lines also, for a feminist reader, acknowledge explicitly the 'sacrifice' of the feminine as the *mater/materia* (a false etymology but one which was nevertheless exploited in the Renaissance) on which the transcendence of the male subject depends (see Irigaray 1985*a*:133ff; Whitford 1991: 150). Donne's second use of 'peece' seems somewhat more sexually connotative, although such a meaning could not have been uppermost in Donne's mind as it would be offensive to Elizabeth's parents. 'Piece' as an absolute, 'without "of" and specification of the substance', was and is used to refer to a person generally (*OED* II.9), and is used frequently by Donne in his *Devotions* and *Letters* to describe 'man' as an isolated unit in need of community. But 'piece' was also used to indicate a woman or girl, often with connotations of sexual looseness on her part, the ultimate sexual object (*OED* II.9.b). 'Demolish'd' in line 8 of the funeral elegy into 'those peeces' by line 28, Elizabeth is now 'this [sexual] peece' over whom men fought until she disappears altogether, only to be re-membered again and again in Donne's speculations. In her patriarchal culture, if she can be 'no bodies else' (L. *alius*, 'other'), like Overbury's '*Adopted-Selfe*' (p. 149, above), 'she' cannot be 'she'.

In the conclusion to *An Anatomy of the World*, Donne uses the analogy of an anatomical procedure to explain why he cannot possibly rehearse all of the world's ills:

> But as in cutting up a man that's dead,
> The body will not last out to have read
> On every part, and therefore men direct
> Their speech to parts, that are of most effect. (435–8)

A choice must be made then. In articulating the meaning of Elizabeth Drury's life or re-membering her, which of her 'parts' does Donne 'read on', and can we accept that the parts to which he directs his speech are those 'of most effect'? Donne uses the word 'effect' in its sense of that which is most subject to the effects of death; that is, that which rots first (see Allen 1943b: 322–42). The word is 'affect' in modern spelling, or 'the way in which a thing is physically affected or disposed; especially, the actual state or disposition of the body' (*OED* II.5); 'a state of body opposed to the normal; indisposition, distemper, malady, disease' (II.6). D. C. Allen quotes the English translation of DeVigo's *The Most Excellent Works of Chirurgerye* (London, 1543), which states that of every body to be dissected, four choices are made as to the parts to be studied: 'The fyrst is of membres nutritive, for they ben more apte to receyve putrefactions or rottynges then other. The second election is of membres spirituall, as of the hart, of the pannicles or thynne skynnes, of the longes. The thyrde election is, of the membres animale, that is to say of the heade, and hys partes. The fourth of the extremities of the bodye, as of the armes, the legges, and theyr partes'. De Vigo does not mention 'membres' generative here as a possible choice for dissection.[17] Even by 1618, Helkiah Crooke, physician to King James, supplies a lengthy justification for his consideration of these generative parts, 'veyled by Nature, and through our unseasonable modesty not sufficiently uncovered', yet urges that of the parts of generation belonging unto women, 'wee would advise no man to take further know-ledge then shall serve for his good instruction' (1618: 197, 199). In Chapter 1 I quoted several invocations of a modest Muse, but as I have been arguing, Elizabeth began to be studied by suitors just before she died and continues to be read as text after her death. My discussion of the female 'parts' of Elizabeth Drury—both her anatomy and those mental attributes which were con-sidered uniquely or predominantly female traits—and her feminine 'part'—her gender role in society—will hopefully serve for 'man's' good instruction. I want to ask which parts of Elizabeth

---

[17] In many Renaissance medical treatises, the sexual organs were referred to in the context of their primary procreative function. Sexual pleasure was Nature's bribe, a way of coaxing human beings into replicating themselves, especially women who would otherwise not bear the pain and danger of childbirth. Helkiah Crooke answers the question 'Why there is so great pleasure in the emission of seede?' (the 'seede' believed to issue from both men and women) with this very reason (1618: 286).

Drury, both those to which Donne directs his speech and those which are conspicuous by their absence, most effect or define feminine and masculine identities in phallocentric discourse and which are most affected by that same discourse.

Let me summarize my argument thus far. In the eyes of Donne and the patriarchy, Elizabeth's premature closure of her virginal body could be viewed as a 'strategy' of *dilatio*, an 'erotics of prolongation', deferring the inevitable marriage and devirgination which would be her destiny as sole heiress of her family's fortune. Her hymen is a kind of dividing wall or partition between her body, the fortune attached to it, and the suitors which appear to vie for her in 'A Funerall Elegie'. Elizabeth has thus avoided the definitive function of women, God's command to 'increase and multiply', a dictum which was also applied to rhetorical dilation or the amplification of discourse, especially in the art of preaching on the compressed or 'closed' texts of the scriptures. Donne in turn enacts this rhetorical application of *dilatio* in talking about the virginal body of Elizabeth as a text, in order to present her as an example to be imitated by good Christians; hence, she complies with the command to 'increase and multiply', with Donne's help, but as text. Her early death has left blank spaces in the book of destiny which must be filled. The act of filling these spaces is a kind of rhetorical defloration of Elizabeth which is perpetrated with each act of reading Donne's poem and with each resultant active imitation of Elizabeth's example. Moreover, Donne makes Elizabeth's body visible to a public audience as text and/or thought, using metaphors of libraries and scrolls to describe her so that she progresses throughout the poems from closed, virginal body to blank space (the removed hymen), to Protestant text—a double-sided scroll—and finally to the bodiless possessor of two souls. It is these passages I want to look at now.

In the lines immediately following Donne's description of Elizabeth as possessing a soul of 'Gold' and a body of 'Electrum' in *The Second Anniversary*, he declares of Elizabeth:

> we understood
> Her by her sight, her pure and eloquent blood
> Spoke in her cheekes, and so distinckly wrought,
> That one might almost say, her bodie thought,
> Shee, shee, thus richly, and largely hous'd, is gone. (243–7)

These lines are slippery in the way they negotiate the dualism of mind and body. On the one hand, especially in the context of his culture and the direction of the poems as a whole (if we take Donne's advice about endings), Donne presents here only a subtler reconfiguration of dualism in which the dominant term elevates the lesser: to see her is to know her, indeed to comprehend her; there is no need for contact. The female body articulates itself, but it does so according to script, with a blush. Elizabeth does not speak, nor does anyone return her speech. Some of the most commented upon and quoted lines of Donne's *Anniversaries*, critics have tended to read them as presenting a perfect balance between body and spirit. For example, John Carey writes that 'Donne achieves an integration of body and mind. He conceives of Elizabeth's body as an intellectual thing, and he does so in the teeth of deeply entrenched traditions. For centuries Western Christianity had seen the soul as the prisoner of the body—a bird in a cage, an angel trapped on a dunghill. Donne collapses, in an instant, this age-old dualism' (1990: 149). But in his description of Elizabeth's body Donne goes only half way, if that. The materiality of the body is absorbed by a function of the intellect so that, in effect, it ceases to become a body.

On the other hand, Elizabeth's eloquent body shares some aspects of the sensible transcendental which Irigaray offers as an alternative to dualism, in which the god is 'conjur[ed] . . . up among us, within us, as resurrection and transfiguration of blood, of flesh, through a language and an ethics that is ours' (1993*a*: 129), that is, 'yours and mine'. Certainly, as Carey notes, Donne's description of Elizabeth is another manifestation of his insistence that the body and soul are interdependent. And in a sermon Donne exults in the advantage humans will have over Angels: 'yet man cannot deliberately wish himselfe an Angel, because he should lose by that wish, and lacke that glory, which he shall have in his body. . . . In that wherein we can be like [Angels], we shall be like them, in the exalting and refining of the faculties of our soules; But they shall never attaine to be like us in our glorified bodies' (vi. 297). Here is something very close to the situation Irigaray envisions in which 'both angel and body [are] found together' (1993*a*: 17). But crucially, Donne puts off this radical collapsing of dualistic categories until after death. 'Immortality has already been put off until death and does not figure as one of our constant tasks as mortals, a transmutation that is endlessly incumbent upon us here, now—its possibility having been inscribed in the body, which is capable of becoming divine' (1993a: 29). Donne insists on the body and asserts 'heaven needs bodies', but he more often rails against the sinful flesh (granted a more complex term than 'body'), 'the mother of sin' (*Sermons*, vii. 106), and perpetuates the notion of the body as a prison, as we saw in *Deaths Duell*. Donne's description of Elizabeth as 'richly' housed shows the potential for true dwelling, rather than the '*internal exile*' which she inevitably suffered. Such dwelling places, however, are still the domain of phallocentric language.

If Elizabeth does not speak, does not have access to language and so only blushes beneath the gaze of Donne, she is barred from reading in his next conceit. Elizabeth is 'learned' (*SA* 302), but as one

> who all Libraries had throughly red
> At home, in her owne thoughts, And practised
> So much good as would make as many more:
> . . .
> Shee, who in th'Art of knowing Heaven, was growen
> Here upon Earth, to such perfection,
> That shee hath, ever since to Heaven shee came,
> (In a far fairer print,) but read the same. (303–5, 311–14)

Here she is even closer to becoming text, the example of her virtue—however the unspecified 'practise' was carried out—making 'many more' good. Line 303 seems perhaps the most hyperbolic claim of all in the light of Renaissance educational practices for girls with the exception of a privileged few, until we read in the following (deflatory) line that Elizabeth is locked up 'At home' and then not even allowed access to that library but only to 'her owne thoughts'. And in lines I have already quoted, it turns out that indeed she is the 'worthiest booke' which, one might suggest, she must steal from the library and take to the more accommodating reading room of heaven.

Neither speaking nor reading, by the end of *The Second Anniversary* Elizabeth no longer even thinks virtuous thoughts,

> for shee rather was two soules,
> Or like to full, on both sides written Rols,
> Where eies might read upon the outward skin,
> As strong Records for God, as mindes within. (503–6)

There is no need even for a see-through body because there is no female body requiring full disclosure, but even so, Donne is not able or chooses not to shed her body entirely, and 'eies' continue to 'read . . . the outward skin'. Donne plays on the etymology of vellum again in a sermon: 'In the outward beauty, These be the Records of velim, these be the parchmins, the endictments, and the evidences that shall condemn many of us, at the last day, our *own skins*; . . . all this is bound up in this velim, in this parchmin, in this skin of ours, and we neglect book, and image, and character, and seal, and all for the covering' (iii. 103–4). Anthony Raspa argues that Donne's image of the two-sided scroll in *The Second Anniversary* 'inscribe[s] the record of her material existence, intelligible in purely historical terms, and on the other side is written her mystical significance in the Register of the Elect' (Donne 1987: p. xxxi), yet ironically there is, precisely, no record of Elizabeth's material, historical existence except for the dates of her baptism and burial.

Elizabeth's crucial re-membering occurs at the beginning of *The Second Anniversary*:

> All have forgot all good,
> Forgetting her, the maine Reserve of all,
> Yet in this Deluge, grosse and generall,
> Thou seest mee strive for life; my life shalbe,
> To bee hereafter prais'd, for praysing thee,
> Immortal Mayd, who though thou wouldst refuse
> The name of Mother, be unto my Muse,
> A Father since her chast Ambition is,
> Yearely to bring forth such a child as this.
> These Hymes may worke on future wits, and so
> May great Grand-children of thy praises grow
> . . .
> For thus, Man may extend thy progeny,
> Untill man doe but vanish, and not die. (28–38; 41–2)

Donne re-members Elizabeth here by giving her a male member, the Phallus. There is the same gender fluidity among Muses, poets, and subjects as we saw in the early verse letters of Donne and the Woodward brothers and the same fantasy of male parthenogenesis. Here, the daughter adopts 'the patronym in which daughters reject the legacy of their mothers and reinforce their father's power' (Sabine 1992: 100). Donne states explicitly that his life depends on recognition 'for praysing thee', and so he allows Elizabeth to step in as Father to his Muse, yet Elizabeth is still put to the task of reproduction. Elizabeth's 'dilation' and the multiplication of Christian souls has been accomplished without resorting to the body itself; no 'trial of intercourse' has occurred. Paradoxically, Elizabeth is both a virgin and a mother/father through Donne's multivalent applications of *dilatio* and *partitio* in the poetic culmination of his writing about the feminine as it functions in hom(m)osexual discourse.

We must decide whether Donne positions himself as a parody of what Irigaray would call the 'between' or an 'angel' (1993a: 15 ff.), his phallic discourse functioning as bridge. He stands at the threshold of the hymen, mediating between two houses of language: the heavenly body and voice of Elizabeth Drury and the language people will understand and participate in as they 'listen' or read.[18] But is Donne a true messenger/angel figure, 'tell[ing] of the passage between the envelope of God and that of the world as micro- or macrocosm' (Irigaray 1993a: 16)? Or are his poems more selfishly motivated, more concerned with promoting his virtuosity and fame? A further scriptural model related to dilation and partition presents itself when we survey Donne's commemoration of Elizabeth Drury within the context of their reception. Joan Webber observes that for Donne, 'words and combinations of words have a validity nearly equal to that of things' and that a biblical text is 'a compression of something expanded in the sermon into a solid structure' (1963: 127, 138). I have already raised the question as to whether Donne creates a structure to glorify and promote his own powers of language in the eyes of the Court from whom he so desperately sought employment, or whether he wrote *The Anniversaries* anticipating his ordination as Anglican priest and his preacherly role. In *Words with Power*, Northrop Frye discusses two biblical models in Genesis which concern the power of language to link heaven and the members of an earthly community: the Tower of Babel and Jacob's Ladder (1990: 154 ff.). Donne's poems can be read as sincere

---

[18] Thomas Docherty identifies a dynamic operating between three concepts involving a female 'part' in Donne's writings and *The Anniversaries*: hymen, medium, and angel (1986: 227–31). Docherty, as Sabine suggests in relation to her own argument (1992: 259 n. 30) comes to similar conclusions to my own but via a different path.

attempts to convey an urgent message to the people of a decaying world, hence functioning as a kind of Jacob's Ladder, Donne being the angel messenger ascending and descending between heaven and earth with Elizabeth as song, proclamation, and angel singing in the heavenly choir. Donne's hyperbole is so extreme, however, his manipulation of language so virtuosic that it becomes suspect and confusing to many of his readers, indeed 'blasphemous' to at least one, Ben Jonson. The structure he creates might thus be seen as a Tower of Babel which makes his name, not 'hers', famous, but which alienates him from his community, especially his female patrons (see Donne 1977: 238–9), even further. Donne keeps to the generic confines in the epitaph and elegy in praising and lamenting Elizabeth, but *The Anniversaries* ultimately become self-celebration rather than memorialization (Fox 1972: 533).

Donne begins 'A Funerall Elegie' with what Frank Manley calls a 'complex inversion' of Horace's *Exegi monumentum ære perennius*: while all material things eventually pass away, even funeral monuments, only verse will keep its subject alive eternally. While he is in keeping with generic expectations to point to the tomb's inappropriateness as a lasting monument to the memory of Elizabeth and as a container for her body, the tomb and its failure to house her focuses Donne's central anxiety: the containment of Elizabeth in his verse. Elizabeth functions as the matter for his display, but also as his competitor for renown, much as Sappho and Ovid do in 'Sapho to Philaenis'. Donne must create but contain Elizabeth's excesses; his virtuosity must outdo her virtue:

> Tis lost, to trust a Tombe with such a ghest,
>     Or to confine her in a Marble chest,
> Alas, what's Marble, Jeat, or Porphiry,
>     Priz'd with the Chrysolite of eyther eye,
> Or with those Pearles, and Rubies which shee was?
>     Joyne the two Indies in one Tombe, 'tis glas;
> And so is all to her materials,
>     Though every inche were ten escurials.
> Yet shee's demolish'd: Can we keepe her then
>     In workes of hands, or of the wits of men?
> Can these memorials, ragges of paper, give
>     Life to that name, by which name they must live?
> Sickly, alas, short-liv'd, aborted bee
>     Those Carkas verses, whose soule is not shee.

> And can shee, who no longer would be shee,
>   Being such a Tabernacle, stoope to bee
> In paper wrap't; Or, when she would not lie
>   In such a house, dwell in an Elegie? (1–18)

Donne's use of the word, 'ghest', is both ironic—Elizabeth's dead
body is no wayfarer but will crumble to dust in the tomb—and
theologically correct: in a Christian context this tomb is a temporary resting place for Elizabeth's body until the Last Judgement;
she 'dwells' here only temporarily just as her soul was a guest in
her body: 'Shee, whose faire body no such prison was, | But that a
soule might well be pleas'd to passe | An Age in her' (SA 221–3).
Donne sets his parameters (typically, out of sight) and the vertigin-
ous extremes are dizzying. Donne's proportions are one inch to
ten escurials, the immense palace completed by Philip II of Spain
in 1584 which incorporated a church, a library, art collection,
college, and monastery. Elizabeth's 'incomprehensiblenesse' cannot be contained even by dozens of these massive structures and
yet in the very next line, 'shee's demolish'd'. 'Demolish' (L. , de-
+ moliri, -it, 'build, construct, erect') means to pull down or throw
down a building 'by violent disintegration of its fabric, pull to
pieces, reduce to ruin' (OED 1). In the space of a phrase, Donne
can reduce Elizabeth to rubble, to be rebuilt into structures and
shapes of his own likeness. The anxiety Donne expresses here
becomes, in the process of writing about her, confident bragging
by the end of The First Anniversary: 'Nor could incomprehens-
iblenesse deterre | Me, from thus trying to emprison her. | Which
when I saw that a strict grave could do, | I saw not why verse
might not doe so too'. Yet if we read 'otherwise' (Belsey 1994: 13),
we recognize Elizabeth's imprisonment or confinement is an
'internal exile'; she cannot truly dwell 'in an Elegie' or in
any patriarchal house, because in these spaces she is 'unable to
articulate her difference'. Elizabeth's confinement is achieved in
the very process of Donne shaking off the confines of generic and
decorous limitations. Donne shows that language can be as heavy
and suffocating as any tomb yet it, too, proves not to be escape-
proof.

  Donne ends The First Anniversary implying that verse will keep
Elizabeth's fame alive until the second coming when the grave
gives up the body to be joined once again in heaven with its soul.

But just prior to these lines he has been justifying his choice of verse over chronicle and declaring his bold invasion of 'this great office', so that the 'enrolment' of his fame is also implied. The people who build Babel declare, 'let us build a city and a tower . . . let us make us a name'. Donne published his tower of words and became known throughout his lifetime as the poet of the *Anniversaries*. But if it was Donne's intention to make a name for himself, his intention backfired. The winning of new patrons meant censure by old ones. His readers are rendered confused and unable to communicate with one another across this 'incomprehensible' structure, seeking a way through the labyrinth of these poems with the clue of Elizabeth Drury. By *The First Anniversary*, the tension between Elizabeth's feminine virtue and Donne's masculine virtuosity, and the tension between the etymological root of 'virtue' and its superficial 'semblance' of femininity, is apparent. Elizabeth is 'She, of whom the'Auncients seem'd to prophesie, | When they call'd vertues by the name of shee' (175–6), the female embodiment of virtue and thus Thomas Heywood's worst nightmare, except that Elizabeth is safely dead and unable to use her 'nimble and voluble' 'mothers tongue', nor did she while alive, being 'taciturna' (see her epitaph, below). Yet in the lines immediately following these Donne describes Elizabeth as

> She in whom vertue was so much refin'd,
> That for Allay unto so pure a minde
> Shee tooke the weaker Sex, she that could drive
> The poysonous tincture, and the stayne of *Eve*,
> Out of her thoughts, and deeds; and purifie
> All, by a true religious Alchimy. (177–82)

Elizabeth is so purely 'vertue' that she takes as 'Allay' to this 'gold', the 'weaker Sex'. If 'she' is prophecy fulfilled and the embodiment of virtue, 'she' is so only by being able to counter the 'poyson' of femaleness, like one of the properties of Electrum, according to Paracelsus (see Milgate in Donne 1978: 164).

Further parallels with the Babel story are possible. Elizabeth Drury could be described as Donne's plain of Shinar, the perfect place ('Occasion') on which to build a tower of words, stretching between heaven and earth, demonstrating the ingenuity of its builder. By 1611, Donne had been wandering for almost a decade in a desert of unemployment and increasing debt despite numerous attempts to gain a position at court. The fear of those who built the Tower of Babel—'lest we be scattered abroad upon the face of the whole earth' is very much that of Donne who wrestled with suicide and despair throughout these dark years. Of course Donne's entire *Anniversaries* concern this very possibility: the dissolution and decay of the world, and as Carey observes, changeability was the 'focus of his self-scrutiny throughout his life'; he hungered for 'absolutes and totalities' (1990: 182, 155). Donne's sermons are full of assertions that no matter how decayed our body and scattered into dust and atoms of dust, God can glue us back together again at the Last Judgement (e.g. iii. 109; vi. 156). Donne struggled with the recognition of his own scattered-ness of mind and the perception of a world moving towards dissolution in all of his works, and Elizabeth Drury, or rather the 'shee' of *The Anniversaries*—the woman imagined and 'not as she was'—is perhaps one attempt to bridge the gap between the changeability of earth and the changelessness of heaven. Para-doxically, it is his use of Elizabeth Drury and her metamorphosis within the poems that gives Donne a sense of his own position in the world, because Donne is controlling that change in a creative mode. Thus is he able to justify his role at the end of *The Anniversaries*.

If we think of the poems in terms of structures or buildings, then, Elizabeth is incorporated into the very walls of these towers of words, spiraling towards the heavens, scattered among the other 'matter' Donne anatomizes and breaks down into bits he can use to build his own unique structure, his own house of language. Inasmuch as her female body functions as text within the poems, Elizabeth Drury becomes the marginalized feminine, both ex-cluded from and yet required for, 'place', the sacred space or inner temple of masculine subjectivity, the site of the transmission of the Word. In functioning as both structural matter and as empty space, the 'irony . . . is that the poem is then left to revolve around a centre that, by its very definition, is not there' (Kesler 1990: 121). Once again, the feminine is manifested as a present absence:

Woman is still the place, the whole of the place in which she cannot take possession of herself as such. She is experienced as all-powerful precisely insofar as her indifferentiation makes her radically powerless. She is never here and now because it is she who sets up that eternal elsewhere from which the 'subject' continues to draw his reserves, his re-sources, though without being able to recognize them/her. She is not uprooted from matter, from the earth, but yet, but still, she is already scattered into $x$ number of places that are never gathered together into anything she knows of herself, and these remain the basis of (re)production—particularly of discourse—in all its forms. (Irigaray 1985*a*: 227)

## II. ELIZABETH DRURY'S EPITAPH

I began this chapter with an assertion that that most reductive sign of a human being's existence, the hyphen between dates of birth and death, could not hold up under the weight of Elizabeth's subsequent idealization. Here, I want to point to another sign, or mark, with which Donne describes—indeed circumscribes— Elizabeth in her epitaph: a parenthesis. I will explore the ambiguity of that sign which contains the supposedly 'unnecessary' or 'unessential'. I reconsider its etymological meaning of 'to put in *beside*' as an alternative approach to assigning 'proper place' to this slip of a girl. The epitaph which Donne wrote for Elizabeth Drury's monument in Hawstead Church is almost never included in discussions of *The Anniversaries*. Frank Manley's edition does not include it so that it is not until Wesley Milgate's edition in 1976 that the general reader is given the opportunity to consider Elizabeth's epitaph in the context of the entire group of poems. Interestingly, the editors of the *Variorum* have chosen not to include Elizabeth's epitaph in their edition of *The Anniversaries* and 'A Funerall Elegie' (vol. vi) but to publish it in a separate volume (vol. viii) with Donne's other epitaphs.

Paradoxically, Elizabeth Drury comes into being only after her death. Yet all we have, even so, is the textual mould which Donne and Elizabeth's parents have cast around her dead body; within is an empty space. We have no point of reference for the 'she' of the poems, except for an always prior Donnean text. The lacuna formed by the absence of any historical verities is paradoxically as impenetrable and obfuscating as the marble which surrounds her body. To discuss how Donne writes about Elizabeth Drury in both her absences—her death and the fact of their never having met— would seem to be a task which is both impossible and, to those critics who dismiss her as a 'blank counter' (Manley 1963: 2), 'nothing to Donne' (Williamson 1962/3: 188), or a mere 'pretext'

(Marotti 1986: 243), irrelevant. Yet feminist critics such as Sheila Fisher and Janet Halley are pointing out the degree to which 'early modern women's relationships to the textual record of these periods' is one of absence, 'in both its literal and its literary-theoretical meanings' (1989: 1, 2).[19] To fully understand these relationships requires the application of a kind of 'lost-wax method' of reading, then, whereby the negative spaces which the dominant (male) discourse shapes but cannot or will not occupy must be recuperated. To dismiss the blank space of Elizabeth's historical existence altogether is akin to paving over the tomb of the Unknown Soldier. We cannot allow another kind of incomprehensibleness to deter us from acknowledging the textual constrictions within which flesh and blood females are placed. The assertion of Elizabeth's negligible life, if not death, is made by critics first, on the basis of a lack of evidence, and second, without acknowledging the conditions of her apparent insignificance. We cannot equate absence or *un*-significance with *in*significance, for real women lie buried within the text. Elizabeth has been re-membered, articulated, but the Anatomy or autopsy has allowed Donne, who admits he 'never saw' Elizabeth, both the *auto-opsis*, the seeing for himself, and the seeing of himself in the space he creates with her body. As much as we may be unable to acknowledge the specific historicity of that individual body, it is Elizabeth's body as it is gendered female, or rather as it is en-gendered both female and male which is one of the shaping forces of the poems.

An epitaph, from the Greek, ἐπιτάφιον, for 'written on a tomb' is a fairly loose generic category; aside from its purpose and location it is a shorter form of the funeral elegy. Its content is usually panegyrical, designed to catch the attention of passers-by and compel them to meditate on mortality. Greek and Roman epitaphs ranged from the highly satirical and ribald to the intensely personal and serious and were written in both verse and prose. Epitaphs were a popular genre in the English Renaissance, appealing to the desire to find order even in death, in a world people felt was decaying and returning to chaos. It is in the epitaph that we first observe Elizabeth's body re-placed with words about her

---

[19] Camille Wells Slights has recently responded to Halley in particular on this matter as it relates to Anne More, and argues that we should not too hastily dismiss the possibility of greater female agency in the poems (1996: 66–88). See Halley 1989.

body. Elizabeth becomes 'sexualized' even as we move further away from her physical body. Single-mindedly focused on her body, the epitaph is both visually and verbally at its most compressed in the parenthesis[20] which lies in its very centre:

QVO PERGAS, VIATOR, NON HABES:
AD GADES OMNIVM VENISTI; ETIAM ET AD TVAS:
HIC IACES, SI PROBVS ES, IPSE;
IPSA ETENIM HÎC IACET PROBITAS,
ELIZABETHA:
CVI,
CVM, VT IN PVLCHRITVDINE, ET INNOCENTIA
ANGELOS ÆMVLATA STRENVE FVERAT, ID ET IN HOC PRÆSTARE NISA EST,
VT SINE SEXV DEGERET;
IDEOQVE CORPVS INTACTVM, QVÂ FACTVM EST INTEGRITATE,
(PARADISVM SINE SERPENTE,)
DEO REDDERE VOLVIT,
QVÆ NEC ADEO AVLÆ SPLENDORIBVS ALLICEFACTA, VT A SEMET EXVLARET,
NEC ADEO SIBIMET CŒNOBIVM FACTA, VT SE SOCIETATI DENEGARET,
NEC OB CORPORIS, FORTVNÆVE DOTES, MINVS IN ANIMO
DOTATA,
NEC OB LINGVARVM PERITIAM, MINVS TACITVRNA.

[Thou knowest not, wayfarer, whither thou goest. Thou hast come to the Cadiz of all men, even to thine own. Thou liest here thyself, if thou art virtuous; for indeed here lies Virtue herself, Elizabeth,—in that, as in beauty and innocence she had eagerly vied with the angels, she strove besides to excel them, nay even in this, that she lived sexlessly and wished on that account to restore to God an undefiled body, unimpaired as it was fashioned (an Eden without the serpent), not so much allured by the splendours of that palace that she was banished from her true self, nor so much made a cloister for herself that she denied herself to company, nor for all her endowments of body or fortune less endowed in intellect, nor for all her skill in tongues the less able to hold her peace.] (Donne 1995b: 175, 429–30)[21]

---

[20] While Donne's texts are an editorial nightmare, we can be confident in discussing the following parentheses, the actual physical lines: one is carved in marble, and Donne meticulously supervised the publication of *The First Anniversary*, which contains the second parenthesis I will discuss.

[21] Despite the lengthy relative clause, 'cui' of l. 6 is governed by 'extruendo' in l. 23 which I have not quoted here because of space restrictions. Milgate's translation from Donne 1978 is used by the editors of the *Variorum* and I use it here with a few qualifications.

Representing the point of furthest West, Cadiz is used by Donne as a metaphor for Elizabeth as the locus of extreme virtue. But if Elizabeth is the 'Cadiz of all men', she could never have taken part in the expeditions to Cadiz in which Donne participated as a young man. She could not have ventured beyond her own door-step unaccompanied, enclosed as she would have been within the private sphere of the household. The paradox of Elizabeth's 'achievement' and subsequent praise is that she did, precisely, nothing, as she was expected to do nothing despite her (danger-ous) potential for doing something, such as speaking many lan-guages ('linguarum peritiam'). Women were expected to enact the parable of the talents in reverse, and were praised for burying them, once they were themselves exchanged or commercialized in the 'marriage market'. The epitaph is pervaded by the tension between Elizabeth's (subversive) potential and cultural expecta-tions of generic femaleness. The actual lines of the parenthesis, called lunulæ, from Erasmus, meaning 'little moon' (Lennard 1991: 14), serve both to contain and to expose this tension.

Donne's phrase, 'ut sine SEXU degerent', all on its own line, is intriguing for numerous reasons. What exactly does he mean, that Elizabeth lived 'sine SEXU', 'without sex' or 'sexlessly' as Milgate translates it? The phrase suggests that gender is applied at the moment the (woman) contacts a man, as in the refrain of 'Epi-thalamium [Made at Lincoln's Inn]', and, paradoxically, like the 'earth-creature' of Gen. 2: 18 who is sexually undifferentiated until a 'like-opposite' is created. In the Renaissance, girls and boys tended to remain together in the nursery until the age of 7, when boys were sent to grammar school to learn Latin and Greek. But Elizabeth is obviously beyond this age and the category of a child; in fact she is in a kind of limbo, just past the onset of puberty, which contemporary medical treatises put at the age of 14,[22] and so potentially, if not actively, sexual. We see in 'The Primrose', 'The Relique', 'The Undertaking', and most famously, 'The Ex-stasie', that Donne uses the word 'sex' as the ultimate marker of difference between two individuals so that often the transcend-ence of sexual difference becomes the ultimate goal of true love.

---

[22] 'The Universal time, all men do accord, beginneth for the most part in the second seaven years, that is at 14 yeares olde. . . . At that time men begin to grow hayrie, to have lustfull imaginations and to change their voyce; womens Pappes begin to swell and they to thinke uppon husbands' (Crooke 1618: 261).

Only the misogynistic speaker of 'The Primrose' would presumably consider Elizabeth a 'monster' (18) if 'shee would get above | All thought of sexe' (15–16).

While a generic component of an epitaph is often a description of the general shape of events a person's life took, the content of Elizabeth's epitaph more literally outlines her body, drawing an unbroken line around it. She let nothing in, being 'corpus intactum' and she let nothing out, being 'taciturna'. Donne embarks on a series of negatively constructed compliments, e.g. 'Nec ob linguarum peritiam, minus taciturna [neither for all her skill in languages, the less able to hold her peace]'. Donne uses a stronger word here than Milgate's translation suggests. 'Taciturna' means *silent*, its antonym is *loquax*. In *The First Anniversary*, even Elizabeth could only 'guild' every 'state' with the result that only 'Some women have some taciturnity' (423). Donne's method of praise in the epitaph presents an undesirable situation *in potentia* while at the same time denying its actuality, the same technique used for banishing fears and so forth in epithalamia, as noted in Chapter 3. Elizabeth could speak, indeed skilfully and in different languages, yet she does not. The grammatical construction differs from the one Donne uses in the epitaph for his wife, Anne, where the superlative is used repeatedly to describe her as 'Fæminæ lectissimæ, dilectissimæque; | Coniugi charissimæ, castissimæque; | Matri piisimæ, indulgentissimæque' [a woman most choice/select/read, most beloved/loving/well-read; a spouse most dear, most chaste; a mother most loving/merciful/pious/dutiful, most tender]'.[23] Obviously the emotion driving the language is different in each case, but perhaps the different constructions of praise are also a signal of the different status of the two females, so that because of Elizabeth's age and position on the threshold of womanhood, Donne uses a 'teeter-totter' construction. In line 15, Donne states Elizabeth's fortune and body were matched by her intellect. The phrase which Milgate translates in his edition as 'fortune' is 'fortunæve dotes', more specifically a dowry or marriage portion. Milgate makes it non-specific but one wonders, especially in the light of the hints about marriage matches which Donne makes in the elegy, whether Elizabeth died while marriage plans were in the

---

[23] I quote M. Thomas Hester's translation which aims to show 'as fully as possible . . . Donne's exploitation of the copious variety of the Latin idiom in order to figure forth his "wonder" at the life and death of Anne'. See 1996a: 21 and *passim*.

making. Perhaps Donne uses the word simply because she was an only child and heiress, or perhaps this was the only way one referred to a woman's fortune.

Elizabeth's liminal state is most compressed in Donne's description of her as '(PARADISUM SINE SERPENTE)'. That this statement should have its own line and, except for an interjection near the end, be the only phrase enclosed by a parenthesis is significant. The word, 'paradise', is derived from the Persian for an enclosed park or garden of delight and the lunulæ literally enact such a definition. John Lennard notes the classification of the parenthesis by Elizabethan schoolmasters as a rhetorical figure rather than as a mark of punctuation (1991: 14). George Puttenham in *The Arte of English Poesie* calls them a 'figure of tollerable disorder . . . by an English name the [*Insertour*] and is when ye will seeme for larger information or some other purpose, to peece or graffe in the middest of your tale an unnecessary parcell of speach, which neverthe-/lesse may be thence without any detriment to the rest' (1936: 169). Thus, parentheses act as both containers of a subtext within a text and disrupters of a text by inserting a supposedly 'unnecessary parcell of speach'. Lennard observes that the contents of parentheses are often ignored or trivialized by critics because they are assumed to mark 'extra' words which are 'additional, irrelevant, extraneous, subordinate, or damaging to the clarity of argument'. Indeed, Donne implies as much when he declares in a sermon, 'Devotion is no Marginall note, no interlineary glosse, no Parenthesis that may be left out' (ix. 194). He dismisses the act of dying as a parenthesis in Deaths Duell: 'As the first part of a sentence peeces wel with the last, and never respects, never hearkens after the *parenthesis* that comes betweene, so doth a *good life* here flowe into an *eternall life*' (x. 241; see also iii. 188, 287; v. 78, 345). Lennard asserts that 'a lunula marks a boundary between two textual states, one as it were the tonic, the other parenthetical to the tonic' (242), but which is often especially meaningful, rather than meaningless. In a letter to Sir Henry Goodyer, Donne comes so far as to acknowledge the more than extraneous use of parentheses: 'In the History or style of friendship, which is best written both in deeds and words, a Letter which is of a mixed nature, and hath something of both, is a mixed Parenthesis: It may be left out, yet it contributes, though not to the being, yet to the verdure, and freshnesse thereof' (1977: 114).

The pivotal point to remember is that Elizabeth was still a young girl at the time of her death, just past puberty and on the brink of womanhood, as Donne makes clear in 'A Funerall Elegie': suitors are fighting over her, but 'To scape th'infirmities which waite upone | Woman, shee went away, before sh'was one' (77–8). One need only recollect the refrain of Donne's Lincoln's Inn epithalamium to establish that the wedding night was the *rite de passage* during which a girl or maid became a woman: 'Tonight put on perfection, and a Woman's name'. Yet Elizabeth was not just 'admir'd' (63) but 'desir'd' (64) by her suitors; that is, those 'who ere had worth enough' (64). Hence, she had entered the state which Tertullian called *mulieritas*, 'the state of a woman aware of her own sexual feelings and capable of inspiring sexual feelings in others', a state that began, 'ineluctably, with puberty' (P. Brown 1989: 81). In his treatise, *De virginibus velandis [On the Veiling of Virgins]*, Tertullian states 'ex illo enim virgo desinet ex quo potest non esse [for a *virgin* ceases to be a *virgin* from the time that it becomes possible for her *not* to be one]' (*CSEL* 76/11.1.4; *ANF* 4.34). Thus began a woman's career as 'diaboli ianua [the devil's gateway]' (*CSEL* 70), Tertullian's infamous malediction. Elizabeth is thus poised on the threshold between two utterly different states of being and contains within herself aspects of both: a child innocent of adult sexual shame if nevertheless conceived in original sin, and a 'knowing' sexual woman who recognizes she must be vigilant in maintaining her virtuous reputation. Although essentially passive, Elizabeth is represented as the agent in maintaining the closure of her body's two troubling orifices, and this point is the fulcrum on which Donne balances his lever of praise and power. Elizabeth is lifted up as the exemplary exceptional 'one', 'Virtue herself'. But to present Elizabeth's virginal virtue as unparadoxically ideal is to set a dangerous precedent. Inasmuch as Donne's use of parenthesis suggests the closed virginal body, he also suggests that Elizabeth as a Paradise without the serpent is not part of the main body of the phallogocentric Text. In *Biathanatos*, Donne recounts Aulus Gellius' cautionary propaganda about the virgins of Milesium who began committing suicide in large numbers (1984*b*: 100). They 'had a wantonness of dying', Donne scoffs, hanging themselves, 'for fashion', but more probably they wanted to avoid marriage (see Cantorella 1986: 63). City authorities finally had to threaten the virgins with public display of their dead, naked bodies, to stave off the rash of suicides and restore the supply of marriageable women. Donne's Paradox, 'That Virginity is a Virtue', assigned to his *Dubia* by Peters, in any case usefully indicates that in Protestant England, virginity was considered temporary and preliminary to marriage, not permanent:

*Virginity* is a *vertue*, and hath her Throne in the middle: The extreams are, in *Excesse*, to violate it before marriage; in Defect, not to marry. . . . *Virginity* is an *Embrion*, an unfashioned lump, till it attain to a certain time, which is about twelve years of age in women, fourteen in men, and then it beginneth to have the soule of *Love* infused into it, and to become a *vertue*: There is also a certain limited time when it ceaseth to be a vertue, which in men is about fourty, in women about thirty years of age:. . . . May we not . . . account it a . . . heynous vice, for a *Virgin* to let her Fruit (*in potentia*) consume and rot to nothing, and to let the *vertue* of her *Virginity* degenerate into *Vice*. (1980: 55, 57)

Against such opinions of women who might want to remain virgins and avoid undesirable marriage matches, or continue their education, how are we to read the parenthesis and what it contains in Elizabeth's epitaph? As 'an unnecessary parcell of speech' which serves only to expand the 'narrative'? As physical marks on the 'page' (or tomb) mimicking the closure of her body? Or, as disruptive sub-text? Does Donne parenthesize this statement because of its impossibility, its theological daring, or because such a stage in a female's life could only ever be temporary? We have here, I suggest, what Lennard would call the exploitation of a parenthesis. Just above this line, Elizabeth's body is *'corpus intactum'*, definitive of a virgin, and *'integritate'*, an extremely loaded word in the writings of Ambrose meaning whole or pure, without any mixing or crossing of boundaries (P. Brown 1989: 354). The lunulæ, the prophylactic brackets, contain her body apart from the rest of the text as a kind of *hortus conclusus*, indeed, within which we find the first Garden, but without the serpent.

Donne uses one more phrase which suggests both the influence of Ambrose and hints that as Sabine argues, the Virgin Mary continued to feed his imagination. We move from garden metaphors to other kinds of enclosure. Elizabeth was not 'allured' by *'aulæ splendoribus* [the splendours of that palace]', her body. Peter Brown explains Ambrose's description of the Virgin Mary as an *aula pudoris*, 'a royal hall of undamaged chastity': 'The Imperial palace was a building rendered perpetually sacred by the presence of the Emperor. No private citizen, at any time, could dare to occupy its silent, golden halls.' Thus, according to Ambrose's metaphor, 'an unbreakable "invisible frontier" lay between a virgin's body and the polluting "admixture" of the outside world' (354). There are more connections to be made between Elizabeth and the Virgin Mary. Ambrose asserted the perpetual virginity of Mary, even after having given birth to Jesus. This belief, and that of the Immaculate Conception—the belief that Mary was born without original sin—were two intensely divisive issues in Christian doctrine. Donne is clearly suggesting in this parenthesis that Elizabeth is like Mary in being a 'paradise' which contained no serpent to bring about original sin, and a perpetual virgin who admitted no phallus. Indeed we find the exact same phrase used by the Anglican, Anthony Stafford, in his 1635 paean to the Virgin Mary, *The Femall Glory*. He invites us to 'Feed your eyes with the sight of her whose minde is a Paradice without a Serpent' (1988: 150). Sabine, who edited the facsimile reproduction of *The Femall Glory*, mentions this phrase in her discussion of Donne's negotiations with the figure of Mary, but she does not mention its appearance in Elizabeth's epitaph or indeed the epitaph at all.

Donne clearly liked to imagine paradise in his poetry, and its inhabitants almost always included snakes. In 'Twicknam Garden' the dejected Petrarchan lover declares, 'And that this place may thoroughly be thought | True Paradise, I have the serpent brought' (8–9). Carey points to the phallic double-meaning here which I suggest is also present in the parenthesis describing Elizabeth, especially since 'SINE SERPENTE' echoes 'SINE SEXU' two lines earlier. Donne's parenthesis recalls 'Sapho to Philaenis', when which Sapho attempts to persuade Philaenis that she does not need a man: 'Thy body is a natural paradise, | In whose self, unmanured, all pleasure lies, | Nor needs perfection; why shouldst thou then | Admit the tillage of a harsh rough man?' (35–8). Indeed, Elizabeth is described again in *The Anniversaries* as an 'unvext Paradise' (*FA* 363), and, in a complex analogy (with a dig at courtiers), as 'Shee to whose person Paradise adhear'd, | As Courts to Princes' (*SA* 77–8). The most extended conceit is also found in *The First Anniversary* where Donne describes the new world produced by the active remembrance or 'practise' (78) of Elizabeth Drury's virtue:

> (For all assum'd unto this Dignitee,
> So many weedlesse Paradises bee,
> Which of themselves produce no venemous sinne,
> Except some forraine Serpent bring it in). (81–4)

More than coincidentally, these lines are also enclosed by lunulæ or a parenthesis, so that the 'weedlesse Paradises' are protected from the invasion of the 'forraine Serpent' which is yet, hypothetically, already within the enclosure. There are more references to Paradise in Donne's verse letters to the Countess of Bedford, where in an uncomfortable attempt at flattery, Donne declares, 'Even in you, vertues best paradise, | Vertue hath some, but wise degrees of vice' ('T'have written then', 75–6). It would thus seem, from all these examples, that the idea of paradise and the co-existence of good and evil, potential or actual in one place held great imaginative appeal for Donne, one which he was willing to explore even at the risk of charges of blasphemy.

As I have tried to show, a virgin's *corpus intactum* was only considered to be a temporary state in Protestant England. A Paradisal body without the serpent, or phallus, is one which can never be seduced or deflowered. Perhaps the parentheses indicate that Elizabeth was only to be temporarily a '(PARADISUM SINE SERPENTE)', saved from a (sexual) 'fall' only by her early death. Eventually the parenthesis would be removed and a 'serpent' let in. After all, Donne says in another sermon, '*Paradise* was not walled, nor hedged; and there were serpents in Paradise too' (x. 160). Moreover, what challenge is there in maintaining her *hortus conclusus* if there is no danger to be avoided? In what lies Elizabeth's merit if there is no 'serpent' to reject? Thus, at the centre of Elizabeth's epitaph, Donne places a rhetorical figure which almost works too well, encapsulating the closed state of her body and yet sealing it off from the sexual consummation which was the destiny of any Protestant virgin. It is in the subsequent works, the 'Funeral Elegy' and the *Anniversaries*, that he removes the parenthesis and lets in the serpent, in Elizabeth's extraordinary textual sexualization. Donne's use of parenthesis and other textual signs to both 'emprison her' and yet acknowledge her 'incomprehensiblenesse' is only one example of an endlessly fascinating mind at work on the female body. Even by an epitaph we are reminded that 'no *Jod*' in Donne's writing is 'superfluous', even a parenthesis can keep his readers 'busy'. *The Anniversaries* and all Donne's poetry and prose show the cost to the psyche of the split between body and mind, material and spiritual, the pretermission of the feminine from full creative participation, yet they also intimate that Donne intuited 'on the horizon, a hint . . . of a "world" so inconceivable, so other' (Irigaray 1985a: 228) into which, even in his imagination, he could not fully venture, shackled as he was to a phallocentric tradition. Donne could recognize "Tis all in pieces, all cohærence gone; | All just supply, and all Relation' (*FA* 213–14), but he could not always locate the solution in a reconfiguration of gender relations. He could recognize the error in striving for the 'one' of solitude and singularity where 'every man alone thinkes he hath got | To be a Phœnix, and that there can bee | None of that kinde, of which he is, but hee' (*FA* 216–18), but he perpetuates the exclusion of the one 'other' in the 'Father, Sonne' relation which is anything but 'forgot' (*FA* 215) in patriarchal culture. Rather, as Irigaray asserts (see 1993a: 148) and Donne's Nethersole sermon and his *Devotions* dedication illustrate, it is the debt to the mother which is forgotten, and the fecund couples of father and mother, Spirit and Bride which are still waiting to be recognized.

# Coda

new Philosophy cals all in doubt.
*(The First Anniversary)*

To paraphrase Sapho, What shall we call Donne, then? Clearly (or rather, complicatedly) he is more than the masculine monolith which has become almost a casual observance in criticism of his poetry and prose.[1] A. C. Partridge observes that 'any student who seeks to explicate the writings of Donne must be prepared to amend his [or her] judgments repeatedly' (1978: 11). There are certainly grounds for extending Donne's reputation for originality and iconoclasm to his construction of gender, especially in his exploration of lesbian love, his evocations of mutual love between men and women, and the fluidity of gender boundaries in poems such as the early verse letters. But where does this leave the feminine? Still, 'all in pieces'.

Lamenting Donne's general elusiveness, Judith Herz betrays her residual disappointment in settling for 'solace' in individual 'fragments' of Donne's work, and William Kerrigan suggests this

---

[1] The trend having been started by Donne himself and Thomas Carew, Helen Carr cites examples from the eighteenth and nineteenth centuries of critics who assert and approve of Donne's 'masculine perswasive force'. For example, Coleridge approves of Donne's 'manly harmony' in his satires, as well as his more general 'masculine intellect'; Emerson speaks of Donne's 'masculine' oratory; G. H. Lewes enthuses, 'Honest John Donne—rough—hearty—pointed and sincere . . . was in every sense a man' (Carr 1988: 97). Milgate hails the 'manly lucidity' of Donne's style in his verse letters to men, and then goes on to describe the style of his verse letters to women: 'Donne entertains and also flatters the ladies by the playful wit, the intellectual fantasy, *sometimes (almost) the mild engaging idiocy* with which he elaborates the basically simple thought and imagery from which he begins' (Donne 1967b: p. xxxviii; my italics). Margaret Maurer asserts that as Donne's style matures from his early to his later verse letters, his 'posture of inferiority' disappears and '[t]he tone becomes manfully self-reliant' (1976: 247). Laurence Lerner suggests that 'what Donne takes from Ovid may be above all his masculinity: masculine cynicism, masculine power, masculine brilliance' (1990: 126).

particular difficulty in Donne's work is viewed as contributing to a lack of 'progress'. Though as these critics recognize, the problem lies not in Donne's work but in our own expectations of what it might be asking of us. In other words, we might say less often that Donne is a great poet *in spite of* this or that technical deficiency, his oscillation between points of view, his contradictions, and so forth, and assert that Donne is a great poet *because of* these same elements. I do not suggest that we simply turn the tables on what is or is not accorded value, but rather that we expand our range of possibilities. It seems to me that Donne's significance for constructing new paradigms lies in this larger 'incomprehensibleness' which keeps us constantly wondering. 'The only response one can make to the question of the meaning of the text is: read, perceive, experience. . . . *Who are you?* is probably the most relevant question to ask of a text, as long as one isn't requesting a kind of identity card or an autobiographical anecdote' (1993*c*: 178; Irigaray's ellipsis). Irigaray's notion of style allows us one way of coming to terms with Donne's work as a whole so as to view its difficulty neither as a failure of the artist nor as a failure of interpretation on our part. There is 'a certain style' for Irigaray which 'is not susceptible of reduction to a grill that may be transposed or imposed elsewhere'; which 'resists coding, summary, counting, cataloguing'; which 'cannot be brought down to the level of such oppositions as sense/mind, poetry/ideas . . . masculine/feminine, as these dichotomies have been presented to us so far'; which 'creates without resolving or dissolving into dichotomies, however sophisticated they may be' (1993*c*: 177–8; Irigaray's ellipsis). We need not view Donne as deficient or disappointing in any way because his work, perhaps in spite of himself, constitutes an other means of expression than the patriarchal insistence on linearity, unity, a single position, 'mastery', Truth with a capital 'T', and so on.

Samuel Taylor Coleridge said: 'If you would teach a scholar in the highest form how to *read*, take Donne' (see Brinkley 1955: 521). I would also recommend that 'If you would teach a [feminist] scholar in the highest form how to read, take Donne'. The Latin root of 'incomprehensibleness' was a term used in wrestling to describe a slippery opponent. In my exploration of Donne's various figurations of 'that subtile (k)not which makes us (wo)man'[2]

---

[2] I paraphrase line 64 of 'The Exstasie'.

Donne might seem a slippery opponent, just as the feminine proved incomprehensible to him. But his work cries out for encounter nonetheless, and feminist analysis shows that it is possible to meet not in a relation of opposition, but in an embrace so as to form a 'fecund couple'. If such 'new Philosophy cals all in doubt' it is a doubt which moves, not towards entropy but one which makes room for 'parousia', the coming of the divine in the 'here and now', 'in and through the body' (Irigaray 1993*a*: 147 ff.), a progress of and in love wholly desired by Donne.

# Selected Bibliography

## MANUSCRIPT SOURCES

Bodleian Library, Oxford, MS Ashmole 38.
Bodleian Library, Oxford, MS Ashmole 47.
Bodleian Library, Oxford, MS Eng.poet.f.9.
Bodleian Library, Oxford, MS Eng.poet.e.97.
Bodleian Library, Oxford, MS Malone 14.
Bodleian Library, Oxford, MS Malone 508.
Bodleian Library, Oxford, MS Rawlinson poet.160.
British Library Additional MS 10309.
British Library Additional MS 25707.
National Library of Scotland MS 2067, Hawthornden XV.
New York Public Library, Berg Collection, Westmoreland MS.

## PRINTED BOOKS

Printed works before 1700 are published in London unless otherwise indicated.

Abel, Elizabeth, ed. (1982). *Writing and Sexual Difference*. Brighton: Harvester.

Adams, J. N. (1982). *The Latin Sexual Vocabulary*. London: Duckworth.

Adelman, Janet (1992). *Suffocating Mothers: Fantasies of Maternal Origin in Shakespeare's Plays,* Hamlet *to* The Tempest. New York: Routledge.

Aers, David, and Kress, Gunther (1978). '"Darke Texts Need Notes": Versions of Self in Donne's Verse Epistles'. *Literature and History* 8: 138–58.

—— Hodge, Bob and Kress, Gunther (1981). *Literature, Language and Society in England, 1580–1680*. Totowa, NJ: Barnes & Noble.

Agrippa, Henry Cornelius (1542). *A Treatise of the Nobilitie and excellencye of woman kynde*. Trans. David Clapham.

Akrigg, G. P. V. (1962). *Jacobean Pageants; or, The Court of King James*. Cambridge, Mass.: Harvard University Press.

Allen, D. C. (1943a). 'Dean Donne Sets His Text'. *ELH* 10: 208–29.

Allen, D. C. (1943*b*). 'John Donne's Knowledge of Renaissance Medicine'. *JEGP* 42: 322–42.

—— (1964). 'Donne's "Sapho to Philaenis"'. *ELN* 1: 188–91.

Andreason, N. J. C. (1967). *John Donne: Conservative Revolutionary*. Princeton University Press.

Apollonius Rhodius (1912). *The Argonautica*. Trans. R. C. Seaton. London: Heinemann.

Aretino, Pietro (1971). *Dialogues*. Trans. Raymond Rosenthal. New York: Stein and Day.

Ariès, Phillippe (1981). *The Hour of Our Death*. Trans. Helen Weaver. Harmondsworth: Penguin.

Armstrong, Alan (1977). 'The Apprenticeship of John Donne: Ovid and the Elegies'. *ELH* 44: 419–42.

Armstrong, Nancy, and Tennenhouse, Leonard, eds. (1987). *The Ideology of Conduct: Essays on Literature and the History of Sexuality*. New York: Methuen.

Aughterson, Kate, ed. (1995). *Renaissance Woman: A Sourcebook. Constructions of Femininity in England*. London: Routledge.

Augustine of Hippo, St (1984). *Concerning the City of God against the Pagans*. Trans. Henry Bettenson. Harmondsworth: Penguin.

—— (1982). *On the Literal Meaning of Genesis*. Trans. John Hammond Taylor, SJ. Volumes xli and xlii. *Ancient Christian Writers: The Works of the Fathers in Translation*. Ed. Johannes Quasten, Walter J. Burghardt, Thomas Comerford Lawler. New York: Newman Press.

Aulus Gellius (1928). *The Attic Nights of Aulus Gellius*. Trans. John C. Rolfe. 3 Volumes. London: Heinemann.

Bacon, Sir Francis (1597). *Essayes*.

Bal, Mieke (1986). 'Sexuality, Sin and Sorrow: The Emergence of Female Character (A Reading of Genesis 1–3)' in Suleiman: 317–38.

Bald, R. C. (1951–2). 'Donne's Early Verse Letters'. *HLQ* 15: 283–9.

—— (1959). *Donne and the Drurys*. Cambridge University Press.

—— (1986, first publ. 1970). *John Donne: A Life*. Oxford University Press.

Barclay, Alexander (1928). *The Eclogues of Alexander Barclay: From the original edition by John Cawood*. Ed. Beatrice White. Printed for the Early English Text Society by Oxford University Press.

Barkan, Leonard (1975). *Nature's Work of Art: The Human Body as Image of the World*. New Haven: Yale University Press.

Barnes, Barnabe (1994). *A Divine Centurie of Spirituall Sonnets (1595)*. Cambridge: Chadwyk-Healey *English Poetry Full-Text Database*.

Barnfield, Richard (1595). *Cynthia, with Certaine Sonnets, and the Legend of Cassandra*.

Bastard, Thomas (1598). *Chrestoleros*.

Battersby, Christine (1989). *Gender and Genius: Towards a Feminist Aesthetics*. London: The Women's Press.

Baumlin, James S. (1991). *John Donne and the Rhetorics of Renaissance Discourse.* Columbia: University of Missouri Press.

Beal, Peter, compiler (1980–93). *Index of English Literary Manuscripts.* 2Volumes. London: Mansell.

Behn, Aphra (1992). *Oronooko, The Rover and Other Works.* Ed. Janet Todd. Harmondsworth: Penguin.

Bell, Ilona (1983). 'The Role of the Lady in Donne's *Songs and Sonets*'. *SEL* 23: 113–29.

Belsey, Catherine (1993, first publ. 1985). *The Subject of Tragedy: Identity and Difference in Renaissance Drama.* London: Routledge.

—— (1994). *Desire: Love Stories in Western Culture.* Oxford: Basil Blackwell.

Benet, Diana Treviño (1994). 'Sexual Transgression in Donne's Elegies'. *MP* 92/1: 14–35.

Bennett, Joan (1964). *Five Metaphysical Poets.* 3rd edn. Cambridge University Press.

—— (1967, first publ. 1938 by Oxford University Press). 'The Love Poetry of John Donne: A Reply to Mr. C. S. Lewis' in *Seventeenth Century Studies Presented to Sir Herbert Grierson.* New York: Octagon Books: 85–104.

Berg, Maggie (1991). 'Luce Irigaray's "Contradictions": Poststructuralism and Feminism'. *Signs* 17/1: 50–70.

Berger, Harry (1988). *Revisionary Play: Studies in the Spenserian Dynamics.* With an Introductory Essay by Louis Montrose. Berkeley: University of California Press.

Berry, Philippa (1989). *Of Chastity and Power: Elizabethan Literature and the Unmarried Queen.* London: Routledge.

—— (1994). 'The Burning Glass: Paradoxes of Feminist Revelation in *Speculum*' in Burke, Schor, Whitford: 229–46.

*Biblia Sacra iuxta vulgatem clementiam* (1985). Madrid: Biblioteca de Autores Cristianos.

Black, L. G. (1974). 'Studies in Some Related Manuscript Poetic Miscellanies of the 1580s', D.Phil. thesis (Oxford).

Blank, Paula (1995). 'Comparing Sappho to Philaenis: John Donne's "Homopoetics"'. *PMLA* 110/3: 358–68.

Bloom, Clive, ed. (1988). *Jacobean Poetry and Prose: Rhetoric, Representation and the Popular Imagination.* New York: St. Martin's Press.

Blumenfeld-Kosinski, Renate (1990). *Not of Woman Born: Representations of Cesarean Birth in Medieval and Renaissance Culture.* Ithaca, NY: Cornell University Press.

Boccaccio, Giovanni (1620). *The Decameron. Containing an Hundred pleasant Novels.* [Trans. E. Hutton].

—— (1972). *Genealogia Deorum Gentilium.* Ed. Piero Giorgio Ricci. Volume ix. *La Letteratura Italiana: Storia e Testi.* Milano, Napoli: Riccardo Ricciardi Editore.

244  BIBLIOGRAPHY

Boethius, Anicius Manlius Severinus (1990, 2nd edn., first publ. 1918). *Philosophiae Consolationis*. Trans. S. J. Tester. Cambridge, Mass.: Harvard University Press.

Boose, Lynda E. (1994). 'The 1599 Bishops' Ban, Elizabethan Pornography, and the Sexualization of the Jacobean Stage' in Burt and Archer: 185–200.

Boutcher, Wayne (1996). 'Vernacular Humanism in the Sixteeenth Century' in Jill Kraye, ed. *The Cambridge Companion to Renaissance Humanism*. Cambridge University Press: 189–202.

Bradstreet, Anne (1967). *The Works of Anne Bradstreet*. Ed. Jeannine Hensley. Foreword by Adrienne Rich. Cambridge Mass.: Harvard University Press.

Brântome, Seigneur de (Pierre de Bourdeille) (1666). *Memoires de Messire Pierre du Bourdeille, Seigneur de BRANTOME contenans Les Vies de Dames Galantes de son temps*. Tome I. Aleyde.

Brathwaite, Richard (1615). *A Strappado for the Divell, Epigrams and Satyres alluding to the time, with divers measures of no lesse Delight*.

Bray, Alan (1988). *Homosexuality in Renaissance England*. 2nd edn. Boston: Gay Men's Press.

Brenner, Athalya, ed. (1993). *A Feminist Companion to Genesis*. Sheffield: Sheffield Academic Press.

Brink, Jean R., ed. (1993). *Privileging Gender in Early Modern England*. Kirksville, Mo.: Sixteenth Century Journal Publishers.

Brinkley, Roberta F. (1955). *Coleridge on the Seventeenth Century*. Durham, N. C.: Duke University Press.

Brown, Judith C. (1986). *Immodest Acts: The Life of a Lesbian Nun in Renaissance Italy*. Oxford University Press.

Brown, Peter (1989). *The Body and Society: Men, Women and Sexual Renunciation in Early Christianity*. London: Faber.

Burke, Carolyn (1994). 'Irigaray Through the Looking Glass' in Burke, Schor, Whitford: 37–56.

—— Schor, Naomi and Whitford, Margaret, eds. (1994). *Engaging with Irigaray: Feminist Philosophy and Modern European Thought*. New York: Columbia University Press.

Burt, Richard, and Archer, John Michael, eds. (1994). *Enclosure Acts: Sexuality, Property, and Culture in Early Modern England*. Ithaca, NY: Cornell University Press.

Butler, Judith (1990*a*). *Gender Trouble: Feminism and the Subversion of Identity*. London: Routledge.

—— (1990*b*). 'Gender Trouble, Feminist Theory, and Psychoanalytic Discourse' in Nicholson: 324–40.

—— (1993). *Bodies That Matter: On the Discursive Limits of 'Sex'*. London: Routledge.

—— (1994). 'Bodies That Matter' in Burke, Schor, Whitford: 141–74.

Bynum, Caroline (1982). *Jesus as Mother: Studies in the Spirituality of the High Middle Ages*. Berkeley: University of California Press.

—— (1995). 'Why All the Fuss about the Body? A Medievalist's Perspective'. *CI* 22: 1–33.

Cameron, Allen Barry (1976). 'Donne's Deliberative Verse Epistles'. *ELR* 6: 369–403.

Campling, Arthur (1937). *The History of the Family of DRURY in the Counties of Suffolk and Norfolk from the Conquest*. London: Mitchell Hughes and Clarke.

Cantorella, Eva (1986). 'Dangling Virgins: Myth, Ritual and the Place of Women in Ancient Greece' in Suleiman: 57–67.

Capellanus, Andreas (1960). *The Art of Courtly Love*. Trans. John J. Parry. New York: Columbia University Press.

Carey, John (1960). 'The Ovidian Love Elegy in England', D.Phil. thesis (Oxford).

—— (1990, 2nd edn., first publ. 1981). *John Donne: Life, Mind and Art*. London: Faber and Faber.

Carr, Helen (1988). 'Donne's Masculine Persuasive Force' in C. Bloom: 96–118.

Case, Robert H., ed. (1896). *English Epithalamies*. London: John Lane.

Castiglione, Baldassare (1994). *The Book of the Courtier* [Hoby translation]. Ed. Virginia Cox. London: J. M. Dent.

Castle, Terry (1979). 'La'bring Bards: Birth *Topoi* and English Poetics'. *JEGP* 78: 193–208.

Catullus (1976). *Catullus, Tibullus and Pervigilium Veneris*. Trans. F. W. Cornish. London: Heinemann.

Chamberlain, John (1939). *The Letters of John Chamberlain*. Ed. Norman E. McClure. 2 Volumes. Philadelphia: American Philosophical Society.

Chamberlin, John S. (1976). *Increase and Multiply: Arts-of-Discourse Procedure in the Preaching of Donne*. Chapel Hill: University of North Carolina Press.

Chambers, A. B. (1985). 'Will the Real John Donne Please Rise?' *JDJ* 4/1: 109–20.

Chanter, Tina (1995). *Ethics of Eros: Irigaray's Rewriting of the Philosophers*. New York: Routledge.

Chapman, George (1962). *The Poems of George Chapman*. Ed. Phyllis Brooks Bartlett. New York: Russell & Russell.

Chester, Robert (1601). *Love's Martyr*.

Churchyard, Thomas. (1994). *A light Bondell of Livly discourses called Churchyards charge (1580)*. Cambridge: Chadwyk-Healey *English Poetry Full-Text Database*.

Cirillo, A. R. (1969). 'The Fair Hermaphrodite: Love-Union in the Poetry of Donne and Spenser'. *SEL* 9: 81–95.

Clark, Arthur Melville (1931). *Thomas Heywood: Playwright and Miscellanist*. Oxford: Basil Blackwell.

Clark, Elizabeth A. (1983). *Women in the Early Church*. Collegeville, Minn.: The Liturgical Press.

Clark, Ira (1988). '"How witty's ruine": The Difficulties of Donne's "Idea of a Woman" in the First of his *Anniversaries'*. *South Atlantic Review* 53/1: 19–26.

*Claudian* (1922). Trans. Maurice Platnauer. Volume i. London: Heinemann.

Cogan, Thomas (1589). *The Haven of Health*.

Colie, Rosalie (1972). '"All in Peeces": Problems of Interpretation in Donne's Anniversary Poems' in Fiore: 189–218.

Collins, Adela Yarbro, ed. (1985). *Feminist Perspectives on Biblical Scholarship*. Chico, Calif.: Scholars Press.

Constable, Henry (1960). *The Poems of Henry Constable*. Ed. Joan Grundy. Liverpool University Press.

Corns, Thomas N., ed. (1993). *The Cambridge Companion to English Poetry: Donne to Marvell*. Cambridge University Press.

Correll, Barbara (1995). 'Symbolic Economies and Zero-Sum Erotics: Donne's "Sapho to Philaenis"'. *ELH* 62: 487–509.

Corthell, Ronald J. (1989). 'Donne's "Disparitie": Inversion, Gender, and the Subject of Love in Some Songs and Sonnets'. *Exemplaria* 1/1: 17–42.

Craige, Alexander (1606). *The Amorose Songes, Sonets, and Elegies*.

Cressy, David (1980). *Literacy and the Social Order: Reading and Writing in Tudor and Stuart England*. Cambridge University Press.

Crompton, Louis (1980/1). 'The Myth of Lesbian Impunity: Capital Laws from 1270 to 1791'. *Journal of Homosexuality* 6/1–2: 11–25.

Crooke, Helkiah (1618). *Microcosmographia. A Description of the Body of Man.*

Cullum, Revd Sir John (1784). *The History and Antiquities of Hawsted, In the County of Suffolk*. London: Society of Antiquaries.

Curtius, Ernst Robert (1979, first publ. 1953). *European Literature and the Latin Middle Ages*. Trans. Willard R. Trask. London: Routledge and Kegan Paul. Orig. publ. in German as *Europäische Literatur und lateinisches Mittelalter* by A. Francke AG Verlag, Bern, 1948.

Daniel, Samuel (1965). *Poems and A Defence of Ryme*. Ed. Arthur Colby Sprague. Chicago: University of Chicago Press and Phoenix Books.

Dante Alighieri (1961). *The Divine Comedy*. Italian text with Trans. and Comm. by John D. Sinclair. New York: Oxford University Press.

Datta, Kitty (1977). 'Love and Asceticism in Donne's Poetry: The Divine Analogy'. *CQ* 19/2: 5–25.

Davies, Sir John (1975). *The Poems of Sir John Davies*. Ed. Robert Krueger. Oxford: Clarendon.

Davies of Herford, John (1603). *Microcosmos*.

—— (1605). *Wittes Pilgrimage*.

—— (1610). *The Scourge of Folly*.

—— (1617). *Wits Bedlam*.

Davison, Francis (1603). *A Poetical Rhapsody*.

DeJean, Joan (1989). *Fictions of Sappho: 1546–1937*. University of Chicago Press.

de Lauretis, Teresa (1988). 'Sexual Indifference and Lesbian Representation'. *Theatre Journal* 40: 155–77.

—— (1990). 'Eccentric Subjects: Feminist Theory and Historical Consciousness'. *Feminist Studies* 16/1: 115–50.

DeLuna, Barbara (1967). *Jonson's Romish Plot: A Study of* Catiline *and its Historical Context*. Oxford: Clarendon.

De Stefano, Barbara (1984). 'Evolution of Extravagant Praise in Donne's Verse Epistles'. *SP* 81: 75–93.

Derrida, Jacques (1979). *Spurs: Nietzsche's Styles/Éperons: Les Styles de Nietzsche*. Trans. Barbara Harlow. Intro. by Stefano Agosti. Drawings by François Loubrieu. University of Chicago Press.

—— (1981). *Positions*. Trans. Alan Bass. University of Chicago Press.

Docherty, Thomas (1986). *John Donne, Undone*. London: Methuen.

Donne, John (1912). *The Poems of John Donne*. Ed. Herbert J. C. Grierson. 2 Volumes. Oxford University Press.

—— (1942). *Complete Poems*. Ed. Roger E. Bennett. University of Chicago Press.

—— (1952). *Essays in Divinity*. Ed. Evelyn M. Simpson. Oxford: Clarendon.

—— (1953–62). *Sermons*. Ed. Evelyn M. Simpson and George R. Potter. 10 Volumes. Berkeley: University of California Press.

—— (1965). *The Elegies and the Songs and Sonnets*. Ed. Helen Gardner. Oxford: Clarendon.

—— (1967a). *The Complete Poetry of John Donne*. Ed. John T. Shawcross. New York: Anchor Books.

—— (1967b). *The Satires, Epigrams and Verse Letters*. Ed. W. Milgate. Oxford: Clarendon.

—— (1967c). *Selected Prose*. Chosen by Evelyn Simpson. Ed. Helen Gardner and Timothy Healy. Oxford: Clarendon.

—— (1969). *Ignatius His Conclave*. Ed. T. S. Healy, SJ. Oxford: Clarendon.

—— (1977). *Letters to Severall Persons of Honour* (1651). A Facsimile Reproduction with an Introduction by M. Thomas Hester. Delmar, NY: Scholars' Facsimiles & Reprints.

—— (1978). *The Epithalamions, Anniversaries and Epicedes*. Ed. W. Milgate. Oxford University Press.

—— (1980). *Paradoxes and Problems*. Ed. Helen Peters. Oxford University Press.

—— (1982). *The Divine Poems*. 2nd edn. Ed. Helen Gardner. Oxford: Clarendon.

—— (1983). *The Songs and Sonets of John Donne*. 2nd edn. Ed. Theodore Redpath. London: Methuen.

—— (1984a). *Biathanatos*. Ed. Ernest W. Sullivan II. Newark: University of Delaware Press.

Donne, John (1984*b*). *Biathanatos*. A modern-spelling edition with Intro. and Comm. by Michael Rudick and M. Pabst Battin. New York: Garland Publishing Inc.

—— (1985). *The Complete English Poems of John Donne*. Ed. C. A. Patrides. London: J. M. Dent.

—— (1986). *The Complete English Poems*. Ed. A. J. Smith. Harmondsworth: Penguin.

—— (1987). *Devotions Upon Emergent Occasions*. Ed. Anthony Raspa. New York: Oxford University Press.

—— (1990). *John Donne*. Ed. John Carey. Oxford Authors Series. Oxford University Press.

—— (1995*a*). *The Variorum Edition of the Poetry of John Donne*. Volume vi. *The Anniversaries and the Epicedes and Obsequies*. General Editor: Gary A. Stringer. Bloomington: Indiana University Press.

—— (1995*b*). *The Variorum Edition of the Poetry of John Donne*. Volume viii. *The Epigrams, Epithalamions, Epitaphs, Inscriptions, and Miscellaneous Poems*. General Editor: Gary A. Stringer. Bloomington: Indiana University Press.

Drayton, Michael (1961). *The Works of Michael Drayton*. Ed. J. William Hebel. 5 Volumes. Oxford: Clarendon.

Dubrow, Heather (1976). 'Donne's "Epithalamion made at Lincolnes Inne": An Alternative Interpretation'. *SEL* 16: 131–43.

—— (1986). 'Tradition and the Individualistic Talent: Donne's "An Epithalamion or Mariadge Song on the Lady Elizabeth"' in Summers and Pebworth 1986: 106–16.

—— (1988). '"The Sun in Water": Donne's Somerset Epithalamium and the Poetics of Patronage' in Dubrow and Strier: 197–219.

—— (1990). *A Happier Eden: The Politics of Marriage in the Stuart Epithalamium*. Ithaca, NY: Cornell University Press.

—— (1995). *Echoes of Desire: English Petrarchism and Its Counterdiscourses*. Ithaca. NY: Cornell University Press.

—— and Strier, Richard, eds. (1988). *The Historical Renaissance: New Essays on Tudor and Stuart Literature and Culture*. University of Chicago Press.

El-Gabalawy, Saad (1976). 'Aretino's Pornography in the Later English Renaissance'. *English Miscellany* 25: 97–119.

Eliot, T. S. (1958). 'Donne in Our Time' in Spencer: 3–19.

Ellrodt, Robert (1980). 'Angels and the Poetic Imagination from Donne to Traherne' in *English Renaissance Studies: Presented to Dame Helen Gardner in Honour of her Seventieth Birthday*. Oxford University Press: 164–79.

Empson, William (1995). *Essays on Renaissance Literature*. Volume i. *Donne and the New Philosophy*. Ed. John Haffenden. Cambridge University Press.

*English Poetry Full-Text Database* (1994). Version 3.1. CD-ROM. Cambridge: Chadwyk-Healey.

Erasmus, Desiderius (1965). *The Colloquies of Erasmus*. Trans. Craig R. Thompson. University of Chicago Press.

Estrin, Barbara (1994). *Laura: Uncovering Gender and Genre in Wyatt, Donne and Marvell*. Durham, NC: Duke University Press.

Evans, Robert C., and Little, Anne C., eds. (1995). *'The Muses Female Are': Martha Moulsworth and Other Women Writers of the English Renaissance*. West Cornwall, Conn.: Locust Hill Press.

Faderman, Lillian (1985). *Surpassing the Love of Man: Romantic Friendship and Love Between Women from the Renaissance to the Present*. London: Women's Press.

Ferguson, Margaret W., Quilligan, Maureen and Vickers, Nancy J., eds. (1986). *Rewriting the Renaissance: The Discourses of Sexual Difference in Early Modern Europe*. University of Chicago Press.

Fewell, Danna Nolan, and Gunn, David M. (1993). *Gender, Power, and Promise: The Subject of the Bible's First Story*. Nashville: Abingdon Press.

Fineman, Joel (1986). *Shakespeare's Perjured Eye: The Invention of Poetic Subjectivity in the Sonnets*. Berkeley: University of California Press.

Finkelpearl, Philip J. (1969). *John Marston of the Middle Temple: An Elizabethan Dramatist in His Social Setting*. Cambridge, Mass.: Harvard University Press.

Finucci, Valeria, and Schwartz, Regina, eds. (1994). *Desire in the Renaissance: Psychoanalysis and Literature*. Princeton University Press.

Fiore, Peter Amadeus, ed. (1972). *Just So Much Honor: Essays Commemorating the Four-Hundredth Anniversary of the Birth of John Donne*. University Park: Pennsylvania State University Press.

Fiorenza, Elisabeth Schüssler (1992). *But She Said: Feminist Practices of Biblical Interpretation*. Boston: Beacon Press.

Fish, Stanley (1990). 'Masculine Perswasive Force: Donne and Verbal Power' in Harvey and Maus: 223–52.

Fisher, Sheila, and Halley, Janet E., eds. (1989). *Seeking the Woman in Late Medieval and Renaissance Writings: Essays in Feminist Contextual Criticism*. Knoxville: University of Tennessee Press.

Fitz [Woodbridge], Linda T. (1980). '"What Says the Married Woman?": Marriage Theory and Feminism in the English Renaissance'. *Mosaic* 13: 1–22.

Fletcher, Anthony, and Stevenson, John, eds. (1985). *Order and Disorder in Early Modern England*. Cambridge University Press.

Flynn, Dennis (1995). *Donne and the Ancient Catholic Nobility*. Bloomington: Indiana University Press.

Fortier, Mark (1991). 'The Muse in Donne and Jonson: A Post-Lacanian Study'. *MLS* 24/4: 90–104.

Foucault, Michel (1970). *The Order of Things: An Archaeology of the Human Sciences*. London: Tavistock.

—— (1978). *The History of Sexuality*. Volume i. *An Introduction*. Trans. Robert Hurley. Harmondsworth: Penguin.

Foucault, Michel (1987). *The History of Sexuality.* Volume ii. *The Use of Pleasure.* Trans. Robert Hurley. Harmondsworth: Penguin.

—— (1990). *The History of Sexuality.* Volume iii. *The Care of the Self.* Trans. Robert Hurley. Harmondsworth: Penguin.

Fowler, Alastair (1982). *An Introduction to the Theory of Genres and Modes.* Cambridge, Mass.: Harvard University Press.

Fox, Ruth A. (1972). 'Donne's *Anniversaries* and the Art of Living'. *ELH* 39: 528–41.

Frantz, David O. (1972). '"Leud Priapians" and Renaissance Pornography'. *SEL* 12: 157–72.

—— (1989). *Festum Voluptatis: A Study of Renaissance Erotica.* Columbus: Ohio State University Press.

Freccero, John (1975). 'The Fig Tree and the Laurel: Petrarch's Poetics'. *Diacritics* 5: 34–40.

Freud, Sigmund (1991; first publ. 1964). *New Introductory Lectures on Psychoanalysis.* Trans. James Strachey. Ed. James Strachey and Angela Richards. Harmondsworth: Penguin.

Frontain, Raymond-Jean, and Malpezzi, Frances M., eds. (1995). *John Donne's Religious Imagination: Essays in Honor of John T. Shawcross.* Conway, Ark.: University of Central Arkansas Press.

Frye, Northrop (1990). *Words with Power: Being a Second Study of the Bible and Literature.* Harmondsworth: Penguin.

Fuss, Diana (1989). *Essentially Speaking: Feminism, Nature and Difference.* New York: Routledge.

Garber, Marjorie (1997). 'Out of Joint' in Hillmann and Mazzio: 23–52.

Gardner, Helen (1946). 'Notes on Donne's Verse Letters'. *PMLA* 41/3: 318–21.

—— ed. (1962). *Twentieth Century Views: John Donne, A Collection of Critical Essays.* Englewood Cliffs, NJ: Prentice Hall International.

Gataker, Thomas (1623). *A Good Wife Gods Gift; And, A Wife Indeed. Two Mariage Sermons.*

*Geneva Bible, The. A facsimile of the 1560 edition* (1969). Introduction by Lloyd E. Berry. Madison: University of Wisconsin Press.

Gent, Lucy, and Llewellyn, Nigel, eds. (1990). *Renaissance Bodies: The Human Figure in Renaissance Culture c.1540–1660.* London: Reaktion Books.

Gilbert, Sandra, and Gubar, Susan (1979). *The Madwoman in the Attic.* New Haven: Yale University Press.

Girard, René (1977). *Violence and the Sacred.* Trans. Patrick Gregory. Baltimore: Johns Hopkins University Press.

Goldberg, Jonathan (1983). *James I and the Politics of Literature: Jonson, Shakespeare, Donne and Their Contemporaries.* Baltimore: Johns Hopkins University Press.

—— (1986). 'Fatherly Authority: The Politics of Stuart Family Images' in Ferguson, Quilligan, Vickers: 3–33.

—— (1992). *Sodometries: Renaissance Texts. Modern Sexualities.* Stanford: Stanford University Press.

—— ed. (1994). *Queering the Renaissance.* Durham: Duke University Press.

Goldhill, Simon (1995). *Foucault's Virginity: Ancient Erotic Fiction and the History of Sexuality.* Cambridge University Press.

Goldstein, Laurence, ed. (1991). *The Female Body: Figures, Styles, Speculations.* Ann Arbor: University of Michigan Press.

Gombrich, E. H. (1972). *Symbolic Images: Studies in the Art of the Renaissance.* Oxford: Phaidon.

Gosse, Edmund (1899). *The Life and Letters of John Donne.* 2Volumes. London: William Heinemann.

Gottlieb, Sidney (1983). 'Elegies Upon the Author: Defining, Defending and Surviving Donne'. *JDJ* 2/2: 22–39.

Graves, Robert (1961, 2nd edn., first publ. 1948). *The White Goddess: A Historical Grammar of Poetic Myth.* London: Faber.

*The Greek Anthology* (1970). Trans. W. R. Paton. 5Volumes. London: Heinemann.

Greenblatt, Stephen (1980). *Renaissance Self-Fashioning: From More to Shakespeare.* University of Chicago Press.

—— (1988). *Shakespearean Negotiations: The Circulation of Social Energy in Renaissance England.* Oxford: Clarendon.

Greene, Gayle, and Kahn, Coppelia, eds. (1988). *Making a Difference: Feminist Literary Criticism.* London: Methuen.

Gregory, E. R. (1989). *Milton and the Muses.* Tuscaloosa: University of Alabama Press.

Grosz, Elizabeth (1989). *Sexual Subversions: Three French Feminists.* Sydney: Allen & Unwin.

—— (1994). 'The Hetero and the Homo: The Sexual Ethics of Luce Irigaray' in Burke, Schor, Whitford: 335–50.

Gubar, Susan (1981). '"The Blank Page" and Issues of Female Creativity'. *CI* 8: 243–63.

—— (1984). 'Sapphistries'. *Signs* 10/1: 43–62.

Guibbory, Achsah (1983). 'A Sense of the Future: Projected Audiences of Donne and Jonson'. *JDJ* 2/2: 11–21.

—— (1993). 'John Donne' in Corns: 123–47.

Guilpin, Everard (1598). *Skialetheia; or, A Shadow of Truth.*

—— (1974). *Certaine Epigrams and Satyres.* Ed. D. Allen Carroll. Chapel Hill, NC: University of North Carolina Press.

Hall, Joseph (1969). *The Poems of Joseph Hall.* Ed. Arnold Davenport. Liverpool University Press.

Hallet, Judith P. (1979). 'Sappho and Her Social Context: Sense and Sensuality'. *Signs* 4/3: 447–64.

Halley, Janet E. (1989). 'Textual Intercourse: Anne Donne, John Donne, and the Sexual Poetics of Textual Exchange' in Fisher and Halley: 187–206.

Halperin, David M.(1986). "One Hundred Years of Homosexuality". *Diacritics*: 34–45

—— (1990). *One Hundred Years of Homosexuality: and Other Essays on Greek Love*. New York: Routledge.

——, Winkler, John J., and Zeitlin, Froma, eds. (1990). *Before Sexuality: The Construction of Erotic Experience in the Ancient Greek World*. Princeton University Press.

Hardison, O. B. (1962). *The Enduring Monument: A Study of the Idea of Praise in Renaissance Literary Theory and Practice*. Westport, Conn.: Greenwood Press.

Harington, Sir John (1930). *The Letters and Epigrams of Sir John Harington Together With The Prayse of Private Life*. Ed. with an Introduction by Norman E. McClure. Foreword by Felix E. Schelling. Philadelphia: University of Pennsylvania Press.

—— (n.d.). *The Metamorphosis of Ajax*. Ed. Peter Warlock and Jack Lindsay. London: Fanfrolico Press.

Harriott, Rosemary (1969). *Poetry and Criticism before Plato*. London: Methuen.

Harvey, Elizabeth (1989). 'Ventriloquizing Sappho: Ovid, Donne, and the Erotics of the Feminine Voice'. *Criticism* 31/2: 115–38.

—— (1992). *Ventriloquized Voices: Feminist Theory and English Renaissance Texts*. London: Routledge.

——, and Maus, Katharine Eisaman, eds. (1990). *Soliciting Interpretation: Literary Theory and Seventeenth-Century English Poetry*. University of Chicago Press.

Hazlitt, William (1903). *Lectures on the Comic Writers*. Volume viii. *Complete Works*. Ed. A. R. Waller and Arnold Glover. London: J. M. Dent.

Heath, John (1610). *Two centuries of epigrammes*.

Heidegger, Martin (1971). *Poetry, Language, Thought*. Trans. Albert Hofstadter. New York: Harper & Row.

Henderson, Katherine Usher, and McManus, Barbara F., eds. (1985). *Half Humankind: Contexts and Texts of the Controversy about Women in England 1540–1640*. Chicago: University of Illinois Press.

Herbert, Edward (1665). *Occasional Verses*.

Herz, Judith Scherer (1986). "'An Excellent Exercise of Wit That Speaks So Well of Ill": Donne and the Poetics of Concealment' in Summers and Pebworth 1986: 3–14.

Hesiod (1932). *The Homeric Hymns and Homerica*. Trans. Hugh G. Evelyn-White. Cambridge, Mass.: Harvard University Press.

Hester, M. Thomas (1985). 'Reading Donne's Epigrams: "Raderus"/ "Ralphius"'. *PLL* 21: 324–30.

—— (1990). 'The Titles/Headings of Donne's English Epigrams'. *ANQ* n.s. 3.1: 3–11.

—— (1996a). '"Fæminæ lectissimæ": Reading Anne Donne' in Hester (1996b): 17–34.

—— ed. (1996b). *John Donne's 'desire of more': The Subject of Anne More Donne in His Poetry*. Newark: University of Delaware Press; London: Associated University Presses.

Heywood, Thomas (1602). *How a Man May Chuse a Good Wife From a Bad.*

—— (1613). *A Marriage Triumphe.*

—— (1624). *Gunaikeion; or, Nine Bookes of Various History Concerninge Women.*

—— (1640). *The Exemplary Lives and memorable Acts of nine the most worthy Women of the World.*

Hill, Eugene D. (1987). 'John Donne's Moralized Grammar: A Study in Renaissance Christian Hebraica' in *Papers in the History of Linguistics*. Ed. Hans Aarsfleff, Lonis G. Kelly, and Hans-Josef Niederehe: 189–98.

Hillman, David, and Mazzio, Carla, eds. (1997). *The Body in Parts: Fantasies of Corporeality in Early Modern Europe*. New York: Routledge.

Hirsch, David A. Hedrich (1991). 'Donne's Atomies and Anatomies: Deconstructed Bodies and the Resurrection of Atomic Theory'. *SEL* 31/1: 69–94.

Hobbs, Mary (1989). 'Early Seventeenth-Century Verse Miscellanies and Their Value for Textual Editors' in *English Manuscript Studies 1100–1700.* Volume i. Ed. Peter Beal and Jeremy Griffiths. Oxford: Basil Blackwell.

Hobby, Elaine (1993). 'The Politics of Gender' in Corns: 31–54.

Hodge, Joanna (1994). 'Irigaray Reading Heidegger' in Burke, Schor, Whitford: 191–209.

Hodges, Devon L. (1985). *Renaissance Fictions of Anatomy*. Amherst: University of Massachusetts Press.

Holmlund, Christine (1991). 'The Lesbian, the Mother, the Heterosexual Lover: Irigaray's Recodings of Difference'. *Feminist Studies* 17/2: 283–308.

Holstun, James (1987). '"Will You Rent Our Ancient Love Asunder?": Lesbian Elegy in Donne, Marvell and Milton'. *ELH* 54/5: 835–68.

Homer (1971). *Iliad*. Trans. A. T. Murray. Cambridge, Mass.: Harvard University Press.

Horace (1991, 2nd edn., first publ. 1926). *Satires, Epistles and Ars poetica*. Trans. H. Rushton Fairclough. Cambridge, Mass.: Harvard University Press.

Horne, R. C. (1993). 'An Allusion to Nashe's *Choise of Valentines* in Donne's Second Satire'. *N&Q* 30: 414–15.

Howard, Jean E. (1987). 'The New Historicism in Renaissance Studies' in Kinney and Collins: 3–33.

Hughes, Richard E. (1967). 'The Woman in Donne's *Anniversaries*'. *ELH* 34: 307–26.

—— (1968). *The Progress of the Soul: The Interior Career of John Donne*. New York: William Morrow.

Hull, Suzanne W. (1982). *Chaste, Silent and Obedient: English Books for Women 1475–1640*. San Marino, Calif.: Huntington Library.

Humphries, Jefferson (1991). 'Muse Figures: Notes on Gender Difference in Poetry' in Goldstein: 195–210.

Irigaray, Luce (1981). 'And the One Doesn't Stir Without the Other'. Trans. Hélène Vivienne Wenzel. *Signs* 7/1: 60–7.

—— (1983). *L'Oubli de l'Air chez Martin Heidegger*. Paris: Les Éditions de Minuit.

—— (1985a). *Speculum of the Other Woman*. Trans. Gillian C. Gill. Ithaca, NY: Cornell University Press. Orig. *Speculum de l'autre femme*. Paris: Les Éditions de Minuit, 1974.

—— (1985b). *This Sex Which Is Not One*. Trans. Catherine Porter with Carolyn Burke. Ithaca, NY: Cornell University Press. Orig. *Ce Sexe qui n'en pas un*. Paris: Les Éditions de Minuit, 1977.

—— (1989). 'The Language of Man'. Trans. Erin G. Carlston. *Cultural Critique* 13: 191–202. Orig. 'Le langue de l'homme'. *Revue philosophique* 4(1978).

—— (1990). 'Women's Exile: Interview with Luce Irigaray'. Trans. Couze Venn. *The Feminist Critique of Language: A Reader*. Ed. Deborah Cameron. London: Routledge: 80–96.

—— (1991a). *The Irigaray Reader*. Ed. Margaret Whitford. Oxford: Basil Blackwell.

—— (1991b). *Marine Lover of Friedrich Nietzsche*. Trans. Gillian C. Gill. New York: Columbia University Press. Orig. *Amante Marine*. Paris: Les Éditions de Minuit, 1987.

—— (1992). *Elemental Passions*. Trans. Joanne Collie and Judith Still. London: Athlone. Orig. *Passions élémentaires*. Paris: Les Éditions de Minuit, 1982.

—— (1993a). *An Ethics of Sexual Difference*. Trans. Carolyn Burke and Gillian C. Gill. Ithaca, NY: Cornell University Press. Orig. *Éthique de la différance sexuelle*. Paris: Les Éditions de Minuit 1984.

—— (1993b). *je, tu, nous: Toward a Culture of Difference*. Trans. Alison Martin. New York: Routledge. Orig. *Je, tu nous*. Paris: Éditions Grasset & Fasquelle, 1990.

—— (1993c). *Sexes and Genealogies*. Trans. Gillian C. Gill. New York: Columbia University Press. Orig. *Sexes et Parentés*. Paris: Les Éditions de Minuit, 1987.

—— (1994). *Thinking the Difference for a Peaceful Revolution*. Trans. Karin Montin. New York: Routledge. Orig. *Le Temps De La Différance: Pour une révolution pacifique*. Paris: Librairie Générale Française, 1989.

—— (1996). *I Love to You: Sketches of a Possible Felicity in History*. Trans. Alison Martin. New York: Routledge. Orig. *J'aime à toi*. Paris.

Jacobson, Howard (1974). *Ovid's Heroides*. Princeton University Press.

Jacobus, Mary, Keller, Evelyn Fox, and Shuttleworth, Sally, eds. (1990). *Body/Politics: Women and the Discourses of Science*. London: Routledge.

Jardine, Lisa (1989). *Still Harping on Daughters: Women and Drama in the Age of Shakespeare*. New York: Columbia University Press.

—— (1993). *Erasmus, Man of Letters: The Construction of Charisma in Print*. Princeton University Press.

Jerome, St (1893). *Letters and Selected Works*. Volume vi. *A Select Library of Nicene and Post-Nicene Fathers of the Christian Church*. Second Series. Trans. the Hon. W. H. Fremantle, the Revd G. Lewis, the Revd W. G. Martley. New York: The Christian Literature Company.

Johnson, Barbara (1987). *A World of Difference*. Baltimore: Johns Hopkins University Press.

—— (1994). *The Wake of Deconstruction*. Baltimore: Johns Hopkins University Press.

Johnson, Beatrice (1928). 'Classical Allusions in the Poetry of Donne'. *PMLA* 43: 1098–109. Rpt. in Roberts 1975: 85–92.

Jonson, Ben (1925–52). *Ben Jonson*. Ed. C. H. Herford and Percy and Evelyn Simpson. 11 Volumes. Oxford: Clarendon.

Jordan, Constance (1990). *Renaissance Feminism: Literary Texts and Political Models*. Ithaca, NY: Cornell University Press.

Jordan, Richard Douglas (1989). *The Quiet Hero: Figures of Temperance in Spenser, Donne, Milton, and Joyce*. Washington: Catholic University of America Press.

*Juvenal and Persius* (1993, 2nd edn.). Trans. G. G. Ramsay. Cambridge, Mass.: Harvard University Press.

Kaplan, E. Ann (1984). 'Is the Gaze Male?' in Snitow, Stansell and Thompson: 321–36.

Kauffman, Linda S. (1986). *Discourses of Desire: Gender, Genre and Epistolary Fictions*. Ithaca, NY: Cornell University Press.

Kay, Dennis (1990). *Melodious Tears: The English Funeral Elegy from Spenser to Milton*. Oxford: Clarendon.

Keach, William (1977). *Elizabethan Erotic Narratives: Irony and Pathos in the Ovidian Poetry of Shakespeare, Marlowe, and Their Contemporaries*. New Brunswick, NJ: Rutgers University Press.

Kegl, Rosemary (1994). *The Rhetoric of Concealment: Figuring Gender and Class in Renaissance Literature*. Ithaca, NY: Cornell University Press.

Kelly, Joan (1977). 'Did Women Have a Renaissance?' in R. Bridenthal and C. Koonz, eds. *Becoming Visible: Women in European History*. Boston: Houghton Mifflin: 137–64.

Kelly, Kathleen (1986). 'Conversion of the Reader in Donne's "Anatomy of the World"' in Summers and Pebworth 1986: 147–56.

Kernan, Alvin (1959). *The Cankered Muse: Satire of the English Renaissance*. New Haven: Yale University Press.

Kerrigan, William (1972). 'The Fearful Accommodations of John Donne'. *ELR* 4: 337–63.

—— (1987). 'What Was Donne Doing?' *SCR* 4/2: 2–15.

Kerrigan, William, and Braden, Gordon, eds. (1989). *The Idea of the Renaissance*. Baltimore: Johns Hopkins University Press.

Kesler, R. L. (1990). 'The Idealization of Women: Morphology and Change in Three Renaissance Texts'. *Mosaic* 23/2: 107–26.

Kilgour, Maggie (1990). *From Communion to Cannibalism: An Anatomy of Metaphors of Incorporation*. Princeton University Press.

Kinney, Arthur F., and Collins, Dan S., eds. (1987). *Renaissance Historicism: Selections from* English Literary Renaissance. Amherst: University of Massachusetts Press.

Klause, John L. (1987). 'Donne and the Wonderful'. *ELR* 17/1: 41–66.

Klawitter, George (1987/8). 'John Donne and Woman: Against the Middle Ages'. *Allegorica* 9: 270–7.

—— (1992). 'Verse Letters to T.W. from John Donne: "By You My Love Is Sent"'. *Journal of Homosexuality* 23. Published simultaneously in Summers: 85–102.

—— (1994). *The Enigmatic Narrator: The Voicing of Same-Sex Love in the Poetry of John Donne*. New York: Peter Lang.

Kofman, Sarah (1985). *The Enigma of Woman: Woman in Freud's Writings*. Trans. Catherine Porter. Ithaca, NY: Cornell University Press.

Kolodny, Annette (1980). 'A Map for Rereading: Or, Gender and the Interpretation of Literary Texts'. *New Literary History* 11/3: 451–67.

Kremen, Kathryn R. (1972). *The Imagination of the Resurrection: The Poetic Continuity of a Religious Motif in Donne, Blake, and Yeats*. Lewisburg, Penn.: Bucknell University Press.

Kristeva, Julia (1986). *The Kristeva Reader*. Ed. Toril Moi. Oxford: Basil Blackwell.

—— (1987a). *Desire in Language: A Semiotic Approach to Literature and Art*. Ed. Leon S. Roudiez. Trans. Thomas Gora, Alice Jardine, and Leon S. Roudiez. Oxford: Basil Blackwell.

—— (1987b). *Tales of Love*. Trans. Leon S. Roudiez. New York: Columbia University Press.

Lacan, Jacques (1993). *Écrits: A Selection*. Trans. Alan Sheridan. London: Routledge.

Lamb, Mary Ellen (1986). 'The Countess of Pembroke and the Art of Dying' in Rose: 207–26.

Lanyer, Aemilia (1993). *The Poems of Aemilia Lanyer: Salve Deus Rex Judæorum*. Ed. Susanne Woods. Oxford University Press.

Laqueur, Thomas (1990). *Making Sex: The Body and Gender from the Greeks to Freud*. Cambridge, Mass.: Harvard University Press.

Larson, Deborah Aldrich (1990). *John Donne and Twentieth-Century Criticism*. London: Associated University Presses.

Latt, David J. (1978). 'Praising Virtuous Ladies: The Literary Image and Historical Reality of Women in Seventeenth-Century England' in

Marlene Springer, ed. *What Manner of Woman: Essays on English and American Life and Literature*. Oxford: Basil Blackwell: 39–64.

*Lawes Resolutions of Womens Rights; or The Lawes Provision for Woemen* (1632).

Lebans, W. M. (1972). 'Donne's *Anniversaries* and the Tradition of Funeral Elegy'. *ELH* 39: 545–59.

Leishman, J. B. (1966; first publ. 1951 by Hutchinson & Co., Ltd., London). *The Monarch of Wit: An Analytical and Comparative Study of the Poetry of John Donne*. New York: Harper & Row.

Lennard, John (1991). *But I Digress: The Exploitation of Parentheses in English Printed Verse*. Oxford: Clarendon.

Lerner, Laurence (1990). 'Ovid and the Elizabethans' in Charles Martindale, ed. *Ovid Renewed: Ovidian Influences on Literature and Art from the Middle Ages to the Twentieth Century*. Cambridge University Press: 121–35.

Levin, Carole, and Watson, Jeanie, eds. (1987). *Ambiguous Realities: Women in the Middle Ages and Renaissance*. Detroit: Wayne State University Press.

—— and Robertson, Karen, eds. (1991). *Sexuality and Politics in Renaissance Drama*. Lewiston, NY: Edwin Mellen.

Levine, Jay Arnold (1962). 'The Status of the Verse Epistle Before Pope'. *SP* 59: 658–84.

Lewalski, Barbara Keifer (1973). *Donne's* Anniversaries *and the Poetry of Praise: The Creation of a Symbolic Mode*. Princeton University Press.

—— (1979). *Protestant Poetics and the Seventeenth-Century Religious Lyric*. Princeton University Press.

Lipking, Lawrence (1988). *Abandoned Women and Poetic Tradition*. University of Chicago Press.

Lockwood, Deborah H. (1987). 'Donne's Idea of Woman in the Songs and Sonets'. *Essays in Literature* 14/1: 37–50.

Loraux, Nicole (1987). *Tragic Ways of Killing a Woman*. Trans. Anthony Forster. Cambridge, Mass.: Harvard University Press.

Lorber, Judith (1994). *Paradoxes of Gender*. New Haven: Yale University Press.

Love, Harold (1966). 'The Argument of Donne's "First Anniversary"'. *MP* 64: 125–31.

—— (1993). *Scribal Publication in Seventeenth-Century England*. Oxford: Clarendon.

Low, Anthony (1988). 'Donne and the New Historicism'. *JDJ* 7/1: 125–31.

—— (1993). *The Reinvention of Love: Poetry, Politics and Culture from Sidney to Milton*. Cambridge University Press.

Lucian (1979). *Affairs of the Heart*. Volume viii. Trans. M. D. Macleod. London: Heinemann.

Lui, Yameng (1989). 'The Making of Elizabeth Drury: The Voice of God in "An Anatomy of the World"'. *JDJ* 8/1–2: 89–102.

Lyon, John (1997). 'Jonson and Carew on Donne: Censure into Praise'. *SEL* 37/1: 97–118.

McClung, William A., and Simard, Rodney (1987). 'Donne's Somerset Epithalamion and the Erotics of Criticism'. *HLQ* 50/2: 95–106.

McGowan, Margaret M. (1972). '"As Through a Looking-glass": Donne's Epithalamia and their Courtly Context' in A. J. Smith: 175–218.

McGrath, Lynette (1980). 'John Donne's Apology for Poetry'. *SEL* 20: 73–89.

MacColl, Alan (1972). 'The Circulation of Donne's Poems in Manuscript' in A. J. Smith 1972: 28–46.

Maclean, Ian (1988, first publ. 1980). *The Renaissance Notion of Woman: A Study in the Fortunes of Scholasticism and Medical Science in European Intellectual Life.* Cambridge University Press.

Maclure, Millar (1958). *The Paul's Cross Sermons 1534–1642.* University of Toronto Press.

Manley, Frank, ed. (1963). *John Donne: The* Anniversaries. Baltimore: Johns Hopkins Press.

Mann, Lindsay (1981). 'Radical Consistency: A Reading of Donne's "Communitie"'. *UTQ* 50/3: 285–99.

—— (1985/6). 'Sacred and Profane Love in Donne'. *Dalhousie Review* 65/4: 534–50.

—— (1987). 'The Typology of Woman in Donne's Anniversaries'. *Renaissance and Reformation* 11/4: 337–50.

—— (1992). 'Misogyny and Libertinism: Donne's Marriage Sermons'. *JDJ* 11: 111–32.

Marcus, Leah Sinanoglou (1978). *Childhood and Cultural Despair: A Theme and Variations in Seventeenth-Century Literature.* University of Pittsburgh Press.

Marlowe, Christopher (1987–95). *Complete Works.* Ed. Roma Gill. 4Volumes. Oxford: Clarendon.

Marotti, Arthur (1986). *John Donne: Coterie Poet.* Madison: University of Wisconsin Press.

—— ed. (1994). *Critical Essays on John Donne.* New York: G. K. Hall & Co., Toronto: Maxwell Macmillan.

—— (1995). *Manuscript, Print, and the English Renaissance Lyric.* Ithaca, NY: Cornell University Press.

Marston, John (1961). *The Poems of John Marston.* Ed. Arnold Davenport. Liverpool University Press.

Martial (1993). *Epigrams.* Trans. D. R. Shackleton Bailey. 3Volumes. Cambridge, Mass.: Harvard University Press.

Martialis (1601). *Epigrammatum. Libri XIV. Domitii Calderini Commentariis perpetuis, et Georgii Merulæ observationibus, illustrati.* Paris.

Maurer, Margaret (1976). 'John Donne's Verse Letters'. *MLQ* 37: 234–59.

Maus, Katharine Eisaman (1993). 'A Womb of His Own: Male Renaissance Poets in the Female Body' in J. Turner 1993b: 266–88.

Merrix, Robert P. (1984). 'The Vale of Lillies and the Bower of Bliss: Soft-Core Pornography in Elizabethan Poetry'. *Journal of Popular Culture* 19/4: 3–16.

Middleton, Thomas (1599). *Micro-cynicon: Sixe Snarling Satyres.*

Miles, Margaret R. (1992). *Desire and Delight: A New Reading of Augustine's Confessions.* New York: Crossroad.

Milgate, W. (1950). 'The Early References to John Donne'. *N&Q* 195: 229–31, 246–7, 290–2, 381–3.

Miller, Nancy K., ed. (1986). *The Poetics of Gender.* New York: Columbia University Press.

Mills-Court, Karen (1990). *Poetry as Epitaph: Representation and Poetic Language.* Baton Rouge: Louisiana State University Press.

Mollenkott, Virginia Ramey (1981). 'John Donne and the Limitations of Androgyny'. *JEGP* 80: 22–38.

—— (1993). *The Divine Feminine: The Biblical Imagery of God as Female.* New York: Crossroad.

Montaigne, Michel de (1588). *Essais.* Paris.

—— (1603). *The Essayes or Morall, Politicke and Millitarie Discourses of Lo: Michaell de Montaigne.* 3Bookes. Trans. John Florio.

Mueller, Janel (1975). 'Death and the Maiden: The Metaphysics of Christian Symbolism in Donne's *Anniversaries*'. *MP* 73: 280–6.

—— (1985). '"This Dialogue of One": A Feminist Reading of Donne's *Exstasie*'. *ADE Bulletin* 81: 39–42.

—— (1989). 'Women among the Metaphysicals: A Case, Mostly, of Being Donne For'. *MP* 87: 142–58.

—— (1992). 'Lesbian Erotics: The Utopian Trope of Donne's "Sapho to Philaenis"'. *Journal of Homosexuality* 23/1–2. Published simultaneously in Summers: 103–34.

—— (1993). 'Troping Utopia: Donne's Brief for Lesbianism' in J. Turner 1993*b*: 182–207.

Mueller, William (1962). *John Donne: Preacher.* Princeton University Press.

Munich, Adrienne (1988). 'Notorious Signs, Feminist Criticism and Literary Tradition' in Greene and Kahn: 238–59.

Nashe, Thomas (1958). *The Works of Thomas Nashe.* Ed. Rev. F. P. Wilson. 5Volumes. Oxford University Press.

Neely, Carol Thomas (1988). 'Constructing the Subject: Feminist Practice and the New Renaissance Discourses'. *ELR* 18/1: 5–18.

Newman, Karen (1991). *Fashioning Femininity and English Renaissance Drama.* University of Chicago Press.

Nicholson, Linda J., ed. (1990). *Feminism/Postmodernism.* London: Routledge.

Norbrook, David (1984). *Poetry and Politics in the English Renaissance.* London: Routledge & Kegan Paul.

—— (1990). 'The Monarchy of Wit and the Republic of Letters: Donne's Politics' in Harvey and Maus: 3–36.

Novarr, David (1956). 'Donne's "Epithalamion made at Lincoln's Inn": Context and Date'. *RES* n.s.7: 250–63.

—— (1980). *The Disinterred Muse: Texts and Contexts*. Ithaca, NY: Cornell University Press.

Oliver, P. M. (1997). *Donne's Religious Writing: A Discourse of Feigned Devotion.* London: Longman.

Overbury, Sir Thomas (1968). *The 'Conceited Newes' of Sir Thomas Overbury and His Friends. A Facsimile Reproduction of the Ninth Impression of 1616 of Sir Thomas Overbury His Wife*. Ed. James E. Savage. Gainesville, Fla.: Scholars' Facsimiles and Reprints.

Ovid (1979, 2nd edn.). *The Art of Love and Other Poems*. Trans. J. H. Mosley. Rev. G. P. Goold. Cambridge, Mass.: Harvard University Press.

—— (1986, 2nd edn.). *Heroides and Amores*. Trans. Grant Showerman. Rev. G. P. Goold. 2 Volumes. Cambridge, Mass.: Harvard University Press.

—— (1984, 2nd edn.). *Metamorphoses*. Trans. F. J. Miller. Rev. G. P. Goold. Cambridge, Mass.: Harvard University Press.

Palmer, D. J. (1970). 'The Verse Epistle' in Malcolm Bradbury and David Palmer, eds. *Metaphysical Poetry*. London: Edward Arnold: 73–100.

Park, Katharine (1997). 'The Rediscovery of the Clitoris' in Hillman and Mazzio: 171–94.

—— and Nye, Robert A. (1991). 'Destiny Is Anatomy'. *The New Republic* Feb. 18: 53–7.

Parker, Holt R. (1992). 'Love's Body Anatomized: The Ancient Erotic Handbooks and the Rhetoric of Sexuality' in Amy Richlin, ed. *Pornography and Representation in Greece and Rome*. New York: Oxford University Press: 90–111.

Parker, Michael (1986). 'Diamonds Dust: Carew, King and the Legacy of Donne' in Summers and Pebworth 1986: 191–200.

Parker, Patricia (1987). *Literary Fat Ladies: Rhetoric, Gender, Property*. London: Methuen.

Parrish, Paul (1986). '"A Funeral Elegie": Donne's Achievement in Traditional Form'. *Concerning Poetry* 19: 55–66.

Partridge, A. C. (1971). *The Language of Renaissance Poetry: Spenser, Shakespeare, Donne, Milton*. London: Andre Deutsch.

—— (1978). John Donne: Language and Style. London: André Deutsch.

Partridge, Eric (1990, 3rd edn., first publ. 1947 by Routledge & Kegan Paul Ltd.). *Shakespeare's Bawdy*. London: Routledge.

Patterson, Annabel (1983). 'Misinterpretable Donne: The Testimony of the Letters'. *JDJ* 2: 39–53.

Pebworth, Ted-Larry (1989). 'John Donne, Coterie Poetry and the Text as Performance'. *SEL* 29: 61–75.

—— and Summers, Claude J. (1984). '"Thus Friends Absent Speake": The Exchange of Verse Letters Between John Donne and Henry Wotton'. *MP* 81: 361–77.

Pindar (1989, 3rd edn.). *The Odes of Pindar, Including the Principal Fragments.* Trans. Sir John Sandys. Cambridge, Mass.: Harvard University Press.

Plato (1994, first publ. 1961). *The Collected Dialogues of Plato Including the Letters.* Ed. Edith Hamilton and Huntington Cairns. Bollingen Series LXXI. Princeton University Press.

Pollock, Zailig (1983). '"The Object and the Wit": The Smell of Donne's First *Anniversary*'. *ELR* 13/3: 301–18.

Prior, Mary, ed. (1985). *Women in English Society 1500–1800.* London: Methuen.

Puttenham, George (1936). *The Arte of English Poesie.* Ed. Gladys Doidge Willcock and Alice Walker. Cambridge University Press.

Quinn, Dennis (1969). 'Donne's Anniversaries as Celebration'. *SEL* 9/1: 97–105.

Rackin, Phyllis (1993). 'Historical Difference/ Sexual Difference' in Brink: 37–64.

Radzinowicz, Mary Ann (1988). 'The Politics of Donne's Silences'. *JDJ* 7/1: 1–19.

Revard, Stella P. (1993). 'The Sapphic Voice in Donne's "Sapho to Philaenis"' in Summers and Pebworth: 63–76.

Rich, Adrienne (1979). *On Lies, Secrets and Silence.* New York: Norton.

Ricks, Christopher (1988). 'Donne After Love' in Scarry (1988b): 33–69.

Riley, Denise (1988). *'Am I That Name?': Feminism and the Category of 'Women' in History.* Minneapolis: University of Minnesota Press.

Roberts, John R., ed. (1975). *Essential Articles for the Study of John Donne's Poetry.* Hamden, Conn.: Archon Books.

—— (1982). 'An Assessment of Modern Criticism'. *JDJ* 1/1: 55–67.

Robinson, Sally (1989). 'Deconstructive Discourse and Sexual Politics: The "Feminine" and/in Masculine Self-Representation'. *Cultural Critique* 13: 203–27.

Roebuck, Graham (1996). '"Glimmering lights": Anne, Elizabeth, and the Poet's Practice' in Hester (1996b): 172–82.

Rose, Mary Beth, ed. (1986). *Women in the Middle Ages and the Renaissance: Literary and Historical Perspectives.* Syracuse University Press.

—— (1988). *The Expense of Spirit: Love and Sexuality in English Renaissance Drama.* Ithaca, NY: Cornell University Press.

Rousselle, Aline (1988). *Porneia: On Desire and the Body in Antiquity.* Trans. Felicia Pheasant. Oxford: Basil Blackwell.

Rubin, Gail (1975). 'The Traffic in Women: Notes on the "Political Economy of Sex"' in Rayna R. Reiter, ed. *Towards an Anthropology of Women.* New York: Monthly Review Press: 157–210.

Rubinstein, Frankie (1984). *A Dictionary of Shakespeare's Sexual Puns and their Significance.* New York: Macmillan.

Sabine, Maureen (1992). *Feminine Engendered Faith: The Poetry of John Donne and Richard Crashaw.* London: Macmillan.

Sacks, Elizabeth (1980). *Shakespeare's Images of Pregnancy*. New York: St Martin's.

Sackton, Alexander (1967). 'Donne and the Privacy of Verse'. *SEL* 7: 67–82.

Scarry, Elaine (1988*a*). 'Donne: "But yet the body is his booke"' in Scarry (1988*b*): 70–105.

—— ed. (1988*b*). *Literature and the Body: Essays on Populations and Persons*. Baltimore: Johns Hopkins University Press.

Schindler, Walter (1984). *Voice and Crisis: Invocation in Milton's Poetry*. Hamden, Conn.: Archon Books.

Schleiner, Louise (1994). *Tudor and Stuart Women Writers*. With Verse Translations from Latin by Connie McQuillen, from Greek by Lynn E. Roller. Bloomington: Indiana University Press.

Schor, Naomi (1994). 'This Essentialism Which Is Not One: Coming to Grips with Irigaray' in Burke, Schor, Whitford: 57–78.

Scodel, Joshua (1991). *The English Poetic Epitaph: Commemoration and Conflict from Jonson to Wordsworth*. Ithaca, NY: Cornell University Press.

Scott, Joan W. (1986). 'Gender: A Useful Category of Historical Analysis'. *American Historical Review* 91/5: 1053–75.

Secundus, Joannes (1930). *The Love Poems of Joannes Secundus*. Ed. F. A. Wright. London: George Routledge & Sons.

Sedgwick, Eve Kosofsky (1985). *Between Men: English Literature and Male Homosocial Desire*. New York: Columbia University Press.

—— (1990). *Epistemology of the Closet*. Berkeley: University of California Press.

Selden, Raman (1975). 'John Donne's "Incarnational Conviction"'. *CQ* 17: 55–73.

Shakespeare, William (1988). *The Complete Works*. Ed. Stanley Wells and Gary Taylor. Oxford: Clarendon.

Shami, Jeanne (1995). 'Donne's Sermons and the Absolutist Politics of Quotation' in Frontain and Malpezzi: 380–412.

Shepherd, Simon, ed. (1985). *The Women's Sharpe Revenge: Five Women's Pamphlets from the Renaissance*. London: Fourth Estate.

Sherwood, Terry G. (1984). *Fulfilling the Circle: A Study of John Donne's Thought*. University of Toronto Press.

Showalter, Elaine, ed. (1989*a*). *The New Feminist Criticism: Essays on Women, Literature and Theory*. London: Virago.

—— (1989*b*). *Speaking of Gender*. London: Routledge.

Shuger, Deborah Kuller (1994). *The Renaissance Bible: Scholarship, Sacrifice and Subjectivity*. Berkeley: University of California Press.

Sidney, Sir Philip (1962). *The Poems of Sir Philip Sidney*. Ed. William A. Ringler, Jr. Oxford: Clarendon.

—— (1973). *Miscellaneous Prose of Sir Philip Sidney*. Ed. Katherine Duncan-Jones and Jan Van Dorsten. Oxford: Clarendon.

Simpson, Evelyn M. (1948). *A Study of the Prose Works of John Donne*. 2nd edn.. Oxford: Clarendon.

—— (1986). 'The Literary Value of Donne's Sermons' in Gardner 1962: 137–51.

Simpson, Percy (1930). 'Ben Jonson and Cecilia Bulstrode'. *TLS* Mar. 6: 187.

Slights, Camille Wells (1996). 'A Pattern of Love: Representations of Anne Donne' in Hester (1996*b*): 66–88.

Smith, A. J. (1985). *The Metaphysics of Love: Studies in Renaissance Love Poetry From Dante to Milton*. Cambridge University Press.

—— ed. (1972). *John Donne: Essays in Celebration*. London: Methuen.

—— ed. (1975). *John Donne: The Critical Heritage*. London: Routledge & Kegan Paul.

Smith, Barbara Herrnstein (1968). *Poetic Closure: A Study of How Poems End.* University of Chicago Press.

Smith, Bruce R. (1991). *Homosexual Desire in Shakespeare's England: A Cultural Poetics*. University of Chicago Press.

Smith, C. Gregory, ed. (1904). *Elizabethan Critical Essays*. 2 Volumes. Oxford University Press.

Snitow, Ann, Stansell, Christine and Thompson, Sharon, eds. (1984). *Powers of Desire: The Politics of Sexuality*. London: Virago.

Sparrow, John (1949). 'Two Epitaphs by John Donne'. *TLS* Mar. 26: 208.

Spelman, Elizabeth V. (1982). 'Woman as Body: Ancient and Contemporary Views'. *Feminist Studies* 8/1: 109–31.

Spencer, Theodore, ed. (1958). *A Garland for John Donne: 1631–1931*. Gloucester, Mass.: Peter Smith.

Spender, Dale (1985). *Man Made Language*. 2nd edn. London: Routledge & Kegan Paul.

Spenser, Edmund (1989). *The Yale Edition of the Shorter Poems of Edmund Spenser*. Ed. William A. Oram et al. New Haven: Yale University Press.

—— (1995). *The Faerie Queene*. Ed. A. C. Hamilton. London: Longman.

Stafford, Anthony (1988). *The Femall Glory (1635)*. A Facsimile Reproduction with an Introduction by Maureen Sabine. Delmar, NY: Scholars' Facsimiles Reprints.

Strong, Roy (1983). *The English Renaissance Miniature*. London: Thames and Hudson.

Suleiman, Susan Rubin, ed. (1986). *The Female Body in Western Culture: Contemporary Perspectives*. Cambridge, Mass.: Harvard University Press.

Sullivan, Ernest W. (1993). *The Influence of John Donne: His Uncollected Seventeenth-Century Printed Verse*. Columbia: University of Missouri Press.

Summers, Claude J., ed. (1992). *Homosexuality in Renaissance and Enlightenment England: Literary Representations in Historical Context.* New York: Haworth-Harrington Park.

Summers, Claude J., and Pebworth, Ted-Larry, eds. (1986). *The Eagle and the Dove: Reassessing John Donne*. Columbia: University of Missouri Press.

—— —— eds. (1988). *'The Muses Common-Weale': Poetry and Politics in the Seventeenth Century*. Columbia: University of Missouri Press.

—— —— eds. (1993). *Renaissance Discourses of Desire*. Columbia: University of Missouri Press.

Tayler, Edward W. (1991). *Donne's Idea of a Woman: Structure and Meaning in 'The Anniversaries'*. New York: Columbia University Press.

Teager, Florence (1936). 'Patronage of Joseph Hall and John Donne'. *PQ* 15/4: 408–13.

Thomson, Patricia (1972). 'Donne and the Poetry of Patronage: The *Verse Letters*' in A. J. Smith: 308–23.

Tibullus (1976). *Catullus, Tibullus and Pervigilium Veneris*. Trans. J. B. Postgate. London: Heinemann.

Traub, Valerie (1994). 'The (In)Significance of "Lesbian" Desire in Early Modern England' in Goldberg 1994: 62–83.

—— (1995). 'The Psychomorphology of the Clitoris'. *GLQ* 2: 81–113.

Trible, Phyllis (1978). *God and the Rhetoric of Sexuality*. Philadelphia: Fortress Press.

Tufte, Virginia (1970). *The Poetry of Marriage: The Epithalamium in Europe and Its Development in England*. Los Angeles: Timmon-Brown Inc.

Turberville, George (1567). *The Heroycall Epistles of the Learned Poet Publius Ovidius Naso, In English Verse. With Aulus Sabinus Aunsweres to Certaine of the Same*.

Turner, James Grantham (1993*a*). *One Flesh: Paradisal Marriage and Sexual Relations in the Age of Milton*. Oxford: Clarendon.

—— ed. (1993*b*). *Sexuality and Gender in Early Modern Europe: Institutions, Texts, Images*. Cambridge University Press.

Verducci, Florence (1985). *Ovid's Toyshop of the Heart: Epistulae Heroidum*. Princeton University Press.

Vicary, Thomas (1641). *The English-Mans Treasure. With the true Anatomie of Mans Body*.

Vickers, Nancy J. (1982). 'Diana Described: Scattered Women and Scattered Rhyme' in Abel: 95–110.

Virgil (1960, 2nd edn., first publ. 1916). *Eclogues, Georgics, Aeneid*. Trans. H. Rushton Fairclough. 2 Volumes. Cambridge, Mass.: Harvard University Press.

Vives, Juan (1541). *A Very Fruteful and Pleasant boke callyd* The Instruction of a Christen Woman. Trans. Richard Hyrde.

Waller, Marguerite (1989). 'The Empire's New Clothes: Refashioning the Renaissance' in Fisher and Halley: 160–83.

Walters, Margaret (1972). 'Epistolary Verse and Its Social Context 1590–1640', B. Litt. diss. (Oxford).

Walton, Izaac (1927). *The Lives of John Donne, Sir Henry Wotton, Richard Hooker, George Herbert & Robert Sanderson.* London: Oxford University Press.

Warner, Marina (1987, 2nd edn., first publ. 1985 by Weidenfeld and Nicholson). *Monuments and Maidens: The Allegory of the Female Form.* London: Pan Books Ltd.

Webber, Joan (1963). *Contrary Music: The Prose Style of John Donne.* Madison: University of Wisconsin Press.

Weir, Alison (1991). *The Six Wives of Henry VIII.* New York: Grove Weidenfeld.

Whipple, T. K. (1970). *Martial and the English Epigram from Sir Thomas Wyatt to Ben Jonson.* New York: Phaeton Press.

Whitford, Margaret (1991). *Luce Irigaray: Philosophy in the Feminine.* London: Routledge.

—— (1994). 'Reading Irigaray in the Nineties' in Burke, Schor, Whitford: 15–33.

Williams, Arnold (1948). *The Common Expositor: An Account of the Commentaries on Genesis 1527–1633.* Chapel Hill: University of North Carolina Press.

Williams, Gordon, compiler (1994). *A Dictionary of Sexual Language and Imagery in Shakespearean and Stuart Literature.* 3Volumes. London: Athlone.

Williamson, George (1962/3). 'The Design of Donne's "Anniversaries"'. *MP* 9/3: 181–91.

Willson, D. Harris (1956). *King James VI and I.* London: Jonathan Cape.

Wilson, Gail Edward (1980). 'Donne's Sarcophagal Imagery in "Epithalamion made at Lincoln's Inn", vv. 37–42'. *American N&Q* 18/5: 72–3.

Wilson, Thomas (1994). *The Art of Rhetoric (1560).* Ed. Peter E. Medine. University Park: Pennsylvania State University Press.

Wiltenburg, Robert (1988). '"What need hast thou of me? or of my Muse?": Jonson and Cecil, Politician and Poet' in Summers and Pebworth 1988: 34–47.

Winkler, John J. (1990). *The Constraints of Desire: The Anthropology of Sex and Gender in Ancient Greece.* London: Routledge.

Wither, George (1902). *The Poetry of George Wither.* Volume i. Ed. Frank Sidgwick. London: A H. Bullen.

Wollman, Richard B. (1993). '"The Press and the Fire": Print and Manuscript Culture in Donne's Circle'. *SEL* 33: 85–97.

Woodbridge, Linda (1986, first publ. 1984). *Women and the English Renaissance: Literature and the Nature of Womankind 1540–1620.* Urbana: University of Illinois Press.

Woolf, Virginia (1977, first publ. 1929 by Hogarth Press). *A Room of One's Own.* London: Grafton Books.

Woudhuysen, H. R. (1996). *Sir Philip Sidney and the Circulation of Manuscripts 1558–1640.* Oxford: Clarendon.

Wright, Louis B. (1958). *Middle-Class Culture in Elizabethan England*. Ithaca, NY: Cornell University Press.

Wrightson, Keith (1982). *English Society: 1580–1680*. London: Hutchinson.

Wroth, Sir Thomas (1610). *The Abortive of an Idle Houre: or a Centurie of Epigrams*.

# Index